Security, Privacy, Confidentiality and Trust in Blockchain

Security, Privacy, Confidentiality and Trust in Blockchain

Guest Editors

Mikolaj Karpinski
Oleksandr O. Kuznetsov
Roman Oliynykov

Basel • Beijing • Wuhan • Barcelona • Belgrade • Novi Sad • Cluj • Manchester

Guest Editors

Mikolaj Karpinski
Department of Software
Engineering
University of the National
Education Commission
Krakow
Poland

Oleksandr O. Kuznetsov
Department of Political
Sciences, Communication and
International Relations
University of Macerata
Macerata
Italy

Roman Oliynykov
School of Computer Science
V. N. Karazin Kharkiv
National University
Kharkiv
Ukraine

Editorial Office
MDPI AG
Grosspeteranlage 5
4052 Basel, Switzerland

This is a reprint of the Special Issue, published open access by the journal *Electronics* (ISSN 2079-9292), freely accessible at: https://www.mdpi.com/journal/electronics/special_issues/RDWZKL1466.

For citation purposes, cite each article independently as indicated on the article page online and as indicated below:

Lastname, A.A.; Lastname, B.B. Article Title. *Journal Name* **Year**, *Volume Number*, Page Range.

ISBN 978-3-7258-3307-8 (Hbk)
ISBN 978-3-7258-3308-5 (PDF)
https://doi.org/10.3390/books978-3-7258-3308-5

© 2025 by the authors. Articles in this book are Open Access and distributed under the Creative Commons Attribution (CC BY) license. The book as a whole is distributed by MDPI under the terms and conditions of the Creative Commons Attribution-NonCommercial-NoDerivs (CC BY-NC-ND) license (https://creativecommons.org/licenses/by-nc-nd/4.0/).

Contents

About the Editors vii

Preface ix

Mikolaj Karpinski, Oleksandr Kuznetsov and Roman Oliynykov
Security, Privacy, Confidentiality, and Trust in the Blockchain: From Theory to Applications
Reprinted from: *Electronics* 2025, *14*, 581, https://doi.org/10.3390/electronics14030581 1

Yeajun Kang, Wonwoong Kim, Hyunji Kim, Minwoo Lee, Minho Song and Hwajeong Seo
Malicious Contract Detection for Blockchain Network Using Lightweight Deep Learning Implemented through Explainable AI
Reprinted from: *Electronics* 2023, *12*, 3893, https://doi.org/10.3390/electronics12183893 7

Myeonghyun Kim, Jihyeon Oh, Seunghwan Son, Yohan Park, Jungjoon Kim and Youngho Park
Secure and Privacy-Preserving Authentication Scheme Using Decentralized Identifier in Metaverse Environment
Reprinted from: *Electronics* 2023, *12*, 4073, https://doi.org/10.3390/electronics12194073 22

Cesar E. Castellon, Tamim Khatib, Swapnoneel Roy, Ayan Dutta, O. Patrick Kreidl and Ladislau Bölöni
Energy-Efficient Blockchain-Enabled Multi-Robot Coordination for Information Gathering: Theory and Experiments †
Reprinted from: *Electronics* 2023, *12*, 4239, https://doi.org/10.3390/electronics12204239 44

Seok-Jun Buu and Hae-Jung Kim
Disentangled Prototypical Graph Convolutional Network for Phishing Scam Detection in Cryptocurrency Transactions
Reprinted from: *Electronics* 2023, *12*, 4390, https://doi.org/10.3390/electronics12214390 65

Washington Enyinna Mbonu, Carsten Maple and Gregory Epiphaniou
An End-Process Blockchain-Based Secure Aggregation Mechanism Using Federated Machine Learning
Reprinted from: *Electronics* 2023, *12*, 4543, https://doi.org/10.3390/electronics12214543 78

Rubén Juárez and Borja Bordel
Augmenting Vehicular Ad Hoc Network Security and Efficiency with Blockchain: A Probabilistic Identification and Malicious Node Mitigation Strategy
Reprinted from: *Electronics* 2023, *12*, 4794, https://doi.org/10.3390/electronics12234794 102

Oleksandr Kuznetsov, Nikolay Poluyanenko, Emanuele Frontoni, Sergey Kandiy, Mikolaj Karpinski and Ruslan Shevchuk
Enhancing Cryptographic Primitives through Dynamic Cost Function Optimization in Heuristic Search
Reprinted from: *Electronics* 2024, *13*, 1825, https://doi.org/10.3390/electronics13101825 137

Kyohei Shibano, Kensuke Ito, Changhee Han, Tsz Tat Chu, Wataru Ozaki and Gento Mogi
Secure Processing and Distribution of Data Managed on Private InterPlanetary File System Using Zero-Knowledge Proofs
Reprinted from: *Electronics* 2024, *13*, 3025, https://doi.org/10.3390/electronics13153025 189

Jie Zhang, Gehao Lu and Jia Yu
A Smart Contract Vulnerability Detection Method Based on Heterogeneous Contract Semantic Graphs and Pre-Training Techniques
Reprinted from: *Electronics* **2024**, *13*, 3785, https://doi.org/10.3390/electronics13183786 . . . . . **200**

Peng He and Ming Xu
An NTRU-Based Key Encapsulation Scheme for Underwater Acoustic Communication
Reprinted from: *Electronics* **2025**, *14*, 405, https://doi.org/10.3390/electronics14030405 . . . . . . **222**

About the Editors

Mikolaj Karpinski

Mikolaj Karpinski has received MSc, PhD, and DSc degrees in Electrical Control and Information Technology (1980, 1990, and 1996, respectively), and a Diploma of Full Professor in Cyber Security (2001). Currently, he is a Professor and Head of Department of Software Engineering of the Institute of Security and Computer Science at the University of the National Education Commission, Krakow, Poland, and a Professor in the Department of Cybersecurity at the Ternopil Ivan Puluj National Technical University, Ukraine. From 2006 to 2025 he carried out scientific visits and/or completed internships at institutions including the University of Colorado Boulder, Max Planck Institute for Informatics, HTW Berlin University of Applied Science, TechnoCentre of Coventry University, Samsung Electronics Co., Rolls-Royce plc, Sabaa for Data Science Inc., etc. His research interests include artificial intelligence, cybersecurity, computer and information engineering, computer and sensor networks, industrial electronics, Internet of Things, security of wireless networks, cryptanalysis, cryptography, electrical engineering, lighting engineering, and electric and photometric measurements. He has belonged to the IEEE since 2001. He recently led the project POIR.04.01.04-00-0048/20, funded by the National Centre for Research and Development, Poland, and is a laureate of the Award of the Minister of National Education of Poland: "Medal of the Commission of National Education".

Oleksandr Kuznetsov

Oleksandr Kuznetsov is an Associate Professor at the Faculty of Engineering, eCampus University, Italy, and serves as a Full Professor in the Department of Intelligent Software Systems and Technologies, School of Computer Science and Artificial Intelligence, V.N. Karazin Kharkiv National University, Ukraine. He earned his Doctor of Technical Sciences degree in Information Security Systems and is a recipient of the prestigious Boris Paton National Prize of Ukraine. His research expertise encompasses a broad spectrum of cybersecurity domains, including applied cryptography, blockchain technology, biometric authentication, and artificial intelligence applications in security. Prof. Kuznetsov has made significant contributions to Ukraine's national cryptographic information protection system, leading to the development and standardization of several national cryptographic standards. His current research focuses on decentralized consensus protocols, zero-knowledge proof technologies, and post-quantum cryptographic solutions. With over 200 publications, he continues to advance the field through his work on secure blockchain implementations, privacy-preserving protocols, and AI-driven security systems. His recent achievements include pioneering work in homomorphic encryption for biomedical image protection and the development of innovative decentralized electronic voting protocols.

Roman Oliynykov

Roman Oliynykov is a cryptographer, blockchain researcher, and Professor at V.N. Karazin Kharkiv National University. He graduated from the Kharkiv National University of Radioelectronics in Ukraine with expertise in Computer Engineering and Cybersecurity, and after further research activity obtained his Ph.D. and Dr. Habil. degrees in Cryptology. His professional experience has covered the development and security analysis of decentralized consensus protocols, zk-based cryptographic protocols, tokenomics for cryptocurrencies, and the development of cryptographic primitives, including Ukrainian cryptographic standards the Kalyna block cipher (DSTU 7624:2014) and the Kupyna hash function (DSTU 7564:2014). He has recently led projects on analyses of voting schemes for blockchains and cryptographic protocols for such schemes. His teaching disciplines include software and network security, general crypto, and cryptocurrencies. He has also been involved in the training of Ukrainian cyber police officers.

Preface

The rapid evolution of blockchain technology has created an urgent need for advanced security, privacy, and trust mechanisms. This Special Issue emerged from our recognition of the growing challenges in blockchain implementation across various domains. Our goal was to bring together innovative research that addresses these challenges while maintaining practical applicability.

The research presented in this Reprint covers both theoretical foundations and real-world applications. In particular, we specifically sought contributions that bridge the gap between academic research and industry implementation. The selected papers represent diverse approaches to blockchain security, from post-quantum cryptography to artificial intelligence integration.

This collection is particularly relevant for researchers in cryptography, blockchain technology, and cybersecurity. It also provides valuable insights for industry practitioners implementing blockchain solutions in various sectors. The papers offer both theoretical frameworks and practical implementation guidelines that can inform future development in the field.

We are grateful to all contributing authors who shared their innovative research and insights. Their work collectively advances our understanding of blockchain security challenges and solutions. Special appreciation goes to the reviewers, whose thorough evaluation and constructive feedback significantly enhanced the quality of each contribution. We also thank the Editorial team at *Electronics* for their support throughout the publication process.

As Guest Editors, we believe that this Special Issue provides a comprehensive overview of current advances in blockchain security while highlighting promising directions for future research. We hope that these contributions will inspire further innovations in secure blockchain implementation.

Mikolaj Karpinski, Oleksandr O. Kuznetsov, and Roman Oliynykov
Guest Editors

Editorial

Security, Privacy, Confidentiality, and Trust in the Blockchain: From Theory to Applications

Mikolaj Karpinski [1,2,*], Oleksandr Kuznetsov [3,4,5,*] and Roman Oliynykov [6,7]

[1] Department of Software Engineering, University of the National Education Commission, 30-084 Krakow, Poland
[2] Department of Cybersecurity, Ternopil Ivan Puluj National Technical University, 46001 Ternopil, Ukraine
[3] Department of Cybersecurity of Information Systems, Networks and Technologies, V.N. Karazin National University, 61022 Kharkiv, Ukraine
[4] Department of Political Sciences, Communication and International Relations, University of Macerata, Via Crescimbeni, 62100 Macerata, Italy
[5] Department of Theoretical and Applied Sciences, eCampus University, Via Isimbardi 10, 22060 Novedrate, Italy
[6] Input Output (IOG Singapore Pte Ltd.), 4 Battery Road, Singapore 049908, Singapore; roman.oliynykov@iohk.io
[7] Education and Research Institute of Computer Sciences and Artificial Intelligence, V.N. Karazin Kharkiv National University, 61022 Kharkiv, Ukraine
* Correspondence: mikolaj.karpinski@uken.krakow.pl (M.K.); oleksandr.kuznetsov@uniecampus.it (O.K.)

Received: 27 January 2025
Accepted: 28 January 2025
Published: 1 February 2025

Citation: Karpinski, M.; Kuznetsov, O.; Oliynykov, R. Security, Privacy, Confidentiality, and Trust in the Blockchain: From Theory to Applications. *Electronics* **2025**, *14*, 581. https://doi.org/10.3390/electronics14030581

Copyright: © 2025 by the authors. Licensee MDPI, Basel, Switzerland. This article is an open access article distributed under the terms and conditions of the Creative Commons Attribution (CC BY) license (https://creativecommons.org/licenses/by/4.0/).

1. Introduction

From the financial and medical sectors to various supply chains, most industries have seen a sea change due to the blockchain [1,2]. This transformation poses unparalleled challenges regarding security, privacy, and trust. The decentralized nature of blockchain systems leads to complex security considerations that the incoming solution package needs to address innovatively [3,4].

Recent developments in blockchain applications have pointed to several critical challenges [5–7]: security vulnerability in smart contracts, leakage in the privacy of transaction data, and several attack vectors on consensus mechanisms. Integrating the blockchain with emerging technologies such as the Internet of Things (IoT) and artificial intelligence further aggravates these challenges and has created urgent requirements for efficient security frameworks and privacy preservation mechanisms.

This Special Issue, "Security, Privacy, Confidentiality, and Trust in the Blockchain", addresses the pressing challenges that have arisen with regard to this technology. This Special Issue of *Electronics* brings together recent research contributions related to the theoretical foundations and practical applications of blockchain security. The collected works span several domains, from advanced cryptographic primitives to real-world blockchain applications in underwater communications and autonomous systems.

The papers in this Special Issue introduce new approaches to the enhancement of the security and privacy of blockchains, ranging from NTRU-based encryption schemes to smart contract vulnerability detection methods and novel applications of zero-knowledge proofs. Most of the selected works focus on practical implementations that show exactly how theoretical security notions are implemented into concrete blockchain solutions.

This Special Issue was established as a result of the increasing interest in holistic solutions to blockchain security challenges. The selected papers represent significant advances in addressing these challenges while maintaining the balance between security, efficiency, and usability. We hope that through these contributions, further research and developments in blockchain security will be fostered, leading to more robust and trustworthy blockchain systems.

2. Overview of Contributions

The papers in this Special Issue represent important advances in several domains of blockchain security and privacy. Their contributions can be systematically analyzed from the perspectives of their key technological innovations and practical applications.

In light of such scenarios, one suggested key encapsulation scheme based on NTRU presented by He and Xu (Contribution 1) proposes a completely different approach to secure data transmission underwater. In this scheme, ring sampling techniques are used for compact NTRU trapdoor generation in order to minimize communication overheads without affecting security. Underwater acoustic channel characteristics are integrated, while they propose using temporary identity information in order to guarantee confidentiality and reliability. Their experimental validation shows very good performance metrics, achieving the required ciphertext security while meeting the strict requirements of underwater acoustic communication.

Zhang et al. (Contribution 2) propose an approach for to detection of vulnerabilities in smart contracts. This approach is based on heterogeneous contract semantic graphs combined with the pre-training method, which represents a significant jump compared to classical approaches. The developed technique shows increased precision, recall, and F1 scores while detecting four common and harmful types of smart contract vulnerability.

Other significant contributions in this area of privacy-preserving data management include that by Shibano et al. (Contribution 3), who develop a system for the secure processing of private IPFS. The zero-knowledge proofs, as implemented by these authors with the Groth16 protocol of zk-SNARKs, ensure that the authentication of data occurs with privacy maintained. The ability of this system to prevent unauthorized secondary distribution through recipient name embedding adds an extra layer of grassroot security.

Kuznetsov et al. (Contribution 4) show the state of the art regarding the optimization of cryptographic primitives based on dynamic cost function adjustments performed in heuristic searches. Their approach achieves a success rate of 100% in finding 8-bit bijective S-boxes with maximal nonlinearity. It requires iterations of the order of magnitude of 50,000; this is relatively efficient compared to contributions from previous studies. This is an important contribution to the area of symmetric system security.

Juárez and Bordel (Contribution 5) present a more sophisticated dual-layer blockchain architecture for VANETs. The proposed system can neutralize malicious behaviors with an efficacy of up to 86% thanks to several innovative reputation assessment frameworks combined with Bayesian inference principles. This model succeeds in dealing with some security challenges of vehicular ad hoc networks without losing its operational efficiency.

The work of Mbonu, Maple, and Epiphaniou (Contribution 6) focuses on the security of federated learning by introducing a blockchain-based secure aggregation mechanism. These authors overcome the problem of a single point of failure in the traditional architecture of federated learning using a centralized server and secure model aggregation simultaneously. In addition, the efficiency of training and the model convergence rate are drastically improved by implementing a fault-tolerant server together with a callback mechanism.

This Special Issue also includes innovative work in cryptocurrency security, including the study by Buu and Kim, (Contribution 7) who develop a disentangled prototypical graph convolutional network for phishing scam detection. Their model achieves significant improvements in F1 scores and AUC metrics, demonstrating the effectiveness of combining disentanglement mechanisms with prototypical learning for fraud detection.

In Kim et al.'s (Contribution 8) study, the authors address metaverse security-related challenges with an effective solution—a decentralized identifier-based authentication scheme—that copes relatively well with various private avatar identities in a very secure way, as demonstrated by the rich experimental validation and security analysis performed by the authors.

Castellon et al. (Contribution 9) study blockchain-enabled multi-robot coordination in terms of energy efficiency for information gathering. Their implementation of an energy-efficient protocol as a proof-of-work showed a reduction of up to 14% in energy consumption while maintaining secure coordination among robots. Their work effectively demonstrates practical scalability with up to 10 robots and effectively rejects data that have been tampered with by malicious entities.

Kang et al. (Contribution 10) present a fresh approach to the detection of malicious contracts using a lightweight deep learning model. Their Gredeeptector detects malicious contracts with 92.3% accuracy and simultaneously reduces the model file size by 41.5% compared to baseline approaches. In particular, the implementation of explainable AI for identifying important instructions makes their solution particularly suitable for IoT environments.

Taken together, these findings provide advanced theoretical contributions with practical implementations for blockchain security. Each paper addresses a specific challenge by taking into account a rigorous definition of the security standard to be enforced while considering the application's applicability.

3. Key Findings and Impact

The research presented in this Special Issue highlights some critical milestones achieved in areas of technological advancement in security and privacy in the blockchain. It integrates post-quantum cryptography into the blockchain, mainly through NTRU-based schemes that have shown feasible solutions for protecting blockchain communications in challenging environments. This is important because the emergence of quantum computers threatens modern cryptographic systems.

The security of smart contracts emerges as an important area of concern, and to address this issue new methods of detection can achieve much better accuracy rates. Methods comprising a combination of semantic graph analysis and pre-training techniques provide a leap forward in the field of vulnerability detection. This will directly contribute to addressing highly critical challenges related to the security of the blockchain because of the immutable nature of smart contracts once they are deployed.

Zero-knowledge proofs and secure distributed storage systems provide very significant advances in the preservation of privacy. The successful implementation of these technologies in practice, through novel products like private IPFS, bridges the gap between theoretical and real-world privacy requirements for applications. Among these implementations are those that preserve data authenticity while guaranteeing privacy, an important balance to consider in blockchain systems.

Energy efficiency in blockchain security mechanisms is another major development. The optimization of proof-of-work protocols and the development of lightweight detection models show that the requirements regarding security can be met without excessive computational overheads. This is one of the basic challenges in the adoption of blockchain technology: the trade-off between security and resource consumption.

This Special Issue also discusses the successful applications of blockchain security in emerging domains. From underwater communication to metaverse authentication, research has proven the versatility of blockchains in securing diversified applications. These implementations provide useful blueprints for future security solutions in specialized domains.

It thus follows that cross-domain integration would be one of the research trends in this Special Issue, especially when considering blockchains either combined with artificial intelligence or with IoT. Indeed, many papers show successful fusions resulting in robust and efficient security solutions, thereby also indicating the future research directions in blockchain security research and development.

Taken together, the selected papers provide advanced theoretical contributions with practical implementations for blockchain security. Each paper addresses a specific challenge by taking into account a rigorous definition of the security standard to be enforced while considering the application's applicability.

4. Future Research Directions

This Special Issue brings together several promising areas in which blockchain security may be investigated in the future. The integration of post-quantum cryptography remains to be further advanced, especially regarding optimizations needed for resource-constrained environments. The successes with NTRU-based schemes indicate the possibility of other post-quantum approaches showing promise in blockchain systems.

The security of smart contracts still remains in its development stages. While current approaches for vulnerability detection have great potential, much is yet to be achieved in real-time detection and the automation of correction mechanisms. Combining formal verification approaches with machine learning techniques might help in achieving less vulnerable features.

Another important research direction is privacy preservation in cross-chain interactions. While blockchain systems are becoming increasingly interconnected, establishing how to balance privacy preservation with interoperability represents a very important research direction. Zero-knowledge proof systems should be further optimized for complex cross-chain transactions.

Improving energy efficiency in security mechanisms is a process of continuous innovation. The use of lightweight security protocols that preserve strong protections while minimizing resource consumption remains an open challenge that faces the developers of IoT and edge computing applications.

The metaverse, along with the management of one's digital identity, is where new security risks are arising. The integration of virtual environments with blockchain-based authentication needs to be furthered. Special focus should be provided to scalability, while not compromising either user experience or security.

5. Conclusions

This Special Issue highlights several significant advances regarding the security, privacy, and trust mechanisms in blockchains. The ten papers together therefore show advancements in many domains, ranging from theoretical cryptography to practical applications, and from post-quantum cryptography solutions to energy-efficient security protocols.

The research in this Special Issue presents effective solutions to the critical challenges regarding blockchain security, while also indicating other areas requiring further investigation in future research activities. Meanwhile, these studies also demonstrate the maturity of this topic, because advanced cryptographically strong principles are adapted and combined effectively with practical perspectives. Noteworthy results are presented with regard to smart contract security analysis, privacy provision, and the development of resource-efficient security primitives.

These works lay the foundations for future researchers in studies on blockchain security. They show how strong and efficient security solutions may effectively coexist with or support more practical efficiency improvements. When developing security frameworks and their methodologies in blockchain technology, these studies will act as valuable references for researchers and practitioners.

We would like to thank all the authors, reviewers, and editorial staff who have contributed to this Special Issue. Their contributions have enhanced our understanding of blockchain security and will influence future developments in this rapidly developing area.

Author Contributions: Conceptualization and methodology, writing—original draft preparation, O.K.; formal analysis, M.K.; writing—review and editing, M.K. and R.O. All authors have read and agreed to the published version of the manuscript.

Data Availability Statement: The datasets generated during and/or analyzed during the current study are available from the corresponding author upon reasonable request.

Conflicts of Interest: Author Roman Oliynykov was employed by the company Input Output (IOG Singapore Pte Ltd.). The remaining authors declare that the research was conducted in the absence of any commercial or financial relationships that could be construed as a potential conflict of interest.

List of Contributions

1. He, P.; Xu, M. An NTRU-Based Key Encapsulation Scheme for Underwater Acoustic Communication. *Electronics* **2025**, *14*, 405.
2. Zhang, J.; Lu, G.; Yu, J. A Smart Contract Vulnerability Detection Method Based on Heterogeneous Contract Semantic Graphs and Pre-Training Techniques. *Electronics* **2024**, *13*, 3786.
3. Shibano, K.; Ito, K.; Han, C.; Chu, T.; Ozaki, W.; Mogi, G. Secure Processing and Distribution of Data Managed on Private InterPlanetary File System Using Zero-Knowledge Proofs. *Electronics* **2024**, *13*, 3025.
4. Kuznetsov, O.; Poluyanenko, N.; Frontoni, E.; Kandiy, S.; Karpinski, M.; Shevchuk, R. Enhancing Cryptographic Primitives through Dynamic Cost Function Optimization in Heuristic Search. *Electronics* **2024**, *13*, 1825.
5. Juárez, R.; Bordel, B. Augmenting Vehicular Ad Hoc Network Security and Efficiency with Blockchain: A Probabilistic Identification and Malicious Node Mitigation Strategy. *Electronics* **2023**, *12*, 4794.
6. Mbonu, W.; Maple, C.; Epiphaniou, G. An End-Process Blockchain-Based Secure Aggregation Mechanism Using Federated Machine Learning. *Electronics* **2023**, *12*, 4543.
7. Buu, S.; Kim, H. Disentangled Prototypical Graph Convolutional Network for Phishing Scam Detection in Cryptocurrency Transactions. *Electronics* **2023**, *12*, 4390.
8. Castellon, C.; Khatib, T.; Roy, S.; Dutta, A.; Kreidl, O.; Bölöni, L. Energy-Efficient Blockchain-Enabled Multi-Robot Coordination for Information Gathering: Theory and Experiments. *Electronics* **2023**, *12*, 4239.
9. Kim, M.; Oh, J.; Son, S.; Park, Y.; Kim, J.; Park, Y. Secure and Privacy-Preserving Authentication Scheme Using Decentralized Identifier in Metaverse Environment. *Electronics* **2023**, *12*, 4073.
10. Kang, Y.; Kim, W.; Kim, H.; Lee, M.; Song, M.; Seo, H. Malicious Contract Detection for Blockchain Network Using Lightweight Deep Learning Implemented through Explainable AI. *Electronics* **2023**, *12*, 3893.

References

1. Abou Jaoude, J.; George Saade, R. Blockchain Applications—Usage in Different Domains. *IEEE Access* **2019**, *7*, 45360–45381. [CrossRef]
2. Alruwaili, F.F.; Alabduallah, B.; Alqahtani, H.; Salama, A.S.; Mohammed, G.P.; Alneil, A.A. Blockchain Enabled Smart Healthcare System Using Jellyfish Search Optimization With Dual-Pathway Deep Convolutional Neural Network. *IEEE Access* **2023**, *11*, 87583–87591. [CrossRef]

3. Apat, H.K.; Sahoo, B. A Blockchain Assisted Fog Computing for Secure Distributed Storage System for IoT Applications. *J. Ind. Inf. Integr.* **2024**, *42*, 100739. [CrossRef]
4. Cheng, H.; Lo, S.-L.; Lu, J. A Blockchain-Enabled Decentralized Access Control Scheme Using Multi-Authority Attribute-Based Encryption for Edge-Assisted Internet of Things. *Internet Things* **2024**, *26*, 101220. [CrossRef]
5. Hewa, T.; Ylianttila, M., Liyanage, M. Survey on Blockchain Based Smart Contracts: Applications, Opportunities and Challenges. *J. Netw. Comput. Appl.* **2021**, *177*, 102857. [CrossRef]
6. Shafay, M.; Ahmad, R.W.; Salah, K.; Yaqoob, I.; Jayaraman, R.; Omar, M. Blockchain for Deep Learning: Review and Open Challenges. *Clust. Comput.* **2023**, *26*, 197–221. [CrossRef] [PubMed]
7. Kuznetsov, O.; Sernani, P.; Romeo, L.; Frontoni, E.; Mancini, A. On the Integration of Artificial Intelligence and Blockchain Technology: A Perspective About Security. *IEEE Access* **2024**, *12*, 3881–3897. [CrossRef]

Disclaimer/Publisher's Note: The statements, opinions and data contained in all publications are solely those of the individual author(s) and contributor(s) and not of MDPI and/or the editor(s). MDPI and/or the editor(s) disclaim responsibility for any injury to people or property resulting from any ideas, methods, instructions or products referred to in the content.

Article

Malicious Contract Detection for Blockchain Network Using Lightweight Deep Learning Implemented through Explainable AI

Yeajun Kang, Wonwoong Kim, Hyunji Kim, Minwoo Lee, Minho Song and Hwajeong Seo *

Division of IT Convergence Engineering, Hansung University, Seoul 02876, Republic of Korea; 22213202@hansung.ac.kr (Y.K.); 22213203@hansung.ac.kr (W.K.); 22111401@hansung.ac.kr (H.K.); 23213701@hansung.ac.kr (M.L.); 23213704@hansung.ac.kr (M.S.)
* Correspondence: hwajeong@hansung.ac.kr; Tel.: +82-760-8033

Abstract: A smart contract is a digital contract on a blockchain. Through smart contracts, transactions between parties are possible without a third party on the blockchain network. However, there are malicious contracts, such as greedy contracts, which can cause enormous damage to users and blockchain networks. Therefore, countermeasures against this problem are required. In this work, we propose a greedy contract detection system based on deep learning. The detection model is trained through the frequency of opcodes in the smart contract. Additionally, we implement Gredeeptector, a lightweight model for deployment on the IoT. We identify important instructions for detection through explainable artificial intelligence (XAI). After that, we train the Greedeeptector through only important instructions. Therefore, Greedeeptector is a computationally and memory-efficient detection model for the IoT. Through our approach, we achieve a high detection accuracy of 92.3%. In addition, the file size of the lightweight model is reduced by 41.5% compared to the base model and there is little loss of accuracy.

Keywords: smart contract; greedy contract detection; deep learning; explainable artificial intelligence; lightweight

1. Introduction

Blockchain has recently been used in various fields [1–3]. The reason why blockchain can be used in such a variety of fields is because of smart contracts. A smart contract is a digital contract based on blockchain. Smart contracts allow parties to conclude contracts without the involvement of a third party. However, as a result of analyzing some smart contracts deployed on Ethereum, it was confirmed that greedy contracts are included [4]. A greed contract locks the Ether indefinitely so that it cannot be withdrawn within the contract. Therefore, executing a greedy contract causes enormous damage. There can be events in which the parity multisig wallet is frozen. Due to a code flaw discovered in the multisig wallet library smart contract, approximately 510,000 Ether users were locked indefinitely. Since these problems pose a very critical threat to the blockchain network, they must be prevented.

To prevent this problem, methodologies are needed to prevent malicious activity. There are two main ways to detect malicious activity: malicious node detection and malicious smart contract detection. Among the latter, various malicious smart contract detection models have been proposed [5–7] to detect malicious smart contracts. Most deep-learning-based methods detect malicious smart contracts by learning the features of smart contracts. In addition, research has been conducted to image smart contracts and train them to implement a detection model [8].

However, since the transaction speed is directly related to the scalability of the blockchain, the transaction speed in the blockchain must also be considered. If detection

takes too much time, it incurs computational and memory overhead. However, existing deep-learning-based detection models are designed only to increase accuracy. Therefore, existing deep learning detection models may cause computational and memory overhead. Moreover, a lot of research on IoT blockchain has been conducted recently [9–11]. Therefore, a lightweight detection model as well as a detection rate is essential. In other words, a lightweight deep learning detection model that does not reduce the scalability of blockchain is needed.

In this paper, through XAI, we identify important instructions when deep learning detects greedy contracts. We propose a `Greedeeptector` trained through important instructions. `Greedeeptector` is a lightweight detection model for the Internet of Things (IoT). `Greedeeptector` identifies greedy contracts in a computationally and memory-efficient manner without compromising the scalability of the blockchain or detection accuracy. The efficiency of speed and memory is very important for low-end devices, such as IoT devices. Also, in terms of blockchain scalability, the lower the computational and memory usage, the higher the scalability.

1.1. Contribution

1.1.1. In-Depth Analysis of Greedy Contract Instruction Using Explainable Artificial Intelligence

Through integrated gradient and gradient SHAP, instructions that affect the prediction of the model are identified. We select several important instructions for benign and greedy smart contracts, and we analyze them in depth. In addition, we analyze which instructions have important characteristics and are frequently used in greedy contracts.

1.1.2. Implementation of a Lightweight Neural Network Based on Important Instructions

Important instructions extracted through XAI have fewer data dimensions. We implement a lightweight model using these important instructions for the training process. The lightweight model is about 50% lighter than the previous model. In addition, the lightweight model shows little loss of accuracy.

1.1.3. Improving the Stability of Blockchain Networks through Detection When Executing Contracts

Unlike previous work, our work performs greedy contract detection when the smart contract is executed. That is, detection can be performed not only for newly deployed smart contracts but also for already deployed smart contracts. Thus, it improves the stability of the blockchain network.

The remainder of this paper is organized as follows: In Section 2, related technologies, such as artificial neural networks, smart contracts, and previous work, are presented. In Section 3, the proposed method to detect greedy contracts is introduced. In Section 4, a comparison between the default model and the lightweight model and an in-depth analysis of the contract's instructions are described. Finally, Section 5 concludes the paper.

2. Related Works

2.1. Artificial Neural Networks

An artificial neural network [12] refers to a computer-implemented structure of the neurons in the human brain. Deep learning performs learning by stacking multiple layers of artificial neural networks and consists of an input layer, a hidden layer, and an output layer. The input layer refers to the layer that receives the data to be learned. The hidden layer calculates the weight, and the final result is output through the output layer. Unlike machine learning, deep learning extracts and learns features from data by itself. Due to these characteristics, deep learning is used in various fields, such as computer vision, speech recognition, natural language processing, and signal processing. Multi-layer perceptron (MLP) and convolutional neural networks (CNN) [13] are representative deep learning models and are mainly used for classification problems. In addition, recurrent neural networks (RNNs) [14], which are good for training time-series data, and generative neural networks, such as generative adversarial networks (GANs) [15], also exist.

2.2. Lightweight Deep Learning

Lightweight deep learning is deep learning that reduces the size of the model and reduces computational complexity while maintaining the performance of models with deep and complex layers [16]. If a non-lightweight deep learning model is used in a low-end IoT device, memory overhead may occur in the process of loading numerous parameters. Therefore, such lightweight deep learning is essential for low-end IoT devices with limited computing resources, such as mobile environments, autonomous vehicles, and robots. We utilize XAI to implement lightweight models.

2.3. Explainable Artificial Intelligence (XAI)

Artificial intelligence is a black-box model and inside the model learns complex relationships and characteristics about data. Therefore, it is not clear what the reasons and grounds for decisions made by AI models are. However, in fields where important decisions must be made, such as medicine, finance, and law, a clear basis for the AI output may be required. XAI [17] is a technology created to solve these problems. XAI is a technology that provides the reasons and rationale for decisions made by deep learning models. XAI can increase the reliability of deep learning technology and has the advantage of facilitating debugging to achieve the result requiired [18]. In addition, by improving understanding of the training result, it can be developed into a better model. XAI can determine which features are needed for prediction. That is, it is possible to learn a deep learning model with necessary features only, excluding unnecessary features. In this way, the deep learning model can be optimized and a lightweight model can be implemented. Therefore, XAI is useful for implementing efficient and lightweight models. We used Captum [19] to apply various algorithms. Captum is a unified, open-source model interpretability library for PyTorch. There are several methods of XAI (e.g., integrated gradients and gradient SHAP). We utilize these two algorithms to implement a lightweight deep learning model.

Integrated gradients (IG) [20] is an XAI algorithm that calculates the importance of each feature by accumulating and multiplying the gradient information and the difference between the input and baseline. Since IG calculates the importance of each feature locally, it does not have a global interpretation function. IG satisfies the sensitivity and implementation invariance conditions. The sensitivity condition states that, if the difference between the baseline and the input is only one feature, the model should have non-zero attribution if it makes different predictions for the two inputs. The implementation invariance condition is a condition that when different models predict the same for the same input, the two models must have a constant attribution for the same input. IG has the advantage of being simple to implement and can be applied to various datasets, such as text and images.

Gradient SHAP [21] is an XAI algorithm that approximates Shapley values through gradients. The Shapley value quantifies the contribution of each player participating in the game based on game theory. In other words, the Shapley value represents the contribution of a specific player when they cooperate with all other players. Recently, it has mainly been used to interpret deep learning models. This allows us to interpret how the features contribute to the output. The Shapley value is useful for feature analysis because it can be analyzed both locally and globally. In addition, the Shapley value has the advantage of high accuracy by considering the interaction between inputs. However, it also has the disadvantage that the computation increases exponentially as the number of features increases. To overcome this shortcoming, Gradient SHAP calculates the Shapley values through gradients.

2.4. Blockchain

Blockchain is a peer-to-peer distributed ledger network in which all network participants share the same ledger [22]. All transaction data in the network are included in blocks, and the blocks are linked to each other in a chain form. Blockchain is a decentralized method in which nodes in the network each own a ledger, rather than a method in which a central server manages data. Therefore, as the nodes in the network directly verify the transaction, the transaction is performed without a third party and does not require a server. If hackers want to manipulate data, they must manipulate the blockchains of the majority nodes in the network. However, since this is virtually impossible, the integrity of the transaction is guaranteed. Due to these advantages, blockchain is used in various fields, such as digital asset transactions and medical care.

2.5. Smart Contract

A smart contract is a digital contract based on blockchain [23]. In the past, contracts were made in writing, but smart contracts are implemented through code. Smart contracts are automatically executed only when certain conditions are met. Therefore, the decentralization pursued by the blockchain is realized by the two parties signing a contract through a smart contract without the involvement of a third-party certification authority. Smart contracts can be written in a variety of high-level programming languages, but are typically written in the Solidity language. Code written in a high-level programming language is converted to Ethereum bytecode through a compiler and is then deployed on the blockchain. The Ethereum bytecode consists of an opcode and a value. An opcode represents an instruction to be executed by a computer, and there are currently 140 opcodes in Ethereum. The deployed smart contract is executed through the Ethereum virtual machine (EVM). EVM provides an execution environment for smart contracts and executes smart contracts in the form of a bytecode. In addition, in order to execute a smart contract, it is necessary to have a certain amount of gas, which is used as a fee for the transaction. This is the cryptocurrency paid to miners as the computational cost of smart contract execution.

Once deployed, the smart contract cannot be deleted and its code cannot be modified. This is because smart contracts are deployed on a blockchain that has immutability characteristics. Information stored on the blockchain is permanently maintained and cannot be modified. In other words, even if errors or security vulnerabilities are found in the smart contract code, they cannot be corrected, which can cause big problems.

2.6. Greedy Contract

A greedy contract [4] is a smart contract that can reach a state where it locks indefinitely so that the Ether cannot be withdrawn. A greedy contract can receive the Ether. However, since there is no instruction to process the received Ether or the instruction cannot be reached, the Ether is locked in the contract forever. Therefore, the Ether sent to the greedy contract cannot be recovered even by the node that deployed the contract. Executing a greedy contract can cause enormous damage.

2.7. Malicious Smart Contract Detection

ACSAC '18 classified malicious smart contracts into three types: greedy, suicidal, and prodigal contracts [4]. In addition, the authors implemented `MAIAN`, a tool that detects malicious smart contracts through symbolic analysis. The `MAIAN` tool is the most representative smart contract detection tool. It detects bug-causing transactions by processing the bytecode of smart contracts. In the symbolic analysis method, the symbolic execution is started at the first instruction in the bytecode. Execution then proceeds sequentially until the terminating instruction (e.g., STOP, RETURN) is found. If a function call occurs while tracing an instruction sequence, it is searched considering the branch condition. If the terminating instruction is not valid, it is backtracked in the depth-first search process to try another path. Then, concrete validation is performed to verify the results of symbolic analysis. For this, malicious contract candidates are executed on a fake Ethereum network created through a private fork. In order to distinguish between the three types of malicious contracts, the following procedures are performed: Ether check (prodigal), check if the contract can be killed (suicidal), instruction check (greedy), etc. If the contract is determined to be malicious even after this process, MAIAN finally classifies the contract as malicious.

The MAIAN tool is developed in Python, and it can detect a smart contract in less than 10 s on average.

In [5], the authors proposed a system that detects malicious contracts after first detecting malicious users. This is the latest work in the field of malicious smart contract detection. In this system, if a user deploys a malicious smart contract, the user is classified as a malicious node and can no longer deploy smart contracts. LSTM, GRU, and ANN were used as models to detect malicious smart contracts. The AUCs of LSTM, GRU, and ANN achieved 0.99, 0.99, and 0.97, respectively. In the scenario considered, detection is performed before deploying smart contracts, so detection is not possible for smart contracts that have already been deployed.

In [6], SmartCheck, which analyzes XPath patterns by converting Solidity codes into XML-based intermediate representations, was proposed. SmartCheck detects vulnerabilities in smart contracts by analyzing the XPath. However, a weak smart contract without an XPath pattern has a critical problem in that it is difficult to detect.

In [7], SNC '21 proposed a model that analyzes the vulnerability of smart contracts based on machine learning by introducing a shared child node. The model can predict eight types of vulnerabilities including re-entrancy, arithmetic, access control, unchecked low-level calls, bad randomness, front running, and denial of service. However, the model is not stable because it does not secure enough malicious smart contracts.

3. Greedeeptector

For the well-known MAIAN tool, various detection methods have been proposed. In previous work [5], the latest deep learning-based detection technique is described, which can also detect malicious contracts, but the number of datasets used is very small. Therefore, the reliability is not high, and it is difficult to state that it is robust. Also, the methods cannot perform detection on already deployed smart contracts.

In this paper, we present a robust greedy contract detection system using lightweight deep learning implemented through XAI. Our approach works both for contracts to be deployed and contracts that have already been deployed. Therefore, the proposed method can ensure the safe execution of smart contracts on the current Ethereum network. In addition, we design a lightweight detection system that can operate efficiently on the blockchain. Moreover, in this work, we evaluate and discuss our detection system. Our work is applied to the blockchain network. That is, the deep learning model is run on blockchain nodes (e.g., computers or low-end devices). Evaluation of the execution of the actual blockchain network will be carried out in future work.

Figure 1 and Algorithm 1 show the mechanism of Greedeeptector. nodes on the Ethereum network can obtain information about smart contracts and execute smart contracts. Before executing a smart contract, each node runs Greedeeptector to detect a greedy contract. For this, pre-processing is performed. As mentioned in line 2 of Algorithm 1, the smart contract's bytecodes are converted to opcodes (https://github.com/daejunpark/evm-disassembler accessed on 11 September 2023). Then the frequency for each opcode is counted. Finally, the opcode frequency of the target smart contract is input into Greedeeptector. If the result (*isGreedy*) is 0, then the contract is executed because it is a benign contract. Conversely, if it is a greedy contract, it is not executed. Table 1 represents the key points of the proposed system.

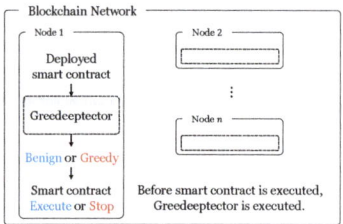

Figure 1. Diagram of our Greedeeptector.

Algorithm 1 Greedeeptector mechanism

Require: Bytecode of smart contract (B_{SC}), Extracted opcodes of smart contract (OP_{sc}), Frequency of opcodes (F_{OP}), Deep learning model for greedy contract detection (Greedeeptector)
$Opcodes$={00:STOP, ..., FF:SELFDESTRUCT}   ▷ Set up dictionary mapping opcodes to bytecodes
for op in B_{SC} **do**
    if op in $Opcodes$ **then**
        OP_{sc}.append(op)   ▷ Bytecode to opcode
    end if
end for
Initialize F_{OP} to zero
for op in OP_{sc} **do**
    $F_{OP}[op] \leftarrow F_{OP}[op]+1$ ▷ Calculate frequency of opcode
end for
$isGreedy \leftarrow$ Greedeeptector (F_{OP})   ▷ Greedy contract detection
if $isGreedy == True$ **then**
    Stop the smart contract
else
    Execute the smart contract
end if

Table 1. Key points of the proposed system.

Key Points	Descriptions
Greedy contracts	Greedy contracts have potential risk (e.g., Ether can be lost.).
Blockchain network	Blockchain network can execute smart contract (e.g., Ethereum, Bitcoin).
Explainable artificial intelligence	Since it can interpret the results of training, it can be used for lightweighting.
Lightweight deep learning	It increases the scalability of blockchain and can be applied to lightweight devices.

3.1. Base Model

In this section, we present the base model of Greedeeptector. Figure 2 shows a diagram of the base model. First, the opcodes are extracted from the smart contract. The extracted opcodes are converted into an array representing the frequency of each opcode. The frequencies for each opcode are input to the neural network, and the neural network classifies greedy and benign contracts. If the target smart contract is classified as a greedy contract, its execution is stopped.

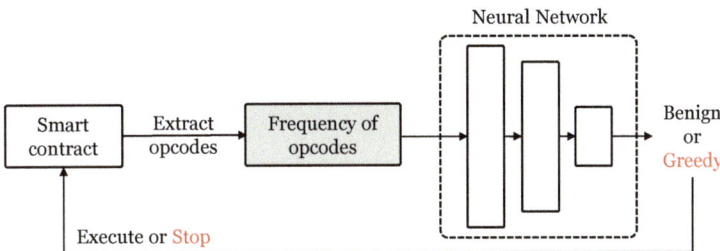

Figure 2. The diagram of the base model.

3.1.1. Pre-Processing

As explained earlier, the frequency of smart contract opcodes is required to detect greedy contracts. Therefore, the frequency of the opcode must be extracted from the bytecode of the smart contract through pre-processing. Figure 3 shows the pre-processing process. A smart contract can be expressed as a bytecode composed of opcodes (instructions) and values used for operation. We extract the opcodes among them. Then, a sequence of opcodes used in the smart contract is generated. Since one opcode is 1 byte, a total of 256 opcodes (00 to FF) can exist. However, Ethereum only provides 140 opcodes. So, we generate an array of length 140 representing the opcode frequency. The index of the frequency array means each opcode and the value means the frequency. That is, it contains information about how many times each opcode is used in a smart contract. The generated array of the opcode frequency is used as a dataset for greedy contract detection.

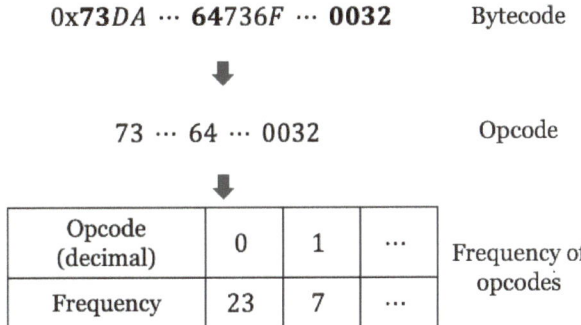

Figure 3. Converting bytecode to the frequency of opcodes in pre-processing.

3.1.2. Detection

The neural network is used to detect greedy contracts. Our proposed system is designed to perform detection without compromising blockchain scalability. Due to the large size of time-series models, like recurrent neural networks, we opted for a more lightweight deep neural network. Figure 4 shows the structure of the deep learning network used in our work. First, the opcode frequency data generated through the pre-processing is input to the deep learning network. Each element of the frequency array is assigned to one neuron of the input layer. That is, the number of neurons in the input layer is equal to the number of opcodes in Ethereum. As a hidden layer, a fully connected layer (linear layer) is used. Before passing to the output layer, it goes through a dropout layer that discards random neurons to prevent overfitting. In the output layer, a value between 0 (benign) and 1 (greedy) is output as a predicted value for the data through the sigmoid activation function. Equation (1) shows the formula for the sigmoid activation function. Finally, the loss between the actual label and the predicted value is calculated through the binary cross-entropy loss function. Equation (2) represents the binary cross-entropy loss formula. y hat means the continuous sigmoid function output value between 0 and 1, and y means the discontinuous actual value. The neural network is updated to minimize the loss. Through this training process, a neural network can distinguish greedy contracts from benign contracts.

$$\sigma(x) = \frac{1}{1+e^{-x}} \tag{1}$$

$$BCE(y, \hat{y}) = -(y \log(\hat{y}) + (1-y) \log(1-\hat{y})) \tag{2}$$

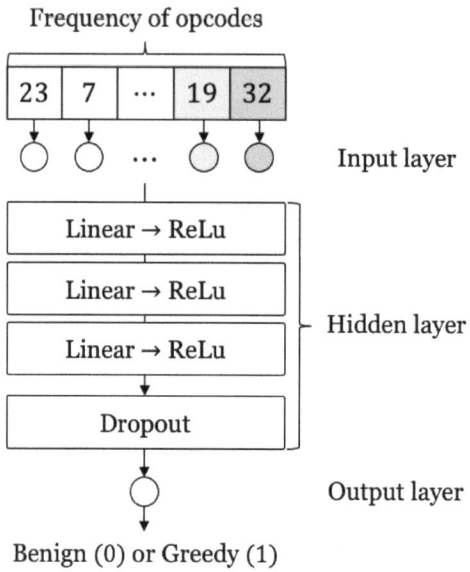

Figure 4. The structure of the base model.

Table 2 shows the hyperparameters of the base model. The hyperparameters of the base model are chosen through experimentation to achieve the optimal performance. To the best of our knowledge, these hyperparameters yield the maximum performance. The number of input layers is 140 (the number of opcodes used). Also, to prevent overfitting, a dropout value of 40% is used, and the epoch is set to 200.

Table 2. Hyperparameters of the base model.

Hyperparameters	Descriptions
Epoch	200
Batch size	256
Units of the input layer	140
Dropout	0.4
Optimizer (learning rate)	Adam (0.0001)

3.2. Lightweight Model Using XAI

We used XAI to design a computation and memory-efficient lightweight model. Figure 5 shows the process of implementing a lightweight model using XAI. We implemented the base model using the frequency of 140 opcodes. Subsequently, we computed the IG and SHAP values of the base model. In Figure 5, the red color in the graph represents the IG values, while the blue represents the SHAP values. Even though there are values for all 140 opcodes, the graph only captures 17 of them. These values indicate the influence each feature of the input data has on the prediction; the larger their absolute value, the more significant the feature becomes. Furthermore, a positive value suggests that the feature contributes to the greedy contract, whereas a negative value implies a contribution to the benign contract. Thus, we can identify opcodes that have a significant impact on the classification between benign and greedy contracts.

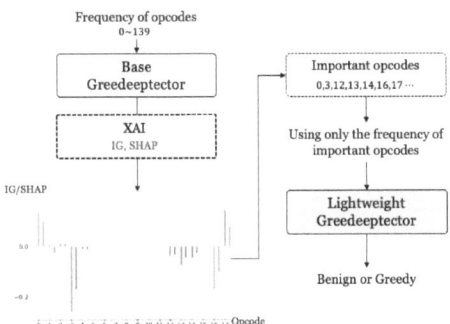

Figure 5. Design of lightweight model; the red color in the graph represents the IG values, while the blue represents the SHAP values.

The lightweight model uses only important opcodes among 140 opcodes. That is, fewer than 140 opcodes can be used. This usually allows the construction of a simpler model, since the number of input data features is reduced. As a result, the number of neurons in the input layer is reduced and the parameters of the neural network are reduced. Here, only opcodes that can reduce the parameters of the model as much as possible without degrading the accuracy should be selected. So, we chose the top n opcodes on the basis of experiment.

However, since a large number of data samples are used for training, some of them may have outliers. If there are outliers, the IG and SHAP values of a specific sample have a large effect on the average. Furthermore, the more positive the IG and SHAP values, the higher the contribution to greedy contracts, whereas the more negative the values indicates a higher contribution to benign contracts. The reliability is then reduced, so outliers should be removed. We use the inter-quantile range (IQR) [24] to remove outliers. In the inter-quartile range (IQR) approach, the dataset is segmented into quartiles, with the 25th percentile denoted as $Q1$ and the 75th percentile as $Q3$. The lower bound is established at $Q1 - 1.5 \cdot IQR$ and the upper bound at $Q3 + 1.5 \cdot IQR$. Any data points falling outside this interval are deemed outliers. The constant multiplied by IQR is usually 1.5. In summary, after removing outliers, our lightweight model can reduce the number of parameters while maintaining accuracy by learning only the top n opcodes from the average IG and SHAP.

Table 3 shows the hyperparameters of the lightweight model designed via XAI. The hyperparameters of the lightweight model are chosen through experimentation to achieve optimal performance. To the best of our knowledge, these hyperparameters yield the maximum performance. In the lightweight model, the same epoch, batch size, dropout rate, optimizer, and learning rate as the base model were used. In other words, the difference in hyperparameters between the lightweight model and the base model is the number of neurons in the input and hidden layers. In this work, the frequency of one opcode is assigned to one neuron. In the lightweight model, the number of units in the input layer is reduced because only the frequency for important opcodes is used as data (it is set experimentally, see Section 4.3). That is, since the number of features of the input data (the number of important opcodes) is reduced, the number of neurons in the model is reduced. As a result, lightweight models can reduce file size and computational complexity.

Table 3. Hyperparameters of the lightweight model.

Hyperparameters	Descriptions
Epoch	200
Batch size	256
Units of the input layer	58
Dropout	0.4
Optimizer (learning rate)	Adam (0.0001)

4. Experiments and Evaluation

For this experiment, we use Google Colaboratory Pro+, a cloud-based service with Ubuntu 20.04.5 LTS and GPU (Tesla T4) 15GB RAM. Python 3.9.16 and PyTorch 2.0.0 are used as the programming environment.

4.1. Dataset

In this experiment, the Google BigQuery dataset (https://cloud.google.com/blog/products/data-analytics/ethereum-bigquery-public-dataset-smart-contract-analytics?hl=en accessed on 11 September 2023) provided by Google is used. The Google BigQuery dataset contains datasets for smart contracts deployed on Ethereum. A dataset of 14,716 benign and greedy contracts is generated through MAIAN, a malicious smart contract detection tool. The training dataset includes both benign contracts and greedy contracts. Additionally, the test dataset also encompasses both benign and greedy contracts. The ratio of benign to greedy contracts is set at 1:1.

4.2. Result for Base Model

Table 4 shows the performance of the base model using 140 Ethereum instructions. The base model achieves an average test F1-score of 92.6%. The number of parameters of the base model is 15,297.

Table 4. Performance of the base model.

Performance Metric	Descriptions
Training F1-score	95.0%
Validation F1-score	92.3%
Test F1-score	92.6%
The number of parameters	15,297

4.3. Result for Lightweight Model

We use XAI to design a lightweight model that is computation- and memory-efficient. The lightweight model consists of a process of extracting important opcodes, removing outliers, and learning the frequency of important opcodes. In this section, we discuss the implementation and performance of the lightweight model.

Extract the Important Instructions Using XAI

Before selecting important opcodes, we need to remove outliers in IG and SHAP. This is because it improves the reliability of selecting important opcodes by reducing the impact of specific data samples on average for IG and SHAP. Figure 6 is an example of removing outliers using the IQR method described above. Most of the values are clustered between −1 and 1, and there are a few outliers. As shown on the right side in Figure 6, we successfully removed outliers.

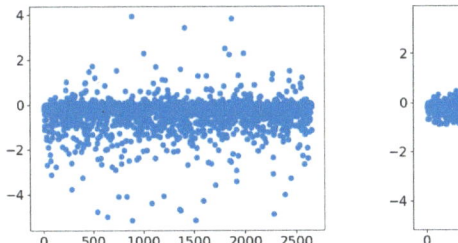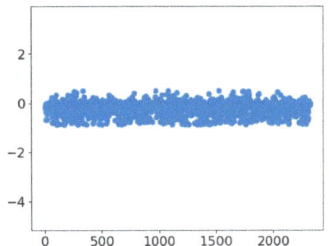

Figure 6. An example of outlier removal using the IQR ; Before (**left**), After (**right**).

The important instructions are selected by calculating IG and SHAP for the base model. The reason for considering both properties is to secure reliability. A total of 50 opcodes are selected from IG and SHAP to reduce the size of the model as much as possible while maintaining accuracy. This is the optimal number of opcodes obtained as a result of experimentation while reducing the number of instructions from 140 opcodes. Then, duplicates are removed from the 50 opcodes selected from IG and SHAP, respectively. This makes it possible to select important opcodes with both IG and SHAP.

However, the important opcodes are slightly different in each experiment. Therefore, it is difficult to obtain stable performance when using important opcodes obtained through one experiment. Therefore, we construct a lightweight model using instructions that appeared more than k times (k = 5, 7, 10) out of 10 trials.

Table 5 shows the experimental results for each case. The experimental findings indicate that the F1-score in Case1 achieved the best accuracy with 92.3%. In Case2 and Case3, the performance was lower than Case1. This seems to be because some opcodes that affect prediction are excluded.

Table 5. Comparison of performance according to the number of opcodes used (Case1, Case2, Case3 (k = 5, 7, 10, respectively)).

	Case1	Case2	Case3
The number of opcodes	58	51	37
Training F1-score	0.93	0.92	0.90
Validation F1-score	0.92	0.92	0.90
Test F1-score	0.92	0.91	0.90
The number of parameters	5855	4861	3167

As the number of opcodes used decreases, the number of neurons in the input layer of the neural network decreases. Accordingly, the number of parameters in the entire model is also reduced. Therefore, Case3 has the smallest number of parameters. However, Case3 is unsuitable for use because of the large loss of accuracy compared to the base model. Therefore, we adopted Case1, which is lightweight with minimal loss of accuracy, as our Lightweight Greedeeptector model.

Table 6 shows the performance of the lightweight model. As noted earlier, the lightweight model has fewer parameters than the base model. Therefore, it is efficient in terms of computational complexity and memory usage. However, performance loss may occur. Nevertheless, the accuracy of the lightweight model was 92.3% So, our lightweight model provides memory and computational efficiency without loss of performance. Therefore, our work has the advantage of reducing computational and memory overhead in a blockchain network when blockchain nodes perform greedy contract detection in a real scenario.

Table 6. Performance of the lightweight model.

Performance Metric	Descriptions
Training F1-score	92.6%
Validation F1-score	91.6%
Test F1-score	92.3%
The number of parameters	5855

4.4. Comparison between Base Model and Lightweight Model

In this section, we report various experiments undertaken to build a lightweight model. We also compare the model size and detection accuracy of the base and lightweight models.

4.4.1. Performance

Table 7 shows a comparison between the base and lightweight model. The lightweight model size is reduced by 41.5%, and the space complexity decreases as the model size decreases. The parameter (weight of the model) is reduced by 61.8%, and the computational complexity decreases as the model has fewer parameters. The model size is a very important advantage in lightweight deep-learning models. A small-size model is equivalent to a deep-learning model with fewer parameters. The fewer the parameters, the smaller the amount of computation. Therefore, a small model size means low computational complexity. Thus, when detecting greedy contracts on the blockchain, our implementation is memory and computationally efficient. The accuracy of the base model and the lightweight model are similar. However, since we reduced the size of the model by 41.5%, this small performance loss is negligible.

Table 7. Comparison between base and lightweight model.

Model	Model Size	Parameters	Speed	F1-Score
Base	0.89 MB	15,297	0.015 ms	92.6%
Lightweight	0.53 MB	5855	0.013 ms	92.3%

In our scenario, our implementation is deployed on each node (IoT device) on the blockchain (currently, it is a prototype.). The efficiency of speed and memory is very important for low-end devices, such as IoT devices. In terms of blockchain scalability, the lower the computational and memory usage, the higher the scalability. In other words, our target node is a low-power node on the blockchain, so the small-size model is a significant advantage on the blockchain.

4.4.2. Instruction Analysis

Tables 8 and 9 show a comparison of the top eight important opcodes for benign and greedy contracts depending on the XAI algorithm. In IG and SHAP, it stands out that instructions related to branching (JUMP, JUMPDEST, JUMPI) are important. JUMP is an unconditional branch instruction, and JUMPI is a conditional branch instruction. JUMPDEST means the branch destination address. The branch instructions related to the benign contract are JUMP and JUMPDEST. Conversely, the branching instruction associated with greedy contracts is JUMPI. JUMPI is a conditional branch instruction, and JUMP and JUMPDEST are instructions that branch regardless of conditions. Due to greedy contract characteristics, the greedy contract uses conditional branch instructions to bypass the ability to process the Ether [4]. In fact, through our experiments, it is confirmed that the JUMPI instruction is an important instruction—it is thought that the JUMPI instruction greatly affects classification as a greedy contract. Conversely, in benign contracts, conditional branch instructions are not an important characteristic.

Table 8. Top 8 important opcodes in the benign contract.

Algorithm	Sorted by Values of IG and SHAP							
	1	2	3	4	5	6	7	8
IG	JUMPDEST	DUP1	SUB	JUMP	EQ	PUSH4	REVERT	SLT
SHAP	DUP1	SUB	JUMP	JUMPDEST	PUSH4	EQ	MLOAD	LT

Table 9. Top 8 important opcodes in the greedy contract.

Algorithm	Sorted by Values of IG and SHAP							
	1	2	3	4	5	6	7	8
IG	JUMPI	CALLVALUE	SWAP1	SWAP2	STOP	CALLDATASIZE	AND	ADDRESS
SHAP	JUMPI	PUSH2	CALLVALUE	SWAP2	POP	STOP	SWAP1	CALLDATASIZE

4.5. Comparison with Existing Method

`MAIAN` detects prodigal, suicidal and greedy contracts. Its file size is very small. However, the disadvantage is that detection takes a long time.

The previous work represents the latest deep-learning-based approach. It categorizes several types of malicious smart contracts into one class. Therefore, various malicious smart contracts can be detected. However, the methods used do not work on blockchain networks and are not valid for already deployed smart contracts. In other words, it is operable only for newly deployed smart contracts. Therefore, it is not suitable for blockchain networks where numerous malicious contracts have already been deployed. In addition, data from a total of 781 contracts (650 benign contracts and 131 malicious contracts) only were used. Therefore, it is considered that the reliability of the previous approach is not high. The elements mentioned in Table 10 are the result of our implementation of the previous model as it is.

Many models have been proposed in previous work, but we reproduce the model with the highest performance. These values are then measured by the reproduced model.

Table 10. Comparison of smart contract detection methods.

Category	MAIAN [4]	Previous Work [5]	This Work (LM)
Smart contracts	Prodigal, suicidal, greedy (3 classes)	Malicious (2 classes)	Greedy (2 classes)
Algorithm	Symbolic analysis, Concrete validation	Deep learning	Deep learning
Parameters	-	54,018	5855
File size	0.232 MB	0.74 MB	0.53 MB
Speed	Within 10 s	Slower than ours	0.013 ms

Our method can classify greedy contracts and benign contracts. However, among the malicious contracts that occur when using a dataset of about 80,000, the proportion of greedy contracts is 93.4% (in the Google BigQuery dataset). Therefore, problems caused by malicious smart contracts in the blockchain can be prevented just by detecting greedy contracts. We increased the reliability and stability of the model by using a dataset 38 times larger than in previous work. Our implementation only detects greedy contracts but has the potential to prevent most malicious smart contracts. Our lightweight model is larger than the `MAIAN`, but can detect contracts significantly faster. Compared to the previous work, the file size and the number of parameters decreased by 28.4% and 89.2%, respectively. Since our work has far fewer parameters, it is fast and memory efficient. These points represent a great advantage for the blockchain network.

5. Conclusions

In this work, we identify and analyze opcodes that significantly impact the model in order to implement a lightweight model. Additionally, based on this, we propose a computationally and memory-efficient lightweight detection model for the IoT. Unlike previous approaches that perform detection at the smart contract deployment phase, the proposed system performs detection at the smart contract execution phase. Therefore, the proposed system can perform the detection of already deployed smart contracts. As a result, the proposed system improves the stability and scalability of blockchain networks.

As a summary of our experimental results, the file size of the lightweight model is reduced by 41.5% compared to the base model. Thus, when our system is running on a blockchain, it is a memory and computationally efficient system. Finally, despite being lightweight, our system has a high detection accuracy of 92.3%.

We tried to detect not only greedy contracts but also various malicious smart contracts, but it is not easy to collect malicious smart contract datasets other than greedy contracts. Therefore, we implemented a model that detects only greedy contracts.

In future work, we plan to implement a model that can detect various malicious smart contracts as well as greedy contracts. Additionally, the lightweight model is implemented to target low-end devices. Therefore, we plan to make the model lighter by using not only XAI but also knowledge distillation, quantization, and pruning methods. Afterwards, we plan to conduct additional experiments by deploying the lightweight model on low-end devices, such as Raspberry Pi.

Author Contributions: Software, Y.K., W.K. and H.K.; Writing—original draft, Y.K.; Writing—review & editing, M.L., M.S. and H.S.; Supervision, H.S. All authors have read and agreed to the published version of the manuscript.

Funding: This work was supported by Institute of Information & communications Technology Planning & Evaluation (IITP) grant funded by the Korea government(MSIT) (No.2022-0-00627, Development of Lightweight BIoT technology for Highly Constrained Devices, 100%).

Conflicts of Interest: The authors declare no conflict of interest.

References

1. Liu, Z.; Jiang, L.; Osmani, M.; Demian, P. Building information management (BIM) and blockchain (BC) for sustainable building design information management framework. *Electronics* **2019**, *8*, 724. [CrossRef]
2. Liu, J.; Liu, Z.; Yang, Q.; Osmani, M.; Demian, P. A Conceptual Blockchain Enhanced Information Model of Product Service Systems Framework for Sustainable Furniture. *Buildings* **2022**, *13*, 85. [CrossRef]
3. Liu, Z.; Wu, T.; Wang, F.; Osmani, M.; Demian, P. Blockchain Enhanced Construction Waste Information Management: A Conceptual Framework. *Sustainability* **2022**, *14*, 12145. [CrossRef]
4. Nikolić, I.; Kolluri, A.; Sergey, I.; Saxena, P.; Hobor, A. Finding the greedy, prodigal, and suicidal contracts at scale. In Proceedings of the 34th Annual Computer Security Applications Conference, San Juan, PR, USA, 3–7 December 2018; pp. 653–663.
5. Shah, H.; Shah, D.; Jadav, N.K.; Gupta, R.; Tanwar, S.; Alfarraj, O.; Tolba, A.; Raboaca, M.S.; Marina, V. Deep Learning-Based Malicious Smart Contract and Intrusion Detection System for IoT Environment. *Mathematics* **2023**, *11*, 418. [CrossRef]
6. Tikhomirov, S.; Voskresenskaya, E.; Ivanitskiy, I.; Takhaviev, R.; Marchenko, E.; Alexandrov, Y. Smartcheck: Static analysis of ethereum smart contracts. In Proceedings of the 1st International Workshop on Emerging Trends in Software Engineering for Blockchain, Gothenburg, Sweden, 27 May 2018; pp. 9–16.
7. Xu, Y.; Hu, G.; You, L.; Cao, C. A novel machine learning-based analysis model for smart contract vulnerability. *Secur. Commun. Networks* **2021**, *2021*, 1–12. [CrossRef]
8. Lohith, J.J.; Anusree Manoj, K.; Guru, N.; Srinivasan, P. TP-Detect: Trigram-pixel based vulnerability detection for Ethereum smart contracts. *Multimed. Tools Appl.* **2023**, 1–15. [CrossRef]
9. Tyagi, A.K.; Dananjayan, S.; Agarwal, D.; Thariq Ahmed, H.F. Blockchain—Internet of Things Applications: Opportunities and Challenges for Industry 4.0 and Society 5.0. *Sensors* **2023**, *23*, 947. [CrossRef] [PubMed]
10. Taloba, A.I.; Elhadad, A.; Rayan, A.; Abd El-Aziz, R.M.; Salem, M.; Alzahrani, A.A.; Alharithi, F.S.; Park, C. A blockchain-based hybrid platform for multimedia data processing in IoT-Healthcare. *Alex. Eng. J.* **2023**, *65*, 263–274. [CrossRef]
11. Sharma, P.; Namasudra, S.; Crespo, R.G.; Parra-Fuente, J.; Trivedi, M.C. EHDHE: Enhancing security of healthcare documents in IoT-enabled digital healthcare ecosystems using blockchain. *Inf. Sci.* **2023**, *629*, 703–718. [CrossRef]
12. Haykin, S. *Neural Networks and Learning Machines, 3/E*; Pearson Education: Chennai, Tamil Nadu, India, 2009.
13. Albawi, S.; Mohammed, T.A.; Al-Zawi, S. Understanding of a convolutional neural network. In Proceedings of the 2017 International Conference on Engineering and Technology (ICET), Antalya, Turkey, 21–23 August 2017; IEEE: Piscataway, NJ, USA, 2017; pp. 1–6.
14. Petneházi, G. Recurrent neural networks for time series forecasting. *arXiv* **2019**, arXiv:1901.00069.

15. Goodfellow, I.; Pouget-Abadie, J.; Mirza, M.; Xu, B.; Warde-Farley, D.; Ozair, S.; Courville, A.; Bengio, Y. Generative adversarial networks. *Commun. ACM* **2020**, *63*, 139–144. [CrossRef]
16. Wang, C.H.; Huang, K.Y.; Yao, Y.; Chen, J.C.; Shuai, H.H.; Cheng, W.H. Lightweight deep learning: An overview. *IEEE Consum. Electron. Mag.* **2022**, 1–12. [CrossRef]
17. Gunning, D.; Stefik, M.; Choi, J.; Miller, T.; Stumpf, S.; Yang, G.Z. XAI—Explainable artificial intelligence. *Sci. Robot.* **2019**, *4*, eaay7120. [CrossRef] [PubMed]
18. Ali, S.; Abuhmed, T.; El-Sappagh, S.; Muhammad, K.; Alonso-Moral, J.M.; Confalonieri, R.; Guidotti, R.; Del Ser, J.; Díaz-Rodríguez, N.; Herrera, F. Explainable Artificial Intelligence (XAI): What we know and what is left to attain Trustworthy Artificial Intelligence. *Inf. Fusion* **2023**, *99*, 101805.
19. Kokhlikyan, N.; Miglani, V.; Martin, M.; Wang, E.; Alsallakh, B.; Reynolds, J.; Melnikov, A.; Kliushkina, N.; Araya, C.; Yan, S.; et al. Captum: A unified and generic model interpretability library for pytorch. *arXiv* **2020**, arXiv:2009.07896.
20. Sundararajan, M.; Taly, A.; Yan, Q. Axiomatic attribution for deep networks. In Proceedings of the International Conference on Machine Learning, PMLR, Sydney, Australia, 6–11 August 2017; pp. 3319–3328.
21. Erion, G.; Janizek, J.D.; Sturmfels, P.; Lundberg, S.M.; Lee, S.I. Learning explainable models using attribution priors. In Proceedings of the International Conference on Learning Representations ICLR 2020, Addis Ababa, Ethiopia, 30 April 2020.
22. Nakamoto, S. Bitcoin: A peer-to-peer electronic cash system. *Decentralized Bus. Rev.* **2008**, *21260*, 1–9.
23. Buterin, V. A next-generation smart contract and decentralized application platform. *White Pap.* **2014**, *3*, 1–2.
24. Whaley, D.L., III. The Interquartile Range: Theory and Estimation. Ph.D. Thesis, East Tennessee State University, Johnson City, TN, USA, 2005.

Disclaimer/Publisher's Note: The statements, opinions and data contained in all publications are solely those of the individual author(s) and contributor(s) and not of MDPI and/or the editor(s). MDPI and/or the editor(s) disclaim responsibility for any injury to people or property resulting from any ideas, methods, instructions or products referred to in the content.

Article

Secure and Privacy-Preserving Authentication Scheme Using Decentralized Identifier in Metaverse Environment

Myeonghyun Kim [1], Jihyeon Oh [1], Seunghwan Son [1], Yohan Park [2], Jungjoon Kim [3] and Youngho Park [1,*]

[1] School of Electronic and Electrical Engineering, Kyungpook National University, Daegu 41566, Republic of Korea; kimmyeong123@knu.ac.kr (M.K.); chldlstnr071@knu.ac.kr (J.O.); sonshawn@knu.ac.kr (S.S.)
[2] School of Computer Engineering, Keimyung University, Daegu 42601, Republic of Korea; yhpark@kmu.ac.kr
[3] School of Electronics Engineering, Kyungpook National University, Daegu 41566, Republic of Korea; jungkim7@ee.knu.ac.kr
* Correspondence: parkyh@knu.ac.kr

Abstract: The metaverse provides a virtual world with many social activities that parallel the real world. As the metaverse attracts more attention, the importance of security and privacy preservation is increasing significantly. In the metaverse, users have the capability to create various avatars, which can be exploited to deceive or threaten others, leading to internal security issues. Additionally, users attempting to access the metaverse are susceptible to various external security threats since they communicate with service providers through public channels. To address these challenges, we propose an authentication scheme using blockchain, a decentralized identifier, and a verifiable credential to enable metaverse users to perform secure identity verification and authentication without disclosing sensitive information to service providers. Furthermore, the proposed approach mitigates privacy concerns associated with the management of personal information by enabling users to prove the necessary identity information independently without relying on service providers. We demonstrate that the proposed scheme is resistant to malicious security attacks and provides privacy preservation by performing security analyses, such as AVISPA simulation, BAN logic, and the real-or-random (ROR) model. We also show that the performance of our proposed scheme is better suited for the metaverse environment by providing greater security and efficiency when compared to competing schemes.

Keywords: metaverse; authentication; blockchain; decentralized identifier

1. Introduction

Various advanced technologies are rapidly evolving and being invented, leading to the emergence of the metaverse concept, which is envisioned as the next iteration of the Internet. Metaverse is a virtual realm that parallels the physical world, where people engage with the metaverse using wearable devices (such as a virtual reality (VR)/augmented reality (AR) devices) and manipulate digital avatars to engage with others. Furthermore, the advancement of cutting-edge communication and networking technologies, including wireless networks and 5G technology, plays an important role in moving the metaverse forward by enabling low-latency, high-speed, and reliable data exchange between devices and the network. In addition, AI technology also contributes to automating the creation of virtual environments and digital items, and extracting valuable insights from the vast amount of data generated within the metaverse [1,2]. Blockchain, serving as a trust infrastructure in decentralized distributed networks, enables individual-centric digital asset transactions for metaverse users, not tied to traditional service providers' platforms. It can also contribute to achieving the compatibility of individual services held by various virtual spaces (or service providers) within the metaverse [3]. The metaverse is anticipated to bring about great innovation in various aspects of life, including e-commerce, medical, education, entertainment, smart factory and other social services [4,5].

In the metaverse, users can create avatars to represent themselves virtually, and they can access various services through these avatars. However, in the current metaverse application, users possess the freedom to create any avatar to serve as their virtual representation, irrespective of their real-world identity. This characteristic presents avenues for malicious users to fabricate a similar avatar and cause serious security problems, such as identity leakage, theft, and virtual asset fraud during avatar interactions. In addition, issues such as stalking, harassment, and sexual assault can pose a threat to users by manipulating the avatar, as well as the potential privacy threat of using AI technology to monitor users, make inferences about them, or engage in impersonation [6–8]. Furthermore, users need to exchange their information and data with third parties to access services offered in various virtual worlds within the metaverse. However, due to the aforementioned characteristics, the identity information of the third parties using the user's information is often unclear, making interactions for users challenging. Examples include qualifications to provide professional services such as medical or educational services, or adult verification to use certain data. Therefore, it is essential to design an authentication scheme that allow users to safely use services in the metaverse and remain secure from other security threats.

In current metaverse application, users have no direct means to verify the identity of other avatars as malicious or not, so they need help from the metaverse service provider. In the process of tracking these manipulators, the service provider mainly utilizes the manipulator's account and password as clues to track the manipulator from a specific avatar identity [9]. However, employing password-dependent methods means that any player who knows the account password can successfully gain access, so if a malicious user obtains the password illegally through various means, he/she can log in illegally and manipulate the avatar of a legitimate player. For more secure user identification and assurance on the metaverse, users can provide a lot of personal information to service providers. However, service providers that collect sensitive information, such as users' voices and motions generated in the metaverse, can abuse this personal information and cause users' privacy violations and huge losses through advertisements, personal tracking, fraud, illegal use, etc. In addition, the users and platform servers communicate through public channels in metaverse environments. Thus, an external adversary can attempt to eavesdrop and forge messages transmitted over public channels and attempt various security attacks, including masquerade, replay and man-in-the-middle attacks. Therefore, sensitive user information should not be disclosed to external parties and should only be shared with specific stakeholders in specific circumstances.

In this paper, we propose a blockchain-based authentication scheme that utilizes decentralized identifiers and verifiable credentials technology to enhance system security and protect users from various security and privacy threats. Decentralized identifiers and verifiable credentials enable trustworthy identity verification and data exchange without intermediaries. We propose an authentication scheme where users can authenticate not only avatars but also real manipulators during the authentication process required before interactions between avatars, using the users' decentralized identifiers and verifiable credentials. Additionally, to ensure secure communication and avatar interactions in the metaverse environment, we propose an authentication method using blockchain between users and platform servers and between avatars. In our proposed scheme, the user and service provider establish security communication channels during the login phase through secure authentication and key agreement. Furthermore, we minimize user information exposed to service providers during interactions with other avatars and enhance user privacy protection by allowing only the necessary personal identification information for verification when interacting with different avatars in the metaverse.

Furthermore, in the metaverse, during the consensus process of validating and recording information on the blockchain, security attacks, such as 51% attacks and Sybil attacks, can occur [10–12]. These attacks can undermine the trustworthiness of information recorded on the actual blockchain. However, in this paper, the consensus process occurs only once when the user initially creates a unique ID and registers it in the system. Subsequently, during the authentication process, users verify the required record information on the blockchain, and at this point, the blockchain's consensus process does not occur, minimizing the consensus process. Additionally, this paper assumes the security of the blockchain consensus process and focuses on security threats and privacy issues during the user registration phase and subsequent use of metaverse services.

1.1. Contributions

The main contributions of paper are as follows:

- In the metaverse environment, users are exposed to threats, such as fraud through fake avatars and the risk of personal information leakage during data transmission through open channels. We propose a secure authentication method for the metaverse environment to ensure security against various threats arising from fake avatars or vulnerabilities in wireless communication channels, and provide forward secrecy, anonymity, and privacy preservation.
- The proposed scheme utilizes decentralized identifiers and verifiable credentials to enhance user privacy protection. Metaverse users can provide only the necessary identity information to stakeholders without disclosing their information to external parties, thereby safeguarding their personal information.
- We perform an informal analysis to ensure that the proposed scheme can provide security against various attacks, including impersonation, session key disclosure, replay, man-in-the-middle, and insider attacks. Additionally, we show that the proposed scheme can achieve mutual authentication, perfect forward secrecy, anonymity and privacy preservation.
- The security of the proposed scheme is analyzed by performing informal and formal analyses, such as Burrows–Abadi–Nikoogadam (BAN) logic, the real-or-random (RoR) model, and the automated validation of internet security protocols and applications (AVISPA) simulation tool. We also compare the performance and security features with the related works to show that the proposed scheme is superior.

1.2. Organization

The organization of the paper is as follows. Section 2 reviews the existing authentication scheme applicable to the metaverse environment. Section 3 introduces relevant preliminaries. Section 4 presents a proposed system model and adversary model. The details of the proposed authentication scheme are depicted in Section 5. Section 6 analyzes the security of the proposed scheme in informal and formal proofs, and Section 7 analyzes the computation and communication costs of the proposed scheme and related works. Finally, we summarize the conclusion and the future works in Section 8.

2. Related Work

With the emergence of metaverse platforms (e.g., roblox and minecraft) and the increasing number of applications that utilize the metaverse, the security of the metaverse environment is discussed in several studies [13–15]. According to the paper proposed by Vu et al. [13], in the virtual world, users may find themselves in a situation where they are required to present identity information in order to obtain certain services and activities. They argued that not only are authentication mechanisms required to ensure that metaverse users can access the platform with appropriate identities but IoT devices in the metaverse infrastructure (e.g., sensors and UAVs) also need effective mechanisms for authentication during operation. They asserted that blockchain technology can address metaverse security and privacy issues, including identity and authentication management. Patwe and Mane [14] argued the necessity of designing a secure authentication mechanism because impersonation, server spoofing, mutual authentication threats, and replay attacks can occur in the metaverse environment. And they proposed a blockchain-based architecture for avatar and user authentication in consideration of the decentralized nature of the metaverse. However, to date, there are no proposed specific system models and mutual authentication schemes for metaverse environments.

In the metaverse environment, where users use virtual services from the service provider's server using wearable devices, such as VR and AR, some mutual authentication methods for the IoT environment can be applied. Panda and Chattopadhyay [16] proposed an elliptic curve cryptography-based mutual authentication protocol to ensure secure communication between IoT devices and cloud servers. They argue that the proposed scheme is secure against various security threats (including impersonation attack, replay attack, etc.) by performing an informal analysis and using the AVISPA simulation tool. However, they did not consider the device-hijacking attack scenario. In the metaverse, there is a risk of maliciously capturing and tampering with a user's XR device to extract sensitive information or impersonate a legitimate user to gain access to the system. Li et al. [17] proposed a mutual authentication scheme based on blockchain for users and servers. Li et al.'s scheme solves the problem of SPoF that occurs in the centralized authentication structure by proposing a blockchain-based decentralized authentication scheme. They claimed that their scheme is secure against impersonation and man-in-the-middle attacks, and that it also provides perfect forward secrecy. However, security features such as insider attacks and anonymity are not covered. These schemes can be applied to authentication between a user's device and a service provider's server. However, it is difficult to apply these schemes to the authentication mechanism required for interactions between avatars in the metaverse environment. Ryu et al. [18] proposed an authentication scheme that can ensure secure communication in a metaverse environment and transparently manage user identification data using blockchain technology. They designed the necessary mutual authentication methods to provide secure communication between platform servers and users as well as secure interactions between avatars. However, users who manipulate avatars in the metaverse need to prove their real-world information (e.g., age, gender, occupation and account) to other avatars in specific situations. Ryu et al.'s avatar authentication scheme can expose a lot of personal information of users to metaverse service providers. If personal information is exposed, it is possible to track the avatar's user, or to impersonate a legitimate user by using a camouflage avatar.

Therefore, there is a need for research on authentication methods that can provide secure communication and privacy protection for users while considering the characteristics of the metaverse. We propose an authentication and key agreement scheme to enable metaverse users to securely utilize services from service providers. Furthermore, within the platform, we propose a secure authentication scheme between avatars that allows users to protect their privacy during avatar interactions without relying on the service provider.

3. Preliminaries

This section briefly introduces a fuzzy extractor, decentralized identifier (DID) and verifiable credential (VC).

3.1. Fuzzy Extractor

The fuzzy extractor [19] is widely acknowledged for confirming biometric validation. A biometric key can be constructed using a biometric outline, such as irises, facial features, and fingerprints. The characteristics of the fuzzy extractor are defined by the following two algorithms, including a probabilistic algorithm $Gen(\cdot)$, and a deterministic algorithm $Rep(\cdot)$:

- $Gen(BIO) = (r, \delta)$: The user's biometric information BIO is accepted as an input parameter to the algorithm. Then, the secret value r is output along with the public reproduction parameter δ.
- $Rep(BIO, \delta) = (r)$: The algorithm accepts a noisy user biometric BIO from the user, controlling the noise using the public reproduction parameter δ. Then, Rep reproduces the original biometric secret value r.

3.2. Decentralized Identifier and Verifiable Credential

The decentralized identifier [20] is a concept designed to uniquely identify the digital identities of users and entities within a distributed network. It allows users to manage and verify their identities in a decentralized manner, without relying on central identity verification authorities. Users can confirm or show their DID ownership by employing cryptographic methods, such as digital signatures. DIDs are stored in conjunction with blockchains, ensuring their immutability and security. The features and operation of DIDs in the proposed scheme are as follows:

1. **Decentralized identifier creation**: Users or entities generate DIDs. DIDs are unique and can be created by users themselves, not centralized authentication authorities.
2. **Integration with blockchain**: DIDs are stored in conjunction with a blockchain. This ensures that DIDs are stored in a distributed registry, making duplication or alteration difficult.
3. **Digital identity verification**: To log in to digital services or applications using their DID, users create a signature using their private key.
4. **Distributed identity management**: Users manage their DIDs and identity information in a distributed network. This information is stored on the blockchain, ensuring immutability, and users share it only when necessary.

A verifiable credential [21] is a concept and technology used to represent and verify personal identities and permissions in the digital realm. Verifiable credentials serve as an alternative to centralized identity verification systems, allowing individuals to manage and share identity information (credentials) issued by identity authorities. The features and operation of VCs in the proposed scheme are as follows:

1. **Creation of VCs**: Users process their identity-related data to generate VCs. These VCs include the user's identity information and the user's signature using the elliptic curve-based signature algorithm.
2. **Issuer of VCs**: VCs are created by the party or institution that issues the information. The issuer verifies the source of the information and signs the VC to ensure its integrity.
3. **Storage and transmission of VCs**: VCs are stored in a digital format, and users share them only when necessary. VCs are securely transmitted and stored, often in encrypted form.
4. **Verification of VCs**: When presenting VCs to a verifier, the verifier uses the issuer's public key to verify the signature of the VC and validate the accuracy of the information. This confirms the authenticity of the VC.
5. **Selective sharing of VCs**: Users can share only the necessary information through VCs, enhancing personal data protection. They provide minimal information to third parties and perform required identity verification.

4. System Model

Our proposed secure and privacy-preserving authentication scheme using a decentralized identifier in the metaverse environment is composed of four entities, including certificate authority, service provider, user, and blockchain. We depict the proposed system model in Figure 1, and describe each entity as give below.

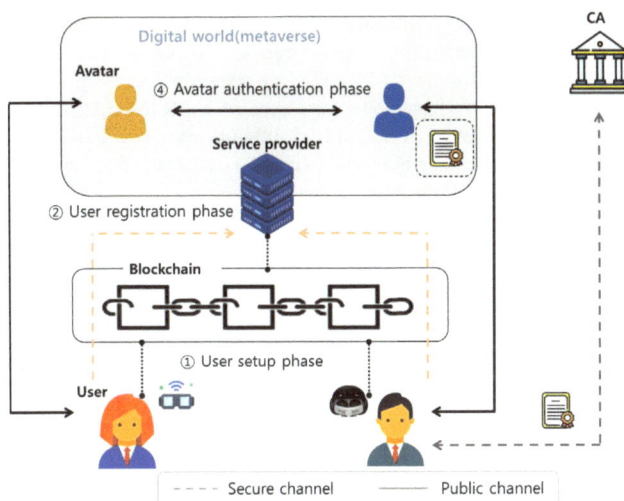

Figure 1. The proposed system model.

- Certificate authority (CA): CA serves as a fully trusted entity that initializes and publishes system parameters. CA receives the user's decentralized identifier and personal information, which require verification. Then, CA verifies both and issues a credential to the user proving the user's personal information (occupation, age, etc.). The credential values must be authenticated between the users/avatars in the metaverse environment.
- Service provider (SP): SPs offer services that enable users to engage in various activities in virtual spaces, such as education, gaming, healthcare, and more. The user first registers on the SP using the decentralized identifier. If a user attempts to access the SP, SP verifies the correct identity of the user. In addition, the SP is responsible for forwarding request and response messages that occur in its own virtual space during the avatar authentication phase.
- User: The user creates his/her own decentralized identifier on the blockchain. The user sends his/her decentralized identifier and personal information to CA to receive credentials to prove their personal information. Then, the user registers with the SP to participate in the metaverse environment. At this time, the user transmits only minimal information to register with the SP, and no other personal information is transmitted. The user can interact with other users by using avatars created in the virtual world, such as exchanging information with other users for various purposes. The user uses DID, public key, and verifiable credentials in the virtual space to mutually authenticate with other users' avatars to achieve secure interaction between avatars and avatars.
- Blockchain: In the proposed authentication scheme, we adopt the public blockchain, which is a fully decentralized infrastructure. In the public blockchain network, every node can easily join blockchain networks without the need for a trusted authority. All blockchain members can read the ledger and upload transitions to the blockchain. To ensure that all entities participating in the system agree on a single source of truth, the public blockchain adopts proof-based consensus algorithms, including proof of work and proof of stake. In our system, the blockchain is adopted to store the information required for authentication, and it does not contain any other information other than DID documents. In the proposed scheme, we assume that the consensus process of the blockchain operates correctly and reliably.

The process flows of the proposed scheme are described as follows:

- **User setup phase:** The user generates their own decentralized identifier. The CA issues a verifiable credential to the user that proves the user's personal information.

- **User registration phase:** The user registers with the SP using his/her own decentralized identifier. The SP verifies that the user's decentralized identifier is valid, and then the user's avatar is generated in virtual space.
- **Login phase:** When the user attempts to access the SP, the user and SP authenticate each other. If the mutual authentication between the user and SP is completed and the session key is agreed upon, the user and SP establish a secure communication channel through the session key.
- **Avatar authentication phase:** In the virtual space, the user can interact with other avatars. For secure avatar-to-avatar interactions, the user provides verifiable credentials, proving the personal information needed to perform the avatar authentication phase.

4.1. Adversary Model

The adversary can have the following capabilities based on the Dolev–Yao (DY) threat model. The Dolev–Yao threat model [22] is widely employed in the analysis of protocol security [23–25]. The capabilities of an adversary are defined as follows:

- An adversary can eavesdrop, intercept, modify, expunge, and forge the transmitted messages through a public channel.
- An adversary can conjecture about either the identity or the password of a legitimate user, but it is incapable of conjecturing about both simultaneously.
- An adversary can physically seize the user's XR devices and infer sensitive data through power analysis attacks [26–28].
- An adversary can attempt to launch various attacks, including impersonation, replay attacks, and man-in-the-middle attacks.
- An adversary can be an insider in the SP.

For this work, we also adopt a more stringent adversary model, known as the "Canetti–Krawczyk (CK) model" [29]. In the CK model, the adversary not only has all the capabilities of the DY model but the adversary can obtain ephemeral session states and long-term values (including secret keys) by performing a session-hijacking attack. The adversary also creates a replica avatar in the metaverse environment to deceive others.

5. Proposed Scheme

This section presents the proposed secure and privacy-preserving authentication scheme using a decentralized identifier for the metaverse. The proposed scheme includes the initialization, user setup, registration, login, and avatar authentication phases. Table 1 describes the symbols used in the scheme.

Table 1. Symbols and their meanings.

Symbol	Description
U_i	i-th user
SP	The service provider
CA	A certificate authority
ID_i, PW_i	Identity and password of U_i
sk_x, PK_x	Secret key and public key of entity x
DID_x	Decentralized identity of entity x
$H(\cdot)$	Hash function
T	Timestamp
$\alpha_i, \beta_x, x_x, a_x$	Random nonces
$\oplus$	XOR operation
$\|\|$	Concatenation operation

5.1. Initialization Phase

First, CA initializes the system parameters. CA generates large prime numbers p, q, an additive group G, elliptic curve EC_p over F_p, a generator P, one-way hash functions $H.$, and a secret key sk_{CA}, and it computes a public key PK_{CA} corresponding to sk_{CA}. After that, CA publishes the system parameters $par = \{p, q, G, EC_p, P, PK_{CA}, h(\cdot)\}$ to the network.

5.2. User Setup

The user generates their own decentralized identifier. CA issues a verifiable credential to the user that proves the user's personal information. This phase is performed over a secure channel. Figure 2 shows the user setup phase and detailed processes steps are as follows.

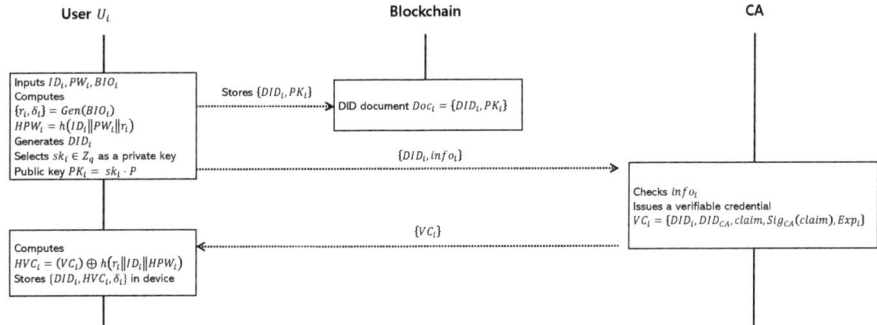

Figure 2. User setup phase of the proposed scheme.

- **US-1:** User U_i inputs a unique ID_j, password sk_j and biometric information BIO_j. Then, U_i selects a random number $sk_i \in Z_q$ as a private key and computes $Gen(BIO_i) = \{r_i, \delta_i\}$, $HPW_i = h(ID_i || PW_i || r_i)$, $PK_i = sk_i \cdot P$. Then, U_i generates the U_i's own DID_i that indicates the location of the DID document $Doc_i = \{DID_j, PK_i\}$ on the blockchain.
- **US-2:** U_i requests CA to issue a credential by sending DID_i, personal information $info_j$. CA checks a U_i's personal information and DID_i, and issues a verifiable credential $VC_i = \{DID_i, DID_{CA}, claim, Sig_{CA}(claim), Exp_i\}$ that vouches for U_i's personal information, such as occupation, age, etc. Then, CA sends VC_i to U_i. After checking VC_i, U_i computes $HVC_i = (VC_i) \oplus h(r_i || ID_i || HPW_i)$ and stores $\{DID_i, HVC_i, \delta_i\}$ in the device.

5.3. User Registration Phase

User U_i registers with SP using his/her own decentralized identifier. SP verifies that the user's decentralized identifier is valid, and then the user's avatar is generated in virtual space. This phase is performed over a secure channel. Figure 3 shows the user registration phase and detailed processes steps are as follows.

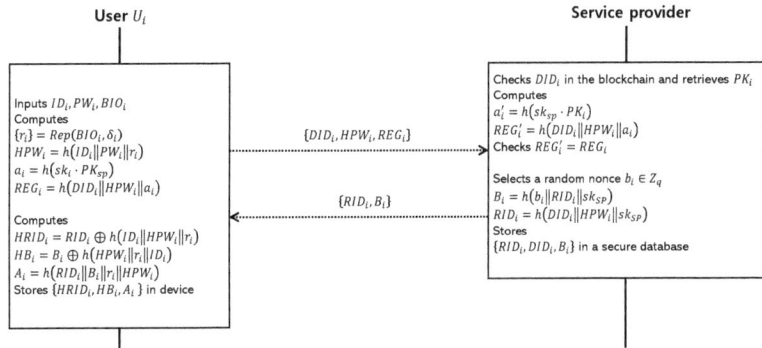

Figure 3. User registration phase of the proposed scheme.

- **UR-1:** U_i inputs a identity ID_i, password PW_i, and imprints a biomatic information BIO_i. Then, U_i computes $\{r_i\} = Rep(BIO_i, \delta_i)$, $HPW_i = h(ID_i||PW_i||r_i)$, $a_i = h(sk_i \cdot PK_{sp})$, $REG_i = h(DID_i||HPW_i||a_i)$, and send $\{DID_i, HPW_i, REG_i\}$ to SP.
- **UR-2:** SP checks the validity of DID_i and retrieves PK_i from the blockchain. If it is valid, SP computes $a_i = h(sk_{sp} \cdot PK_i)$, $REG_i' = h(DID_i||HPW_i||a_i)$ and verifies $REG_i \stackrel{?}{=} REG_i'$. If the equation is correct, SP selects a random nonce $b_i \in Z_q$ and calculates $B_i = h(b_i||RID_i||sk_{sp})$, $RID_i = h(DID_i||HPW_i||sk_{sp})$. After that, SP dispatches $\{RID_i, B_i\}$ to U_i and stores $\{RID_i, DID_i, B_i\}$ in a secure database.
- **UR-3:** U_i computes $HRID_i = RID_i \oplus h(ID_i||HPW_i||r_i)$, $HB_i = B_i \oplus h(HPW_i||r_i||ID_i)$, $A_i = h(RID_i||B_i||r_i||HPW_i)$ and stores $\{HRID_i, HB_i, A_i\}$ in U_i's XR devices.

5.4. Login Phase

When the user U_i attempts to access the SP, the user and SP authenticate each other. If mutual authentication between the user and SP is completed and the session key is established, the user and SP communicate using the session key to guarantee secure communication. Figure 4 presents the login phase and the detailed processes of this phase are as follows.

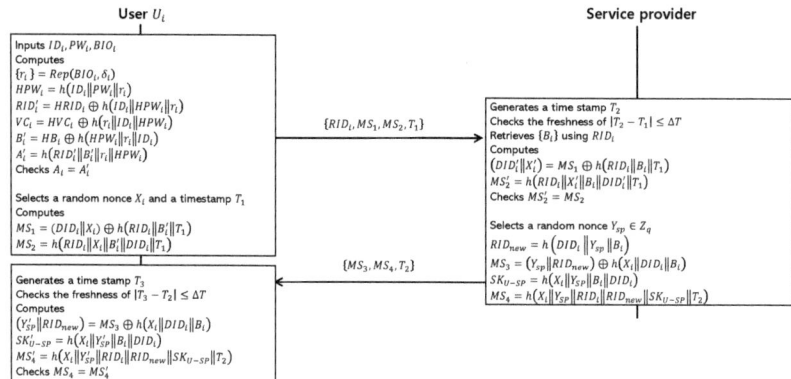

Figure 4. Login phase of the proposed scheme.

- **LA-1:** User U_i first enters ID_i, PW_i, and BIO_i. Then, U_i computes $\{r_i\} = Rep(BIO_i, \delta_i)$, $HPW_i = h(ID_i||PW_i||r_i)$, $RID_i' = HRID_i \oplus h(ID_i||HPW_i||r_i)$, $VC_i = HVC_i \oplus h(r_i||ID_i||HPW_i)$, $B_i' = HB_i \oplus h(HPW_i||r_i||ID_i)$, $A_i' = h(RID_i'||B_i'||r_i||HPW_i)$, and checks the $A_i = A_i'$. If the equation is correct, U_i selects a random nonce X_i and a current timestamp T_1, and computes $MS_1 = (DID_i||X_i) \oplus h(RID_i||B_i'||T_1)$, $MS_2 = h(RID_i||X_i||B_i'||DID_i||T_1)$. After that, U_i sends $\{RID_i, MS_1, MS_2, T_1\}$ to SP.
- **LA-2:** SP generates a current timestamp T_2 and checks the freshness of the timestamp. Next, SP retrieves $\{B_i\}$ from the database using RID_i, and calculates $(DID_i'||X_i') = MS_1 \oplus h(RID_i||B_i||T_1)$, $MS_2' = h(RID_i||X_i'||B_i||DID_i'||T_1)$. SP checks the $MS_2' \stackrel{?}{=} MS_2$, and selects a random nonce $Y_{sp} \in Z_q$ and calculates $RID_{new} = h(DID_i||Y_{sp}||B_i)$, $MS_3 = (Y_{SP}||RID_{new}) \oplus h(X_i||DID_i||B_i)$, $SK_{U-SP} = h(X_i||Y_{SP}||B_i||DID_i)$, $MS_4 = h(X_i||Y_{SP}||RID_i||RID_{new}||SK_{U-SP}||T_2)$. After that, SP transmits $\{MS_3, MS_4, T_2\}$ to U_i.
- **LA-3:** After reception of the messages, U_i checks the freshness of T_2 and computes $(Y_{sp}'||RID_{new}) = MS_3 \oplus h(X_i||DID_i||B_i)$, $SK_{U-SP} = h(X_i||Y_{sp}'||B_i||DID_i)$, $MS_4' = h(X_i||Y_{sp}'||RID_i||RID_{new}||SK_{U-SP}||T_2)$. Then, U_i checks the validity of $MS_4 \stackrel{?}{=} MS_4'$, calculates $HRID_i' = RID_{new} \oplus h(ID_i||HPW_i||r_i)$, and updates $HRID_i$ with $HRID_i'$.

5.5. Avatar Authentication Phase

In the virtual space, user U_i can interact with other avatars U_j. For secure avatar-to-avatar interactions, the user provides the verifiable credentials proving the personal information to perform the avatar authentication phase. Figure 5 shows the avatar authentication phase and the detailed steps are as follows.

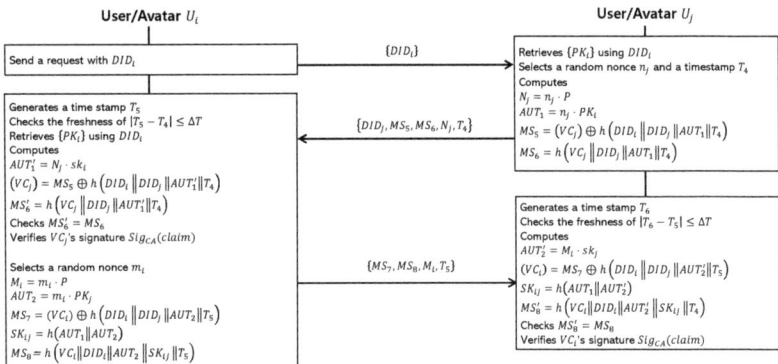

Figure 5. Avatar authentication phase of the proposed scheme.

- **AA-1:** U_i first sends a request including DID_i to U_j. After reception of the request, U_j retrieves $\{PK_i\}$ using DID_i, and selects a random nonce n_j and a current timestamp T_4. Next, U_j computes $N_j = n_j \cdot P$, $AUT_1 = n_j \cdot PK_j$, $MS_5 = (VC_j) \cdot h(DID_i||DID_j||AUT_1||T_4)$, $MS_6 = h(VC_j||DID_j||AUT_1||T_4)$, and sends $\{DID_j, MS_5, MS_6, N_j, T_4\}$ to U_i.

- **AA-2:** After receiving the message $\{DID_j, MS_5, MS_6, N_j, T_4\}$, U_i checks the validity of T_4, and retrieves $\{PK_j\}$ from the blockchain using DID_j. Then, U_i computes $AUT_1' = N_j \cdot sk_i$, $(VC_j) = MS_5 \cdot h(DID_i||DID_j||AUT_1'||T_4)$, $MS_6' = h(VC_j||DID_j||AUT_1'||T_4)$ and verifies the equation $MS_6' \stackrel{?}{=} MS_6$ and the signature $Sig_{CA}(claim)$ of the VC_j. Next, U_i selects a random nonce m_i and calculates $M_i = m_i \cdot P$, $AUT_2 = m_i \cdot PK_j$, $MS_7 = (VC_i) \cdot h(DID_i||DID_j||AUT_2||T_5)$, $MS_8 = h(VC_i||DID_i||AUT_2||h(AUT_1||AUT_2)||T_5)$. And U_i transmits $\{MS_7, MS_8, M_i, T_5\}$ to U_j.

- **AA-3:** Upon reception of message $\{MS_7, MS_8, M_i, T_5\}$, U_j checks the freshness of T_5 and computes $AUT_2' = M_i \cdot sk_j$, $(VC_i) = MS_7 \cdot h(DID_i||DID_j||AUT_2'||T_5)$, $MS_8' = h(VC_i||DID_i||AUT_2'||h(AUT_1||AUT_2')||T_4)$. Finally, U_j checks that $MS_8' \stackrel{?}{=} MS_8$ is correct and verifies VC_i's signature $Sig_{CA}(claim)$.

6. Security Analysis

In this section, we show the resilience of the proposed system against malicious security attacks through an informal analysis and AVISPA simulation. We also utilize BAN logic [30,31], which is a widely accepted formal security analysis, to prove that the proposed scheme is guaranteed for secure mutual authentication. Subsequently, we prove the session key secrecy utilizing the real-or-random (ROR) model.

6.1. Informal Security Analysis

We perform informal security analysis to demonstrate how the proposed protocol fulfills some of the security requirements, such as impersonation, replay, perfect forward secrecy, session key disclosure attacks, mutual authentication, etc.

6.1.1. Stolen XR Device Attack

Under the assumptions in Section 4.1, an adversary Adv can seize the user's XR device and extract the stored parameters $\{DID_i, HVC_i, \delta_i, HRID_i, HB_i, A_i\}$ to obtain sensitive information VC_i, B_i. However, all the stored sensitive information are masked with hash,

XOR operations utilizing identity ID_i, password PW_i, and biometric information BIO_i so that the Adv cannot obtain sensitive information. Thus, the proposed scheme is secure against stolen XR device attacks.

6.1.2. Offline Password-Guessing Attack

The Adv attempts to guess the user's password PW_i using extracted values from the U_i's XR device and intercepts the transmitted messages on public channels. However, it is impracticable for Adv to guess PW_i without knowledge of the real identity ID_i and response value r_i. PW_i is constructed as $HPW_i = h(ID_i||PW_i||r_i)$, where r_i is the response value from a fuzzy extractor with bio-information as the input. Therefore, our scheme is resistant to offline password-guessing attacks.

6.1.3. Impersonation Attack

Adv can create fake login messages $\{RID_i, MS_1, MS_2, T_1\}$ and $\{MS_3, MS_4, T_2\}$ to impersonate legitimate user U_i and gain unauthorized access to the metaverse environment supported by SP. However, Adv cannot forge the request message and compute the session key SK_{U-SP} because it is infeasible for Adv to obtain B_i and random nonces X_i and Y_{sp}, where B_i, X_i, and Y_{sp} are masked and B_i is shared by U_i and the SP only. Therefore, the proposed protocol prevents impersonation attacks.

6.1.4. Avatar Impersonation Attack

In the metaverse, Adv creates a fake avatar in an attempt to impersonate a legitimate user U_i's avatar. Adv should be required to prove ownership of the legitimate U_i's decentralized identifier DID_i and present verifiable credential VC_i to others. However, Adv cannot impersonate the legitimate user of the avatar because Adv cannot obtain the private key corresponding to DID_i and it is difficult to extract VC_i, which is masked with the real identity ID_i and password PW_i. Furthermore, since the user can easily create a new DID, if a problem occurs with the existing DID, the user can obtain a new DID and VC and discard the existing DID. Therefore, the proposed scheme prevents an avatar impersonation attack.

6.1.5. Session Key Disclosure Attack

In the proposed scheme, Adv should obtain the secret value B_i and the random nonces X_i and Y_{sp} to compute a common session key. However, it is infeasible for Adv to compute a valid session key SK_{U-SP} because U_i's secret value B_i is masked with the real identity ID_i, password PW_i, and biomatic information BIO_i. In addition, random nonces X_i and Y_{sp} are masked with B_i and DID_i. Adv also cannot decrypt M_1 without U_i's private key r_{User}. Therefore, the session key $SK_{U-SP} = h(X_i||Y_{SP}||B_i||DID_i)$ disclosure attacks are computationally infeasible in the proposed protocol.

6.1.6. Perfect Forward Secrecy

Even if the long-term secret keys sk_i and sk_{sp} are compromised, Adv does not obtain the previous session key $SK_{U-SP} = h(X_i||Y_{SP}||B_i||DID_i)$. Since DID_i and B_i are not revealed in messages transmitted on public channels, and random nonces X_i and Y_{sp} are refreshed every session, Adv cannot obtain the previous session key. Therefore, the proposed protocol guarantees perfect forward secrecy. Furthermore, if the secret key is compromised, the user can easily invalidate the existing DID associated with that key and create a new DID with a corresponding key pair. Subsequently, by re-registering with the system, the user can obtain a new VC from the CA.

6.1.7. Replay Attack and MITM Attack

Adv attempts replay and man-in-the-middle (MITM) attacks using previously transmitted messages. However, all the transmitted messages include the current timestamps T_x are refreshed with each session, and U_i and SP check the freshness of all transmitted messages. In addition, RID_i is also updated every session. If the received messages are invalid, the receiver terminates the current session. Therefore, the proposed protocol prevents replay and MITM attacks.

6.1.8. Insider Attack

According to Section 4.1, an internal Adv attempts to impersonate U_i's avatar using a fake avatar and intercepted messages DID_i, $\{DID_j, MS_5, MS_6, N_j, T_4\}$ and $\{MS_7, MS_8, M_i, T_5\}$. However, it is infeasible for Adv to calculate $AUT_1 = N_j \cdot PK_j = N_j \cdot sk_i$, $AUT_2 = m_i \cdot PK_j = M_i \cdot sk_j$ without the private keys sk_i, sk_j and random nonces n_j and m_i. Thus, Adv cannot obtain verifiable credential VC without AUT_1, AUT_2. Therefore, Adv cannot disguise itself as another legitimate user in the metaverse without private key sk_i and VC_i corresponding to DID_i.

6.1.9. Ephemeral Secret Leakage Attack

According to Section 4.1, Adv can obtain the ephemeral secret values, such as X_i and Y_{sp}. Then, the adversary can attempt to calculate the session key SK_{U-SP}. However, Adv cannot calculate SK_{U-SP} without B_i and DID_i. Therefore, the proposed protocol has resistance to the ephemeral key leakage attack.

6.1.10. Mutual Authentication

Sections 6.1.3 and 6.1.5 demonstrate that Adv cannot impersonate U_i and obtain the session key. In the login phase, U_i and SP verify all transmitted messages. When SP receives the login request message $\{RID_i, MS_1, MS_2, T_1\}$ from U_i, SP verifies $MS_2' \stackrel{?}{=} MS_2$. If valid, SP authenticates U_i. When U_i receives response messages $\{MS_3, MS_4, T_2\}$ from SP, U_i verifies the equation $MS_4' \stackrel{?}{=} MS_4$. If valid, U_i authenticates SP. Consequently, all entities are mutually authenticated so that the proposed system provides secure mutual authentication.

6.1.11. Anonymity

If Adv intercepts, modifies, and deletes the transmitted messages, it can execute Section 6.1.1 to extract U_i's real identity. However, it is impossible for Adv to obtain real identity ID_i. The user's ID_i is comprised of $RID_i = h(DID_i||HPW_i||sk_{sp})$ by using hash and XOR functions. Therefore, the proposed protocol ensures the anonymity of U_i.

6.1.12. Privacy-Preservation

In the proposed scheme, U_i's identity and sensitive personal information are managed by the user, and it is provided only to other relevant parties when access to specific services and data is required. The SP can only check some of U_i's information as a requirement to access the metaverse environment, and U_i's other information cannot be viewed without user consent. Therefore, the proposed scheme guarantees the privacy preservation of the user.

6.1.13. Untraceability

Nontraceability ensures that an external Adv cannot track the legitimate user U_i. Because all messages are dynamic and unique using temporary identities RID_x, random nonces X_i and Y_j, and timestamps T_x in each session, where each parameters are updated every session in the login phase, the proposed scheme provides untraceability for U_i.

6.1.14. Denial-of-Service (DoS) Attack

The Adv attempts to create a number of login request messages and transmit them to the SP to paralyze the network. However, since the SP checks the RID_i and T_i, which are updated each session, the Adv cannot create new valid messages. Even if the Adv attempts to resend past messages, SP considers them invalid and terminates the connection. Therefore, the proposed scheme ensures safety against DoS attacks.

6.2. Security Analysis Using BAN Logic

Over the BAN logic analysis, we prove that the proposed scheme guarantees secure mutual authentication between the user U_i and SP. We also define the rules, goals, idealized forms, and assumptions for performing BAN logic analysis. Table 2 introduces the BAN logic notations.

Table 2. Notations for BAN logic.

Notation	Description
$\alpha \mid \equiv X$	α **believes** statement X
$\#X$	Statement X is **fresh**
$\alpha \triangleleft X$	α **sees** statement X
$\alpha \Rightarrow X$	α **controls** statement X
$\alpha \mid \sim X$	α once **said** X
$\{X\}_K$	X is **encrypted** under key K
$<X>_Y$	Formula X is **combined** with formula Y
$\alpha \stackrel{K}{\leftrightarrow} \beta$	α and β may use **shared key** K to communicate
$\stackrel{K}{\to}\beta$	β has K as a **public key**
SK	Session key used in the current session

BAN Logic Rules

The BAN logic rules are as follows:

1. Message meaning rule:
$$\frac{\alpha \mid \equiv \alpha \stackrel{K}{\leftrightarrow} \beta,\ \alpha \triangleleft \{X\}_K}{\alpha \mid \equiv \beta \mid \sim X}$$

2. Nonce verification rule:
$$\frac{\alpha \mid \equiv \#(X),\ \alpha \mid \equiv \beta \mid \sim X}{\alpha \mid \equiv \beta \mid \equiv X}$$

3. Jurisdiction rule:
$$\frac{\alpha \mid \equiv \beta \mid \Longrightarrow X,\ \alpha \mid \equiv \beta \mid \equiv X}{\alpha \mid \equiv X}$$

4. Freshness rule:
$$\frac{\alpha \mid \equiv \#(X)}{\alpha \mid \equiv \#(X, Y)}$$

5. Belief rule:
$$\frac{\alpha \mid \equiv (X, Y)}{\alpha \mid \equiv X.}$$

6.3. Goals

We present the following security goals to show that the proposed system guarantees a secure mutual authentication.

Goal 1: $User \mid \equiv (User \stackrel{SK}{\leftrightarrow} SP)$

Goal 2: $User \mid \equiv SP \mid \equiv (User \stackrel{SK}{\leftrightarrow} SP)$

Goal 3: $SP \mid \equiv (User \stackrel{SK}{\leftrightarrow} SP)$

Goal 4: $SP \mid \equiv User \mid \equiv (User \stackrel{SK}{\leftrightarrow} SP)$

6.3.1. Idealized Forms

The idealized forms are the following:

Msg_1: $User \to SP$: $(RID_i, MS_1, MS_2, T_2)_{B_i}$

Msg_2: $SP \to User$: $(MS_3, MS_4, T_2)_{B_i}$

6.3.2. Assumptions

We define the following initial assumptions for the BAN logic proof.

A_1: $SP \models \#(T_1)$

A_2: $User \models \#(T_2)$

A_3: $User \models (SP \xleftrightarrow{B_i} User)$

A_4: $SP \models (User \xleftrightarrow{B_i} SP)$

A_5: $SP \models \#(X_i)$

A_6: $User \models \#(Y_{sp})$

A_7: $User \models SP \Rightarrow (User \xleftrightarrow{SK} SP)$

A_8: $SP \models User \Rightarrow (User \xleftrightarrow{SK} SP)$

6.3.3. Proof Using BAN Logic

The detailed steps of the BAN logic proof are as follows:

Step 1: From Msg_1,
$$S_1 : SP \triangleleft (RID_i, MS_1, MS_2, T_2)_{B_i}$$

Step 2: Upon the message meaning rule with S_1 and A_4,
$$S_2 : SP \models User \mid\sim (RID_i, MS_1, MS_2, T_2)$$

Step 3: Using the freshness rule with A_1,
$$S_3 : SP \models \#(RID_i, MS_1, MS_2, T_2)$$

Step 4: Using the nonce verification rule with S_2 and S_3,
$$S_4 : SP \models User \models (RID_i, MS_1, MS_2, T_2)$$

Step 5: Since the session key $SK_{U-SP} = h(X_i||Y_{SP}||B_i||DID_i)$, from S_4 and A_5,
$$S_5 : SP \models User \models (User \xleftrightarrow{SK} SP) \textbf{ (Goal 4)}$$

Step 6: Upon the jurisdiction rule with S_6 and A_8,
$$S_6 : SP \models (User \xleftrightarrow{SK} SP) \textbf{ (Goal 3)}$$

Step 7: Using the Msg_2,
$$S_7 : User \triangleleft (b_1, ID_{SP}, T_2)_{a_1}$$

Step 8: From the message meaning rule with S_8 and A_3,
$$S_8 : User \models SP \mid\sim (b_1, ID_{SP}, T_2)_{a_1}$$

Step 9: Using the freshness rule with A_2,

$$S_9 : User \mid\equiv \#(b_1, ID_{SP}, T_2)_{a_1}$$

Step 10: Upon the nonce verification rule with S_9 and S_{10},

$$S_{10} : User \mid\equiv SP \mid\equiv (b_1, ID_{SP}, T_2)_{a_1}$$

Step 11: Since the session key $SK_{U-SP} = h(X_i||Y_{SP}||B_i||DID_i)$, from S_{11} and A_6,

$$S_{11} : User \mid\equiv SP \mid\equiv (User \xleftrightarrow{SK} SP) \textbf{ (Goal 2)}$$

Step 12: Utilizing the jurisdiction rule with S_{13} and A_7,

$$S_{12} : User \mid\equiv (User \xleftrightarrow{SK} SP) \textbf{ (Goal 1)}$$

Therefore, the proposed protocol achieves secure mutual authentication between the user and SP.

6.4. ROR Model

The ROR model, which is based on probabilistic game theory, is widely used to analyze the semantic security of an authenticated key agreement [32–34]. Using the ROR model, we demonstrate that our proposed scheme ensures session key security against a malicious adversary within probabilistic polynomial time. We first present the fundamentals of the ROR model in Table 3. We follow this by proving the session key security of our proposed scheme.

Table 3. Various queries and descriptions.

Query	Description
$Execute(\mathcal{P}_U^t, \mathcal{P}_{SP}^t)$	$\mathcal{A}$ using this query to tap the communication messages transmitted between $\mathcal{P}_U^t$ and $\mathcal{P}_{SP}^t$.
$Send(\mathcal{P}^t, M)$	$\mathcal{A}$ sends a messages to the $\mathcal{P}^t$ and receives a response messages from $\mathcal{P}^t$.
$Reveal(\mathcal{P}^t)$	$\mathcal{A}$ gets a current session key between $\mathcal{P}^t$ and its partner.
$Test(\mathcal{P}^t)$	$\mathcal{A}$ guesses the probabilistic outcome for a flipped unbiased coin C. If the session key is fresh, $\mathcal{A}$ receives $C = 0$. If the session key is not fresh, $\mathcal{A}$ receives $C \neq 0$. Otherwise, $\mathcal{A}$ obtains null value ($\perp$).
$Corrupt(\mathcal{P}_U^t)$	This query presumes an active attack. $\mathcal{A}$ extracts secret values stored in the XR devices by executing a power analysis.

In the ROR model, adversary $\mathcal{A}$ interacts with the t−th instance of an executing participant, $\mathcal{P}^t$. Then, we define $\mathcal{P}_U^t$ and $\mathcal{P}_{SP}^t$ as the participants of t-th U_i and t-th SP. In the ROR model, the adversary can execute *Execute*, *Send*, *Reveal*, *Test*, and *Corrupt* to consider different queries presuming actual security attacks. The descriptions of each query are introduced in Table 3. Furthermore, a query of the collision-resistant one-way hash function is denoted as *Hash*.

Theorem 1. *Before proving the session key security of the proposed scheme, we define q_{hash} and q_{send} as the number of Hash and Send queries, and $|Hash|$ as the range space of the hash function. C and s denote Zipf's parameters [35], and l_B is the number of bits in the biometric secret key r_i. When adversary $\mathcal{A}$ obtains the session key in polynomial time, the adversary $\mathcal{A}$ breaches the* semantic security of the proposed scheme, and its advantage is represented by $Adv_\mathcal{A}(t)$. $Adv_\mathcal{A}(t)$ is estimated by

$$Adv_\mathcal{A}(t) \leq \frac{q_{hash}^2}{|Hash|} + 2\, max\{C' \cdot q_{send}^s, \frac{q_{send}}{2^{l_B}}\}. \tag{1}$$

Proof. We consider the following games $G_i, i = [0, 3]$, and assume that $Pr[Succ_{G_i}]$ is $\mathcal{A}$'s advantage of winning the game G_i. The detailed descriptions of each game are discussed as follows. □

- **Game 0:** G_0 presents the $\mathcal{A}$'s real attacks against our proposed scheme in the ROR model. $\mathcal{A}$ selects the bit c at the starting of G_0. $Adv_\mathcal{A}(t)$ is as follows.

$$Adv_\mathcal{A}(t) = |2Pr[Succ_{G_0}] - 1|. \tag{2}$$

- **Game 1:** G_1 is modeled such that $\mathcal{A}$ implements an eavesdropping attack. In this game, $\mathcal{A}$ executes the $Execute(\cdot)$ query to steal the communicated messages $\{RID_i, MS_1, MS_2, T_1\}$ and $\{MS_3, MS_4, T_2\}$ between U_i and SP. At the end of this game, $\mathcal{A}$ executes $Reveal$ and $Test$ queries to check whether the derived session key SK_{U-SP} is an actual or random key. $\mathcal{A}$ needs the long-term secret values (such as the private keys sk_i and sk_{sp}), and the short-term secret values (such as the random nonces X_i and Y_{sp}) to extract the SK_{U-SP}. However, it is impracticable for $\mathcal{A}$ to obtain these secret values, even if $\mathcal{A}$ obtains all communicated messages. As shown, the eavesdropping messages $\{RID_i, MS_1, MS_2, T_1\}$ and $\{MS_3, MS_4, T_2\}$ do not increase the probability of a winning game G_1. Therefore, because games G_1 and G_0 are indistinguishable, we obtain

$$Pr[Succ_{G_1}] = Pr[Succ_{G_0}]. \tag{3}$$

- **Game 2:** G_2 is modeled as an active attack. In this game, $\mathcal{A}$ executes the $Send$ and $Hash$ queries to guess the hash collision. However, all exchanged messages are protected using the one-way hash function $h(\cdot)$ and consist of secret credentials and random numbers. Moreover, it is difficult for Adv to derive secret credentials and a random nonce because it is a computationally infeasible problem depending on the properties of $h(\cdot)$. So, using the birthday paradox, we obtain the following inequality:

$$|Pr[Succ_{G_1}] - Pr[Succ_{G_2}]| \leq \frac{q_{hash}^2}{2|Hash|}. \tag{4}$$

- **Game 3:** G_3 is modeled such that an active attack is implemented by $\mathcal{A}$. In this game, $\mathcal{A}$ executes the $Corrupt(\mathcal{P}_V^t, \mathcal{P}_{EP}^t)$ query to extract the secret values $\{DID_i, HVC_i, \delta_i, HRID_i, HB_i, A_i\}$ from the user's XR devices. Subsequently, to derive credential VP_i and U_i's secret key sk_i, $\mathcal{A}$ must guess the unknown password PW_i through operating the $Send$ query. However, it is computationally infeasible for $\mathcal{A}$ to guess the password PW_i through the $Send$ query without V_i's identity ID_i and secret nonce x_i. In the absence of password-guessing attacks, games G_2 and G_3 are identical. The probability of $\mathcal{A}$ winning the game G_4 using Zip's law is

$$[Pr[Succ_{G_3}] - Pr[Succ_{G_4}] \leq max\{C' \cdot q_{send}^s, \frac{q_{send}}{2^{l_B}}\}. \tag{5}$$

After all of the games are executed, $\mathcal{A}$ conjectures the correct bit c. Hence, we obtain

$$Pr[Succ_{G_3}] = \frac{1}{2}. \tag{6}$$

Considering Equations (2) and (3), we obtain

$$\frac{1}{2}Adv_{\mathcal{A}}(t) = |Pr[Succ_{G_0}] - \frac{1}{2}|$$
$$= |Pr[Succ_{G_1}] - \frac{1}{2}|. \tag{7}$$

Then, we consider Equations (4) and (5) and obtain the following inequality:

$$\frac{1}{2}Adv_{\mathcal{A}}(t) = |Pr[Succ_{G_1}] - Pr[Succ_{G_4}]|$$
$$\leq \frac{q_{hash}^2}{2|Hash|} + max\{C' \cdot q_{send}^s, \frac{q_{send}}{2^{l_B}}\}. \tag{8}$$

Consequently, the stipulated result $Adv_{\mathcal{A}}(t)$ is presented by multiplying both sides of Equation (8):

$$Adv_{\mathcal{A}}(t) \leq \frac{q_{hash}^2}{|Hash|} + 2\,max\{C' \cdot q_{send}^s, \frac{q_{send}}{2^{l_B}}\}. \tag{9}$$

6.5. Avispa Simulation Tool

AVISPA is a well-known security simulation tool that analyzes the protocols' ability to resist replay and MITM attacks [36–38]. The AVISPA tool employs the high-level protocols specifications language (HLPSL) for outlining the actions of each participant. Afterword, the HLPSL code of the protocol is converted into the intermediate format (IF) through the HLPSL2IF translator. Then, IF data are input to implement AVISPA on one of four backends, such as "the CL-based attack searcher (CL-AtSe)", "the on-the-fly-model checker (OFMC)", "the tree Automata-based protocol analyzer (TA4SP)", and "the SAT-based model checker (SATMC)". When IF data are passed through the selected backend, the simulation result is output following the output format (OF). In this paper, we perform AVISPA simulations of the proposed scheme using OFMC and the CL-AtSe backend, which provide the XOR operation. In OF, if the SUMMARY segment indicates SAFE, it means that the analyzed scheme is resistant to replay and MITM attacks.

Figure 6 describe the user's role in HLPSL code form. The other parties (service provider and certificate authority) are also coded in a format similar to Figure 6. Figure 7 indicates the goals and environment of the proposed protocol and the role of the session. Figure 8 presents the AVISAP simulation result of the proposed protocol using CL-AtSe and OFMC. The results under the CL-AtSe and OFMC backends show that the proposed protocol is safe. Therefore, the proposed protocol can be resilient against man-in-the-middle and replay attacks.

```
%%%%%%% Role UA %%%%%
role usera(UA,SP,CA : agent, SKuanc,SKuans :symmetric_key, H,ADD,MUL: hash_func, SND, RCV : channel(dy))
played_by UA
def=
local State: nat,
        IDi,PWi,BIOi,DIDi,PKi,SKi,RRi,INFOi,HPWi,HVCi,AAi,REGi,HRIDi,HBii,Aii,Xi,T1,MS1,MS2,SKus:text,

VCi,P: text,
        RIDi,SKsp,PKsp,BBi,Bii,Ysp,RIDnew,MS3,MS4,SKsu,T2:text

const sp1,sp2,sp3,sp4,ua_sp_xi,sp_ua_ysp: protocol_id
init State:=0
transition
%%%%% Set up phase %%%%%%%
1. State=0 /\RCV(start)=|>
State':=1 /\SKi':=new()
        /\DIDi':=new() /\RRi':=new() /\PKi':=MUL(SKi.P)
        /\SND({DIDi'.INFOi}_SKuanc)
        /\secret({IDi.PWi.BIOi.SKi'.RRi'},sp1,{UA})
        /\secret({INFOi},sp2,{UA,CA})
2. State=1 /\RCV({VCi'}_SKuanc)=|>
State':=2 /\HPWi':=H(IDi.PWi.RRi') /\HVCi':=xor(VCi',H(RRi'.IDi.PWi))
%%%%% Registration phase %%%%%
        /\AAi':=H(MUL(SKi'.PKsp')) /\REGi':=H(DIDi'.HPWi'.AAi')
        /\SND({DIDi'.HPWi'.REGi'}_SKuans)
3. State=2 /\RCV({H(DIDi'.H(IDi.PWi.RRi').SKsp).H(BBi'.H(DIDi'.H(IDi.PWi.RRi').SKsp).SKsp)}_SKuans)=|>
State':=3 /\HRIDi':=xor(H(DIDi'.H(IDi.PWi.RRi').SKsp),H(IDi.HPWi'.AAi'))
        /\HBii':=xor(H(BBi'.H(DIDi'.H(IDi.PWi.RRi').SKsp).SKsp),H(HPWi'.RRi'.IDi))
        /\Aii':=H(H(DIDi'.H(IDi.PWi.RRi').SKsp).H(BBi'.H(DIDi'.H(IDi.PWi.RRi').SKsp).SKsp).RRi'.HPWi')
%%%%% Login phase %%%%%%
/\Xi':=new() /\T1':=new()
/\MS1':=xor(Xi',H(H(DIDi'.H(IDi.PWi.RRi').SKsp).H(BBi'.H(DIDi'.H(IDi.PWi.RRi').SKsp).SKsp).T1'))
/\MS2':=H(H(DIDi'.H(IDi.PWi.RRi').SKsp).Xi'.H(BBi'.H(DIDi'.H(IDi.PWi.RRi').SKsp).SKsp).DIDi'.T1')
/\SND(H(DIDi'.H(IDi.PWi.RRi').SKsp),MS1',MS2',T1')
/\witness(UA,SP,ua_sp_xi,Xi')
4. State=3 /\RCV(xor({Ysp'.H(DIDi'.Ysp'.Bii')},H(Xi'.DIDi'.Bii')),H(Xi'.Ysp'.RIDi'.H(DIDi'.Ysp'.Bii').H(Xi'.Ysp'.Bii'.DIDi').T2'),
T2')=|>
State':=4
        /\SKus':=H(Xi'.Ysp'.H(DIDi'.H(IDi.PWi.RRi').SKsp).H(DIDi'.Ysp'.Bii').DIDi')
        /\request(UA,SP,sp_ua_ysp,Ysp')
end role
```

Figure 6. Role of user.

```
%%%%%%%%%    session  %%%%%%
role session(UA,SP,CA : agent, SKuanc,SKspnc,SKuans :symmetric_key, H,ADD,MUL:
hash_func)

def=
local SND1, SND2, SND3, RVC1, RVC2, RVC3 : channel(dy)
composition
usera(UA,SP,CA,SKuanc,SKuans,H,ADD,MUL,SND1,RCV1)
/\serviceprovider(UA,SP,CA,SKspnc,SKuans,H,ADD,MUL,SND2,RCV2)
/\certificateauth(UA,SP,CA,SKuanc,SKspnc,H,ADD,MUL,SND3,RCV3)
end role

%%%%%  environments and goals  %%%%%%
role environment()

def=
const ua,sp,ca : agent,
skuanc,skspnc,skuans :symmetric_key,
h,add,mul: hash_func,
idi,pwi,bioi,didi,pki,ski,rri,infoi,hpwi,hvci,aai,regi,hridi,hbii,aii,xi,t1,ms1,ms2,skus:text,
vci,p: text
ridi,skksp,pksp,bbi,bii,ysp,ridnew,ms3,ms4,sksu,t2:text
ua_sp_xi,sp_ua_ysp: protocol_id,
sp1,sp2,sp3,sp4: protocol_id

intruder_knowledge = {ua,sp,ca,didi,pki,pksp,ms1,ms2,ms3,ms4,t1,t2,h,add,mul}

composition
session(ua,sp,ca,skuanc,skspnc,skuans,h,add,mul)
/\session(i,sp,ca,skuanc,skspnc,skuans,h,add,mul)
/\session(ua,i,ca,skuanc,skspnc,skuans,h,add,mul)
/\session(ua,sp,i,skuanc,skspnc,skuans,h,add,mul)
end role

goal
secrecy_of sp1,sp2,sp3,sp4
authentication_on ua_sp_xi
authentication_on sp_ua_ysp
end goal

environment()
```

Figure 7. Role of session, environment, and goal.

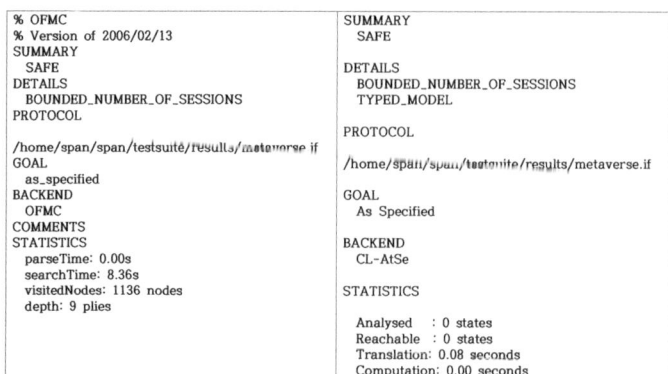

Figure 8. Result of AVISPA simulation.

7. Performance Analysis

We analyze the detailed comparative analysis of the proposed scheme with related schemes [16–18] in terms of the computation costs and the communication costs.

7.1. Analysis of Computation Cost

We compare the computation costs of the proposed scheme with the related schemes [16–18]. In this paper, we follow the execution time of the cryptographic operation measured by [39] using 2048 MB of RAM, Intel Pentium Dual CPU E2200 2.20 GHz, and the Ubuntu 12.04.1 LTS 32bit operating system. The cyclic group G_1 is a subgroup of $E(F_q) : y^2 = x^3 + x$, and G_2 is a subgroup of F_q^2. The group order of G1 is 160 bits, and the order of the base field is 512 bits. Depending on [39–41], we assume that the computation costs of 'a one-way hash function', 'biohasing function', 'elliptic curve point addition', 'elliptic curve scalar point multiplication', 'bilinear pairing', 'random nonce generation', and 'fuzzy extraction' are $T_H \approx 0.0023$ ms, $T_{BH} \approx 0.01$ ms [40], $T_{EA} \approx 0.0288$ ms, $T_{EM} \approx 2.226$ ms, $T_P \approx 5.811$ ms, $T_R \approx 0.539$ ms, $T_F \approx 2.68$ ms [41], respectively. We estimate the computation costs of the proposed scheme and related schemes and compare them. The comparison results are shown in Table 4. Because the proposed technique is designed based on XOR and Hash while minimizing the use of ECC, it shows much lower computation costs than the other existing schemes.

Table 4. Computation costs for authentication scheme: a comparative summary.

Schemes	User	Service Provider
Panda and Chattopadhyay [16]	$5T_{EM} + T_{EA} + 6T_H \approx 36.7759$ ms	$5T_{EM} + 2T_{EA} + 3T_H \approx 36.7837$ ms
Li et al. [17]	$7T_{EM} + 5T_H \approx 51.4723$ ms	$2T_P + 6T_{EM} + T_{EA} + 5T_H \approx 88.2458$ ms
Ryu et al. [18]	$4T_{EM} + T_{EA} + 8T_H + 2T_{BH} \approx 29.4438$ ms	$5T_{EM} + T_{EA} + 5T_H \approx 36.7755$ ms
The proposed scheme	$T_R + T_F + 11T_H \approx 3.2443$ ms	$T_R + 6T_H \approx 0.5528$ ms

7.2. Analysis of Communication Cost

We assume that the bit sizes of the identity, hash output, random nonce, timestamp, and elliptic curve point are 160, 160, 160, 32, and 320, respectively. We present the comparison of the proposed scheme and existing schemes in Table 5. Under the results of the communication cost comparison, the proposed scheme provides a more efficient computation cost compared with the other existing schemes.

Table 5. Communication costs for each scheme: a comparative summary.

Schemes	Costs
Panda and Chattopadhyay [16]	1440 bits
Li et al. [17]	1888 bits
Ryu et al. [18]	1344 bits
Our scheme	1024 bits

7.3. Security and Functionality Comparison

In terms of security and functionality features, we compare the proposed scheme with other related schemes [16–18]. The security features of the proposed scheme and related schemes are presented in Table 6.

Table 6. A comparison of security and functionality features.

	Panda and Chattopadhyay [16]	Li et al. [17]	Ryu et al. [18]	Our Scheme
Stolen IoT devices(XR) attack	—	—	√	√
Offline password guessing attack	√	—	√	√
Impersonation attack	√	√	√	√
Avatar impersonation attack	—	—	√	√
Session key disclosure attack	√	√	√	√
Perfect forward secrecy	√	√	√	√
Replay attack	√	√	√	√
MITM attack	√	√	√	√
Insider attack	√	—	√	√
Ephemeral secret leakage attack	×	√	√	√
Mutual authentication	×	√	√	√
Anonymity	√	×	√	√
Privacy-preservation	—	—	×	√
Untraceability	√	×	√	√
Denial-of-Service (DoS) Attack	×	√	×	√

√: scheme is secure or provides functionality feature ; ×: scheme is insecure and does not provide functionality feature; —: cannot be considered.

The results of our performance and security feature comparisons with related works indicate that our proposed scheme is more efficient in terms of computation and communication costs and satisfies a higher number of security requirements compared to existing schemes. Therefore, the proposed protocol can provide users with a secure service in the metaverse environment and is a lightweight protocol that takes into account the resource constraints of XR devices.

8. Conclusions

In this paper, we propose a secure authentication scheme for metaverse environments to provide a secure avatar interactions and prevent against various security attacks. In our scheme, users can utilize DID and VC to prove their identity to other avatars in the metaverse without revealing irrelevant personal information to service providers. Furthermore, the proposed scheme provides a secure communication channel against various attacks through secure authentication and key agreement between the user and service provider. The proposed scheme is resistant to various security attacks (including stolen XR devices, offline password guessing, user and avatar impersonation, etc.) by performing the ROR oracle security analyses, the well-known AVISPA simulation, and BAN logic analyses. Next, the proposed scheme provides lower computation and communication costs than other related schemes for the metaverse environment by the comparison of computation costs and communication costs. Therefore, the proposed scheme can be applied to practical metaverse environments to provide high security and privacy preservation. In the future, we intend to research authentication protocols for a secure and trusted metaverse environment, taking into consideration potential security issues that may arise in the blockchain.

Author Contributions: Conceptualization, M.K.; formal analysis, M.K. and S.S.; methodology, M.K. and Y.P. (Yohan Park); software M.K. and J.O.; validation, M.K., Y.P. (Yohan Park) and Y.P. (Youngho Park); writing—original draft, M.K.; writing—review and editing, J.K. and Y.P. (Youngho Park); supervision, Y.P. (Youngho Park). All authors have read and agreed to the published version of the manuscript.

Funding: This research was supported by the National Research Foundation of Korea (NRF) funded by the Ministry of Education under grant 2020R1I1A3058605.

Data Availability Statement: Not applicable.

Conflicts of Interest: The authors declare no conflict of interest.

References

1. Xu, M.; Ng, W.C.; Lim, W.Y.B.; Kang, J.; Xiong, Z.; Niyato, D.; Yang, Q.; Shen, X.; Miao, C. A full dive into realizing the edge-enabled metaverse: Visions, enabling technologies, and challenges. *IEEE Commun. Surv. Tutor.* **2023**, *25*, 656–700. [CrossRef]
2. Yang, Q.; Zhao, Y.; Huang, H.; Xiong, Z.; Kang, J.; Zheng, Z. Fusing blockchain and AI with metaverse: A survey. *IEEE Open J. Comput. Soc.* **2022**, *3*, 122–136. [CrossRef]
3. Huynh-The, T.; Gadekallu, T.R.; Wang, W.; Yenduri, G.; Ranaweera, P.; Pham, Q.V.; Costa, D.B.; Liyanage, M. Blockchain for the metaverse: A review. *Futur. Gener. Comp. Syst.* **2023**, *143*, 401–419. [CrossRef]
4. Bansal, G.; Rajgopal, K.; Chamola, V.; Xiong, Z.; Niyato, D. Healthcare in metaverse: A survey on current metaverse applications in healthcare. *IEEE Access* **2022**, *10*, 119914–119946. [CrossRef]
5. Park, S.; Kim, Y. A metaverse: Taxonomy, components, applications, and open challenges. *IEEE Access* **2022**, *10*, 4209–4251. [CrossRef]
6. A Researcher's Avatar was Sexually Assaulted on a Metaverse Platform Owned by Meta, Making Her the Latest Victim of Sexual Abuse on Meta's Platforms, Watchdog Says. Available online: https://www.businessinsider.com/researcher-claims-her-avatar-was-raped-on-metas-metaverse-platform-2022-5 (accessed on 20 September 2023).
7. Wang, Y.; Su, Z.; Zhang, N.; Xing, R.; Liu, D.; Luan, T.H.; Shen, X. A survey on metaverse: Fundamentals, security, and privacy. *IEEE Commun. Surv. Tutor.* **2023**, *25*, 319–352. [CrossRef]
8. Falchuck, B.; Loeb, S.; Neff, R. The social metaverse: Battle for privacy. *IEEE Technol. Soc. Mag.* **2018**, *37*, 52–61. [CrossRef]
9. Li, Y.; Cheng, Y.; Meng, W.; Li, Y.; Deng, R.H. Designing leakage-resilient password entry on head-mounted smart wearable glass devices. *IEEE Trans. Inf. Forensic Secur.* **2020**, *16*, 307–321. [CrossRef]
10. Sayeed, S.; Pitropakis, N.; Buchanan, W.J.; Markakis, E.; Papatsaroucha, D.; Politis, I. TRUSTEE: Towards the creation of secure, trustworthy and privacy-preserving framework. In Proceedings of the 18th International Conference on Availability, Reliability and Security, Benevento, Italy, 29 August–1 September 2023; pp. 1–10.
11. Tu, S.; Yu, H.; Badshah, A.; Waqas, M.; Halim, Z.; Ahmad, I. Secure internet of vehicles (IoV) with decentralized consensus blockchain mechanism. *IEEE Trans. Veh. Technol.* **2023**, *72*, 11227–11236. [CrossRef]
12. Sayeed, S.; Marco-Gisbert, H. Assessing blockchain consensus and security mechanisms against the 51% attack. *IEEE Commun. Surv. Tutor.* **2019**, *9*, 1788. [CrossRef]
13. Truong, V.T.; Le, L.; Niyato, D. Blockchain meets metaverse and digital asset management: A comprehensive survey. *IEEE Access* **2023**, *11*, 26258–26288. [CrossRef]

14. Patwe, S.; Mane, S. Blockchain enabled architecture for secure authentication in the metaverse environment. In Proceedings of the 2023 IEEE 8th International Conference for Convergence in Technology (I2CT), Lonavla, India, 7–9 April 2023; pp. 1–8.
15. Huang, Y.; Li, Y.J.; Cai, Z. Security and privacy in metaverse: A comprehensive survey. *Big Data Min. Anal.* **2023**, *6*, 234–247. [CrossRef]
16. Panda, P.K.; Chattopadhyay, S. A secure mutual authentication protocol for IoT environment. *J. Reliable Intell. Environ.* **2020**, *6*, 79–94. [CrossRef]
17. Li, Y.; Xu, M.; Xu, G. Blockchain-based mutual authentication protocol without CA. *J. Supercomput.* **2022**, *78*, 17261–17283. [CrossRef]
18. Ryu, J.; Son, S.; Lee, J.; Park, Y.; Park, Y. Design of secure mutual authentication scheme for metaverse environments using blockchain. *IEEE Access* **2022**, *10*, 98944–98958. [CrossRef]
19. Dodis, Y.; Reyzin, L.; Smith, A. Fuzzy extractors: How to generate strong keys from biometrics and other noisy data. In Proceedings of the International Conference on the Theory and Applications of Cryptographic Techniques, Interlaken, Switzerland, 2–6 May 2004; pp. 523–540.
20. Decentralized Identifiers (DIDs) v1.0 Core Architecture, Data Model, and Representations. Available online: https://www.w3.org/TR/did-core/ (accessed on 22 August 2023).
21. Verifiable Credentials Data Model 1.1. Available online: https://www.w3.org/TR/vc-data-model/ (accessed on 22 August 2023).
22. Dolev, D.; Yao, A. On the security of public key protocols. *IEEE Trans. Inf. Theory* **1983**, *29*, 198–208. [CrossRef]
23. Masud, M.; Gaba, G.S.; Choudhary, K.; Hossain, M.S.; Alhamid, M.F.; Muhammad, G. Lightweight and anonymity-preserving user authentication scheme for IoT-based healthcare. *IEEE Internet Things J.* **2022**, *9*, 2649–2656. [CrossRef]
24. Kim, M.; Lee, J.; Oh, J.; Kwon, D.; Park, K.; Park, Y.; Park, K.H. A secure batch authentication scheme for multiaccess edge computing in 5G-enabled intelligent transportation system. *IEEE Access* **2022**, *10*, 96224–96238. [CrossRef]
25. Bhattacharya, M.; Roy, S.; Chattopadhyay, S.; Das, A.K.; Jamal, S.S. ASPA-MOSN: An efficient user authentication scheme for phishing attack detection in mobile online social networks. *IEEE Syst. J.* **2023**, *17*, 234–245. [CrossRef]
26. Kocher, P.; Jaffe, J.; Jun, B. Differential power analysis. In Proceedings of the Annual International Cryptology Conference (CRYPTO), Santa Barbara, CA, USA, 15–19 August 1999; pp. 388–397.
27. Son, S.; Kwon, D.; Lee, S.; Jeon, Y.; Das, A.K.; Park, Y. Design of secure and lightweight authentication scheme for UAV-enabled intelligent transportation systems using blockchain and PUF. *IEEE Access* **2023**, *11*, 60240–60253. [CrossRef]
28. Kim, M.; Lee, J.; Park, K.; Park, Y.; Park, K.H.; Park, Y. Design of secure decentralized car-sharing system using blockchain. *IEEE Access* **2021**, *9*, 54796–54810. [CrossRef]
29. Canetti, R.; Krawczyk, H. Universally composable notions of key exchange and secure channels. In Proceedings of the International Conference on the Theory and Applications of Cryptographic Techniques, Amsterdam, The Netherlands, 28 April–2 May 2002; pp. 337–351.
30. Soni, P.; Pardhan, J.; Pal, A.K.; Islam, S.K.H. Cybersecurity attack-resilience authentication mechanism for intelligent healthcare system. *IEEE Trans. Ind. Inform.* **2023**, *19*, 830–840. [CrossRef]
31. Oh, J.; Yu, S.; Lee, J.; Son, S.; Kim, M.; Park, Y. A secure and lightweight authentication protocol for IoT-based smart homes. *Sensors* **2021**, *21*, 1488. [CrossRef] [PubMed]
32. Hosseinzadeh, M.; Ahmed, O.H.; Ahmed, S.H.; Trinh, C.; Bagheri, N.; Kumari, S.; Lansky, J.; Huynh, B. An enhanced authentication protocol for RFID systems. *IEEE Access* **2020**, *8*, 126977–126987. [CrossRef]
33. Lee, J.; Kim, G.; Das, A.K.; Park, Y. Secure and efficient honey list-based authentication protocol for vehicular ad hoc networks. *IEEE Trans. Netw. Sci. Eng.* **2021**, *8*, 2412–2425. [CrossRef]
34. Chen, C.M.; Chen, Z.; Kumari, S.; Lin, M.C. LAP-IoHT: A lightweight authentication protocol for the internet of health things. *Sensors* **2022**, *22*, 5401. [CrossRef]
35. Wang, D.; Cheng, H.; Wang, P.; Huang, X.; Jian, G. Zipf's law in passwords. *IEEE Trans. Inf. Forensics Secur.* **2017**, *12*, 2776–2791. [CrossRef]
36. AVISPA. Automated Validation of Internet Security Protocols and Applications. Available online: http://www.avispa-project.org/ (accessed on 22 August 2023).
37. SPAN: A Security Protocol Animator for AVISPA. Available online: https://people.irisa.fr/Thomas.Genet/span/ (accessed on 22 August 2023).
38. Yu, S.; Lee, J.; Park, Y.; Park, Y.; Lee, S.; Chung, B. A secure and efficient three-factor authentication protocol in global mobility networks. *Appl. Sci.* **2020**, *10*, 3565. [CrossRef]
39. Kilinc, H.H.; Yanik, T. A survey of SIP authentication and key agreement schemes. *IEEE Commun. Surv. Tutor.* **2013**, *16*, 1005–1023. [CrossRef]
40. Ravanbakhsh, N.; Nazari, M. An efficient improvement remote user mutual authentication and session key agreement scheme for E-health care systems. *Multimed. Tools Appl.* **2018**, *77*, 55–88. [CrossRef]
41. Gope, P.; Sikdar, B. Lightweight and privacy-preserving two-factor authentication scheme for IoT devices. *IEEE Internet Things J.* **2019**, *6*, 580–589. [CrossRef]

Disclaimer/Publisher's Note: The statements, opinions and data contained in all publications are solely those of the individual author(s) and contributor(s) and not of MDPI and/or the editor(s). MDPI and/or the editor(s) disclaim responsibility for any injury to people or property resulting from any ideas, methods, instructions or products referred to in the content.

Article

Energy-Efficient Blockchain-Enabled Multi-Robot Coordination for Information Gathering: Theory and Experiments [†]

Cesar E. Castellon [1], Tamim Khatib [1], Swapnoneel Roy [1], Ayan Dutta [1,*], O. Patrick Kreidl [1] and Ladislau Bölöni [2]

[1] School of Computing, University of North Florida, Jacksonville, FL 32224, USA
[2] Department of Computer Science, University of Central Florida, Orlando, FL 32816, USA
* Correspondence: a.dutta@unf.edu; Tel.: +1-904-620-1313
[†] This paper is an extended version of our paper published in ICRA 2022, Philadelphia, PA, USA, 23–27 May 2022.

Abstract: In this work, we propose a blockchain-based solution for securing robot-to-robot communication for a task with a high socioeconomic impact—information gathering. The objective of the robots is to gather maximal information about an unknown ambient phenomenon such as soil humidity distribution in a field. More specifically, we use the proof-of-work (PoW) consensus protocol for the robots to securely coordinate while rejecting tampered data injected by a malicious entity. As the blockchain-based PoW protocol has a large energy footprint, we next employ an algorithmically-engineered energy-efficient version of PoW. Results show that our proposed energy-efficient PoW-based protocol can reduce energy consumption by 14% while easily scaling up to 10 robots.

Keywords: multi-robot system; blockchain; security; energy

1. Introduction

Mobile robots are becoming a standard for information gathering from large geographic areas. Applications of this include data collection about the state of the crop for precision agriculture, current data sampling for ocean monitoring, and hotspot detection for search and rescue, among others [1–3]. In a classical information-gathering task, the robot is equipped with an information collection sensor, e.g., an NDVI camera, and a soil acidity measurement sensor, among others. The robot goes to k locations in the environment and uses its sensor to measure values at those locations. Given the robot has a limited onboard battery power supply, the robot cannot go to all the locations in the environment. Similarly, if the geographic area is large, one robot might not be enough, and multiple (n) robots need to be deployed that will coordinate among themselves while covering $n \cdot k$ locations. The objective is to infer the sensor measurements in the remaining unvisited locations conditioned on these collected $n \cdot k$ measurements. This is possible if the sensor measurements are correlated. For example, if one location $l_1 = (x_1, y_1)$ has the presence of weeds, then another location $l_2 = (x_2, y_2)$ will have high probabilities of having weeds if $\|l_1 - l_2\| < \mathbf{d}$, where $\mathbf{d}$ is a positive constant. The robots should collect these measurements while coordinating (e.g., via communication) with each other during the collection process to decide the best places to collect the measurements from. These measurements are then used by the end users, e.g., farmers, to make more informed decisions about their applications.

Although this seems like an attractive toolkit for automated information gathering, this approach has some challenges as well. First, the optimal information gathering with n robots is shown to be NP-hard [4,5]. Secondly, these robots are often accumulated from untrusted sources for deployment. Therefore, like other cyber-physical systems, these robots are vulnerable to cyber-attacks. Examples include denial of service, jamming, and data tampering attacks, among others. In this paper, we focus on one of these attacks, namely *data integrity attacks*. In these attacks, one or more malicious entities inject tampered or falsified information into the network. This might cause an irrecoverable negative socioeconomic impact. An example of this would be spraying herbicides on good crops and not on weeds, which would kill the crops. Currently, there is no standard for robot security, and the way to go is the hardware or software-based security mechanism. In this paper, we take the software route—we employ a blockchain-based proof-of-work (PoW) consensus protocol to secure the sensed data by the robots from being tampered with.

Standard blockchain-based schemes for crypto-currencies do not readily apply to multi-robot applications, since the robot network topology changes over time as the robots move around in the environment. Furthermore, one or more robots might be completely out of communication with the rest of the group for a considerable amount of time before regaining connectivity. Therefore, there is a need for a tailor-made blockchain-based PoW protocol to solve the multi-robot information-gathering problem. On the other hand, these security mechanisms are known to be power-hungry, and therefore, the robots might become non-operational if they run these security protocols on top of their prescribed sensing and computation routines. To this end, we employ an algorithmically-engineered blockchain-based PoW that reduces the energy requirement while guaranteeing the same level of security as the original protocol. This energy-efficient PoW version, which is premised upon an energy-optimized implementation of the SHA-256 encryption algorithm, has recently been published by us; the reader is referred to [6] for full details.

In this paper, we have tested our proposed energy-efficient blockchain-enabled multi-robot information-gathering technique with up to 10 simulated robots using MATLAB and Python 3. Experimental results show that robots can save up to 14% energy consumption with our energy-optimized version of SHA-256 used in place of the standard SHA-256. We further extrapolate our findings to more real-world scenarios involving a multi-robot system. We acknowledge that adding a layer of blockchain-based security protocol adds to the run times for decision-making and overall mission execution. However, it is a necessary step to make the data exchanged among the robots tamper-proof. Our results show that the amount of added time for this depends on the connectivity mechanism and the difficulty of the PoW consensus mechanism, among other factors. Figure 1 illustrates a sample multi-robot secure information-gathering scenario.

A preliminary version of this work appeared in ICRA 2022 [7]. We have extended the conference paper version mainly by employing an energy-efficient PoW protocol on the robots, whereas our conference paper assumed that the robots only have access to the traditional PoW protocol. Energy consumption of blockchain has been a major issue limiting its usage. While our preliminary results [7] show how blockchain can be useful in the context of robotics systems, the current work further complements it by making blockchain energy-efficient. The primary contributions of this paper are as follows:

1. This is the first study that integrates blockchain-based data security techniques against data tampering attempts into a multi-robot information-gathering framework under continuous, periodic, and opportunistic connectivity.
2. We employ an energy-efficient version of the blockchain-based proof-of-work (PoW) consensus protocol that is up to 14% more efficient than the original PoW implementation in terms of energy consumption.
3. Our proposed techniques in this paper study the security aspects in the multi-robot information-gathering problem setup from the novel perspectives of model estimation error, data vulnerability and its impact, and energy efficiency.

Figure 1. Illustration of a multi-robot information-gathering scenario. The links between the robots indicate the availability of communication. If all the links are present at every time, then the robots have continuous connectivity (CC). If all the links become available (or if the links create a connected network via a different topology) periodically, the robots then follow periodic connectivity (PC). On the other hand, if the white or the orange link is available, but there is no guarantee that all of them are available at any time, then we have opportunistic connectivity (OC). We want these communication protocols among the robots to be secure as well as energy-efficient.

The remainder of the paper is organized as the following. First, in Section 2, we discuss the state of the art in multi-robot information-gathering and security aspects in robotics, while comparing and contrasting our work in this paper against them. In Section 3, we summarize the information-gathering problem (i.e., models and assumptions) using the notation appearing later in the paper. Section 4 discusses the proposed secure communication algorithms and their energy-efficient versions are presented in Section 5. In Section 6, we present and discuss our experimental results and, finally, we conclude in Section 7.

2. Literature Review

Mobile robots can be used to autonomously gather meaningful information based on which future actions can be taken. Due to its sheer practical significance, the domain of information sensing using autonomous mobile robots has recently received considerable attention [1,8–16]. In this problem setup, the goal of the robot(s) is to plan paths of lengths k such that the maximum amount of information can be collected from the environment. The goal locations might or might not be decided in the beginning. In this paper, we study a setting that is more suited for lifelong monitoring—the robots are not given any specific goal locations. Instead, they can finish their exploration anywhere in the environment [9,12,17]. Unlike coverage path planning, where the robots have to go through all the locations in the environment, here, the robots' goal would be to infer the sensor measurements at the locations that they have not visited and collected information from. It is also popular in the literature to assume that the robots have been given pre-defined goal locations, and their goal in that setting would be to plan k-length paths from the start to the goal locations while maximizing the amount of collected information [5,18–20]. Gaussian process (GP) regression is the most used information modeling and inference tool in information-gathering studies [21]. Following GP, information theoretic measures such as entropy or mutual information can be used to send the robots to the most informative locations in the environment [5,22,23]. Similar to our setting in this paper, many prior studies have started with dividing the environment into n sub-regions so that n robots can be uniquely assigned to them [5,22–24]. If the different parts of the environment have different information measures, the robots can communicate their findings, e.g., share their GP models and/or their sensor observations so far to "fuse" their inference models. This has been shown to perform better than using no such coordination [2,12]. For fusing the models, Gaussian mixture models with the Expectation Maximization algorithm [25] can be employed [2,12].

Advancements in multi-agent deep reinforcement learning (DRL) and its applications in robotics have also been applied to the problem of information gathering [26]. One of the first such works is by Said et al. [17], who used recurrent neural networks along with GP for information modeling with up to 10 robots. They have used a mean-field DRL [27] technique to effectively reduce the n-robot learning problem to a 2-agent learning problem. Wei and Zheng [28] proposed an independent learning technique with credit assignment to solve this notoriously difficult problem. Pan, Manjanna, and Hsieh [29] recently proposed a policy gradient-based DRL for multi-robot information sampling. Unlike the prior studies, they do not use GP as the underlying information inference tool. Viseras and Garcia [30] also proposed a DRL-based information-gathering technique for a multi-robot team that can exploit existing accurate information models.

Although communication is a costly operation in terms of energy consumption and robots' communication ranges (via WiFi, for example) are limited, most of the studies assume that the robots can maintain a continuously connected network among themselves so that data sharing is always possible. On the other hand, Dutta, Ghosh, and Kreidl [1] previously showed the computation-intensive nature of such maintenance algorithms. Maintaining periodic connectivity brings up another challenge: reconnection planning with a group of n mobile robots, even in a tree-like environment, is an NP-hard problem [31]. Under these circumstances, opportunistic connectivity is the go-to option. In this case, the robots are not required to maintain communication with others, but if two or more robots are within each other's communication ranges, they will form an ad hoc network to share data as required. Opportunistic connectivity has been shown to be effective in multi-robot tasks [9,10,32]. For a survey of available connectivity models and their applications in multi-robot systems, the reader is referred to [33].

The information collected by the robots might be sensitive, and therefore, protecting the integrity of such data is of the utmost importance. However, there is no standard security protocol for multi-robot coordination, although communication attacks have been approached from the point of view of fault diagnosis (e.g., [34–36]). One of the first works on blockchain-based PoW for protecting the data shared among the robots is by [37], where a swarm of robots is controlled using blockchain-based smart contracts. In our prior work [38], we also used PoW-based tamper-proof technology for multiple robots to collect information. Both of these studies assume a connected robot, unlike this paper, where other connectivity strategies such as periodic and opportunistic are also tested while the blockchain-based security protocol is enabled. PoW is one of the most popular consensus protocols in cryptocurrencies [39]. However, it is known to be significantly resource-intensive [40–42]. This poses a challenge in robotics, as the robots run on a limited onboard power supply. Proof-of-stake (PoS), another blockchain-based consensus protocol, has recently been shown to consume only a fraction of the energy required by

PoW (https://bit.ly/3zlq3aS). Which consensus protocol suits a multi-robot application the best has yet to be explored. For more information on consensus protocols, refer to [43].

3. Problem Setup

We have a set of n homogeneous robots $R = r_1, r_2, \cdots, r_n$ that explore a shared environment. The environment is discretized into a planar graph $G_p = \{V, E\}$, where the node set V represents the information collection locations, and the connections among them are denoted by the edge set E. Each robot r_i has its unique sub-region for exploration, $\mathcal{V}_i$, and $\mathcal{V}_i \cap \mathcal{V}_j = \emptyset$. We have pre-calculated $\mathcal{V}_i$ using K-medoids clustering [44]. An example is shown in Figure 2a. r_i is equipped with an on-board sensor which allows it to sense and collect information (e.g., radiation detector). The robots' observations are modeled to be noisy. A robot r_i starts from a node $v_i^0 \in \mathcal{V}_i$. The path or sequence of nodes $(v_i^0, v_i^1, v_i^2, \ldots)$ that each robot r_i follows determines the sensed locations of the ambient environment $\mathcal{Z}$; specifically, we denote by v_i^t the node that robot r_i enters at time step t and by $\mathcal{Z}(v_i^k)$ the associated (scalar, real-valued) measurement received by robot r_i.

We use a Gaussian process (GP) to model the uncertain environment and noisy measurement process. Let $\mathbf{X}$ denote a Gaussian random vector of length $|V|$ with prior mean vector μ and covariance matrix Σ, where μ and Σ represent the (minimum mean-square-error) prediction over node set V and its corresponding uncertainty, respectively [21]. For any given $GP = (\mu, \Sigma)$, the volumetric measure of uncertainty is calculated by an information-theoretic metric, (differential) entropy, which is formally defined as $H(\mathbf{X}) = \frac{1}{2} \log |\Sigma| + \frac{|V|}{2} \log(2\pi e)$, where $|\Sigma|$ denotes the covariance matrix's determinant, while $|V|$ denotes the vertex set's cardinality. It is a standard assumption in kernel-based parameterizations of GPs that the correlation between two nodes is inversely proportional to the distances between them [4,10,21]. We exploit this property when computing entropy by approximating the computationally intensive matrix determinant $|\Sigma|$ by the product of the per-node variances (σ_v^2) along the diagonal of Σ. In turn, the associated entropy $H(\mathbf{X})$ decomposes additively across the nodes, with each per-node term given by:

$$H(X_v) = \frac{1}{2} \log\left(2\pi e \sigma_v^2\right). \tag{1}$$

These per-node entropies, with their sum (via the Hadamard inequality) serving as the upper bound for the true global entropy $H(\mathbf{X})$, drive the robots towards opportune locations for information collection. In each move cycle, the information value of past measurements is reflected in these entropies by virtue of optimal updates to the underlying GP statistics during each sensing cycle.

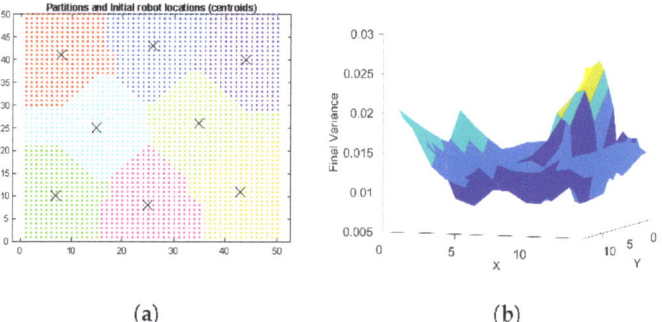

Figure 2. (a) A 50×50 grid environment is divided into eight non-overlapping sub-regions (shown using different colors) using K-medoids clustering. The centroids of these regions ('x') are the robots' initial positions. (b) An example of the final average variance map calculated by four robots in a 14×14 environment using a greedy strategy is shown, where the initial variance of the information model was 0.14. This shows the quality of the inference strategy.

Let us first summarize the sequential sense/move cycle of multi-robot information gathering in the context of initial time step 0. Assume each robot starts with a common initial GP model, called $GP = (\mu, \Sigma)$, and then takes measurement $\mathcal{Z}(v_i^0)$ at its start node $v_i^0 \in V$. Such prior statistics are typically derived pre-deployment from a training dataset and transferred onto each robot r_i before it is deployed to start node v_i^0. We also assume the measurements are subject to additive white Gaussian noise $\epsilon \in \mathcal{N}(0, \sigma_n)$, in which case the updated local GP for robot r_i is given by the posterior statistics:

$$\begin{aligned} \Sigma_i^0 &= \Sigma - \Sigma \mathbf{C} v_i^{0'} \left[\mathbf{C} v_i^0 \Sigma \mathbf{C} v_i^{0'} + \sigma_n^2 \right]^{-1} \mathbf{C} v_i^0 \Sigma \\ \mu_i^0 &= \mu + \Sigma_i^0 \mathbf{C} v_i^{0'} \left[\mathcal{Z}(v_i^0) - \mathbf{C} v_i^0 \mu \right], \end{aligned} \quad (2)$$

where $\mathbf{C} v_i^0$ denotes the length-$|V|$ row vector of all zeros except for a one in component v_i^0, and $\mathbf{C} v_i^{0'}$ is its matrix transpose. During periodic or opportunistic connectivity, the posterior statistics will sometimes evolve on a batch of measurements, which is easily accommodated by appropriate augmentation of the output matrix $\mathbf{C}(\cdot)$; the reader is referred to [10] for more details. As the sensing step concludes, and each robot now possesses its updated GP statistics $GP_i^0 = (\mu_i^0, \Sigma_i^0)$ via Equation (2), the per-node rewards using Equation (1) are calculated. In a greedy fashion, robot r_i then chooses the next adjacent node $v_i^* \in \mathcal{V}_i$ that provides the (approximation of) maximum entropy:

$$v_i^* = \arg\max_{v \in adj(v_i^0)} H(v | GP_i^0)) \quad \text{s.t. } v \in \mathcal{V}_i. \quad (3)$$

In the absence of inter-robot communication, each robot repeats the above sense-and-move cycle until it runs out of the given budget B. Such information-gathering strategies, interleaving GP-based sensor measurement processing with greedy entropy-based movement decisions, are well-studied in the literature and in certain conditions yield performance even provably bounded within constant factors of optimal [4,5,45]. In scenarios permitting inter-robot communication, connected robots during any cycle may also share actual measurements and/or GP statistics through which better-coordinated movement decisions become theoretically possible. Distributed multi-robot information gathering remains the subject of active research, with important considerations including questions of who talks to whom, how often, and how much, as well as how to integrate whatever information does get shared to ideally guarantee improved collective performance. The next section summarizes prior work in this area in the context of the blockchain-based security measures that the rest of this paper seeks to make more energy efficient.

4. Secure Communication Algorithms

Under periodic connectivity (PC) assumptions, the robots will form a connected network after every $\mathcal{F}$ cycle, where $\mathcal{F}$ refers to the coordination frequency [3,13]. (The reader seeking more details on how to reconnect the robots periodically is referred to [3,31].) Observe that the case of $\mathcal{F} = 1$ recovers the standard continuous connectivity (CC) assumptions. Opportunistic connectivity (OC) is distinctly different because the robots are not guaranteed to form connected communication networks; instead, the robots communicate only if and when at least two robots are within each other's communication ranges. Note that, for connectivity discussions, we consider continuous connectivity (CC) as the baseline and, therefore, we first discuss blockchain's proof-of-work (PoW) consensus for CC and discuss PC and OC thereafter.

4.1. Proof-of-Work (PoW) Consensus Protocol in CC

In an insecure version, each robot receives information from other robots and updates its local GP model using Equation (2) [1] (Algorithm 1). A malicious entity can attack this data-sharing system via data-tampering attempts [46,47]. To prevent other robots from incorporating such fake data for their future decision-making, we have used a blockchain-based security protocol. Blockchain is a tamper-resistant digital ledger that the robots maintain in a distributed fashion [43]. In a blockchain, the data are stored in discrete units, called blocks, that are linked (chained) to each other by having the hash of one block as part of the data of the next block. Similar to [38], each robot r_i maintains a local blockchain C_i. Each block $b_{idx} \in C_i$ contains five primary components $< D, T, idx, N, H_{last} >$, where D denotes the collected measurement(s), T represents the current timestamp, idx is the index of the block, N is an integer called nonce, and H_{last} represents the previous block b_{idx-1}'s hash.

Algorithm 1: Energy-efficient blockchain-enabled information gathering

1 $v_i^* \leftarrow r_i$'s next location;
2 **while** *budget* ≥ 0 **do**
3   Go to v_i^* and gather information;
4   Create a block with these;
5   Share this block with the other robots (either periodically with PC or every cycle with CC or OC);
6   Receive blocks from other robots if applicable;
7   Decide whether the received information can be added to the local blockchain using the energy-efficient PoW (Algorithm 2);
8   Update the local GP with the new data using Equation (2) and recalculate entropy using Equation (1);
9   Decide v_i^* using Equation (3);

Algorithm 2 presents the pseudocode of the PoW algorithm. After r_i measures $\mathcal{Z}(v_i^*)$ at v_i^*, it puts them in D. The nonce is initially set to zero. The robot creates a block with it and finds its corresponding hash. To mine this block, r_i checks whether the hash has the required *difficulty* or not. In our implementation, a difficulty is first determined by counting the number of leading or trailing zeros in a block's hash value. Finding the hash value becomes harder the more zeros there are. The nonce is initialized to 0 and raised by 1 inside of a for loop—this is utilized to find this hash value. The loop terminates when the correct nonce is determined, i.e., the number of zeros matches the number of zeros in the hash value of the nonce variable. SHA-256 is used to calculate the hash value. A maximum loop number (MAX_STEPS, line 3 of Algorithm 2) is set. If the correct nonce cannot be identified by the maximum loop number, the nonce is reset to 0, and the software throws an error. *Mining* is the process of obtaining a correct nonce whose hash value satisfies the desired difficulty level. The specific details of different parameters are discussed next.

Algorithm 2: Proof-of-work (PoW) algorithm

Data: Block b, Nonce N, Difficulty d
Result: b.hash, N
1 $N \leftarrow 0$;
2 $diff \leftarrow fill("0", d)$;   /* #0s correspond to difficulty */
3 **while** *MAX_STEPS not reached* **do**
4   b.hash $\leftarrow$ Find the hash using SHA-256;
5   **if** *diff is matched* **then**
6   break;   /* Found desired hash */
7   **else**
8   **if** $i = 2^{256}$ **then**
9              $N \leftarrow 0$;   /* Nonce N is reset */
10   break;
11   Increment N by 1 and retry;

Once this mining process is over, the block is placed into r_i's local blockchain C_i. With CC, the robots share their newly created blocks with each other after every cycle of sense and measurement. The robots replace their local blockchains with the received blockchains if the blocks are validated and, as a result, at the end of each coordination cycle, every robot will have other robots' valid new blocks along with their existing blocks in their local blockchains [38] (Algorithm 2). Note that the verification of the hash is straightforward. A robot looks at the nonce in a particular block, finds its corresponding hash, and checks whether the hash has the desired difficulty level. If not, the block is rejected; otherwise, it is validated. Therefore, increasing the difficulty reduces the probability of it being compromised, while the time and energy required by the robots increase significantly.

4.2. PoW Consensus Protocol in PC and OC

With PC, r_i creates D with the last $\mathcal{F}$ measurements. As the robots coordinate periodically, they do not get a chance to share their collected information every cycle. Therefore, each block will contain $\mathcal{F}$ measurements in PC, whereas it contains only one in CC. The other components in the block are calculated in the same way as in CC. Having a larger block size has one advantage—the robots do not need to share information in every cycle, and therefore, the communication and mining overheads are significantly less. On the other hand, in a bandwidth-limited environment, sharing a larger block might be prohibitive. Furthermore, as the robots are not aware of others' collected data, the quality of their informative paths might be sub-par compared to CC.

With OC, when two or more robots $\bar{R} \subseteq R$ come within each other's communication ranges, they share their local blockchains, and the coordination happens in the same way as in CC. Each robot $r_i \in \bar{R}$'s local blockchain contains its observed data and any valid data it has received earlier from $r_j \in R$. As the robots are collecting data from disjoint sub-regions in the environment, they might have mutually exclusive local blockchains. This might lead to *orphan* blocks. An orphan block is a block that was mined and placed in the blockchain at some point. However, over time, a new blockchain was generated that did not include this block, leaving it abandoned. Orphan blocks only exist in OC. For example, suppose robot r_i has a local blockchain containing the following blocks $\{a, b, c, d\}$, and robot r_j has a local blockchain of $\{a, b, c, e, f, g\}$. Next, these two robots come within C distance. Following our algorithm, r_i will accept the longer blockchain of r_j, causing block d to be abandoned, namely, an orphan block. While block d, in particular, will no longer be used, the data within it will be extracted and put back into a memory buffer known as unconfirmed data that r_i maintains in OC for such scenarios. Note that this is *not* the same as block d; the data D are the same, but the previous hash, the timestamp, and the nonce will all be different. Also, block d was still a valid block but was left out of the blockchain simply due to asynchronous coordination in OC and not because of malicious data. Although the data in block d are preserved, the block itself will stay orphaned, meaning the mining effort put into it is lost. Using our proposed algorithm, the robots will not lose any collected data. For proof of this statement, please see [7] (Lemma 2).

5. Optimizing Energy Consumption of the Robotics System

The blockchain-based solution for the integrity problem in robotics communication comes with the cost of energy consumption. Due to its distributed, decentralized, integrity-preserving, and auditable features, blockchain technology has recently been recognized as a crucial tool for solving network and cybersecurity issues [48–51]. Unfortunately, when applied, the blockchain's intricate workflow uses a lot of electricity (energy), defeating the purpose of many real-world applications while making it difficult to meet the demands of low-energy robotics applications. For instance, energy use in Bitcoin, a typical blockchain application, will soon exceed 7.67 GW annually, which is close to Austria's annual energy consumption (8.2 GW) [52]. Recent techniques for reducing energy consumption in blockchain include developing new blockchain-based system software [53–55], operating systems [56,57], hypervisors [16,58], and hardware [59,60]. While these approaches have yielded significant improvements in reducing energy consumption levels in blockchain, to the best of our knowledge, the solutions do not approach the problem from an algorithmic perspective. In this work, we employ an energy-efficient version of PoW proposed in [6], albeit re-engineered for robotic networks. An illustration is shown in Figure 3.

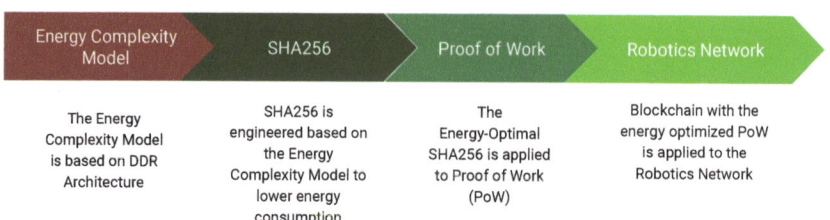

Figure 3. Our approach toward having an energy-optimized PoW for multi-robot communication [6].

Figure 3 summarizes our flow of actions. The energy complexity model (ECM) [61] yields the maximum savings in energy consumption (since it is the only process running on which ECM is applied) when applied to SHA-256. The energy-optimized SHA-256 when applied to PoW yields a lesser decrement in energy consumption levels. This is because the PoW algorithm's computations other than SHA-256 add to the overall energy overhead. This is further evident when incorporated into the blockchain-based robotics network [7].

5.1. The Energy Complexity Model (ECM)

The energy complexity model (ECM), which has been applied to SHA-256 in this work, uses as its reference architecture the Double Data Rate Synchronous Dynamic Random Access Memory (DDR SDRAM). As illustrated in Figure 4, the main memory of DDR is divided into banks containing a fixed number of chunks. Although DDR specifications use the term *block*, we prefer the term *chunk* in the context of SHA-256 to avoid ambiguity. Data are distributed in chunks in each bank. Every bank also has a unique chunk known as the *sense amplifier*. Every data access requires bringing the chunk containing the desired data inside the sense amplifier of the appropriate bank. The current chunk must be returned to its bank before a fresh one can be brought in for the next access, since each sense amplifier can only contain one chunk at a time. As each bank has its sense amplifier, only one chunk of each bank can be accessed at once; however, chunks from various banks can be accessed simultaneously. Therefore, for a P bank DDR memory, we can always access P chunks. In the DDR3 version of the DDR architecture, the sensing amplifier is referred to as the per-bank cache.

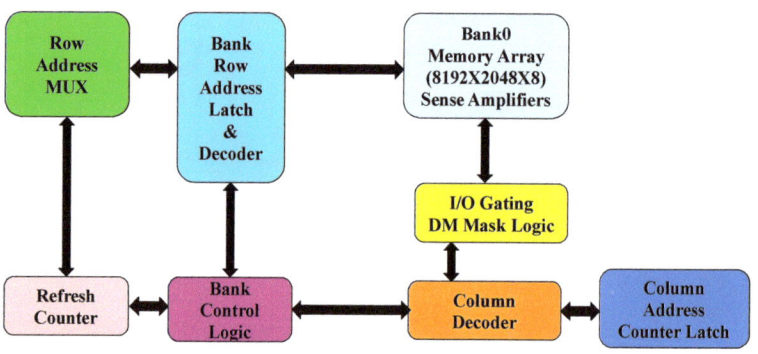

Figure 4. Block diagram of an internal DDR SDRAM memory chip.

A given DDR3 SDRAM's P banks are identified by the ECM as $M_1, M_2, \ldots, M_P$. Each bank M_i contains a cache C_i and several chunks of size nB (in bytes). Figure 5 shows an example with $P = 4$ banks and only 4 chunks per bank. The chunks were given labels with the values $1, 2, \ldots, 16$. The access patterns $(1, 2, 3, 4)$ or $(5, 6, 7, 8)$ are examples of totally serial execution given the restriction in DDR that only one chunk may be placed inside a certain cache C_i at any one time, whereas $(1, 5, 9, 13)$ or $(3, 8, 10, 13)$ are examples of completely parallel execution.

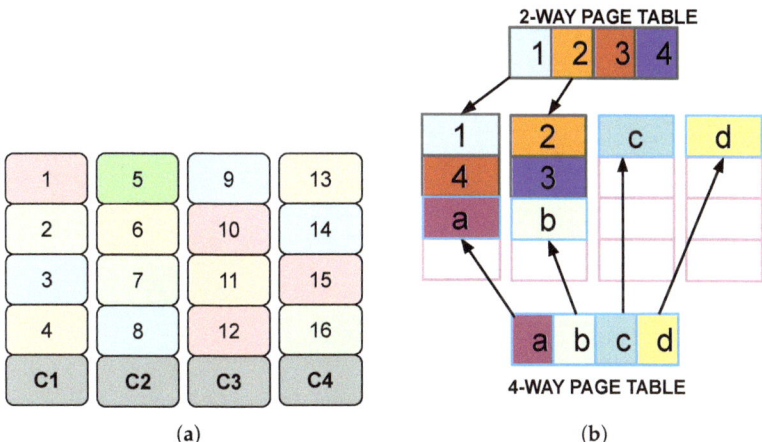

Figure 5. (a) An example of ECM for DDR3 with $P = 4$ banks; (b) Memory layout for different parallelization levels with $P = 4$.

Technically, according to a [61]-derived formula, the amount of energy used by an algorithm $\mathcal{A}$ with the execution time τ for a P bank DDR3 architecture with B bytes per chunk is provided by:

$$E(\mathcal{A}) = \tau + (P \times B)/I. \qquad (4)$$

The so-called *parallelization index*, represented by I, is effectively the number of parallel block accesses done by $\mathcal{A}$ across different memory banks for every P block access made overall. ECM states that an algorithm's potential for energy savings is inversely proportional to the extent to which it can be built to parallelize memory accesses.

5.2. Engineering SHA-256 Algorithm Using ECM

In this work, the underlying PoW hash algorithm SHA-256 has been engineered to use less energy by basing it on ECM. Initially, we describe how any algorithm $\mathcal{A}$ can be parallelized using ECM. Next, we show how SHA-256, the PoW's underlying hash algorithm, is designed for parallelization via ECM.

5.2.1. Parallelizing an Arbitrary Algorithm $\mathcal{A}$

The most frequent memory access sequence made by algorithm $\mathcal{A}$ during execution for a particular input is first noted. The vector created by this access sequence is then designed to have the required amount of parallelism by constructing a logical mapping over memory blocks that house the data that $\mathcal{A}$ has accessed. The physical location of the input (chunks) in the memory is fixed and is managed by the DDR memory controller. However, for various levels of parallelization, the order of access over chunks varies. Each time, a separate page table vector, or $\mathbf{V}$, is framed to perform a different level of access parallelization over physical chunks. The order of access among chunks is defined by $\mathbf{V}$ (Figure 5b).

The page table vector $\mathbf{V}$ contains the pattern $(1, 2, 3, 4, \ldots)$ for 1-way access and $(1, 5, 9, 13, \ldots)$ for 4-way access. The pattern of the page table vector $\mathbf{V}$ is then mapped to the input's original physical places using a function. The function to construct an ordering among the chunks is presented in [6] (Algorithm 2). Based on how we wish to access the chunks (P-way would signify full parallel access), the ordering is determined. By selecting chunks with *jumps*, the page table is filled. Jumps of P are chosen for P-way access to guarantee that consecutive chunk accesses are in P distinct banks. In accordance with the aforementioned example, jumps of 1 ensure that 4 successive chunk accesses occur in the same bank (bank 1 of Figure 5) for $P = 1$. In contrast, jumps of 4 ensure that 4 successive chunk accesses lie in 4 different banks for $P = 4$ (banks 1 through 4 of Figure 5).

5.2.2. Parallelizing SHA-256

As seen in Figure 6a, the SHA-256 algorithm divides the input into fixed-size message blocks that are then delivered sequentially to different compression methods. This block sequence is recognized in accordance with the SHA-256 algorithm's access pattern, which we subject to engineering using the ECM. The SHA-256 input vector (Figure 6a) is pre-processed into a different vector by using [6] (Algorithm 2). After that, the mapping is kept in a page table to be used in later hash computations.

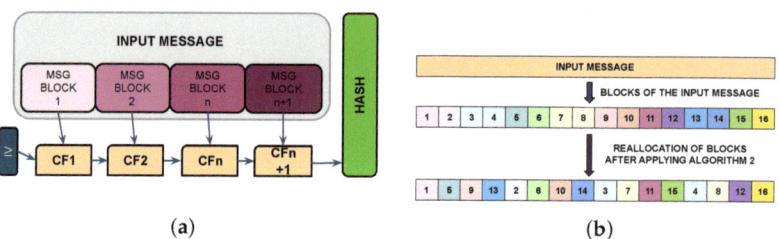

Figure 6. (**a**) An illustration of the original SHA-256 algorithm; (**b**) Access pattern re-engineering of blocks.

In Figure 6b, part of this procedure for 16 blocks and a parallelization index (jump) of 4 is displayed. The result of engineering the SHA-256 algorithm based on ECM is shown in Figure 7a. Note that the complexity of SHA-256 does not change because of this engineering [6] (Theorem 1). The parallelization index is set to $I = 8$, and an 8-bank DDR3 SDRAM is utilized in our experimentation. This basically means that we established a virtual mapping using the methods given in [61] to make sure that each set of 8 consecutive block access in SHA-256 occurs across all 8 banks.

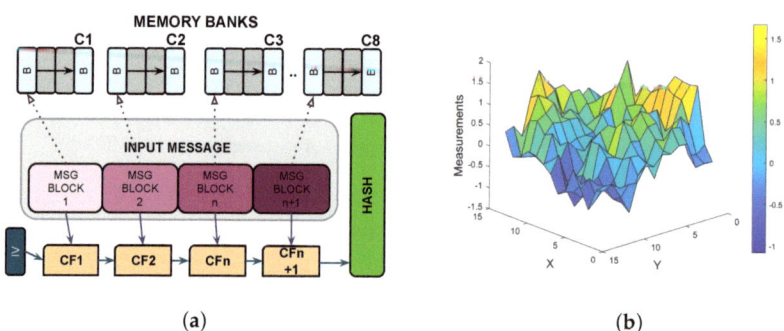

Figure 7. (**a**) An illustration of ECM-enhanced SHA$-$256; (**b**) The scalar information field used in the experiments.

5.3. *Incorporating Energy-Optimized SHA-256 into PoW & Using Energy-Efficient PoW*

Algorithm 2 employs SHA-256 in line 4 for PoW. Applying [6] (Algorithm 2) pre-processes the input vector in line 4 of the Algorithm 2, which is the concatenation of the string (b.Params) and the nonce (line 4 of Algorithm 2). This is how the energy-optimized SHA-256 is used in our work, which is indicated by the green SHA-256 call in line 4. This energy-efficient PoW is then incorporated in this work for the robotics network for the cases of continuous (Section 4.1), periodic, and opportunistic connectivity (Section 4.2), respectively. To summarize, Algorithm 1 is executed in this work with the energy-efficient PoW algorithm for experiments wherever applicable.

6. Experiments

6.1. Setup and Results: Without Considering Energy Model

The parameters used in our experiments are listed in Table 1. The adversarial robot can inject fake data randomly sampled between $[-10, +10]$ in place of the original sensor measurement. The exact information field used in this paper is presented in Figure 7b.

Table 1. Parameters used in our experiments and their values.

Parameter	Value
Language	MATLAB and Python
Environment	Grid
Actions	8
Budget	20
Noise in sensing	$\mathcal{N}(0, 0.25)$
GP kernel	Exponential
Baselines	No Attack (no malicious data tampering) and Insecure (no security protocol in place)
	for energy-efficient PoW
RAM architecture	DDR3
Energy measurement software	pyRAPL [62]
OS	Linux Mint
Processor	Intel i5-2410M, 64-bit
C compiler	gcc 8.3.1

To first illustrate the effect of injecting fake data into a robotic information-gathering system and the impact of our secure technique to nullify that, we choose the mean-square-error (MSE) metric, which indicates how accurate the predicted information model is, to analyze the consequences of data integrity assaults on multi-robot information sampling. Figures 8 and 9a present the findings. The PC and OC results versus the results for CC [38] are also shown.

The PC version of MSE consistently outperforms the insecure version when statistically compared to its results. Similar to CC, the blockchain-based proposed solution will not be able to prevent efforts at data manipulation if the difficulty is set to a low value such as 1. The probability that the hash satisfies the difficulty 1 condition is $\frac{1}{16}$, which is relatively low, and as a result, the malicious robot can occasionally tamper with global data sharing. This is because there are 16 possible hash values per digit, and only one digit is an acceptable value for the prefix (0). The robots performed better—i.e., the final MSE was lower—when they communicated more frequently (for example, $\mathcal{F} = 2$ is better than $\mathcal{F} = 5$ when we compare the PC results with varying $\mathcal{F}$). Although this trend was constant, it is noteworthy that big differences in MSE were infrequently the result. We think that the reason there is such a modest variation in MSE outcomes across frequencies is that the robots that coordinate more frequently have more opportunities to modify their exploration plans (see Figure 9a for reference). Because of the aforementioned factor, it is often true that the connection model performs better in terms of MSE the closer it is to the CC. Be aware that this increases computing time, which we shall address in more detail later in the section.

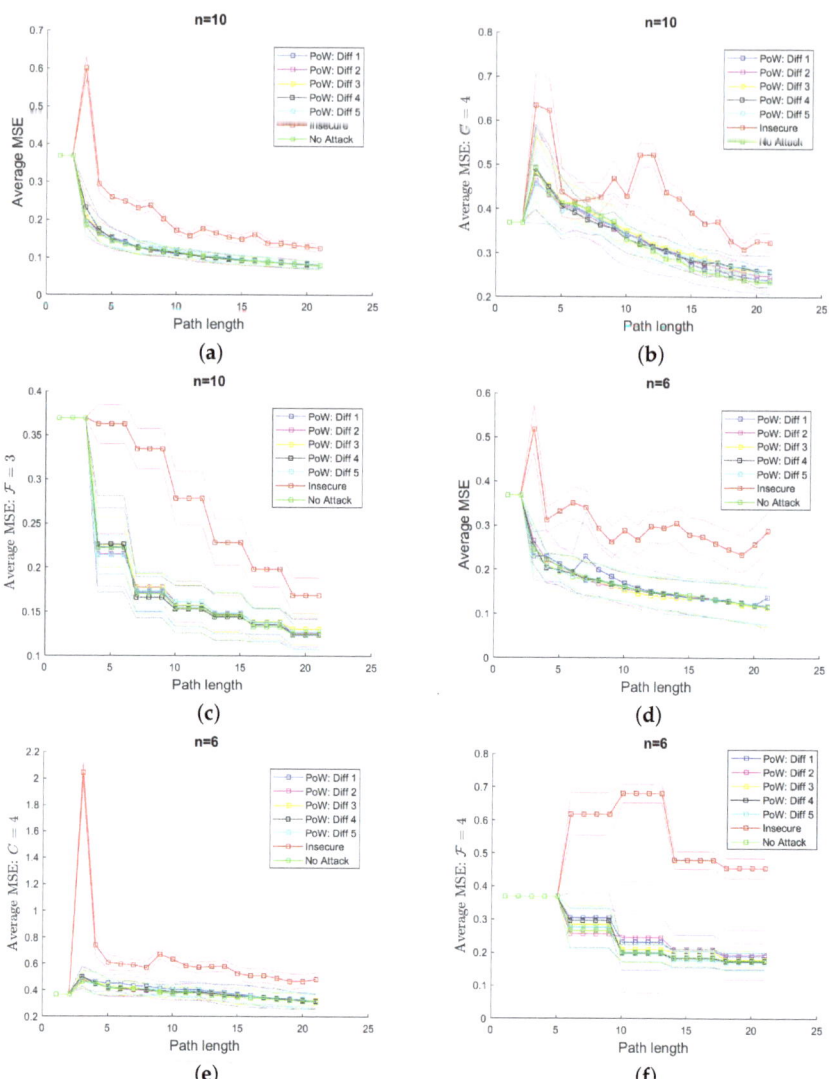

Figure 8. Single attacker: MSE comparison (the lower the better) among various connectivity models used: (**a,d**) CC with $n = 10$ and 6; (**b,e**) OC with $n = 10$ and 6; and (**d,f**) PC with $n = 10$ and 6.

Similar to CC and PC, the OC model almost always outperforms the insecure version statistically, with the exception of a few occasions where it performs less well (with difficulty 1) for the previously mentioned reasons. We have discovered that the MSE is lower with a bigger C compared to a smaller C. With different communication ranges, the MSE varies significantly. For instance, when the difficulty is 4 and n is set to 4, the final MSE value is 0.33 with $C = 4$ and 0.14 with $C = 12$. In almost every experiment, $C = 12$ performed statistically significantly better than $C = 4$. The MSEs with a range of 8 look more comparable to the range 4 than $C = 12$ with 2 robots. Because a third robot can still communicate with two robots that are out of range if there is one in range of the other two, communication range becomes less important as more robots are present. Therefore, the difference between having a range of 8 and 12 was significantly greater (up to 5.5 times when n increases from 4 to 8 with difficulty 4). The robots needed less run time since they had less new data for PoW if they often interacted.

PC consistently beat CC in terms of algorithm run time (Figure 9b–d). Furthermore, when robots coordinate less frequently with PC, the run time is shorter. For instance, the run times for PC with $\mathcal{F} = 2$ and 5 are, respectively, 34.04 and 15.50 s, and the run time for CC is 59.76 s for the same $n = 10$ and difficulty 4.

On the other side, OC consistently outperformed CC but fell short of PC. Additionally, while OC typically performed better with a wider range, this is not always the case. This is due to the fact that, on some occasions, the time saved through coordinating less frequently was offset by the time required to redo PoW for the orphaned blocks.

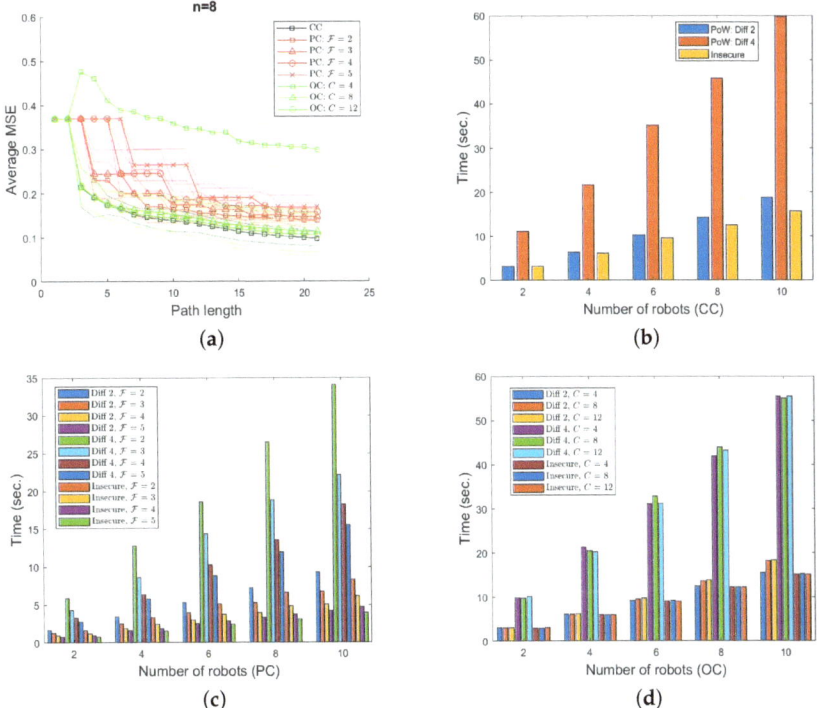

Figure 9. Single attacker: (**a**) comparison of MSE values among all the connectivity models with $n = 8$; run time comparison (the lower the better) between our proposed secure techniques and the implemented benchmark algorithms: (**b**) CC; (**c**) PC; and (**d**) OC.

6.2. Setup and Results: Considering the Energy Model

The specific parametric details for the energy-efficient PoW implementations are listed in Table 1. Remember that the ECM needs hardware with DDR RAMs.

6.2.1. Numeric Results

In our experiments, we performed three different lines of comparison for energy consumption.

1. We had the SHA-256 operation in PoW in our system implemented in two different programming languages, C and Python, for comparison. Furthermore, the energy-optimized SHA-256 was implemented only in C. Therefore, we had three different implementations for energy consumption comparison: (1) the standard implementation of SHA-256 using Python [P]; (2) the standard implementation of SHA-256 using

C [S-C]; and (3) the engineered SHA-256 based on ECM for energy optimization using C [O-C].
2. We set three different difficulty levels for PoW (2, 3, and 4). Each difficulty level accounts for the number of leading 0s the generated hash needs to have to satisfy the condition in Algorithm 2. Next is the proof-of-work complexity index. As implied by Algorithm 2, a higher difficulty level accounts for more resource intensiveness in execution.
3. We have also accounted for energy consumption (and optimization) for the three kinds of connectivity of robots, as illustrated in Figure 1. Robots have a continuous connection (CC) when all linkages are present at all times. Robots will then adhere to periodic connectivity (PC) if all links periodically become available (or if links connect to a network via a different topology). Opportunistic connectivity (OC) is what we have in contrast if either the white or orange link in Figure 1 is available, but there is no assurance that they will all be at any given time.

Figure 10 respectively compares the energy consumption of the robotics system using an energy-optimized and standard implementation of SHA-256 in the PoW algorithm. As mentioned before, we also add a standard Python implementation of SHA-256 in our experiments and measurements. The energy measurements of the Python implementation provide insights into how expensive Python is energy-wise compared to C for the same SHA-256 implementation. We have not engineered the Python implementation of SHA-256 for energy optimization. The energy-optimized version of SHA-256 consistently accounts for lower energy consumption as compared to the standard implementation of SHA-256 in C across Figure 10. The standard Python implementation of SHA-256, as expected, accounts for higher energy consumption than the standard C implementation of SHA-256. The only anomaly observed is in the opportunistic connectivity cases of Figure 10b,c. This can be explained by the randomness involved in opportunistic connectivity. The energy consumption in the case of opportunistic connectivity can be biased in experiments caused by the randomness involved.

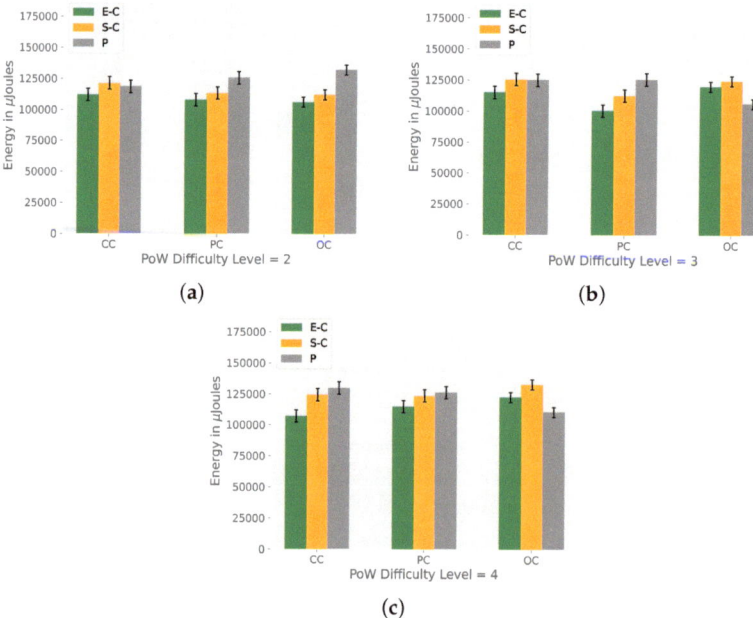

Figure 10. (**a**) C2, (**b**) C3, (**c**) C4 (with 1-sigma standard deviation over 500 trials).

Figure 11a summarizes the average energy savings across difficulty levels 2, 3, and 4 for different connectivity modes (CC, PC, and OC) in comparing the standard and energy-optimized versions of SHA-256 in C (the Python implementation has not been taken into account in Figure 11a). We observe energy savings up to 14% (in the case of CC with difficulty level 4). Section 6.2.2 provides an approximate estimation of energy savings in different similar real-world systems based on Figure 11a.

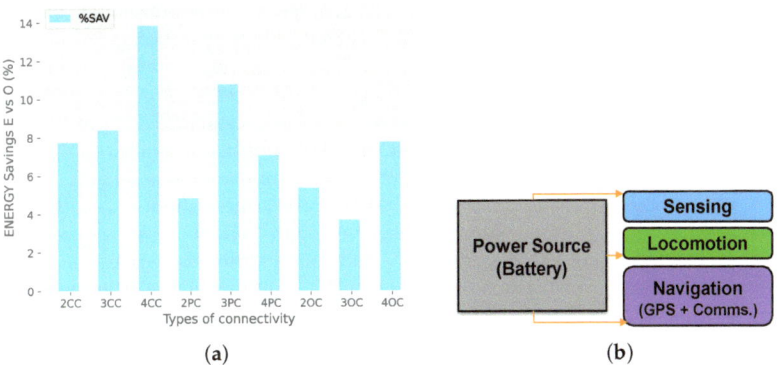

Figure 11. (**a**) Average energy savings (over 500 trials); (**b**) block diagram of energy consumption sources for unmanned devices.

6.2.2. Energy Savings Extrapolation over Real-World Systems

McNulty et al. in [63] establish the energy consumption for unmanned vehicle devices (UVD) to be divided into three subsystems: (1) navigation, (2) sensing, and (3) locomotion, as shown in Figure 11b. In our work, the communications module is part of the navigation subsystem. The total energy consumption of an unmanned device can therefore be expressed by $E_T = E_L + E_P + E_N$, where E_T stands for the total energy consumption, and E_L, E_P, and E_N stand for the energy consumed, respectively, by the locomotion, sensing, and navigation subsystems. Furthermore, $E_N = E_{gps} + E_{comm}$, where E_{gps} stands for energy consumed by the global positioning system and E_{comm} for the energy consumed by communications. Finally, $E_{comm} = E_{trx} + E_{sec}$, where E_{trx} stands for energy consumed by the transmission/reception process, and E_{sec} stands for energy consumed by the security tools implemented. E_{sec} will be equal to $0J$ for a system with no security. On the other hand, E_{sec} adds to the total energy consumption for security applications implemented within the system.

We provide an estimation of the distance a robot can cover in a full battery cycle for different kinds of robots in Table 2. In Table 2, the maximum distance a robot can cover (D_{max}) is for the case in which it has no security ($E_{sec} = 0$ J). The other two columns, $D_{O\text{-}SHA}$ and $D_{E\text{-}SHA}$, estimate the distances covered when robots are implemented over the blockchain network using, respectively, the standard SHA and the energy-optimized SHA for PoW.

We used the following parameters from the robots' specification to estimate the amount of energy consumption per unit distance covered (we use the terms robot and UVD with the same meaning interchangeably in this section): (1) battery power capacity (BWh) expressed in watts per hour, (2) current output amp expressed in milli-amperes, (3) operating voltage vol expressed in volts, and (4) the maximum distance autonomy (D_{max}) expressed in meters. The total battery energy (TE) is calculated as [64]: $TE = amp \times vol \times 3600$. The energy a robot consumes to cover the unit distance (1 m), E_{unit}, is given by $E_{unit} = \frac{TE}{D_{max}}$. If we have security measures implemented for the robots (as a blockchain in our work), the distance covered by each robot over a full battery cycle will be less than D_{max} due to the energy consumed by security applications (E_{sec}). Let us call the distance a robot can go with security in place D_{sec}. Clearly, $D_{sec} < D_{max}$. The total distance cost, D_{cost}, which is the distance that might have been covered with the energy consumed by security applications, can be estimated as $D_{cost} = \frac{E_{sec}}{E_{unit}}$. Finally, $D_{sec} = D_{max} - D_{cost}$.

In Table 2, we estimate D_{sec} when using the standard SHA-256, ($D_{O\text{-}SHA}$) and the energy-optimized SHA-256 ($D_{E\text{-}SHA}$) for the blockchain. To estimate E_{sec} in our work, since the blockchain is used as a security mechanism, we consider the energy consumption per block generated. A block is generated and added each time a robot communicates with another robot. A block generation and insertion in the blockchain involves a full cycle of Merkle tree generation and a subsequent PoW execution. Let us denote the energy consumption of each block operation (generation and insertion) by E_{block}. In [65], the authors estimated E_{block} to be, respectively, 2800 J and 2500 J for an input size of 256 B when standard SHA-256 and energy-optimized SHA-256 were used for the operation. Therefore, E_{sec} in our work can be estimated as a function of the number of block operations (B_{num}) performed by robots during communication: $E_{sec} = E_{block} \times B_{num}$. B_{num} for a specific robot depends on the number of times that the robot communicates (i.e., exchanges information) with other robots throughout D_{max}. In Table 2, we assume each robot to communicate once every 5 m. That is how E_{sec} has been calculated for the two cases (standard SHA-256 and energy-optimized SHA-256) and, in turn, the respective values of distances traveled by each robot during these two cases ($D_{O\text{-}SHA}$ and $D_{E\text{-}SHA}$) have been estimated for the different kinds of robots listed in the table.

Table 2. Distance comparison for various types of hardware available for multi-robot implementation and research.

Type	Name	D_{max}	$D_{O\text{-}SHA}$	$D_{E\text{-}SHA}$
Aerial	DJI3	14,000	13,492	13,546
Aerial	Anafi Ai	32,640	27,101	27,695
Aerial	Bebop 3	9900	7359	7631
Aerial	Matrice RTK	75,900	51,008	53,675
Ground	TurtleBot4	7200	4960	5200
Ground	Jackal	28,800	27,725	27,840
Ground	Husky	10,800	10,498	10,530
Ground	TurtleBot Waffle Pi	1872	1773	1784

As depicted in Table 2, the use of blockchain as a solution to integrity problems in multi-robot communication is costly in terms of energy consumption and in terms of the distance covered by robots per battery cycle. The use of the energy-efficient SHA-256 in blockchain reduces the cost of energy while keeping the same level of security as the standard SHA-256.

7. Conclusions

In this paper, we study the problem of data collection from an unknown environment using a group of mobile robots. As opposed to traditional assumptions in this domain, our robots are vulnerable to cyber-attacks. In particular, we study data-tampering attempts, which can lead to unwanted actions taken by human operators. We have proposed a proof-of-work-based consensus protocol that has the foundation of a blockchain to secure the data shared among the robots. Although we have applied the proposed securing mechanism to a multi-robot information-gathering application, we believe our proposed technique can be used for numerous other applications where multi-robot communication is required for meaningful coordination. Furthermore, we have employed an energy-efficiency technique to reduce the energy footprint of PoW. Results show that our proposed security technique scales up to 10 robots while reducing the energy consumption of the employed PoW protocol by up to 14%. Unsurprisingly, our results show that adding a blockchain-based security mechanism adds to the overall execution time. This additional time is mostly notable in the case of continuous connectivity, and is least notable in the case of opportunistic. Although this added time is up to three-fold, this is necessary for secure multi-robot coordination. Furthermore, we found that, even with 10 robots and a difficulty level of 4, the execution time was less than one minute—a relatively moderate number. This study proves that this is a promising direction of research in securing multi-robot coordination.

In the future, we plan to explore other avenues of data security that do not necessarily rely on blockchains to investigate whether it is possible to develop a more energy-efficient protocol while ensuring the security of the collected information. This will lead to further solutions to robotic communication problems with viable security and efficiency in terms of time and energy. We will also explore techniques leading to the detection of tampered data, such as in the case where intruders introduce tampered data before storing it in the blockchain, e.g., through sensor hardware tampering. Additionally, the current work generically simulates real-world robotics networks. Future research directions include implementing the blockchain network on real-world robotics networks to validate the simulation results presented in this paper.

Author Contributions: Conceptualization, all; methodology, C.E.C., S.R. and T.K.; software, C.E.C., S.R. and T.K.; validation, C.E.C., S.R. and T.K.; formal analysis, C.E.C. and S.R.; investigation, C.E.C. and S.R.; resources, S.R., A.D. and O.P.K.; data curation, C.E.C., S.R. and T.K.; writing—original draft preparation, all; writing—review and editing, all; visualization, C.E.C., S.R., T.K. and A.D.; supervision, S.R., A.D., O.P.K. and L.B.; project administration, S.R. and A.D.; funding acquisition, S.R., A.D., O.P.K. and L.B. All authors have read and agreed to the published version of the manuscript.

Funding: This work is supported in part by National Science Foundation (NSF) CPS Grants #1932300 and #1931767.

Data Availability Statement: Not applicable.

Conflicts of Interest: The authors declare no conflict of interest.

References

1. Dutta, A.; Ghosh, A.; Kreidl, O.P. Multi-robot Informative Path Planning with Continuous Connectivity Constraints. In Proceedings of the 2019 International Conference on Robotics and Automation (ICRA), Montreal, QC, Canada, 20–24 May 2019; pp. 3245–3251.
2. Dutta, A.; Roy, S.; Kreidl, O.P.; Bölöni, L. Multi-robot information gathering for precision agriculture: Current state, scope, and challenges. *IEEE Access* **2021**, *9*, 161416–161430. [CrossRef]
3. Hollinger, G.A.; Singh, S. Multirobot coordination with periodic connectivity: Theory and experiments. *IEEE Trans. Robot.* **2012**, *28*, 967–973. [CrossRef]
4. Krause, A.; Singh, A.; Guestrin, C. Near-optimal sensor placements in Gaussian processes: Theory, efficient algorithms and empirical studies. *J. Mach. Learn. Res.* **2008**, *9*, 235–284.
5. Singh, A.; Krause, A.; Guestrin, C.; Kaiser, W.J. Efficient informative sensing using multiple robots. *J. Artif. Intell. Res.* **2009**, *34*, 707–755. [CrossRef]
6. Castellon, C.E.; Roy, S.; Kreidl, O.P.; Dutta, A.; Bölöni, L. Toward a Green Blockchain: Engineering Merkle Tree and Proof of Work for Energy Optimization. *IEEE Trans. Netw. Serv. Manag.* **2023**, *19*, 3847–3857.
7. Samman, T.; Dutta, A.; Kreidl, O.P.; Roy, S.; Bölöni, L. Secure Multi-Robot Information Sampling with Periodic and Opportunistic Connectivity. In Proceedings of the 2022 International Conference on Robotics and Automation (ICRA), Philadelphia, PA, USA, 23–27 May 2022; pp. 4951–4957.
8. Banfi, J.; Li, A.Q.; Rekleitis, I.; Amigoni, F.; Basilico, N. Strategies for coordinated multirobot exploration with recurrent connectivity constraints. *Auton. Robot.* **2018**, *42*, 875–894. [CrossRef]
9. Dutta, A.; Bhattacharya, A.; Kreidl, O.P.; Ghosh, A.; Dasgupta, P. Multi-robot informative path planning in unknown environments through continuous region partitioning. *Int. J. Adv. Robot. Syst.* **2020**, *17*, 1729881420970461. [CrossRef]
10. Dutta, A.; Patrick Kreidl, O.; O'Kane, J.M. Opportunistic multi-robot environmental sampling via decentralized markov decision processes. In *Distributed Autonomous Robotic Systems*; Springer: Cham, Switzerland, 2021; pp. 163–175.
11. Gao, C.; Ma, J.; Li, T.; Shen, Y. Hybrid swarm intelligent algorithm for multi-UAV formation reconfiguration. *Complex Intell. Syst.* **2023**, *9*, 1929–1962. [CrossRef]
12. Luo, W.; Sycara, K. Adaptive sampling and online learning in multi-robot sensor coverage with mixture of gaussian processes. In Proceedings of the 2018 IEEE International Conference on Robotics and Automation (ICRA), Brisbane, Australia, 21–25 May 2018; pp. 6359–6364.
13. Lauri, M.; Heinänen, E.; Frintrop, S. Multi-robot active information gathering with periodic communication. In Proceedings of the 2017 IEEE International Conference on Robotics and Automation (ICRA), Singapore, 29 May–3 June 2017; pp. 851–856.

14. Trejo, J.A.V.; Ponsart, J.C.; Adam-Medina, M.; Valencia-Palomo, G.; Theilliol, D. Distributed Observer-based Leader-following Consensus Control for LPV Multi-agent Systems: Application to multiple VTOL-UAVs Formation Control. In Proceedings of the 2023 International Conference on Unmanned Aircraft Systems (ICUAS), Warsaw, Poland, 6–9 June 2023; pp. 1316–1323.
15. Viseras, A.; Xu, Z.; Merino, L. Distributed multi-robot cooperation for information gathering under communication constraints. In Proceedings of the 2018 IEEE International Conference on Robotics and Automation (ICRA), Brisbane, Australia, 21–25 May 2018; pp. 1267–1272.
16. Zhang, S.; Lim, W.Y.B.; Ng, W.C.; Xiong, Z.; Niyato, D.; Shen, X.S.; Miao, C. Towards Green Metaverse Networking: Technologies, Advancements and Future Directions. *IEEE Netw.* **2023**, 1–10. [CrossRef]
17. Said, T.; Wolbert, J.; Khodadadeh, S.; Dutta, A.; Kreidl, O.P.; Bölöni, L.; Roy, S. Multi-robot information sampling using deep mean field reinforcement learning. In Proceedings of the 2021 IEEE International Conference on Systems, Man, and Cybernetics (SMC), Melbourne, Australia, 17–20 October 2021; pp. 1215–1220.
18. Hollinger, G.A.; Sukhatme, G.S. Sampling-based robotic information gathering algorithms. *Int. J. Robot. Res.* **2014**, *33*, 1271–1287. [CrossRef]
19. Ma, K.C.; Ma, Z.; Liu, L.; Sukhatme, G.S. Multi-robot informative and adaptive planning for persistent environmental monitoring. In *Distributed Autonomous Robotic Systems*; Springer: Cham, Switzerland, 2018; pp. 285–298.
20. Wei, Y.; Zheng, R. Informative path planning for mobile sensing with reinforcement learning. In Proceedings of the IEEE INFOCOM 2020-IEEE Conference on Computer Communications, Toronto, ON, Canada, 6–9 July 2020; pp. 864–873.
21. Rasmussen, C.E. Gaussian processes in machine learning. In *Advanced Lectures on Machine Learning*; Springer: Berlin/Heidelberg, Germany, 2003; pp. 63–71.
22. Ma, K.C.; Liu, L.; Sukhatme, G.S. Informative planning and online learning with sparse gaussian processes. In Proceedings of the 2017 IEEE International Conference on Robotics and Automation (ICRA), Singapore, 29 May–3 June 2017; pp. 4292–4298.
23. Singh, A.; Krause, A.; Kaiser, W.J. Nonmyopic Adaptive Informative Path Planning for Multiple Robots. In Proceedings of the 21st International Joint Conference on Artificial Intelligence (IJCAI 2009), Pasadena, CA, USA, 11–17 July 2009; Boutilier, C., Ed.; 2009; pp. 1843–1850.
24. Kemna, S.; Caron, D.A.; Sukhatme, G.S. Adaptive informative sampling with autonomous underwater vehicles: Acoustic versus surface communications. In Proceedings of the OCEANS 2016 MTS/IEEE Monterey, Monterey, CA, USA, 19–23 September 2016; pp. 1–8.
25. Dempster, A.P.; Laird, N.M.; Rubin, D.B. Maximum likelihood from incomplete data via the EM algorithm. *J. R. Stat. Soc. Ser. B (Methodol.)* **1977**, *39*, 1–22. [CrossRef]
26. Orr, J.; Dutta, A. Multi-Agent Deep Reinforcement Learning for Multi-Robot Applications: A Survey. *Sensors* **2023**, *23*, 3625. [CrossRef] [PubMed]
27. Yang, Y.; Luo, R.; Li, M.; Zhou, M.; Zhang, W.; Wang, J. Mean Field Multi-Agent Reinforcement Learning. In Proceedings of the 35th International Conference on Machine Learning, ICML 2018, Stockholm, Sweden, 10–15 July 2018; Dy, J.G., Krause, A., Eds.; Volume 80, pp. 5567–5576.
28. Wei, Y.; Zheng, R. Multi-robot path planning for mobile sensing through deep reinforcement learning. In Proceedings of the IEEE INFOCOM 2021-IEEE Conference on Computer Communications, Vancouver, BC, Canada, 10–13 May 2021; pp. 1–10.
29. Pan, L.; Manjanna, S.; Hsieh, M.A. MARLAS: Multi Agent Reinforcement Learning for cooperated Adaptive Sampling. *arXiv* **2022**, arXiv:2207.07751.
30. Viseras, A.; Garcia, R. DeepIG: Multi-robot information gathering with deep reinforcement learning. *IEEE Robot. Autom. Lett.* **2019**, *4*, 3059–3066. [CrossRef]
31. Banfi, J.; Basilico, N.; Amigoni, F. Multirobot reconnection on graphs: Problem, complexity, and algorithms. *IEEE Trans. Robot.* **2018**, *34*, 1299–1314. [CrossRef]
32. Andre, T.; Bettstetter, C. Collaboration in multi-robot exploration: To meet or not to meet? *J. Intell. Robot. Syst.* **2016**, *82*, 325–337. [CrossRef]
33. Amigoni, F.; Banfi, J.; Basilico, N. Multirobot exploration of communication-restricted environments: A survey. *IEEE Intell. Syst.* **2017**, *32*, 48–57. [CrossRef]
34. Ghiasi, M.; Niknam, T.; Wang, Z.; Mehrandezh, M.; Dehghani, M.; Ghadimi, N. A comprehensive review of cyber-attacks and defense mechanisms for improving security in smart grid energy systems: Past, present and future. *Electr. Power Syst. Res.* **2023**, *215*, 108975. [CrossRef]
35. Xu, H.; Sun, Z.; Cao, Y.; Bilal, H. A data-driven approach for intrusion and anomaly detection using automated machine learning for the Internet of Things. *Soft Comput.* **2023**, *27*, 14469–14481. [CrossRef]
36. Zhou, H.; Zheng, Y.; Jia, X.; Shu, J. Collaborative prediction and detection of DDoS attacks in edge computing: A deep learning-based approach with distributed SDN. *Comput. Netw.* **2023**, *225*, 109642. [CrossRef]
37. Strobel, V.; Castelló Ferrer, E.; Dorigo, M. Blockchain technology secures robot swarms: A comparison of consensus protocols and their resilience to byzantine robots. *Front. Robot. AI* **2020**, *7*, 54. [CrossRef]

38. Samman, T.; Spearman, J.; Dutta, A.; Kreidl, O.P.; Roy, S.; Bölöni, L. Secure Multi-Robot Adaptive Information Sampling. In Proceedings of the 2021 IEEE International Symposium on Safety, Security, and Rescue Robotics (SSRR), New York, NY, USA, 25–27 October 2021; pp. 125–131. [CrossRef]
39. Nakamoto, S. Bitcoin: A Peer-to-Peer Electronic Cash System. 2008. Available online: https://www.ussc.gov/sites/default/files/pdf/training/annual-national-training-seminar/2018/Emerging_Tech_Bitcoin_Crypto.pdf (accessed on 27 August 2023).
40. Dittmar, L.; Praktiknjo, A. Could Bitcoin emissions push global warming above 2 °C? *Nat. Clim. Chang.* **2019**, *9*, 656–657. [CrossRef]
41. Egiyi, M.A.; Ofoegbu, G.N. Cryptocurrency and climate change: An overview. *Int. J. Mech. Eng. Technol. (IJMET)* **2020**, *11*, 15–22.
42. Mora, C.; Rollins, R.L.; Taladay, K.; Kantar, M.B.; Chock, M.K.; Shimada, M.; Franklin, E.C. Bitcoin emissions alone could push global warming above 2 °C. *Nat. Clim. Chang.* **2018**, *8*, 931–933. [CrossRef]
43. Salimitari, M.; Chatterjee, M.; Fallah, Y.P. A survey on consensus methods in blockchain for resource-constrained IoT networks. *Internet Things* **2020**, *11*, 100212. [CrossRef]
44. Kaufmann, L. Clustering by means of medoids. In Proceedings of the Statistical Data Analysis Based on the L1-norm and Related Methods, Neuchatel, Switzerland, 31 August–4 September 1987; pp. 405–416.
45. Cao, N.; Low, K.H.; Dolan, J.M. Multi-robot informative path planning for active sensing of environmental phenomena: A tale of two algorithms. In Proceedings of the International Conference on Autonomous Agents and Multi-Agent Systems, Saint Paul, MN, USA, 6–10 May 2013; Gini, M.L., Shehory, O., Ito, T., Jonker, C.M., Eds.; pp. 7–14.
46. Gupta, M.; Abdelsalam, M.; Khorsandroo, S.; Mittal, S. Security and privacy in smart farming: Challenges and opportunities. *IEEE Access* **2020**, *8*, 34564–34584. [CrossRef]
47. Krishna, C.L.; Murphy, R.R. A review on cybersecurity vulnerabilities for unmanned aerial vehicles. In Proceedings of the 2017 IEEE International Symposium on Safety, Security and Rescue Robotics (SSRR), Shanghai, China, 11–13 October 2017; pp. 194–199.
48. Issa, W.; Moustafa, N.; Turnbull, B.; Sohrabi, N.; Tari, Z. Blockchain-based federated learning for securing internet of things: A comprehensive survey. *ACM Comput. Surv.* **2023**, *55*, 191. [CrossRef]
49. Laghari, A.A.; Khan, A.A.; Alkanhel, R.; Elmannai, H.; Bourouis, S. Lightweight-BIoV: Blockchain Distributed Ledger Technology (BDLT) for Internet of Vehicles (IoVs). *Electronics* **2023**, *12*, 677. [CrossRef]
50. Rajasekar, V.; Sathya, K. Blockchain utility in renewable energy. In *Blockchain-Based Systems for the Modern Energy Grid*; Elsevier: Amsterdam, The Netherlands, 2023; pp. 115–134.
51. Gupta, S.S. *Blockchain for Secure Healthcare Using Internet of Medical Things (IoMT)*; Springer Nature: Cham, Switzerland, 2023.
52. Luo, H.; Liu, S.; Xu, S.; Luo, J. LECast: A Low-Energy-Consumption Broadcast Protocol for UAV Blockchain Networks. *Drones* **2023**, *7*, 76. [CrossRef]
53. Li, S.; Li, J.; Pei, J.; Wu, S.; Wang, S.; Cheng, L. Eco-CSAS: A Safe and Eco-Friendly Speed Advisory System for Autonomous Vehicle Platoon Using Consortium Blockchain. *IEEE Trans. Intell. Transp. Syst.* **2023**, *24*, 7802–7812. [CrossRef]
54. Oudani, M.; Sebbar, A.; Zkik, K.; El Harraki, I.; Belhadi, A. Green Blockchain based IoT for secured supply chain of hazardous materials. *Comput. Ind. Eng.* **2023**, *175*, 108814. [CrossRef]
55. Qi, L.; Tian, J.; Chai, M.; Cai, H. LightPoW: A trust based time-constrained PoW for blockchain in internet of things. *Comput. Netw.* **2023**, *220*, 109480. [CrossRef]
56. Gupta, M.; Patel, R.; Jain, S. Analysis of Blockchain Integration with Internet of Vehicles: Challenges, Motivation, and Recent Solution. In *Role of Data-Intensive Distributed Computing Systems in Designing Data Solutions*; Springer: Cham, Switzerland, 2023; pp. 129–163.
57. Praveena, B.; Reddy, P.V.P. Blockchain based Sensor System Design For Embedded IoT. *J. Comput. Inf. Syst.* **2023**, 1–18. [CrossRef]
58. Ali, M.H.; Jaber, M.M.; Khalil Abd, S.; Alkhayyat, A.; Q, M.R.; Ali, M.H. Application of internet of things-based efficient security solution for industrial. *Prod. Plan. Control.* **2023**, 1–15. [CrossRef]
59. Alshahrani, H.; Islam, N.; Syed, D.; Sulaiman, A.; Al Reshan, M.S.; Rajab, K.; Shaikh, A.; Shuja-Uddin, J.; Soomro, A. Sustainability in Blockchain: A Systematic Literature Review on Scalability and Power Consumption Issues. *Energies* **2023**, *16*, 1510. [CrossRef]
60. Kohli, V.; Chakravarty, S.; Chamola, V.; Sangwan, K.S.; Zeadally, S. An analysis of energy consumption and carbon footprints of cryptocurrencies and possible solutions. *Digit. Commun. Netw.* **2023**, *9*, 79–89. [CrossRef]
61. Roy, S.; Rudra, A.; Verma, A. An energy complexity model for algorithms. In Proceedings of the 4th Conference on Innovations in Theoretical Computer Science, New York, NY, USA, 9–12 January 2013; pp. 283–304.
62. Santos, M.; Saraiva, J.; Porkoláb, Z.; Krupp, D. Energy Consumption Measurement of C/C++ Programs Using Clang Tooling. In Proceedings of the 6th Workshop of Software Quality, Analysis, Monitoring, Improvement, and Applications, Belgrade, Serbia, 11–13 September 2017.
63. McNulty, D.; Hennessy, A.; Li, M.; Armstrong, E.; Ryan, K.M. A review of Li-ion batteries for autonomous mobile robots: Perspectives and outlook for the future. *J. Power Sources* **2022**, *545*, 231943. [CrossRef]

64. Caballero, L.; Perafan, A.; Rinaldy, M.; Percybrooks, W. Predicting the Energy Consumption of a Robot in an Exploration Task Using Optimized Neural Networks. *Electronics* **2021**, *10*, 920. [CrossRef]
65. Castellon, C.; Roy, S.; Kreidl, P.; Dutta, A.; Bölöni, L. Energy efficient merkle trees for blockchains. In Proceedings of the 2021 IEEE 20th International Conference on Trust, Security and Privacy in Computing and Communications (TrustCom), Shenyang, China, 20–22 October 2021; pp. 1093–1099.

Disclaimer/Publisher's Note: The statements, opinions and data contained in all publications are solely those of the individual author(s) and contributor(s) and not of MDPI and/or the editor(s). MDPI and/or the editor(s) disclaim responsibility for any injury to people or property resulting from any ideas, methods, instructions or products referred to in the content.

Article

Disentangled Prototypical Graph Convolutional Network for Phishing Scam Detection in Cryptocurrency Transactions

Seok-Jun Buu [1] and Hae-Jung Kim [2,*]

1 Department of Computer Science, Gyeongsang National University, Jinju-si 52828, Republic of Korea; sj.buu@gnu.ac.kr
2 Department of Computer Science, Kyungil University, Gyeongsan-si 38428, Republic of Korea
* Correspondence: hjkim325@kiu.kr

Abstract: Blockchain technology has generated an influx of transaction data and complex interactions, posing significant challenges for traditional machine learning methods, which struggle to capture high-dimensional patterns in transaction networks. In this paper, we present the disentangled prototypical graph convolutional network (DP-GCN), an innovative approach to account classification in Ethereum transaction records. Our method employs a unique disentanglement mechanism that isolates relevant features, enhancing pattern recognition within the network. Additionally, we apply prototyping to disentangled representations, to classify scam nodes robustly, despite extreme class imbalances. We further employ a joint learning strategy, combining triplet loss and prototypical loss with a gamma coefficient, achieving an effective balance between the two. Experiments on real Ethereum data showcase the success of our approach, as the DP-GCN attained an F1 score improvement of 32.54%p over the previous best-performing GCN model and an area under the ROC curve (AUC) improvement of 4.28%p by incorporating our novel disentangled prototyping concept. Our research highlights the importance of advanced techniques in detecting malicious activities within large-scale real-world cryptocurrency transactions.

Keywords: scam detection; node classification; graph neural network; representation learning; blockchain; cryptocurrency transaction network

1. Introduction

Blockchain technology has revolutionized the digital transaction landscape, offering decentralized ledger systems that record transactions across multiple computers, to ensure data integrity and transparency. Initially conceptualized for cryptocurrency transactions, blockchain technology has seen rapid adoption across various industries, resulting in an explosion of transaction data and complex interactions [1]. Challenges of efficiently processing and analyzing the massive volume of data generated within blockchain networks accompany this growth.

One such blockchain network is Ethereum, a platform allowing the creation of customizable, self-executing contracts (smart contracts) and decentralized applications (DApps). As Ethereum gains traction, the vast and intricate web of transactions between accounts (nodes) becomes increasingly complex [2,3]. Ethereum accounts, either externally owned or controlled by smart contract code, interact through transactions, forming a dynamic and complex network structure that constantly evolves with the execution of the smart contracts.

The Ethereum transaction network poses unique challenges due to its sheer size and intricate interactions. The network generates massive amounts of data from high transaction volumes [4], with its ledger containing hundreds of millions of transactions. Extreme class imbalance in the network makes it difficult to accurately identify malicious activities, as certain classes, such as scam nodes, are underrepresented [4]. Traditional machine learning techniques struggle to capture high-dimensional topological and transactional patterns [5].

A concrete illustration of this challenge is shown in Figure 1. This figure visualizes the Ethereum transaction graph, highlighting a suspicious transaction pattern. The transaction sequence marked in red depicts a possible case of wash trading, in which an NFT is minted and this is followed by a series of sales where the final sale that may be artificially inflated, including a loop indicating potential wash trading. This example underscores the need for advanced techniques capable of identifying subtle malicious activities within the complex transaction network of Ethereum.

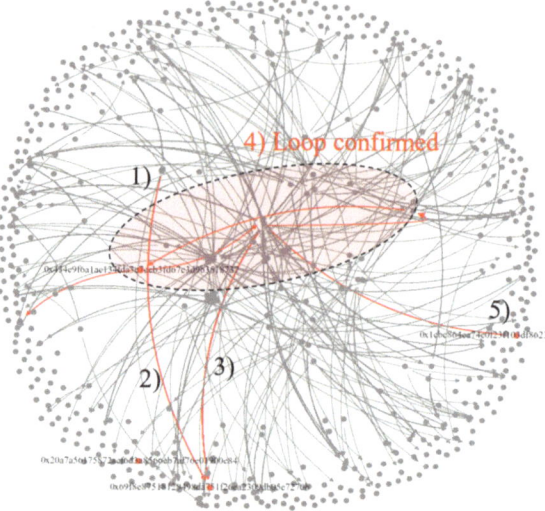

1) NFT Minted → 2) First sell → 3) Second sell
→ 4) Third sell: Loop indicates potential wash trading
→ 5) Fourth sell: Potentially inflated

Figure 1. Ethereum transaction graph showcasing a suspicious transaction pattern, highlighted in red, indicative of potential wash trading and an artificially inflated sale.

Understanding and addressing these challenges is crucial for ensuring Ethereum's security and integrity and for promoting trust and confidence in blockchain technology adoption. In the context of extreme class imbalance and massive, noisy real-world graph structures, there is a pressing need for advanced methods to model the Ethereum transaction network, disentangle transaction features, and tackle account classification and fraud detection challenges.

In this research, we introduce the disentangled prototypical graph convolutional network (DP-GCN) for account classification in Ethereum transaction records. Our method employs a novel approach, which we term disentangled prototyping, to enhance pattern recognition in Ethereum transaction networks. The contributions of our work can be summarized as follows:

- Disentangled Prototyping: We propose a new approach that uses disentangled prototyping to effectively recognize patterns in Ethereum transaction networks by isolating relevant features and leveraging prototypical networks, to enhance account classification.
- Joint Learning: We incorporate a joint learning strategy that combines curriculum learning, triplet loss, and prototypical loss with an adjustable gamma coefficient for optimal performance.
- Empirical Success: Our method achieved significant improvements over existing methods in experiments on real Ethereum transaction data, demonstrating its practical effectiveness in analyzing large-scale cryptocurrency transactions.

2. Related Works

The analysis of blockchain transaction graphs has received significant attention in the literature, with various methods employed to achieve different objectives. Table 1 provides an overview of the relevant literature, detailing the approach, objective, method, transaction network, and performance.

Earlier research explored graph traversing techniques for analyzing blockchain transaction data. For instance, Lin et al. utilized a graph representation method that captures time-dependent patterns in Ethereum transaction networks by encoding temporal information into walk strategies [3]. This approach provides a robust representation of time-evolving blockchain transaction graphs [6]. Similarly, Ofori-Boateng et al. employed a topological analysis technique to detect anomalous transaction patterns in Ethereum and Ripple networks [5]. Their method highlights the importance of topological features in blockchain anomaly detection. Further advancing the field, Bai et al. adopted temporal graphs to capture dynamics in the Ethereum transaction network [6]. By incorporating temporal information, their approach provides a comprehensive analysis of blockchain networks.

The use of graph embedding techniques has become increasingly prevalent in recent research. Jin et al. combined a graph convolutional network (GCN) with hierarchical feature augmentation (HFAug) to detect Ponzi schemes in blockchain networks [7]. Their approach underscores the effectiveness of augmenting node features for improved performance in graph-based anomaly detection. Expanding upon this idea, Liu et al. proposed a feature augmentation-based graph neural network (FA-GNN) for account classification in Ethereum transaction data [8]. Their method emphasizes the significance of feature augmentation in achieving accurate blockchain account classification.

Meanwhile, Xia et al. introduced an ego-graph embedding approach coupled with a skip-gram model for phishing detection [9]. Their method demonstrated enhanced pattern recognition capabilities in blockchain transaction graphs. Building on the concept of graph embedding, Huang et al. developed an edge heterogeneous graph convolutional network (EH-GCN) for account classification in Ethereum transaction data [2]. Their approach highlights the importance of modeling edge heterogeneity for accurate node classification in blockchain networks. Lastly, Zhou et al. designed Ethident for de-anonymization across multiple Ethereum transaction datasets [10]. Their method showcased the benefits of a unified approach to de-anonymization across various types of transactions.

In this study, we propose a unique disentanglement and prototyping process, employing a custom loss function that enables the separation of transaction features into interpretable and meaningful representations. By isolating distinct transactional behaviors and interactions within the network, our method allows for the creation of accurate and informative prototypes.

Table 1. Summary of approaches and methods for transaction graph modeling in cryptocurrency networks.

Approach	Objective	Method	Transaction Network	Performance
Traversing	Graph representation	Temporal Walk Strategies [3]	Ethereum	AUC 0.9383
	Anomaly Detection	Clique Persistent Homology [5]	Ethereum, Ripple	Acc. 0.9540
Traversing Embedding	Ponzi Scheme Detection	GCN with HFAug [7]	Ethereum	Success rate 0.8405
	Account Classification	FA-GNN [8]	Ethereum	F1-Score 0.8880
Embedding	Phishing Detection	Ego-Graph Embedding, Skip-gram Model [9]	Ethereum	F1-Score 0.8199
	Account Classification	EH-GCN [2]	Ethereum	Acc. 0.8620
	De-Anonymization	Ethident [10]	ETH-Mining, ETH-Exchange, ETH-Phish	F1-Score 0.9798

Unlike the existing approaches, our method combines the power of unsupervised learning with a carefully designed loss function, which allows the model to capture non-trivial, high-level patterns in the transaction graphs. This process enhances the interpretability of the embeddings, making it easier to discern relationships and anomalies within the data.

3. Proposed Method

3.1. Overview of the Proposed Method

Our proposed method, the disentangled prototypical graph convolutional network (DPGCN), is a novel approach to detecting fraudulent transactions in cryptocurrency transaction networks. It integrates disentangled representation learning and prototypical networks within a graph convolutional framework, aiming to provide a robust and interpretable mechanism for classifying nodes as either scam or benign. Figure 2 illustrates the structure of the proposed DPGCN, showcasing the flow of information from the transaction network to the disentangled prototypes.

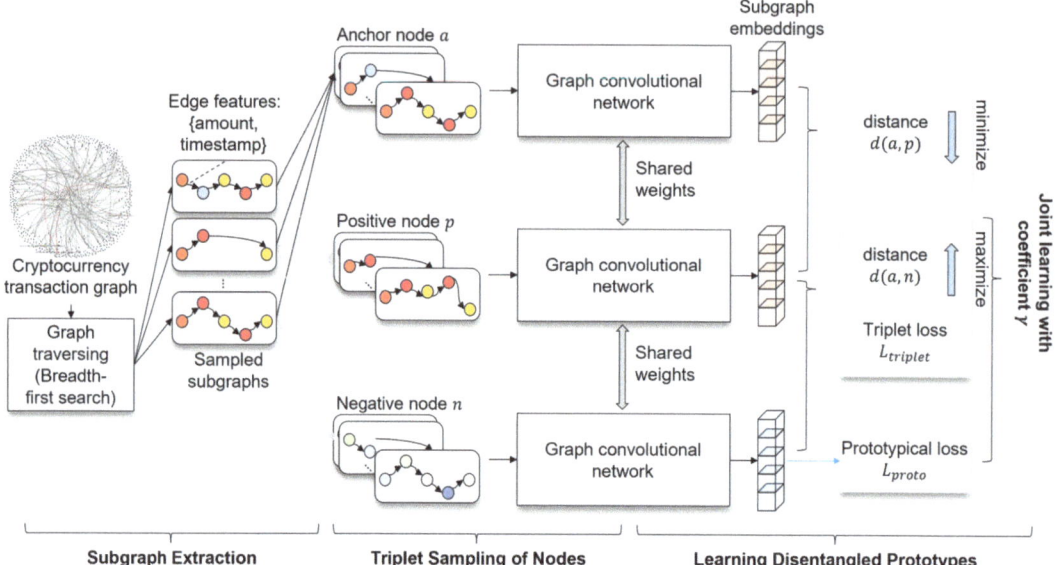

Figure 2. Overview of the disentangled prototypical graph convolutional network (DPGCN) architecture.

The DPGCN model operates in three main stages: subgraph extraction, triplet sampling of nodes, and learning disentangled prototypes. We utilize a graph convolutional network (GCN) to learn node embeddings [11,12], which captures both transactional and topological features from the Ethereum transaction network. Given a graph $G = (V, E)$, where V is the set of nodes and E is the set of edges, the GCN layer computes the embeddings for each node using the following equation:

$$H^{(l+1)} = \sigma\left(\tilde{D}^{-\frac{1}{2}} \tilde{A} \tilde{D}^{-\frac{1}{2}} H^{(l)} W^{(l)}\right) \quad (1)$$

where $H^{(l)}$ is the node feature matrix at layer l, $\tilde{A}$ is the adjacency matrix with added self connections, $\tilde{D}$ is the degree matrix of $\tilde{A}$, $W^{(l)}$ is the weight matrix at layer l, and σ is the activation function. This formula allows the DPGCN model to capture complex patterns within the transaction graph by aggregating information from neighboring nodes and transforming the node features through multiple GCN layers.

3.2. Disentangled Prototyping of a Transanction Network

The disentanglement mechanism within our disentangled prototypical graph convolutional network (DPGCN) is achieved by employing a triplet loss function. Given an anchor node a, a positive node p sharing similar characteristics with a, and a negative node n that is dissimilar to a, the triplet loss function aims to ensure that the embeddings of similar (same class) nodes are closer in the latent space than the embeddings of dissimilar nodes, by at least a margin of α:

$$\mathcal{L}_{\text{triplet}} = \max\left(0, \|e_a - e_p\|_2^2 - \|e_a - e_n\|_2^2 + \alpha\right) \qquad (2)$$

where e_a, e_p, and e_n are the embeddings of the anchor, positive, and negative samples, respectively, and α is the margin parameter.

Once the disentangled embeddings are learned, our next step is to prototype these embeddings for the task of scam node detection. Prototyping involves learning a representative embedding for each class (i.e., scam or benign), which serves as a "prototype" in the embedding space. The prototype P_c of class c is computed as the mean of the embeddings of the samples in that class:

$$P_c = \frac{1}{N_c} \sum_{i=1}^{N_c} e_i \qquad (3)$$

where e_i is the embedding of the ith sample in class c and N_c is the number of samples in class c.

To classify a node, we measure the distance between its embedding and the prototypes of all classes, assigning it to the class with the closest prototype:

$$y_i = \arg\min_c \|e_i - P_c\|_2^2 \qquad (4)$$

where y_i is the predicted class of node i.

During training, we minimize the prototypical loss:

$$\mathcal{L}_{\text{proto}} = \frac{1}{N} \sum_{i=1}^{N} -\log\left(\frac{\exp\left(-\|e_i - P_y\|_2^2\right)}{\sum_{c=1}^{K} \exp\left(-\|e_i - P_c\|_2^2\right)}\right) \qquad (5)$$

where L_{proto} is the prototypical loss, N is the total number of samples, and K is the number of classes.

To put the disentanglement and prototyping process into practice, we employed Algorithm 1, which trained our DPGCN on the Ethereum transaction graph (ETG) with disentangled embeddings. This algorithm utilized curriculum weighting to gradually shift the emphasis between the triplet loss and the prototypical loss over the training epochs.

3.3. Joint Learning with Gamma Coefficient and Curriculum Learning

The overall loss of our model L is a linear combination of the prototypical loss L_{proto} and the triplet loss $L_{triplet}$. The coefficient γ is introduced to modulate the weight between the two losses, where a higher γ emphasizes prototypical loss and a lower γ emphasizes triplet loss:

$$\mathcal{L} = \gamma \mathcal{L}_{\text{proto}} + (1 - \gamma)\mathcal{L}_{\text{triplet}} \qquad (6)$$

To smoothly transition the emphasis between the two losses, we adopted a sigmoidal curriculum weighting scheme to adjust the weights at different training epochs:

$$w(t) = \frac{1}{1 + \exp(-\kappa(t - \tau))} \qquad (7)$$

where $w(t)$ is the curriculum weight at epoch t, κ is the sigmoid scaling factor, and τ is the sigmoid shift parameter.

Algorithm 1: Disentangled Prototypical Graph Convolutional Network (DPGCN) Training

---

Training a DPGCN on the Ethereum transaction graph with disentangled embeddings, utilizing curriculum weighting to balance emphasis between triplet and prototypical losses during the training epochs.

Input:
- ETG: Ethereum Transaction Graph
- transaction_features: Features for each transaction in ETG
- num_classes: Number of different classes (or types) of transactions
- num_epochs: Number of training epochs
- α: Margin for triplet loss
- γ_init: Initial value for dynamic gamma adjustment
- γ_final: Final value for dynamic gamma adjustment
- τ: Epoch threshold for aggressive γ adjustment

Output:
- dpgcn_model: Trained DPGCN model for disentangled embeddings

Initialization
1: function train_DPGCN(ETG, transaction_features, num_classes, num_epochs, α, γ_init, γ_final, τ)
2: Initialize DPGCN model parameters with disentangling mechanisms specific to transaction characteristics.
3: Initialize class_prototypes as zero vectors of embedding dimension.

Main Training Loop
4: for epoch = 1 to num_epochs do

Dynamic Gamma Adjustment
5:    if epoch < τ then
6:       γ = γ_init + (epoch/τ) * (0 − γ_init)
7:    else
8:       γ = 0 + ((epoch − τ)/(num_epochs − τ)) * (γ_final − 0)
9:    end if

Disentangled Prototyping
10:    embeddings = []
11:    triplets = sample_triplets(ETG, transaction_features, num_classes)
12:    for triplet in triplets do
13:       anchor, positive, negative = triplet
14:       //Compute disentangled embeddings for each node in triplet and extend embeddings list
15:       embeddings.extend([DPGCN(node, transaction_features) for node in [anchor, positive, negative]])
16:    end for
17:    //Compute prototypes for each class by averaging embeddings
18:    for c = 1 to num_classes do
19:       class_members = get_transactions_of_class(ETG, c)
20:       class_prototype[c] = average(embeddings[class_members])
21:    end for

Loss Computation and Model Update
22:    //Compute triplet loss
23:    triplet_loss = compute_triplet_loss(embeddings, α)
24:    //Compute prototypical loss
25:    prototype_loss = compute_prototypical_loss(embeddings, class_prototypes)
26:    //Total DPGCN loss
27:    loss = ((1 − γ) * triplet_loss + (1 + γ) * prototype_loss)
28:    Update DPGCN model parameters using backpropagation with the computed loss.
29: end for
30: return dpgcn_model

The sigmoidally weighted triplet loss $L_{triplet}$ and prototypical loss L_{proto} are defined as below, respectively:

$$\mathcal{L}_{\text{triplet}}^{w} = w(t)\mathcal{L}_{\text{triplet}} \qquad (8)$$

$$\mathcal{L}_{\text{proto}}^{w} = (1 - w(t))\mathcal{L}_{\text{proto}} \qquad (9)$$

The curriculum weight $w(t)$ dynamically determines the contribution of each loss to the overall training objective. The gamma coefficient γ serves as a hyperparameter that regulates the balance between the two loss components, where a higher value γ corresponds to greater emphasis on prototypical loss, and vice versa.

Algorithm 2 illustrates the process of detecting potentially fraudulent transactions in an Ethereum transaction graph (ETG) using disentangled embeddings from the trained DPGCN model. By comparing transaction embeddings to class prototypes, the algorithm classifies each transaction as a scam or benign.

Algorithm 2: Transaction Scam Detection using Disentangled Prototypical Graph Convolutional Network

Algorithm 2 outlines the process of detecting potentially fraudulent transactions in the Ethereum transaction graph using disentangled embeddings from DPGCN. By comparing transaction embeddings to class prototypes, the algorithm classifies each transaction as scam or benign.

Input:
- ETG: Ethereum Transaction Graph
- transaction_features: Features for each transaction in ETG
- dpgcn_model: Pre-trained Disentangled Prototypical Graph Convolutional Network model

Output:
- scam_labels: Predicted scam/benign labels for transactions in ETG

```
1:  function ScamDetection(ETG, transaction_features, dpgcn_model)
2:      //Obtain disentangled embeddings for all transactions
3:      embeddings = dpgcn_model.get_embeddings(ETG, transaction_features)
4:      //Calculate class prototypes
5:      class_prototypes = dpgcn_model.compute_class_prototypes(embeddings)
6:      scam_labels = []
7:      for each transaction in ETG do
8:          //Derive its disentangled embedding
9:          transaction_embedding = embeddings[transaction]
10:         //Determine its class by the nearest prototype
11:         nearest_class = find_nearest_prototype(transaction_embedding, class_prototypes)
12:         if nearest_class is scam:
13:             scam_labels.append('scam')
14:         else:
15:             scam_labels.append('benign')
16:         end if
17:     end for
18:     return scam_labels
19: end function
```

---

4. Experimental Results

4.1. Dataset and Preprocessing

We conducted our experiments on the Ethereum transaction history, focusing on a large connected component of the transaction graph. The dataset utilized in this study was obtained from the research conducted by Chen et al. [13], which offered an in-depth description of the data collection and preprocessing techniques. This connected component was extracted through initiating random walks from 1165 source nodes, resulting in a subgraph that encompassed 2,973,382 nodes and 13,551,214 edges. Among these nodes, 1157 were labeled as phishing nodes.

In the context of this study, when we refer to the graph size, we are specifically alluding to the number of nodes in the graph. While both the node and edge counts provide vital insights into the structure and characteristics of a graph, we chose the number of nodes to represent the graph's size for clarity and simplicity.

The average degree of a node provides another essential metric. This signifies the average number of edges connected to a node in a graph. For a directed graph with $|V|$ nodes and $|E|$ edges, the average degree D can be mathematically expressed as $D = \frac{|E|}{|V|}$. Within our Ethereum transaction dataset, this metric offers insight into the average transactional connectivity of an entity in the network.

To ensure a comprehensive and consistent evaluation of our models, we selected the largest connected component of the transaction graph. We deliberately excluded other connected components, to mitigate potential biases that could arise from analyzing smaller, disconnected transaction patterns. The expansive nature of this component allows it to aptly capture the intricate relationships embedded within the Ethereum transaction network.

To establish experimental samples, we embarked on random walks, starting each from a unique node, with the aim of generating subgraphs of varying sizes. For this research, we zeroed in on subgraphs encompassing 30,000, 40,000, and 50,000 nodes, aligning with the comparative methods adopted. Such a methodological approach facilitated an exploration into the performance of our proposed model against a backdrop of diverse graph sizes, each reflecting differing complexity levels of the Ethereum transaction history. Table 2 offers a summarized view of our dataset specifications and the subgraph sizes we engaged in our experiments.

Table 2. Specifications of the Ethereum transaction dataset used in the experiments, detailing the dataset collection period and graph sizes.

# Nodes (Scam)	# Edges	Average Degree
Ethereum transaction history (7 August 2015–19 January 2019)		
2,973,382 (1165)	13,551,214	9.1147
Subgraph [13]		
30,000 (113)	774,379	51.6252
40,000 (134)	994,410	49.7205
50,000 (172)	1,388,156	55.5262

4.2. Implementation Details and Evaluation Metrics

For the implementation of our experiments, we used the Python deep learning library PyTorch (version 2.0.1) in conjunction with the graph deep learning library Spektral (version 1.3.0), TensorFlow-gpu (version 2.9.0), and Scikit-learn (version 1.3.0) for preprocessing and evaluation purposes. We conducted our experiments on NVIDIA Tesla V100 GPUs.

For the node features, we opted to use an identity matrix, due to the lack of available node data other than class labels. Edge features, however, were constructed using the transaction amount and timestamp associated with each transaction.

As for the hyperparameters, we set the margin parameter α for the triplet loss to 0.2. The embedding vector used for calculating the prototypes was set to a dimension of 16. To ensure a robust evaluation, all experiments were conducted with 5-fold cross-validation, with 20% of the data reserved for testing in each fold. In each experiment, the number of triplets was fixed at 2000. Given the high class imbalance in our dataset, we used precision, recall, and F1 score as the primary evaluation metrics.

Considering the significant class imbalance inherent in our dataset, we anchored our evaluation around precision, recall, and the F1 score. It is pertinent to highlight that the F1 score serves as the harmonic mean of the precision and recall, acting as a balanced metric between the two, particularly in scenarios with an imbalanced class distribution. The formula for the F1 score is given by $F1 = \frac{2 \times precision \times recall}{precision + recall}$.

AUC offers insight into the classifier's ability to discern between the classes, indicating the probability that a randomly selected positive instance is ranked higher than a randomly selected negative one. This metric becomes especially invaluable when dealing with imbalanced datasets.

4.3. Performance Comparison

Table 3 presents a comparison of precision, recall, and F1 scores for different graph sizes (30,000, 40,000, and 50,000). We compared our proposed DPGCN method with Deep Walk, Node2Vec, and LINE for graph traversing and embedding, as well as GNN, GAT, and GCN. Additionally, we assessed variants of our proposed method, such as DPGCN w/o prototyping and DPGCN w/o disentanglement.

Table 3. Precision, recall, and F1 score comparison of the different methods for graphs of sizes 30,000, 40,000, and 50,000.

Model	Graph Size = 30,000			Graph Size = 40,000			Graph Size = 50,000		
	Precision	Recall	F1	Precision	Recall	F1	Precision	Recall	F1
	Graph traversing/embedding								
Deep Walk [14]	0.1251	0.7108	0.2049	0.1453	0.5754	0.2227	0.1575	0.5945	0.2426
Node2Vec [15]	0.1094	0.6956	0.1832	0.1424	0.6689	0.2267	0.1554	0.6475	0.2426
LINE [16]	0.1409	0.5352	0.2163	0.1332	0.5597	0.2087	0.1726	0.5222	0.2538
	Comparatives								
GNN	0.8447	0.5536	0.5658	0.6382	0.6267	0.6117	0.6458	0.6284	0.6079
GAT	0.8483	0.5662	0.5818	0.6629	0.6485	0.6381	0.6717	0.6392	0.6338
GCN [2]	0.8748	0.5714	0.5949	0.6419	0.6520	0.6466	0.6494	0.6449	0.6471
	Ours								
DPGCN	0.9637	0.8898	0.9203	0.9666	0.8958	0.9250	0.9394	0.9410	0.9402
w/o prototyping	0.9060	0.5984	0.6384	0.9022	0.6028	0.6433	0.8825	0.6073	0.6535
w/o disentanglement	0.9168	0.6712	0.7293	0.9037	0.6753	0.7339	0.6882	0.9004	0.7801

Several state-of-the-art graph embedding and traversing methods served as benchmarks in our comparative analysis against DPGCN. Deep Walk [14] is a popular approach that generates embeddings by simulating random walks across a graph, allowing a deep representation of vertex sequences. Node2Vec [15], an extension of Deep Walk, provides a more flexible and generalized random walk, offering enhanced node homophily and structural equivalence. LINE [15], on the other hand, focuses on large-scale information network embeddings, striving to preserve both local and global network structures. On the graph neural network (GNN) front, GAT and GCN [2] stand out as prominent models. GAT introduces attention mechanisms, enabling nodes to weigh their neighbors' features, while GCN focuses on creating a layered propagation model to effectively represent graph-structured data. Our proposed DPGCN aims to advance beyond these methods by introducing disentangled prototyping, enabling refined embeddings, particularly for a Ethereum transaction graph.

From Table 3, several insights can be drawn. First, the overall performance improved as the graph size increased, with the highest performance achieved when the graph size was 50,000. This was likely due to the extremely sparse and class-imbalanced nature of the dataset. Furthermore, the graph-traversing or embedding methods such as Deep Walk, Node2Vec, and LINE exhibited relatively low performance, likely due to their inability to effectively model edge information (transaction amount and timestamp), which is crucial in this dataset. In contrast, the graph neural networks such as GNN, GAT, and GCN displayed significantly better performance, as they effectively model edge information.

The proposed DPGCN model, along with its variants (DPGCN w/o prototyping and DPGCN w/o disentanglement), consistently achieved the highest F1 scores across all graph sizes compared to the conventional GCN and other methods. Specifically, our method experimentally demonstrated the validity of the disentangled prototyping strategy for this problem, achieving a maximum F1 score of 0.9402, in comparison to the GCN method, which scored 0.6471 F1. This result highlights the effectiveness of disentangled prototyping in classifying transactions in the Ethereum transaction graph.

4.4. Effects of Disentangled Prototyping

To further investigate the effectiveness of our disentangled prototyping approach, we visualized the feature space using the t-SNE technique and compared the AUC scores for different models.

Figure 3 provides a visualization of the feature space for (a) the input space, (b) the GCN embedded space, and (c) our DPGCN model, using the t-SNE technique. The visualization highlights the differences in the feature spaces across the three cases. In the input space, the features are likely to be scattered randomly with no discernible pattern. In the GCN-embedded space, while there may be some clustering, the features are still likely to be entangled, making it challenging to distinguish between classes. In contrast, the DPGCN model produces a feature space that is clearly distinguishable and less entangled. This visualization emphasizes the advantages of our disentangled prototyping approach, which can help in creating more informative and less entangled feature spaces for better classification.

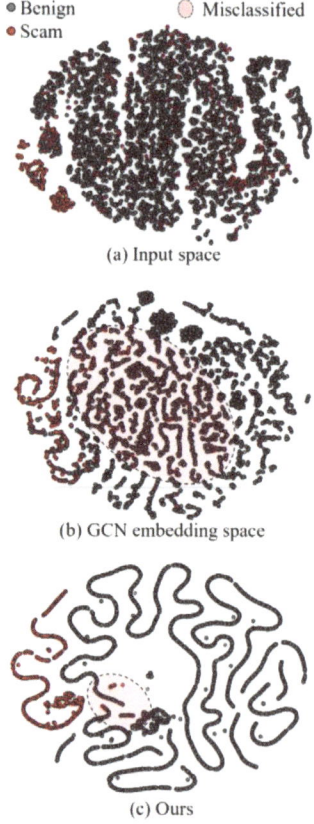

Figure 3. Feature space visualization using the t-SNE technique for (**a**) input space, (**b**) GCN[2]-embedded space, and (**c**) our DPGCN model.

Figure 4 compares the area under the ROC curve (AUC) for DPGCN and DPGCN w/o disentangled prototyping. A higher AUC indicates a better model, as it measures the model's ability to distinguish between positive and negative classes. As shown in the figure, DPGCN achieved a higher AUC compared to DPGCN w/o disentangled prototyping. This result further validates the effectiveness of the disentangled prototyping in our proposed model. By disentangling the feature space, our DPGCN model could more effectively differentiate between the classes, leading to an improved classification performance.

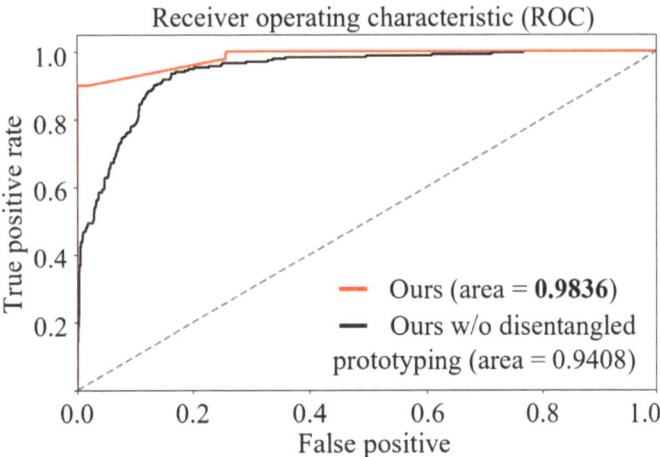

Figure 4. Comparison of area under the ROC curve (AUC) for DPGCN and w/o disentangled prototyping.

4.5. Discussion

We consider the implications of our experiments by performing case analyses on transactions with differing classifications between the GCN model and our DPGCN model, as presented in Table 4.

Table 4. Case analysis of transactions, showing differences in classification between GCN and our DPGCN method, providing node name, block number, from and to destination, and transaction value information.

	Node Name	Reported as	Block	from	To	Value (ETH)
Case 1 (Misclassified by GCN but correct in Ours)	0 × 950bb8abd2419da2c867 97a23d43bbb2da067848	Phishing scam	4200269	Self	0 × 7965...F29A	372.999
			4186015	Enigma presale	Self	373.000
	0 × 8760d59d64fc8082d278 8f1e17e844f4e47230fe	Fraud	7795229	Self	Spindle Token	0.000
			7795217	Self	Playgame Token	0.000
			7042857	Self	Exchange (Malaysia)	0.000
Case 2 (Both misclassified)	0 × 9844f5c5f9aa7146a74f fc7b9227742acfa71dea	Phishing scam	5986398	Self	Other scam node	4.144
			5985936	Exchange (Bittrex, Seattle, WA, USA)	Self	0.084
			5976675	Other scam node	Self	1.000

- Case 1: DPGCN effectively detected scams associated with presale, low-quality tokens, and transfers to small exchanges. Despite limited information (amount and timestamp), our method captured and differentiated scam and benign transactions, successfully classifying such cases. This ability is crucial for robust fraud detection.
- Case 2: A scam node transaction transferred to the large exchange Bittrex was falsely detected. This highlights the limitations of our model in the absence of destination information. Incorporating additional transfer destination data could improve classification for such cases.

In summary, our DPGCN model offers advantages over the GCN method for detecting fraudulent Ethereum transactions, demonstrated by its ability to effectively separate scam and benign transaction histories. Incorporating additional features could further enhance its performance.

In the pursuit of refining our DPGCN model and enhancing Ethereum transaction security, we must also be cognizant of broader implications. Ethical considerations come to the forefront, especially as cryptocurrency transactions bear significant legal and moral weight. The repercussions of false positives, which could unjustly tarnish legitimate entities, are as concerning as the dangers posed by false negatives, which may let malicious activities go unchecked. Moreover, while our model aims to distinguish transaction patterns, there is an inherent risk of infringing upon the privacy rights of users, even if indirectly. Ensuring network integrity is vital, but it should not come at the cost of the very principles of privacy and fairness that underpin the cryptocurrency world.

5. Conclusions

In this study, we introduced the disentangled prototypical graph convolutional network (DPGCN) for identifying fraudulent Ethereum transactions. Our approach combines the strengths of prototypical networks, disentangled representations, and graph convolutional networks for effective transaction network modeling and enhanced fraud detection. Using a real-world Ethereum dataset, we demonstrated the superiority of our model over conventional graph traversal methods and comparatives, such as GNN, GAT, and GCN. Our results highlighted the ability of our method to accurately distinguish between scam and benign transaction histories, showcasing the potential of disentangled prototypical representations.

As we look ahead, several avenues emerge to refine our model further. The potential of integrating richer destination information is evident; however, this comes with challenges, such as assessing the authenticity of these addresses. While our results advocate for the inclusion of more intricate features into the graph for improved performance, it is pivotal to weigh the benefits of adding meta-information, such as transaction frequency or associated notes. This could enhance the model's precision, albeit with the task of filtering potential data noise. Additionally, as we aspire to synergize enhanced graph features, harmonization with the disentangled prototypical loss framework necessitates careful evaluation. Moving forward, we are driven to develop more advanced graph neural networks that can handle vast and intricately complex graphs, beyond only Ethereum transaction analysis, and to unlock further insights in the realm of large-scale network data.

Author Contributions: Conceptualization, S.-J.B.; Formal analysis, H.-J.K.; Funding acquisition, H.-J.K.; Investigation, S.-J.B.; Methodology, S.-J.B. and H.-J.K.; Visualization, S.-J.B.; Writing—review and editing, H.-J.K. All authors have read and agreed to the published version of the manuscript.

Funding: This work was supported by the National Research Foundation of Korea (NRF) grant funded by the Korea government(MSIT) (No. NRF-2021R1F1A1063085).

Data Availability Statement: Xblock datasets (http://xblock.pro/#/search?types=datasets).

Conflicts of Interest: The authors declare no conflict of interest.

References

1. Wang, Z.; Huang, B.; Tu, S.; Zhang, K.; Xu, L. DeepTrader: A deep reinforcement learning approach for risk-return balanced portfolio management with market conditions Embedding. *Proc. AAAI Conf. Artif. Intell.* **2021**, *35*, 643–650. [CrossRef]
2. Huang, T.; Lin, D.; Wu, J. Ethereum account classification based on graph convolutional network. *IEEE Trans. Circuits Syst. II Express Briefs* **2022**, *69*, 2528–2532. [CrossRef]
3. Lin, D.; Wu, J.; Yuan, Q.; Zheng, Z. Modeling and understanding ethereum transaction records via a complex network approach. *IEEE Trans. Circuits Syst. II: Express Briefs* **2020**, *67*, 2737–2741. [CrossRef]
4. Martin, K.; Rahouti, M.; Ayyash, M.; Alsmadi, I. Anomaly detection in blockchain using network representation and machine learning. *Secur. Priv.* **2022**, *5*, e192. [CrossRef]

5. Ofori-Boateng, D.; Dominguez, I.S.; Akcora, C.; Kantarcioglu, M.; Gel, Y.R. Topological anomaly detection in dynamic multilayer blockchain networks. In Proceedings of the Machine Learning and Knowledge Discovery in Databases. Research Track: European Conference, ECML PKDD 2021, Bilbao, Spain, 13–17 September 2021; Proceedings, Part I 21; pp. 788–804.
6. Bai, Q.; Zhang, C.; Liu, N.; Chen, X.; Xu, Y.; Wang, X. Evolution of transaction pattern in Ethereum: A temporal graph perspective. *IEEE Trans. Comput. Soc. Syst.* **2021**, *9*, 851–866. [CrossRef]
7. Jin, C.; Jin, J.; Zhou, J.; Wu, J.; Xuan, Q. Heterogeneous feature augmentation for ponzi detection in ethereum. *IEEE Trans. Circuits Syst. II Express Briefs* **2022**, *69*, 3919–3923. [CrossRef]
8. Liu, J.; Zheng, J.; Wu, J.; Zheng, Z. FA-GNN: Filter and augment graph neural networks for account classification in ethereum. *IEEE Trans. Netw. Sci. Eng.* **2022**, *9*, 2579–2588. [CrossRef]
9. Xia, Y.; Liu, J.; Wu, J. Phishing detection on ethereum via attributed ego-graph embedding. *IEEE Trans. Circuits Syst. II Express Briefs* **2022**, *69*, 2538–2542. [CrossRef]
10. Zhou, J.; Hu, C.; Chi, J.; Wu, J.; Shen, M.; Xuan, Q. Behavior-aware account de-anonymization on ethereum interaction graph. *IEEE Trans. Inf. Forensics Secur.* **2022**, *17*, 3433–3448. [CrossRef]
11. Liu, X.; Tang, Z.; Li, P.; Guo, S.; Fan, X.; Zhang, J. A graph learning based approach for identity inference in dapp platform blockchain. *IEEE Trans. Emerg. Top. Comput.* **2020**, *10*, 438–449. [CrossRef]
12. Yu, L.; Zhang, F.; Ma, J.; Yang, L.; Yang, Y.; Jia, W. Who Are the Money Launderers? Money Laundering Detection on Blockchain via Mutual Learning-Based Graph Neural Network. In Proceedings of the 2023 International Joint Conference on Neural Networks (IJCNN), Gold Coast, Australia, 18–23 June 2023; pp. 1–8.
13. Chen, L.; Peng, J.; Liu, Y.; Li, J.; Xie, F.; Zheng, Z. Phishing scams detection in ethereum transaction network. *ACM Trans. Internet Technol. (TOIT)* **2020**, *21*, 1–16. [CrossRef]
14. Huo, X.; Li, M.; Zhou, Z.-H. Control flow graph embedding based on multi-instance decomposition for bug localization. *Proc. AAAI Conf. Artif. Intell.* **2020**, *34*, 4223–4230. [CrossRef]
15. Grover, A.; Leskovec, J. node2vec: Scalable feature learning for networks. In Proceedings of the 22nd ACM SIGKDD International Conference on Knowledge Discovery and Data Mining, San Francisco, CA, USA, 13–17 August 2016; pp. 855–864.
16. Tang, J.; Qu, M.; Wang, M.; Zhang, M.; Yan, J.; Mei, Q. Line: Large-scale information network embedding. In Proceedings of the 24th International Conference on World Wide Web, Florence, Italy, 18–22 May 2015; pp. 1067–1077.

Disclaimer/Publisher's Note: The statements, opinions and data contained in all publications are solely those of the individual author(s) and contributor(s) and not of MDPI and/or the editor(s). MDPI and/or the editor(s) disclaim responsibility for any injury to people or property resulting from any ideas, methods, instructions or products referred to in the content.

Article

An End-Process Blockchain-Based Secure Aggregation Mechanism Using Federated Machine Learning

Washington Enyinna Mbonu, Carsten Maple * and Gregory Epiphaniou *

WMG, University of Warwick, Coventry CV4 7AL, UK; washington.mbonu@warwick.ac.uk
* Correspondence: cm@warwick.ac.uk (C.M.); gregory.epiphaniou@warwick.ac.uk (G.E.)

Abstract: Federated Learning (FL) is a distributed Deep Learning (DL) technique that creates a global model through the local training of multiple edge devices. It uses a central server for model communication and the aggregation of post-trained models. The central server orchestrates the training process by sending each participating device an initial or pre-trained model for training. To achieve the learning objective, focused updates from edge devices are sent back to the central server for aggregation. While such an architecture and information flows can support the preservation of the privacy of participating device data, the strong dependence on the central server is a significant drawback of this framework. Having a central server could potentially lead to a single point of failure. Further, a malicious server may be able to successfully reconstruct the original data, which could impact on trust, transparency, fairness, privacy, and security. Decentralizing the FL process can successfully address these issues. Integrating a decentralized protocol such as Blockchain technology into Federated Learning techniques will help to address these issues and ensure secure aggregation. This paper proposes a Blockchain-based secure aggregation strategy for FL. Blockchain is implemented as a channel of communication between the central server and edge devices. It provides a mechanism of masking device local data for secure aggregation to prevent compromise and reconstruction of the training data by a malicious server. It enhances the scalability of the system, eliminates the threat of a single point of failure of the central server, reduces vulnerability in the system, ensures security, and transparent communication. Furthermore, our framework utilizes a fault-tolerant server to assist in handling dropouts and stragglers which can occur in federated environments. To reduce the training time, we synchronously implemented a callback or end-process mechanism once sufficient post-trained models have been returned for aggregation (threshold accuracy achieved). This mechanism resynchronizes clients with a stale and outdated model, minimizes the wastage of resources, and increases the rate of convergence of the global model.

Keywords: artificial intelligence; deep learning; federated learning; blockchain; secure aggregation

Citation: Mbonu, W.E.; Maple, C.; Epiphaniou, G. An End-Process Blockchain-Based Secure Aggregation Mechanism Using Federated Machine Learning. *Electronics* **2023**, *12*, 4543. https://doi.org/10.3390/electronics12214543

Academic Editors: Mikolaj Karpinski, Oleksandr O. Kuznetsov and Roman Oliynykov

Received: 19 September 2023
Revised: 31 October 2023
Accepted: 1 November 2023
Published: 5 November 2023

Copyright: © 2023 by the authors. Licensee MDPI, Basel, Switzerland. This article is an open access article distributed under the terms and conditions of the Creative Commons Attribution (CC BY) license (https://creativecommons.org/licenses/by/4.0/).

1. Introduction

The introduction of the Internet of Things (IoT) has resulted in the massive growth in the number of intelligent devices. With strong hardware and dedicated sensors, these devices can collect and process data at high speed. Artificial Intelligence (AI) and Machine Learning (ML) flourish in data. These data are generated by billions of IoT devices and smart phones. By generating these large amounts of data, the IoT has effectively enhanced the training of Deep Learning (DL) models. However, IoT devices cannot independently execute DL algorithms because of their resource-constrained nature. Traditionally, a DL approach entails data collection from various sources and storing them in a centralized location. These stored data are then used to train the DL model. However, privacy legislations such as European Commission's General Data Protection Right (GDPR) and the U.S. Consumer Privacy Bill of Right require that in certain cases, data collection may not be feasible. To address this issue, Federated Learning (FL) was introduced. FL is a distributed DL technique that creates a global model through the local training of multiple decentralized edge devices. It enables distributed ML to be effectively accomplished between various edge devices or participants. Moreso, it promotes the exchange of big data and tends to enhance the privacy preservation of users' data within the confinement of the law [1,2].

The FL algorithm permits the decentralized training of data, but the central server aggregates the model and process planning. In traditional FL, the central server sends to each participating device/client an initial/pre-trained model for training. Using their own local dataset, each participating device trains the model locally and sends it back to the central server for aggregation. The server aggregates the returned trained model to produce an updated global model that is sent back to the participating devices for another round of local training [3]. This client–server interaction [4] continues until model convergence is achieved or a specific number of iterations (rounds) are attained. However, this centralized approach of model aggregation and process planning in traditional FL makes the central server a single point of failure [5]. This threat of a single point of failure (SPOF) on the server could be because of unforeseen external attacks, purposeful unfair aggregation, unexpected failure in network connection, etc. This strong dependence on the central server is a significant drawback to this technique because if there exist a problem with the server or it fails, the training process will stop and as mentioned earlier, the resource-constrained end devices will not be able to independently execute the aggregation process [6]. Several risks and issues arise in such a centralized model: (1) *Communication failure*: To collect model updates and distribute the updated model, the central server depends on communication with end devices. If there is a communication failure, it can interrupt the training process and delay model updates. (2) *Scalability and overload issues*: The central server might face scalability issues in a large network with several end devices. If the model updates and requests from end devices cannot be effectively handled by the central server, it may be overloaded and slow down or crash. This will lead to training disruption. (3) *Security breach*: A security breach on the central server could result in malicious actors gaining unauthorized access to sensitive data or model updates, leading to privacy issues or tampering with the model updates. (4) *Server downtime*: The central server may experience hardware failures or software issues which could result in downtime, making it unavailable to end devices. During this period, model updates cannot be aggregated, and the FL process will stop. (5) *Aggregation bias*: To form an updated global model, the central server aggregates updates from various end devices. If the aggregation is biased, it could favour certain end devices over others, leading to a skewed model result.

Furthermore, the privacy leakage in FL could put updates from the end devices at risk due to fairness and trust issues from the central server, and this could be because of the following: (1) *Central server integrity*: The central server orchestrates the training and aggregation of model updates from end devices. If the server is compromised, it could change or alter the model updates, resulting in influenced or poisonous models being dispersed to end devices. (2) *Model poisoning*: Without thorough validation, the central server may aggregate model updates from a malicious participant in the training process. The malicious participant may attempt to poison the global model by intentionally sending updates that degrade the model performance. (3) *Data bias*: Data distribution across end devices may not be evenly distributed, resulting in bias or data imbalance. This imbalanced distribution could result in less accurate models and be unfair to a subset of the end devices. (4) *Data privacy and security*: In as much as FL aims to preserve the privacy of the user data by not sharing raw data with the central server, there is still risk of data exposure during model updates. The gradients sent to the server may accidentally reveal sensitive information about the local data. Moreso, a malicious central server might compromise or gain sensitive intuitions of the updates from the end devices because of its capability to successfully reconstruct the original data due to non-scrutinized, constant, and direct communication with the end devices. Recent works have shown that a malicious server can use the gradient information to infer the sensitive content about the clients' training data. Through a Generative Adversarial Network (GAN), the distribution of the training data can be recovered by the malicious server [7]. Also, attacks on the server can alter the global model [8]. Furthermore, attacks on the end devices could manipulate local models, and this can result in errors in the global model generated from such altered local models. In like manner, the integrity of the generated global model should be verified before use by the edge devices. FL was integrated with Blockchain technology to ensure transparency and enhance its privacy preservation, security, and performance [9,10].

To address this SPOF threat, privacy, trust, fairness, transparency, and security, Blockchain is integrated into FL methodology to mitigate against vulnerability in the FL centralized approach of model aggregation and process planning. Blockchain is used as a reliable orchestrating memory that eliminates the need for a central coordinating unit and provides a secured, certified, and validated exchange of information. The three fundamental security considerations identified in Ref. [11] are confidentiality, integrity, and availability. As identified in Refs. [12,13], FL suffers from insufficient incentives, poisoning attacks, privacy preservation, etc.

In Blockchain, transactions are unaltered and timestamped. As a distribute ledger, Blockchain can act as an append-only database that offers data integrity. Also, it can act as a hybrid Blockchain that guarantees data confidentiality to only authenticated and permitted users. Blockchain allows the storage and exchange of data in a decentralized approach using digital blocks, increasing FL fault tolerance capacity [14]. These digital blocks are chained together using cryptographic hashes to form a distributed ledger. Blockchain is a type of distributed ledger that is shared among all devices in a federated network. This ensures that data are immutable, visible, traceable, transparent, and non-repudiated. These unique characteristics of Blockchain make it an ideal technology to combine with FL to safeguard the privacy and security of aggregated data.

This paper aims to implement a callback/end-process Blockchain-based secure aggregation mechanism for FL through the masking of model updates. For each iteration of the FL training process by the central server, the Blockchain enables the masking and tracking of local models, where devices mask their local model to train the global model, and post-trained models are sent back to the server for model aggregation. When a certain percentage of post-trained models have been returned by the clients, the server will implement a callback aggregation and issue a force stop to lessen training time, reduce communication rounds, and speed up the convergence of the global model. Similarly, if this percentage as stated by the FL server is not met and a deadline has been reached, an end-process strategy will be issued to the clients yet to return their post-trained models to avoid the issue of infinite loop or endless waiting.

In both cases (callback/end-process), devices at the stage of model training will be forced to synchronize with the central server. The main contributions of this paper are as follows:

- Formulate a mechanism of masking the local models to train the global model for aggregation by the server to prevent the compromise and reconstruction of the data used to train the model.
- Implement a Blockchain network for transparent communication within an FL environment which eliminates the threat of SPOF, ensures transparency, and enhances the security and privacy preservation of data.
- To lessen training time due to dropouts that might occur in the FL environment, a callback function will be synchronously implemented by the FL server once sufficient post-trained models have been returned.

The rest of the paper is organized as follows: In Section 2, we examine related works in the field. Section 3 is the background information of Blockchain technology. Section 4 illustrates the distribution of the global model, consensus mechanism, masking of device local data, and model aggregation. Section 5 introduces the system architecture, synchronization process, client selection update, and FL loss function. Section 6 illustrates the callback function and end-process aggregation mechanism in FL. Section 7 presents the Results, Discussion, and performance evaluation. Finally, Conclusions are drawn in Section 8.

2. Related Work
2.1. Secure Aggregation in FL

To guarantee privacy and security using FL, the following proposals [15,16] on secure aggregation mechanisms have been proposed. Fereidooni et al. [15] proposed a secure aggregation for private Federated Learning. This approach tends to impede inference attacks on FL by prohibiting access and tampering with trained model updates. They utilized a Secure Multipath Computation (SMC) encryption technique to prevent the aggregator from accessing the model updates used for the training of the Machine Learning model. Similarly, Wu et al. [16] proposed a secure aggregation mechanism for model updates in FL to prevent inference and inversion attacks that can obtain sensitive information from local model updates. Their approach utilized matrix transformation to protect each clients' model updates by preventing the attacker from gaining sensitive information using encryption of a little part of the model update to avoid heavy encryption that could result in low accuracy. Their aggregation mechanism functions with an acceptable overhead. However, both approaches suffer the threat of the SPOF of the central server which orchestrates the training process [5].

Huang et al. [7] proposed a secure aggregation mechanism for Federated Learning that utilized ransom masking code to ensure the confidentiality of local gradients. Their proposed mechanism ensures the confidentiality of local gradients and verifiability of aggregated gradients. However, this mechanism is not communication- and bandwidth-efficient when several clients are involved in the training process. Also, it suffers from the threat of SPOF in the aggregator and verification servers. To protect against Byzantine adversarial that could compromise the performance and convergence of the global model, Zhao et al. [17] proposed a secure aggregation mechanism in FL. This mechanism used intel SGX primitives to ensure privacy preservation of the local models by providing a recovery key to the encrypted models. This technique ensures that sensitive information is not revealed to the aggregation server. However, it still suffers the threat of SPOF of the aggregation server that could halt the training process.

2.2. Blockchain-Based Federated Learning

Traditional FL mechanisms depend on the central server for coordination and orchestration. This central server dependence may result in SPOF, trust issues, and unwanted behaviours of the server. To ensure effective decentralization, trust, transparency, and reliability, Blockchain technology has emerged. Blockchain technology has been implemented by many researchers to eliminate the threat of SPOF in traditional FL [18,19].

To guarantee data authenticity and privacy protection, the authors in Ref. [18] implemented an FL framework using Blockchain in self-driving cars. In Ref. [20], they implemented a private Blockchain FL using an interstellar file system to minimize high storage costs in Blockchain, inference, and poisoning attacks in FL. As seen in Ref. [21], they implemented a private Blockchain for secure model aggregation in FL using a consensus process for traffic prediction. In Ref. [19], the author proposed a Blockchain-enabled FL where the security and privacy of the user's information were protected by encrypting and encoding it in the cloud. All these research works mentioned above makes use of Blockchain technology for the aggregation of a trained model, which incurs huge bandwidth and complexity in computation. Most of the contributions are based on a private Blockchain, where the entire process is not decentralized, which could result in trust issues.

For the local evaluation and global aggregation of parameters, Sun et al. [22] proposed the use of Blockchain in FL to lessen the effect of end-point adversarial training data. In this work, the method of selecting a committee member is not feasible and was not fully analysed. Furthermore, if there are more users participating in the network, the method may experience a decrease in classification accuracy. To facilitate the model update and guarantee secure aggregation of the global model, Mallah et al. [23] proposed a Blockchain-enabled Federated Learning that selects only reliable IoT devices for global aggregation. Their approach ensures the aggregation of the global model through optimized behaviour monitoring of the devices, increasing the convergence time of FL processes while preserving network performance. However, there is a trade-off in time and bandwidth efficiency, and the scalability of this technique in variable network topology is not guaranteed. To guarantee a secure aggregation mechanism that will ensure trust, security, and integrity of the global model, the following approaches [24,25] have been proposed.

Kalapaaking et al. [24] proposed a Blockchain-based FL secure aggregation mechanism to guarantee the security and integrity of the global model. Their technique ensured a trusted aggregation of the local model to generate a global model. However, they failed to consider how to handle stragglers and dropouts in Industrial IoT (IIoT). Their assumption was that all the IIoT will successfully return their trained model, which is practically impossible. Chen et al. [25] proposed a Blockchain-based FL for the secure aggregation and efficient sharing of medical data. Their technique enhanced the sharing of medical data in a privacy-preserved manner. However, the use of a contribution-weighted aggregation mechanism, as seen in Ref. [25], will incur huge bandwidth and complexity in computation, which makes the technique not feasible within a resource-constrained setting. To minimize the impact of the attacks from malicious clients or a poisonous server and preserve privacy in FL, Refs. [26,27] have been proposed.

Li et al. [26] proposed a Blockchain-based decentralized FL with committee consensus to solve the issues of SPOF, privacy, and security. Their technique solves the threat of SPOF, prevents malicious attacks, prevents models from been exposed to poisoning or unauthorized devices, and the burden of consensus computing is reduced. However, the validation consumption is increased, and the consensus committee selection could result in security issues if not properly selected. Miao et al. [27] proposed an FL privacy preserving scheme based on a Blockchain network. Their approach mitigates against a poisoning attack from malicious clients and ensures a transparent process using the Blockchain network. However, they did not provide mechanisms on how to deal with stragglers and dropouts that may exist within the devices.

In comparison with above-mentioned research works, our approach is scalable and eliminates the threat of SPOF with traditional FL while retaining the central server for the aggregation of post-trained models. This significantly reduces the computational burden and communication cost of aggregating the trained model using the Blockchain network. Additionally, our technique handles the issues associated with stragglers and dropouts in IoT systems within an FL environment.

3. Background Information on Blockchain Technology

Distributed Ledger Technology (DLT) is an umbrella technology of Blockchain in the sense that every Blockchain is a DLT but not every DLT is a Blockchain. Previously, Blockchain was primarily designed for digital transactions and used as currency, but recently, researchers have found various ways of using the technology or combining it with other methodologies for the greater good. In a distributed ledger, data are independently held and updated by end devices within the network. This eliminates the need for a central authority to perform the orchestration. Rather, each end device is given access to the transaction lists, where each individually and autonomously updates the distributed ledger. Implementing Blockchain with FL will provide additional protection, strong robustness, and privacy preservation.

In Ref. [28], the Blockchain technology components were identified as the Blockchain, Blockchain network, and distributed consensus mechanism. A Blockchain network comprises two computation nodes, namely, the verifier and normal nodes. The former hold an entire record of the Blockchain structure and transaction validations, implement smart contracts, ensure data security, and require high storage and computational capability, while the latter do not keep a record of the Blockchain ledger due to limited computational and storage capability but obtain a little knowledge from the full nodes about the Blockchain status. In private and distributed data, Blockchain has proven to be a secure aggregation mechanism for edge computing in a federated Machine Learning (FML) environment.

There exist three types of Blockchain: (1) Public Blockchain: This type gives free access to the public or any person to partake in the core activities. It is a democratically decentralized Blockchain operation. The disadvantage with this type of Blockchain is that deceptive participants may exist that could execute malicious activities on core functions. (2) Private Blockchain: In this type, only chosen and validated participants are allowed to join. A control function is put on who can partake in the core activities. These types of Blockchain are not essentially decentralized because the distributed ledger is operated by central supervisors and could result in trust issues. (3) Hybrid Blockchain: this combines public and private contributors. It could involve external parties that carefully implement network restrictions and control contributor activities in their respective roles. The immutability data structure of Blockchain makes it a viable technology when implemented in an FL framework. To deal with operational changes or issues such as stragglers or dropouts in an FL environment, Blockchain offers an efficient ecosystem in handling such issues. In a bid to identify malicious activities within a data auditing scheme, Ref. [29] described Blockchain as a DLT that keeps track of the activities of all the nodes in a Blockchain network using a smart contract. The advancement of Blockchain technology has aided the implementation of smart contract technology. Smart contracts are treaties between various entities based on a particular matter that is meant to be implemented by computer programs. Using smart contracts, more users are encouraged to participate in FL training, facilitating the management and control of the entire process [30]. Blockchain members validate and verify codes in the form of smart contracts to protect relationships over computer networks. Smart contracts are used by Blockchain members to make a treaty in a distribution ledger without involving a central third party to implement the treaty. Using interaction records between nodes on a Blockchain network, smart contracts can effectively and automatically identify violations based on the records [31]. To ensure the correctness of the smart contracts, nodes within the Blockchain network must run the same smart contracts, and through a consensus agreement strategy, results are accepted. With Blockchain and smart contracts, various fields have been expanded and improved [32].

3.1. Structure of Blockchain

There are five logical layers of Blockchain, and they are as follows:

- *Application layer*: In Blockchain structure, this is the uppermost layer. The application layer serves as a channel for the Blockchain to connect to the real world. It comprises the chain code, smart contracts, and distributed applications (dApps). The two sub-layers of the application layer are the presentation and execution layers.
- *Consensus layer*: In this layer, consensus algorithms are used to validate transactions. A method of agreement must be reached to generate a new block on a single data block comprising multiple insecure numbers of nodes. These methods of agreement are termed consensus algorithms. They are used to validate transactions and to determine the node to generate a new block. The consensus mechanisms are Proof of Work (PoW), Proof of Stake (PoS), Proof of Elapsed Time (PoET), Proof of Authority (PoA), and Byzantine Fault Tolerance (BFT). We adopted PoA as a consensus mechanism for this framework.
- *Network layer*: In a Blockchain network, the network layer provides communication between nodes. This is also referred to as a Point-to-Point (P2P) network. Network failures are avoided in P2P networks because the nodes regularly communicate with each other. P2P networks help filter out illegal transactions. Full nodes and light nodes are the two types of nodes in P2P networks.
- *Data layer*: This is the basic layer of the Blockchain structure. The data layer comprises data blocks, a digital signature, transactions, a Merkle tree, and hash functions.
- *Infrastructure layer*: This layer is also known as the hardware structure. It contains the services that enable data exchange. Within the infrastructure layer exist services, virtual machines, messaging, and containers.

3.2. Performance Evaluation of Blockchain

The performance of Blockchain can be evaluated with the following factors:

- *Decentralization*: The decentralization nature of Blockchain effectively eliminates SPOF and solves the bottleneck problem of a central authority. The operation of a Blockchain network is unaltered by the disruption of a single node in the network because data exist in multiple nodes on the P2P network. This p2p network configuration ensures the immutability and authenticity of data. The decentralization nature of a Blockchain network effectively handles dropouts or offline nodes without compromising the security and availability of the network.
- *Transparency*: There is great transparency in Blockchain transaction histories because nodes in the network share the same documents. The shared documents must be modified through a consensus where every node in the network must agree. Any alteration of a single record will require the modification of subsequent records for the entire network. With transparency, the integrity of the network is protected, and there is a complete reduction in data alteration.
- *Improved security*: There is enhanced security in Blockchain technology implementation because an agreement must be reached in advance before a transaction takes place. After a transaction is approved, it becomes encrypted and connected to the previous one. To avoid any potential security breaches, the data are not stored on a single server but are instead distributed across a network of computers. Private/public key infrastructures are used to improve the security of the Blockchain network, and it is mathematically impossible to devise these keys because they are randomly generated strings and numbers. Through this process, the security of the network is strengthened, and there is a significant reduction in data leakage.
- *Immutability*: Using cryptographic hashes and timestamps, Blockchain ensures that data remain immutable. After validation, the hash function restricts data altering, updating, and removal. Any change in the transaction data can be identified easily.
- *Data privacy*: In a Blockchain network, data are protected against alteration using digital signatures. Immutable hash chains ensure that transactions are monitored by nodes across the network to preserve data rights.
- *Anonymity*: The data on the chain in a Blockchain network are public. However, Blockchain uses encryption techniques to achieve the privacy preservation of the end devices' private data to avoid exposure to another node on the network.

3.3. Technical Limitations

The technical limitations of Blockchain include the following:

- *Computational complexity*: There is a high computational cost involved in completing a transaction. It entails several steps, such as validation, scrutiny, and security checks across multiple nodes. This computational complexity consumes a significant amount of power and resource-constrained IoT devices will need help to meet resource demands. Also, the sophisticated architecture will demand high computational capabilities that could result in an increase in implementation and running costs.
- *Privacy and security issues*: Blockchain can resist security attacks such as Distributed Denial-of-Service (DDoS), Ransomware, and Sybil attacks. However, there are integral security shortcomings in existing Blockchain networks. If the computing resources can be controlled by more than half of the nodes running Blockchain, consensus processes could be altered for malicious reasons. This is known as a 51% attack. Furthermore, if transactions are not robustly supervised, Blockchain could suffer network interruption and data loss.
- *Scalability issues*: The limited scalability of Blockchain is caused by restricted throughput and high computational costs. This negatively impacts the overall system performance due to the limited block size and increased block time. These complications arise when processing large amounts of data on the Blockchain, especially in large IoT systems where massive amounts of data are generated [33].

According to Ref. [34], Blockchain is defined as a decentralized and distributed technology that can be used and employed in applications involving daily living, such as healthcare systems, supply chain management, digital currencies, etc.

3.4. Blockchain Technology Applications

The applications of Blockchain technology include the following:

- *Secured digital payment system*: Blockchain technology ensures a secured digital payment system and facilitates a reduction in intermediaries' fees as compared to traditional digital payments, where organizations such as credit card companies and financial institutions act as intermediaries. Also, the transaction time is drastically reduced using automated validation and verification systems [35].
- *Automated governance*: Blockchain uses E-governance to provide automated government services. These services include tax collection, conducting elections, issuing certificates, implementing social security, etc. These services are enhanced, and personal data privacy is preserved using Blockchain technology. It gives adequate control functions and supports the efficient management of these services.
- *Data redundancy*: Blockchain facilitates efficient data distribution. Distributed data storage is one of the features of Blockchain and it helps to easily spot data alteration and facilitates recovery from peer nodes. This attribute helps to keep good audit records of data and ensures data integrity and confidentiality.
- *Supply chain management*: This involves business processes that go through various steps to supply the needs of customers and add value to stakeholders. It involves the synchronization of complex processes that require efficient monitoring and accountability.

Having examined the analysis of the Blockchain technology, the next section will showcase global model distribution and the performance evaluation of the Blockchain technology through the masking of device local data for privacy preservation and mitigation against the reconstruction of device local data by a malicious server.

4. Global Model Distribution, Consensus Mechanism, Masking of Device Local Data, and Model Aggregation

4.1. Global Model Distribution

The aggregator server (central server) initiates the training process by sending an initial or pre-trained model to the clients through the Blockchain network. The Blockchain network, using the nodes, verifies the model, validates it, and reaches a consensus.

4.2. Consensus Mechanism

We implemented a private Blockchain setting and adopted PoA as a consensus mechanism. Using trustworthy validators, transactions and blocks are validated. These validators are also tasked with the responsibility of creating new blocks and transaction confirmation. In a consensus mechanism using PoA, not all the nodes are allowed to participate in the consensus process; rather, validators are chosen based on attributes such as investment in the system, identity verification, and reputation. Based on these attributes, PoA depends on a pre-selected group of nodes as validators. Unlike PoW, where there is competition to solve a puzzle, there exist no competition to create a block among validators in PoA. Rather, validators take turns based on a set schedule or a round-robin fashion.

In our architectural framework, the global model sent from the aggregator server to the clients is checked and validated and a consensus is reached before it is sent to the clients as a smart contract. Using a pre-selected group of nodes as validators and turn taking based on a set schedule or a round-robin fashion, the speed of the transaction verification process is significantly increased. Once transactions are confirmed and validated by validators, they are added to the next block. This process ensures trust and security because validators have a strong incentive to correctly validate transactions, or their reputation will be at stake. However, through governing processes, malicious validators can be removed from the network by other validators.

Regarding speed and scalability, transactions are processed faster in PoA networks than in PoW and PoS because PoA does not require stake-based competitions and computations that are resource-intensive. In energy efficiency, PoA is more environmentally friendly because it does not depend on resource-intensive mining. Furthermore, block creation and transaction validation are more predictable with a set schedule and known validators. There is reduced centralization risk in PoA. In an FL setting like our architectural framework, where trust among clients can be established and maintained, PoA offers a balance between efficiency and decentralization.

4.3. Masking of Device Local Data

The essence of masking the local model is the privacy preservation of a device's local data and mitigation against the server from reconstructing the data used to train the model. To illustrate the masking of the device local model using common seeds, keeping each device local model private and secure using a Blockchain network, the following assumptions are made:

Assume M_{12}, M_{13}, and M_{14} as the masks (M) indiscriminately created based on common seeds by (*device*1 and *device*2), (*device*1 and *device*3), and (*device*1 and *device*4), respectively. This is such that $(M_{12} = M_{21})$, $(M_{13} = M_{31})$, and $(M_{14} = M_{41})$, respectively. Similarly, $(M_{23}, M_{24},$ and $M_{34})$ are assumed to be the masks indiscriminately created based on common seeds by (*device*2 and *device*3), (*device*2 and *device*4), and (*device*3 and *device*4), respectively. In like manner, $(M_{23} = M_{32})$, $(M_{24} = M_{42})$, and $(M_{34} = M_{43})$, respectively. Using a key agreement protocol, these common seeds are decided prior to training amongst a pair of devices. The following equations ensued to further illustrate the individual device and the secure aggregation protocol.

Let device = D.
Global model = θ_G.
Device local model = $\beta_1, \beta_2, \beta_3, \ldots, \beta_n$.
Training samples/dataset = $x_1, x_2, x_3, \ldots, x_n$.

$$D_1 = \beta_1 x_1 + M_{12} + M_{13} + M_{14} \tag{1}$$

$$D_2 = \beta_2 x_2 - M_{21} + M_{23} + M_{24} \tag{2}$$

$$D_3 = \beta_3 x_3 - M_{31} - M_{32} + M_{34} \tag{3}$$

$$D_4 = \beta_4 x_4 - M_{41} - M_{42} - M_{43} \tag{4}$$

Combining (1) to (4) will result in the mask cancelling out, i.e., $(M_{12} - M_{21} = 0)$, $(M_{13} - M_{31} = 0)$, $(M_{14} - M_{41} = 0)$, $(M_{23} - M_{32} = 0)$, $(M_{24} - M_{42} = 0)$, and $(M_{34} - M_{43} = 0)$.

$$\sum D_i = D_1 + D_2 + D_3 + D_4 = \beta_1 x_1 + \beta_2 x_2 + \beta_3 x_3 + \beta_4 x_4 \tag{5}$$

$$\theta_G = \sum \frac{D_i}{\sum x_i} = \sum \frac{(\beta_i x_i)}{\sum x_i (i > 3)} \tag{6}$$

In summary, the local model masked at device i is as follows:

$$D_i = \beta_i x_i + \sum_{1<2} M_{12} - \sum_{1>2} M_{21} \tag{7}$$

4.4. Aggregation of Masked Trained Model

Figure 1 illustrates how the device masked trained models are aggregated at the server. As a secured end-process Blockchain-based aggregation mechanism, only returned post-trained models are needed for aggregation. An end-process or a callback function mechanism forces the devices to synchronize with the server. During aggregation, the callback or end-process mechanism eliminates the problem of complicated handling of stragglers and dropouts masked using double masking and Shamir's t-out-of-n Secret Sharing [21]. This mechanism ensures that only returned post-trained models are needed for aggregation.

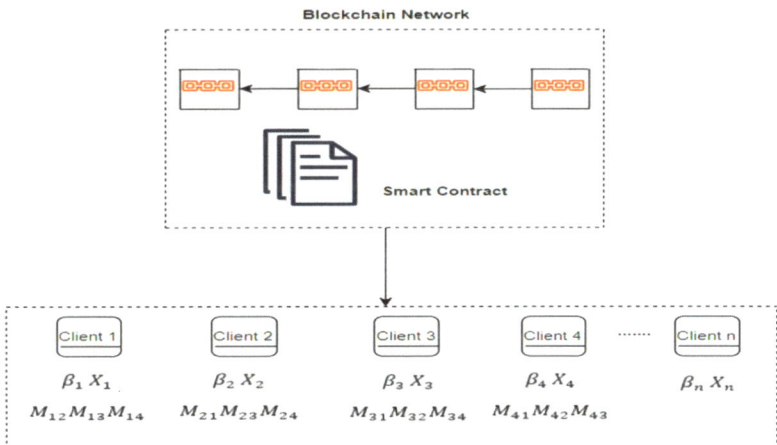

Figure 1. Example of masking of the global model using the Blockchain.

The aggregated global model is as follows:

$$\theta_G = \frac{(\beta_1 \cdot x_1 + \beta_2 \cdot x_2 + \beta_3 \cdot x_3 + \cdots \beta_n \cdot x_n)}{(x_1 + x_2 + x_3 + \cdots x_n)} \tag{8}$$

$$\theta_G = \frac{\sum (\beta_i x_i)}{\sum x_i} \tag{9}$$

where $i = 1, 2, 3, \ldots, n$.

As shown in Figure 2, the masked models will be sent to the server for aggregation. The server periodically sends the intermediate results of the aggregated model to the Blockchain network, and the Blockchain, through the fault-tolerant server, sends an encrypted update of the clients' situation to the aggregator server. This process will be fully illustrated in the next section. The local model trained at device i (β_i) using its local dataset (x_i) trains the model, and the updates are sent to the aggregator server for aggregation as masked model updates. The masked model updates are aggregated and unmasked to create a new global model. The new global model is sent back to the devices through the Blockchain network for further training, and this iteration continues until convergence or the desired accuracy is achieved, as shown in Figure 2.

A new global model emerges as follows:

$$\theta_G = \sum \frac{D_i}{\sum x_i} \tag{10}$$

At the server, the mask is cancelled, resulting in the following:

$$\theta_G = \frac{\sum \beta_i \, x_i}{\sum x_i} \tag{11}$$

where $i = 1, 2, 3, \ldots, n$.

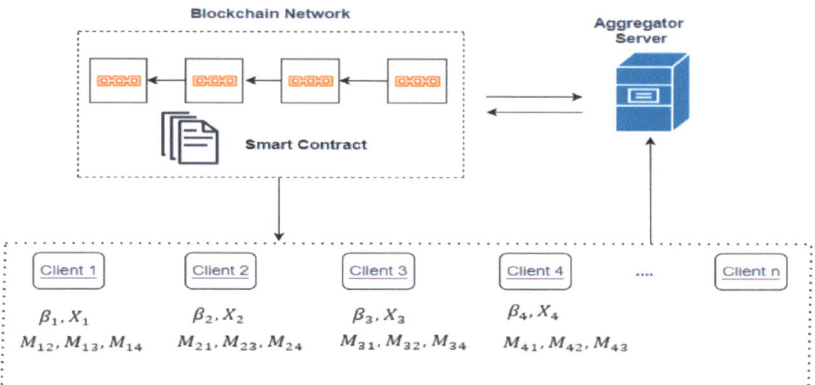

Figure 2. Local model masking and secure aggregation mechanism in FL.

5. System Architecture, Synchronization Process, Client Situation Update, and Loss Function

5.1. System Architecture

In this section, a brief description of all the entities that make up the architectural framework as illustrated in Figure 3 is given, followed by a general explanation of the system architecture, client situation updates (CSUs), and how the loss function is minimized using federated averaging (FedAvg). From Figure 3, the Blockchain-based secure aggregation system architecture consists of four entities: the *aggregator server*, *blockchain network*, *fault-tolerant server*, and *clients*. Their roles are described as follows:

- *Aggregator server*: This is a central server that is tasked with aggregating the model updates from the clients. It generates the initial global model needed for training and sends it to the clients through the Blockchain network.
- *Blockchain network*: The Blockchain network ensures trust and transparency and enables the masking of the global model for local model training. The intermediate results are sent to the Blockchain network for an efficient and transparent computation process.
- *Fault-tolerant server*: In the context of the Blockchain, this entity acts like the PoA, a variation of PoS that is less energy-intensive and requires less computing power when compared with PoW. It ensures that the failure of certain clients or clients going offline does not prevent the operation of the network. For every iteration, the clients' situation updates are communicated to the fault-tolerant server in a privacy-preserved manner. These updates are used within the network to handle the issues associated with stragglers and dropouts.
- *Clients*: They are data owners that train the global model. They send their model updates to the central server and status report (active, stragglers, and dropouts) to the fault-tolerant server in a privacy-preserved manner.

From Figure 3, an initial or pre-trained global model from the *aggregator server* is sent to the clients through the Blockchain network for model training and aggregation. The trustworthy nodes in the *blockchain network* verify the model, reach a consensus using PoA, mask the global model, and send it to the clients as smart contracts. This ensures the security, transparency, tamper-proofness, and privacy-preservation of data. Each client uses their local data to train the model and send a masked update to the central server for aggregation. The masking of device local data and secure aggregation is illustrated using Algorithm 1.

Algorithm 1: Masking Local Data and Secure Aggregation

Input: Device D, global model θ_G, device local model $\beta_1, \beta_2, \beta_3, \dots, \beta_n$, training sample $x_1, x_2, x_3, \dots, x_n$, masks M, number of training rounds T
Output: The aggregated final model θ_T

1 **Initialization**:
2 (a). The global model θ_G from the aggregator server is sent to the clients/devices for model training through the Blockchain network;
3 (b). The Blockchain establishes a secure and transparent channel between the aggregator server and the clients;
4 (c). θ_G is validated using trustworthy validators;
5 (d). Consensus is reached using PoA;
6 (e). Initialize the training round index by t = 1.
7 **Procedure**:
8 **for** t ≤ T **do**
9   (I). **For Blockchain network**:
10   **repeat**
11   **for** each device **do**
12   (a). Decide a key agreement protocol amongst pair of devices;
13   (b). Mask (M) indiscriminately between device1 and device2 such that $M_{12} = M_{21}$;
14   (c). Mask for all connected devices (M_{12}, M_{13}, M_{14}), (M_{21}, M_{23}, M_{24}), (M_{31}, M_{32}, M_{34}), (M_{41}, M_{42}, M_{43}) as represented in Figure 1;
15   (d). Split the masked model using a secret sharing scheme across the Blockchain network;
16   (e). Store model shares on the Blockchain to ensure decentralization and transparency;
17   (f). Send to the devices using smart contract;
18   **end**
19   **until** The local mask model is as (9);
20   (II). **For devices**:
21   **for** ∀D_i ∈ D_n **do**
22   (a). Devices train the model using their local data ($D_i = \beta_i x_i$);
23   (b). Each device sends its trained models to the aggregator server according to (3)–(6);
24   **end**
25   (III). **For the aggregator server**:
26   **for** θ_G **do**
27   (a). Aggregate and unmask according to (8);
28   (b). Dynamically initiate a callback or end-process aggregation mechanism or get update about the device status as per Algorithm 2;
29   (c). Generate a new global model according to (11);
30   **end**
31   t ← t + 1.
32 **end**
33 **return** The aggregated final model θ_T.

There is constant communication between the central server and the *fault-tolerant server* through the Blockchain network. The clients communicate their status updates to the fault-tolerant server in a privacy-preserved manner. As illustrated in Algorithm 2, the fault-tolerant server handles stragglers and dropouts in an efficient manner by ensuring that the unavailability of participating clients does not stop the training process because other clients can step in and take their place. The client's status feedback is communicated to the central server through the Blockchain network in a privacy-preserved manner. The central server uses this information to decide when to initiate a callback function or end-process aggregation mechanism. These aggregation mechanisms effectively handle stale model updates which could occur when clients experience connectivity issues or delays in sending model updates to the central server. Also, it resynchronizes clients that experience a temporary drop-out and then reconnects with an outdated model to receive the latest global model. The entire FL training process is recorded in the Blockchain network, and this technique addresses the threat of an SPOF, privacy, trust, and security. Furthermore, the aggregation of post-trained models (model updates) is carried out by the aggregator server, which greatly reduces the computing burden on the Blockchain network. Furthermore, the clients' status communications to the fault-tolerant server help to manage the issues associated with stragglers and dropouts.

Algorithm 2: Client Situation Update

Input: Device D, set of clients A, selected clients B, crash clients C, Post-trained P, selection fraction S, number of training rounds T.
Output: Crash ratio C_r
$|P| = S.|A|$
1 **Initialization**:
2 a). Initialize the training round index by t = 1.
3 **Procedure:**
4 **for** t ≤ T **do**
5   (I). **For clients**:
6   Send status update according to (12);
7   (II). **For fault tolerant server**:
8   (a). Compute C_r according to (13);
9   **if** $C_r > |P|$ **then**
10   send C_r update to the Blockchain network;
11   **else**
12   do nothing;
13   **end**
14   (III). **For the Blockchain network**:
15   (a). Update aggregator server;
16   (b). Add D;
17   **end**
18   t ← t + 1.
19 **end**
20 **return** C_r

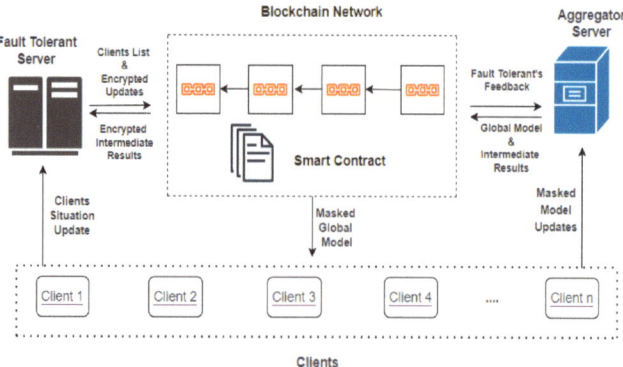

Figure 3. Architecture of the proposed framework.

5.2. Synchronization Process

The synchronization of the Blockchain with the other components in the architectural framework is in real time. Once the global model updates are aggregated by the central server, a hash of the update or summary is recorded on the Blockchain. This provides an immutable record of the model update. A consensus is reached by the validators on the validity of the recorded model updates. This record becomes a permanent part of the Blockchain. Synchronization is achieved through periodic communication between the servers and the immutable records on the Blockchain. The two servers (fault-tolerant server and aggregator server) periodically synchronize with the Blockchain to check for new records and status updates. In an unexpected failure of the central server, the Blockchain immutable records can serve as a reference point to continue the training. The Blockchain serves as a traceable, consistent, transparent, and a trusted reference point across all components in the architectural framework.

5.3. Client Situation Updates (CSUs)

In this context, stragglers and dropouts will be classified as crashed clients. To avoid infinite loops and handle crashed clients, the aggregator server does not need to wait for all the clients to return their post-trained models but will dynamically be able to implement a callback or end-process aggregation once sufficient updates have been returned. This mechanism enhances round efficiency in situations where there is a high probability of crash of clients. CSUs are carried out in a privacy-preserved manner.

Available clients = A.
Selected clients = B.
Crashed clients = C.

$$SU = \frac{|B - B \cap C|}{|A|} \quad (12)$$

After every round of training, the crash ratio is determined using the following:

$$C_r = \frac{C}{A} \quad (13)$$

where C_r is the crash ratio.

In every training round, the fault-tolerant server will send these updates to the aggregator server through the Blockchain network. The aggregator server uses these updates to dynamically evaluate when to implement a callback or end-process mechanism. These updates will enable the Blockchain network during the selection of clients for training to make the decision to allow other clients to step in and take the place of the crashed clients.

5.4. Federated Learning Loss Function

The loss function is a means of evaluating the model's performance on the data it has been trained on. The loss function used in this FL is the cross-entropy loss, a standard supervised learning loss function that examines the difference in the anticipated probability distribution and the actual probability distribution of device data. The loss function of each device is calculated, and the results are aggregated to update the global model. This ensures that the global model is a true representation of the device data. To minimize the expected loss across all devices, FedAvg is used. FedAvg is a technique where multiple devices store training data locally, and the aggregated local updates from these devices are used to train a model.

Let model parameters = w.
Number of devices = n.
Loss function = L.
Loss function for the ith device = $li(w)$.
Learning rate = η.
Derivative function = ∇.

The FedAvg loss function can be expressed as follows:

$$L(w) = \frac{1}{n} * \sum_{i=1}^{n} li(w) \tag{14}$$

The FedAvg goal is to reduce the loss function based on the model parameter w. Using the following update rule, the FedAvg algorithm minimizes the loss function by iteratively updating the model parameters.

$$w_{new} = w_{old} + \eta * \nabla(L(w_{old})) \tag{15}$$

$\nabla(L(w_{old}))$ is the gradient of the loss function with respect to the model parameter w_{old}, and it is computed as the aggregated local gradients of each device.

$$\nabla(L(w_{old})) = \frac{1}{n} * \sum_{i=1}^{n} \nabla(li(w_{old})) \tag{16}$$

With respect to the model parameter w_{old}, $\nabla(li(w_{old}))$ is the gradient of the loss function for the ith device. Applying the update rule iteratively, the FedAvg algorithm minimizes the overall loss function across the devices by converging to a set of model parameters.

6. Illustration of Callback Function and End-Process Mechanism in Federated Learning

Based on the partitioning sample, the strategies that can be adopted to implement FL are Vertical Federated Leaning (VFL), Horizontal Federated Learning (HFL), and Federated Transfer Learning (FTL) [36,37].

(1) VFL: This is a scenario where the sample identities (IDs) are the same, but the sample spaces shared by the datasets are different. There is quite a huge gap in the user–space intersection due to differences in feature space. VFL is also called feature-based FL.

Let S_y, F_y, and L_y denote the yth sample ID space, the yth feature space, and the yth label space, respectively. Consequently, let the data held by each data owner y be represented by the matrix M_y. Then, VFL can be summarized as follows:

$$S_y = S_z, F_y \neq F_z, L_y \neq L_z, \forall M_y, M_z, y \neq z \tag{17}$$

The zth expression is the same as that of the yth.

(2) HFL: In this category, data samples are different but share the same feature space. In this scenario, each device shares an identical feature space, which makes the user–space intersection less significant. HFL represents a real-life scenario, and most FL studies are based on this strategy. HFL can be summarized as follows:

$$S_y \neq S_z, F_y = F_z, L_y = L_z, \forall M_y, M_z, y \neq z \tag{18}$$

(3) FTL: This is a combination of the VFL and HFL strategies, and it is applicable when there are differing data samples and feature spaces of two device datasets. This can be summarized as follows:

$$S_y \neq S_z, F_y \neq F_z, L_y \neq L_z, \forall M_y, M_z, y \neq z \tag{19}$$

The architecture in Figure 4 utilizes a synchronous HFL strategy. The technique is to implement an end-process aggregation, called the deadline aggregation mechanism. This aggregation mechanism is dynamically implemented based on the updates from the fault-tolerant server. When the devices have returned a certain sufficient percentage of post-trained models, the server will implement a callback and issue a force stop to devices yet to return their post-trained models. On the other hand, if this sufficient percentage of the post-trained model, as specified by the FL server, is not yet achieved and a deadline has been reached, a force stop will be issued to the selected devices so that the issue of an infinite loop or endless waiting could be avoided. The assumption made in Figure 4 is to use five devices, but in a real use case scenario, it will involve hundreds of thousands of devices. β_1, β_2, β_3, β_4, and β_5 represent the post-trained models of devices 1, 2, 3, 4, and 5, respectively, while θ_G represents the global model.

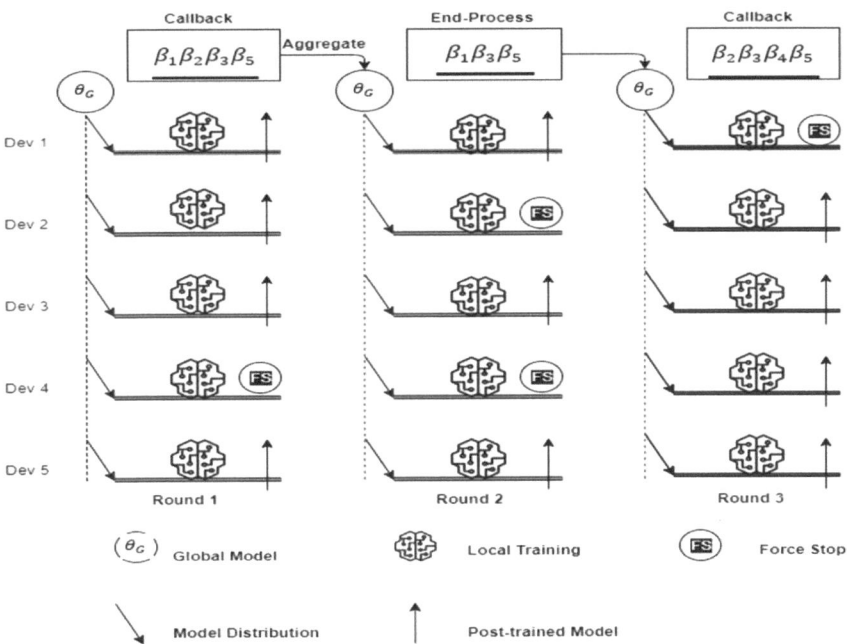

Figure 4. Example of FL model training and aggregation process.

In each round of training, the FL server, through the Blockchain network, sends a global model to all participating devices for local training. In round 1, a callback was initiated because a certain percentage of the post-trained models ($\beta_1\beta_2\beta_3\beta_5$) was returned to the server, and a force stop was issued to the remaining devices yet to return their post-trained models, in this case, device 4. As illustrated in Figure 2 and using (10), the secured aggregated masked post-trained models are unmasked by the aggregator server to produce a new global model used for the next round of training. It is worth noting that only returned post-trained models are needed for unmasking and aggregation. In the second round of training (round 2), a callback was not issued because the percentage of post-trained models, as specified by the server, was not met. At the expiration of the deadline, a force stop is issued to devices yet to return their post-trained models. The returned post-trained models ($\beta_1\beta_3\beta_5$) are unmasked and aggregated to produce a new global model needed for the next round of training. In the third round (round 3), a callback was issued by the server because the percentage of the returned post-trained model was met, and a force stop was issued before the deadline was reached. A new model emerges from the secure aggregation of the returned post-trained models ($\beta_2\beta_3\beta_4\beta_5$) of dev 2, dev 3, dev 4, and dev 5, respectively, as shown in Figure 4. The iteration continues until convergence is reached and a final global model is produced.

7. Results, Discussion, and Performance Evaluation

In this section, we conduct an experiment to demonstrate our proposed framework's performance in model update, secure aggregation, and evaluation of the trained model. This is with respect to the clients and the aggregator server.

7.1. Implementation

The model training was implemented through Python on a Linux operating system using Tensorflow Federated (TFF) libraries. FL training was carried out on a laptop configuration of 8 GB RAM, 500 GB HDD, and 1.3 GHz processor. Using TFF libraries, an FL model was trained on the EMNIST dataset. This dataset was pre-processed by defining a pre-processed function. Pre-processing steps were carried out so that the image pixels and labels could be converted into suitable format for training a keras model. For efficient training, the input data were pre-processed by reshaping the images and labels, batching the data. Using keras, a Convolutional Neural Network (CNN) model was created, which consisted of convolution, pooling, flattening, and dense layers. To enable FL, the model was wrapped with TFF.

The FedAVG process was built, specifying the model function, server, and client optimizers. The training state was initialized, and the training process was executed in multiple rounds. The model was trained repeatedly using data from various clients in a federated manner. During each round of training, the progress was monitored, and metrics such as accuracy and loss were analysed. This process continued until sufficient post-trained models (desired accuracy threshold was achieved) were returned to the server, or the maximum number of rounds was reached. After the training process, the model was evaluated on the test dataset, the test data were batched, and the accuracy was computed. Finally, the training progress was visualized by plotting the accuracy against the number of rounds and the accuracy against loss.

To achieve better convergence, we implemented a learning rate scheduler that decreased the learning rate (lr) over iterations. We achieved speedy convergence by implementing an exponential decay learning rate scheduler. Furthermore, the feedback loop of our framework enhanced speedy convergence and reduced communication cost. The exponential decay learning rate formular is as follows:

$$decayed\_lr = (init\_lr) \times (decay\_rate)^{step/decay\_steps} \qquad (20)$$

where:

$decayed\_lr$: exponential decay learning rate.
$init\_lr$: the starting learning rate.
$decay\_rate$: the base of the exponential function.
$step$: the current round of FL training.
$decay\_steps$: the decay step.

7.2. Results

In Figure 5, we can see a graph that displays the accuracy of the model versus the number of training rounds. As the training continues, the accuracy of the model changes, providing valuable information on how well the model performs for a specific task. A closer look at the graph will identify the trend in the accuracy improvement over time. This gives an understanding of whether the model is converging or if further training is required. To hasten model convergence and avoid an infinite loop or endless waiting, a callback was initiated once enough post-trained models (desired accuracy threshold) had been returned to the server. In this case, 75% accuracy was achieved. Considering the unreliable nature of IoT (stragglers and drop-offs) and to reduce the communication cost, callback at a 75% accuracy threshold (three quarter of the clients) will guarantee a good model and could be a good feat within a resource-constrained setting.

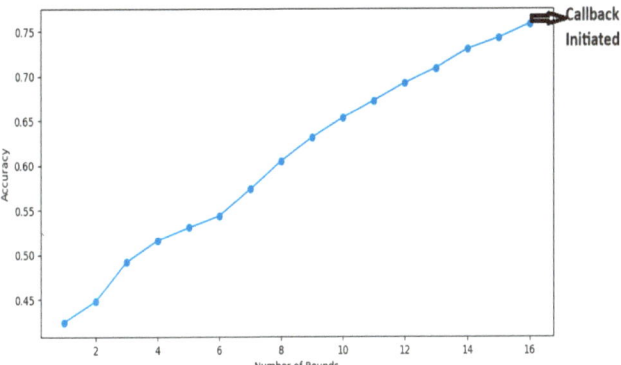

Figure 5. A plot of accuracy and number of rounds.

Figure 6 shows the relationship between the accuracy of the model and loss during the training process. The accuracy indicates how well the model is performing, while the loss indicates the ability of the model to minimize prediction loss. Using the graph, an analysis of the trade-off between accuracy and loss can be achieved. With every iteration, the model learns, and the loss should decrease, leading to improved accuracy. By a closer examination of the graph, we can identify patterns, such as decreasing loss accompanying increasing accuracy. From Figure 6, the model performance can be assessed, and it will also assist in finding an optimal balance between accuracy and loss.

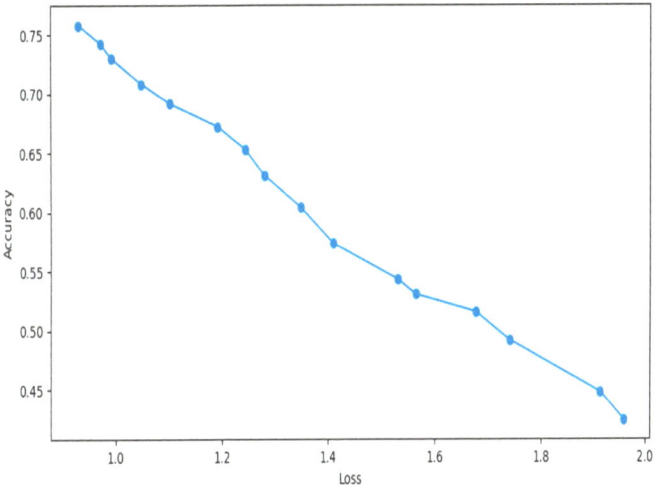

Figure 6. A plot of accuracy and loss to access the model performance at every iteration.

7.3. Comparison

Here, we compare our scheme with several existing related schemes in terms of secure aggregation and model performance. Table 1 gives a functional comparative evaluation of our scheme and previous schemes from the following viewpoints: the ability to handle dropouts, computational complexity, scalability, and communication cost. It can be observed that our scheme successfully achieved all functionalities.

Table 1. A comparative evaluation of our scheme and previous schemes.

Schemes	Handle Dropouts	Computational Complexity	Scalable	Communication Cost
[7]	YES	NO	NO	Low
[15]	YES	NO	NO	Low
[16]	NO	YES	NO	Low
[17]	NO	NO	NO	High
[21]	NO	YES	NO	High
[24]	NO	YES	NO	High
[25]	NO	YES	NO	High
OURS	YES	NO	YES	Low

In handling stragglers and dropouts, the client situation updates are communicated to the fault-tolerant server in a privacy-preserved manner for each round of training. These updates are used within the network to estimate the training time and make decisions on when to end the training process of each round to avoid an infinite loop. These updates will assist in deciding on the number of clients to select for each round of training. If there are more dropouts in each round, the tendency to achieve an accuracy threshold (initiating callback) will be low. The aggregator server uses these updates to set an end-process time if a callback is not yet initiated.

As shown in Figure 7, the computational cost is a measure of the time it takes for each training round. It is a measure of the difference between the start and end times of the training process for each round. The computational complexity of our scheme is not high because the aggregation of the returned trained models is carried out using the aggregator server rather than the Blockchain network. The computational complexity associated with aggregating each round of the training using the Blockchain is eliminated. Here, we retain the central server's ability to aggregate returned trained models to eliminate the complexity associated with aggregation using the Blockchain network. Figure 7 shows the performance of our scheme in terms of communication round complexity in seconds, and it needs just two rounds of communication. The first one is the clients sending their model updates to the aggregator server for aggregation, while the second is sending their status update to the fault-tolerant server for managing dropouts and stragglers. Our communication round can only be compared to Ref. [7], which made use of two communication rounds.

Figures 8 and 9 illustrate the scalability tests of accuracy and loss, respectively. They show various curves that represent the accuracy and loss of models trained with varying number of clients, such as 50, 100, 150, 200, and 250 clients. Across training rounds, the accuracy and loss metrics change when there is variation in the number of clients available for training. After several training rounds and across all client counts, the accuracy generally increases and stabilizes, while the loss decreases. The early training rounds of both figures indicate a period of rapid correction or adjustment according to Equation (20) in the FL process before stabilization. This correction or adjustment is also based on the feedback loop of our architectural framework. From a careful observation of our architectural framework and previous schemes in Table 1, it appears that only our scheme has a feedback loop after every communication round. The feedback loop of our framework provides the status update and performance of the clients in a privacy-preserved manner. This gives an overview of the training process and ensures that more clients are introduced in the next round of training when there are more stragglers and dropouts in the preceding round. Across different numbers of clients in both figures, the variability in curves does not show drastic differences. Rather, it indicates that the model is relatively stable despite an increase in the number of clients. An increase in the number of clients did not result in a dramatic decrease in accuracy or a considerable increase in loss. Consequently, when the number of clients is increased, the accuracy and loss seem to stabilize. The accuracy curves indicate that the training stability converged as the number of clients increases; it remained stable until the desired accuracy was attained or callback was implemented. Our framework shows positive scalability traits across varying client distributions. This indicates that our framework is capable of handling more clients without degradation in performance.

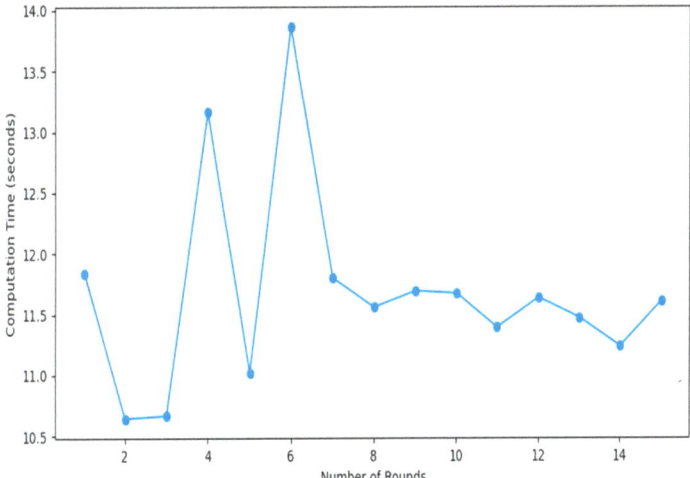

Figure 7. Computational cost of model updates performed in each round.

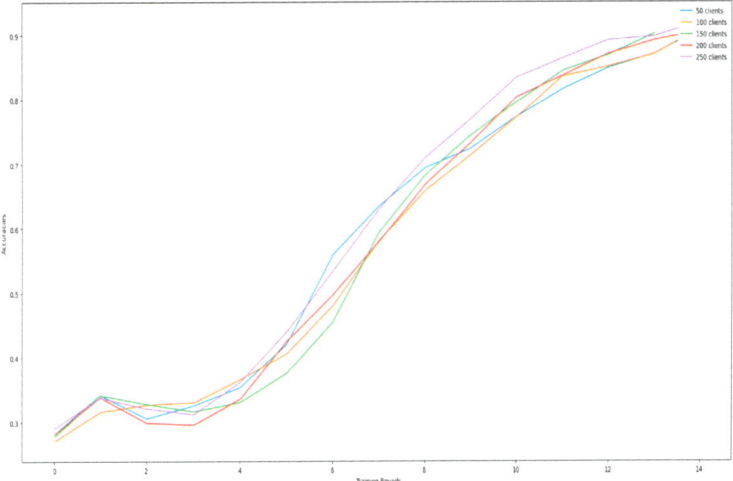

Figure 8. Scalability test of accuracy.

In a scalability assessment that considers factors such as fault tolerance and secure aggregation strategies, our scheme's architectural framework (Figure 3) indicates that secure aggregation could be carried out using the aggregator (central) server or fault-tolerant server. It could also be reconfigured to use the Blockchain network for aggregation. This distinguishes our scheme from previous schemes in terms of fault tolerance and secure aggregation strategies. The constant communication between the aggregator server and Blockchain network ensures that the latest updates are stored in the Blockchain network. Therefore, the abrupt failure of the aggregator server will not lead to a total collapse of the training process because the Blockchain network or fault-tolerant server could continue orchestrating the training process from the point of a sudden or unforeseen breakdown of the aggregator server. Our framework prevents the loss of training time and wastage of resources due to the unexpected failure of the central server.

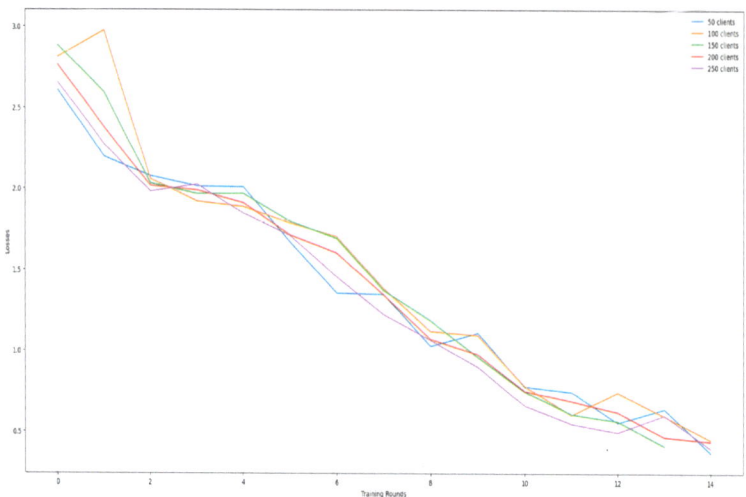

Figure 9. Scalability test of loss.

Finally, our scheme's trust, transparency, and privacy-preservation mechanism enable adequate participation in the model training. With more active clients participating in the model training, speedy convergence of the global model is achieved, the number of iterations (training time) is reduced, and communication costs are low because of callback or the end-process mechanism of aggregation.

8. Conclusions

In this article, a secured Blockchain-based aggregation mechanism using FL has been proposed. The model utilizes Blockchain technology as a means of masking local data of end devices within an FL framework to avoid the reconstruction of local data by a malicious server. Blockchain as a distributed ledger offers an immutable data structure, enhanced security, faster settlement in payment systems, and a consensus protocol. Blockchain provides a unique system of accumulating data in a chronological and privacy-preserved manner because the greatest resource of any organization is data. Using Blockchain, the model tends to solve the threat of SPOF, ensures the privacy preservation of end devices' local data, eliminates the issues of vulnerability, and ensures trust, transparency, fairness, and security. The callback or end-process mechanism eliminates the need for endless waiting that could arise because of the issue of stragglers and dropouts, which is evident in the FL scenario. The secure aggregation mechanism of the masked models using a callback function/end-process technique ensures that only returned post-trained models are needed for aggregation. This mechanism prevents the problem of complicated handling of local masked models of stragglers and dropouts by the FL server during aggregation to produce a global model. The framework enables immutable, efficient, transparent, and secure communication between the FL server and devices within the federated network. The limitation of Blockchain technology, as observed in most research, is the computational complexity in maintaining security and privacy preservation when there is increase in the network. With this technique, the computational complexity is greatly reduced because the Blockchain network does not perform aggregation; rather, the aggregator server aggregates the returned post-trained model. Finally, only returned post-trained models are needed for aggregation, which benefits resource-constrained IoT devices.

Author Contributions: Writing—original draft, W.E.M.; Writing—review & editing, C.M. and G.E.; Supervision, C.M. and G.E. All authors have read and agreed to the published version of the manuscript.

Funding: EP/R007195/1 (Academic Centre of Excellence in Cyber Security Research—University of Warwick); EP/N510129/1 (The Alan Turing Institute); and EP/S035362/1 (PETRAS National Centre of Excellence for IoT Systems Cybersecurity).

Data Availability Statement: Data available on request.

Acknowledgments: This work has been supported by UKRI through the grants: Academic Centre of Excellence in Cyber Security Research—University of Warwick (EP/R007195/1), The Alan Turing Institute (EP/N510129/1), and PETRAS National Centre of Excellence for IoT Systems Cybersecurity (EP/S035362/1). We also acknowledge the constructive criticisms, feedback, and suggestions from the reviewers, which have improved the manuscript. We are also grateful to colleagues whose expertise, insights, and suggestions shaped this work.

Conflicts of Interest: The authors declare no conflict of interest.

References

1. Hussain, G.K.J.; Manoj, G. Federated Learning: A Survey of a New Approach to Machine Learning. In Proceedings of the 2022 1st International Conference on Electrical, Electronics, Information and Communication Technologies, ICEEICT 2022, Trichy, India, 16–18 February 2022; Institute of Electrical and Electronics Engineers Inc.: New York, NY, USA, 2022. [CrossRef]
2. Abdulrahman, S.; Tout, H.; Ould-Slimane, H.; Mourad, A.; Talhi, C.; Guizani, M. A survey on federated learning: The journey from centralized to distributed on-site learning and beyond. *IEEE Internet Things J.* **2021**, *8*, 5476–5497. [CrossRef]
3. Wang, S.; Sahay, R.; Brinton, C.G. How Potent Are Evasion Attacks for Poisoning Federated Learning-Based Signal Classifiers? 2023. Available online: http://arxiv.org/abs/2301.08866 (accessed on 22 July 2023).
4. Rahman, K.M.J.; Ahmed, F.; Akhter, N.; Hasan, M.; Amin, R.; Aziz, K.E.; Islam, A.K.M.M.; Mukta, S.H. Challenges, Applications and Design Aspects of Federated Learning: A Survey. *IEEE Access* **2021**, *9*, 124682–124700. [CrossRef]
5. Chen, H.; Asif, S.A.; Park, J.; Shen, C.-C.; Bennis, M. Robust Blockchained Federated Learning with Model Validation and Proof-of-Stake Inspired Consensus. 2021. Available online: www.aaai.org (accessed on 22 July 2023).
6. Bhatia, L.; Samet, S. Decentralized Federated Learning: A Comprehensive Survey and a New Blockchain-based Data Evaluation Scheme. In Proceedings of the 2022 4th International Conference on Blockchain Computing and Applications, BCCA 2022, San Antonio, TX, USA, 5–7 September 2022; Institute of Electrical and Electronics Engineers Inc.: New York, NY, USA, 2022; pp. 289–296. [CrossRef]
7. Huang, C.; Yao, Y.; Zhang, X.; Teng, D.; Wang, Y.; Zhou, L. Robust Secure Aggregation with Lightweight Verification for Federated Learning. In Proceedings of the 2022 IEEE 21st International Conference on Trust, Security and Privacy in Computing and Communications, TrustCom 2022, Wuhan, China, 9–11 December 2022; Institute of Electrical and Electronics Engineers Inc.: New York, NY, USA, 2022; pp. 582–589. [CrossRef]
8. Liu, P.; Xu, X.; Wang, W. Threats, attacks and defenses to federated learning: Issues, taxonomy and perspectives. *Cybersecurity* **2022**, *5*, 4. [CrossRef]
9. Li, D.; Han, D.; Weng, T.-H.; Zheng, Z.; Li, H.; Liu, H.; Castiglione, A.; Li, K.-C. Blockchain for federated learning toward secure distributed machine learning systems: A systemic survey. *Soft Comput.* **2022**, *26*, 4423–4440. [CrossRef] [PubMed]
10. Salim, S.; Turnbull, B.; Moustafa, N. A Blockchain-Enabled Explainable Federated Learning for Securing Internet-of-Things-Based Social Media 3.0 Networks. *IEEE Trans. Comput. Soc. Syst.* **2021**, 1–17. [CrossRef]
11. Manvith, V.S.; Saraswathi, R.V.; Vasavi, R. A performance comparison of machine learning approaches on intrusion detection dataset. In Proceedings of the 3rd International Conference on Intelligent Communication Technologies and Virtual Mobile Networks, ICICV 2021, Tirunelveli, India, 4–6 February 2021; Institute of Electrical and Electronics Engineers Inc.: New York, NY, USA, 2021; pp. 782–788. [CrossRef]
12. Qu, Y.; Pokhrel, S.R.; Garg, S.; Gao, L.; Xiang, Y. A Blockchained Federated Learning Framework for Cognitive Computing in Industry 4.0 Networks. *IEEE Trans. Ind. Inform.* **2021**, *17*, 2964–2973. [CrossRef]
13. Passerat-Palmbach, J.; Farnan, T.; McCoy, M.; Harris, J.D.; Manion, S.T.; Flannery, H.L.; Gleim, B. Blockchain-orchestrated machine learning for privacy preserving federated learning in electronic health data. In Proceedings of the 2020 IEEE International Conference on Blockchain, Blockchain 2020, Rhodes, Greece, 2–6 November 2020; Institute of Electrical and Electronics Engineers Inc.: New York, NY, USA, 2020; pp. 550–555. [CrossRef]
14. Ullah, I.; Deng, X.; Pei, X.; Jiang, P.; Mushtaq, H. A verifiable and privacy-preserving blockchain-based federated learning approach. *Peer Peer Netw. Appl.* **2023**, *16*, 2256–2270. [CrossRef]
15. Fereidooni, H.; Marchal, S.; Miettinen, M.; Mirhoseini, A.; Mollering, H.; Nguyen, T.D.; Rieger, P.; Sadeghi, A.-R.; Schneider, T.; Yalame, H.; et al. SAFELearn: Secure Aggregation for private FEderated Learning. In Proceedings of the 2021 IEEE Symposium on Security and Privacy Workshops, SPW 2021, San Francisco, CA, USA, 27 May 2021; Institute of Electrical and Electronics Engineers Inc.: New York, NY, USA, 2021; pp. 56–62. [CrossRef]

16. Wu, D.; Pan, M.; Xu, Z.; Zhang, Y.; Han, Z. Towards Efficient Secure Aggregation for Model Update in Federated Learning. In Proceedings of the 2020 IEEE Global Communications Conference, GLOBECOM 2020—Proceedings, Taipei, Taiwan, 7–11 December 2020; Institute of Electrical and Electronics Engineers Inc.: New York, NY, USA, 2020. [CrossRef]
17. Zhao, L.; Jiang, J.; Feng, B.; Wang, Q.; Shen, C.; Li, Q. SEAR: Secure and Efficient Aggregation for Byzantine-Robust Federated Learning. *IEEE Trans. Dependable Secur. Comput.* **2022**, *19*, 3329–3342. [CrossRef]
18. Pokhrel, S.R.; Choi, J. Federated Learning with Blockchain for Autonomous Vehicles: Analysis and Design Challenges. *IEEE Trans. Commun.* **2020**, *68*, 4734–4746. [CrossRef]
19. Guo, X. Implementation of a Blockchain-enabled Federated Learning Model that Supports Security and Privacy Comparisons. In Proceedings of the 2022 IEEE 5th International Conference on Information Systems and Computer Aided Education, ICISCAE 2022, Dalian, China, 23–25 September 2022; Institute of Electrical and Electronics Engineers Inc.: New York, NY, USA, 2022; pp. 243–247. [CrossRef]
20. Zhang, P.; Liu, G.; Chen, Z.; Guo, J.; Liu, P. A study of a federated learning framework based on the interstellar file system and blockchain: Private Blockchain Federated Learning. In Proceedings of the 2022 3rd International Conference on Computer Vision, Image and Deep Learning and International Conference on Computer Engineering and Applications, CVIDL and ICCEA 2022, Changchun, China, 20–22 May 2022; Institute of Electrical and Electronics Engineers Inc.: New York, NY, USA, 2022; pp. 267–273. [CrossRef]
21. Zhang, Q.; Palacharla, P.; Sekiya, M.; Suga, J.; Katagiri, T. Blockchain-based Secure Aggregation for Federated Learning with a Traffic Prediction Use Case. In Proceedings of the 2021 IEEE Conference on Network Softwarization: Accelerating Network Softwarization in the Cognitive Age, NetSoft 2021, Tokyo, Japan, 28 June–2 July 2021; Institute of Electrical and Electronics Engineers Inc.: New York, NY, USA, 2021; pp. 372–374. [CrossRef]
22. Sun, Y.; Esaki, H.; Ochiai, H. Blockchain-Based Federated Learning against End-Point Adversarial Data Corruption. In Proceedings of the 19th IEEE International Conference on Machine Learning and Applications, ICMLA 2020, Miami, FL, USA, 14–17 December 2020; Institute of Electrical and Electronics Engineers Inc.: New York, NY, USA, 2020; pp. 729–734. [CrossRef]
23. Al Mallah, R.; López, D.; Halabi, T. Blockchain-enabled Efficient and Secure Federated Learning in IoT and Edge Computing Networks. In Proceedings of the 2023 International Conference on Computing, Networking and Communications, ICNC 2023, Honolulu, HI, USA, 20–22 February 2023; Institute of Electrical and Electronics Engineers Inc.: New York, NY, USA, 2023; pp. 511–515. [CrossRef]
24. Kalapaaking, A.P.; Khalil, I.; Rahman, M.S.; Atiquzzaman, M.; Yi, X.; Almashor, M. Blockchain-based Federated Learning with Secure Aggregation in Trusted Execution Environment for Internet-of-Things. *IEEE Trans. Ind. Inform.* **2023**, *19*, 1703–1714. [CrossRef]
25. Chen, Y.; Lin, F.; Chen, Z.; Tang, C.; Jia, R.; Li, M. Blockchain-based Federated Learning with Contribution-Weighted Aggregation for Medical Data Modeling. In Proceedings of the 2022 IEEE 19th International Conference on Mobile Ad Hoc and Smart Systems, MASS 2022, Denver, CO, USA, 19–23 October 2022; Institute of Electrical and Electronics Engineers Inc.: New York, NY, USA, 2022; pp. 606–612. [CrossRef]
26. Li, Y.; Chen, C.; Liu, N.; Huang, H.; Zheng, Z.; Yan, Q. A Blockchain-Based Decentralized Federated Learning Framework with Committee Consensus. *IEEE Netw.* **2021**, *35*, 234–241. [CrossRef]
27. Miao, Y.; Liu, Z.; Li, H.; Choo, K.K.R.; Deng, R.H. Privacy-Preserving Byzantine-Robust Federated Learning via Blockchain Systems. *IEEE Trans. Inf. Forensics Secur.* **2022**, *17*, 2848–2861. [CrossRef]
28. Adhikari, N.; Ramkumar, M. IoT and Blockchain Integration: Applications, Opportunities, and Challenges. *Network* **2023**, *3*, 115–141. [CrossRef]
29. Zhang, C.; Xu, Y.; Hu, Y.; Wu, J.; Ren, J.; Zhang, Y. A Blockchain-Based Multi-Cloud Storage Data Auditing Scheme to Locate Faults. *IEEE Trans. Cloud Comput.* **2022**, *10*, 2252–2263. [CrossRef]
30. Li, C.; Yuan, Y.; Wang, F.Y. Blockchain-enabled federated learning: A survey. In Proceedings of the 2021 IEEE 1st International Conference on Digital Twins and Parallel Intelligence, DTPI 2021, Beijing, China, 15 July–15 August 2021; Institute of Electrical and Electronics Engineers Inc.: New York, NY, USA, 2021; pp. 286–289. [CrossRef]
31. Christina, K.; Kesavamoorthy, R. Evolution of Blockchain and Smart Contracts: A State of the Art Review. In Proceedings of the 2023 International Conference on Intelligent Systems for Communication, IoT and Security, ICISCoIS 2023, Coimbatore, India, 9–11 February 2023; Institute of Electrical and Electronics Engineers Inc.: New York, NY, USA, 2023; pp. 235–240. [CrossRef]
32. Xu, Y.; Zhang, C.; Zeng, Q.; Wang, G.; Ren, J.; Zhang, Y. Blockchain-Enabled Accountability Mechanism against Information Leakage in Vertical Industry Services. *IEEE Trans. Netw. Sci. Eng.* **2021**, *8*, 1202–1213. [CrossRef]
33. Sadath, L.; Mehrotra, D.; Kumar, A. Scalability in Blockchain—Hyperledger Fabric and Hierarchical Model. In Proceedings of the 2022 IEEE Global Conference on Computing, Power and Communication Technologies, GlobConPT 2022, New Delhi, India, 23–25 September 2022; Institute of Electrical and Electronics Engineers Inc.: New York, NY, USA, 2022. [CrossRef]
34. Le, H.T.; Nguyen, T.T.L.; Nguyen, T.A.; Ha, X.S.; Duong-Trung, N. BloodChain: A Blood Donation Network Managed by Blockchain Technologies. *Network* **2022**, *2*, 21–35. [CrossRef]
35. Ahmed, M.R.; Meenakshi, K.; Obaidat, M.S.; Amin, R.; Vijayakumar, P. Blockchain Based Architecture and Solution for Secure Digital Payment System. In Proceedings of the IEEE International Conference on Communications, Montreal, QC, Canada, 14–23 June 2021; Institute of Electrical and Electronics Engineers Inc.: New York, NY, USA, 2021. [CrossRef]

36. Imteaj, A.; Thakker, U.; Wang, S.; Li, J.; Amini, M.H. A Survey on Federated Learning for Resource-Constrained IoT Devices. *IEEE Internet Things J.* **2022**, *9*, 1–24. [CrossRef]
37. Jia, B.; Zhang, X.; Liu, J.; Zhang, Y.; Huang, K.; Liang, Y. Blockchain-Enabled Federated Learning Data Protection Aggregation Scheme With Differential Privacy and Homomorphic Encryption in IIoT. *IEEE Trans. Ind. Inform.* **2022**, *18*, 4049–4058. [CrossRef]

Disclaimer/Publisher's Note: The statements, opinions and data contained in all publications are solely those of the individual author(s) and contributor(s) and not of MDPI and/or the editor(s). MDPI and/or the editor(s) disclaim responsibility for any injury to people or property resulting from any ideas, methods, instructions or products referred to in the content.

Article

Augmenting Vehicular Ad Hoc Network Security and Efficiency with Blockchain: A Probabilistic Identification and Malicious Node Mitigation Strategy

Rubén Juárez and Borja Bordel *

Department of Informatics Systems, Universidad Politécnica de Madrid, 28031 Madrid, Spain; ruben.juarez@alumnos.upm.es
* Correspondence: borja.bordel@upm.es; Tel.:+34-910673699

Abstract: This manuscript delineates the development of an avant garde dual-layer blockchain architecture, which has been meticulously engineered to augment the security and operational efficacy of vehicular ad hoc networks (VANETs). VANETs, which are integral to the infrastructure of intelligent transport systems, facilitate the critical exchange of information between vehicular nodes. Despite their significance, these networks confront an array of formidable security vulnerabilities. Our innovative approach, employing a dual blockchain framework—the event chain and the reputation chain—meticulously tracks network activities, thereby significantly enhancing the trustworthiness and integrity of the system. This research presents a transformative dual-layer blockchain architecture, which was conceived to address the intricate security challenges pervasive in VANETs. The architecture pivots on a sophisticated reputation assessment framework, thus leveraging the principles of Bayesian inference and the analytical rigor of historical data to markedly diminish observational errors, as well as elevate the accuracy of reputation evaluations for vehicular nodes. A salient feature of our methodology is the implementation of an attenuation factor, which has been deftly calibrated to modulate the impact of historical behaviors on current reputation scores, thereby ensuring their relevance and alignment with recent vehicular interactions. Additionally, the numerical threshold serves as an indispensable mechanism, thus establishing a definitive criterion for the early identification of potentially malicious activities and enabling the activation of proactive security measures to safeguard the network's integrity. Empirical validation of our dual-layer blockchain model has yielded a remarkable 86% efficacy in counteracting malevolent behaviors, thus significantly outperforming extant paradigms. These empirical outcomes underscore the model's potential as a vanguard in the domain of secure and efficient reputation management within VANETs, thereby heralding a substantial advancement in the sphere of intelligent transportation systems.

Keywords: vehicular ad hoc networks (VANETs); blockchain; probabilistic identification; network threat mitigation; reputation assessment; network efficiency; connected vehicle security

Citation: Juárez, R.; Bordel, B. Augmenting Vehicular Ad Hoc Network Security and Efficiency with Blockchain: A Probabilistic Identification and Malicious Node Mitigation Strategy. *Electronics* **2023**, *12*, 4794. https://doi.org/10.3390/electronics12234794

Academic Editors: Mikolaj Karpinski, Oleksandr O. Kuznetsov and Roman Oliynykov

Received: 1 October 2023
Revised: 21 November 2023
Accepted: 25 November 2023
Published: 27 November 2023

Copyright: © 2023 by the authors. Licensee MDPI, Basel, Switzerland. This article is an open access article distributed under the terms and conditions of the Creative Commons Attribution (CC BY) license (https://creativecommons.org/licenses/by/4.0/).

1. Introduction

The Internet of Vehicles (IoVs) represents an emerging application scenario for Internet of Things (IoTs) technology. At the heart of this technological evolution are vehicular ad hoc networks (VANETs), which facilitate communication between vehicles and between vehicles and infrastructures, thus constituting a key subset of the IoVs. VANETs have emerged as one of the most exciting research fields within intelligent transport systems, thereby providing safety and convenience information for drivers [1]. These networks can communicate the complex and dynamic data generated by vehicles, humans, and the environment in real time, such as traffic conditions, traffic accidents, road construction, and congestion. However, VANETs are especially vulnerable to a variety of security threats, including malicious attacks and the distribution of unreliable information, which can have severe consequences, such as traffic accidents.

Additionally, the distinct characteristics of VANETs introduce significant challenges in terms of security management, privacy, and reliability in their design [2,3]. So, creating an efficient anonymous authentication system with low computational cost [4] in a vehicular ad hoc network (VANET) represents a considerable challenge [5].

Specifically, in the realm of vehicular ad hoc networks (VANETs), the development of an efficient anonymous authentication system that maintains low computational costs poses significant challenges due to several intrinsic characteristics of these networks:

1. High Vehicle Mobility: The highly dynamic nature of VANETs, which are characterized by vehicles moving at high speeds, results in frequent changes in network nodes. This demands an authentication system that is capable of rapidly adapting to changes in network topology without compromising on security or performance.
2. Resource Limitations in Vehicles: Despite being equipped with advanced technologies, modern vehicles still face limitations in terms of processing power and storage capacity. An efficient authentication system must operate within these resource constraints, thereby ensuring light computational loads.
3. Anonymity and Privacy Needs: Given the sensitive nature of vehicular data, such as location and movement patterns, ensuring user anonymity and privacy is paramount. Achieving this without significantly increasing the computational burden adds complexity to system design.
4. Diversity and Scalability: VANETs support a wide array of applications, from road safety to infotainment services, each with its unique security requirements. The authentication system must be versatile enough to cater to these diverse needs and scalable to handle the increasing number of connected vehicles.
5. Resistance to Attacks and Frauds: Authentication systems in VANETs must be robust against various security threats, including impersonation attacks, Sybil attacks, and data manipulation. Designing a system that can effectively counter these threats without imposing excessive computational demands is a significant challenge.

For these reasons, developing an efficient and low-cost computational anonymous authentication system for VANETs is not only crucial for ensuring security and privacy within these networks, but also poses substantial technical challenges. Our research aims to address these challenges through an innovative approach that balances security, efficiency, and practicality.

On the other hand, the incorporation of blockchain technology in VANETs presents a paradigm shift from traditional centralized systems to a more resilient, transparent, and decentralized framework. The blockchain, known for its immutable and secure ledger, is leveraged to enhance the tracking and verification of vehicular movements and interactions. This technology has shown promise in mitigating the inherent vulnerabilities of VANETs, thereby providing a robust platform for secure vehicular communication.

With the growing adoption of blockchain technology across various sectors, including transportation [6], this technology has also shown promise in resolving the challenges within VANETs. Blockchain technology provides a decentralized, secure, and trustworthy database maintained by network nodes [7,8]. In this way, it can be used to track, organize, and verify interactions among vehicles in the network.

In addition, blockchain technology can be also employed for securization purposes.

Cybersecurity threats to vehicular ad hoc networks (VANETs) have escalated in recent years, primarily due to their critical role in managing sensitive vehicular data [9]. The conventional centralized systems, typically operated by vehicle service providers, have demonstrated several security shortcomings. These systems often fail to offer the robust defense mechanisms necessary to protect against sophisticated cyberthreats, thus resulting in notable vulnerabilities within vehicular networks [10].

Additionally, the proliferation of wireless connected devices has exponentially increased the complexity of ensuring secure vehicular communications [11]. The intricate web of data exchange within VANETs demands a security solution that transcends the capabilities of traditional centralized systems. Herein lies the potential of blockchain technology—it offers a decentralized approach that inherently enhances the security, performance, and scalability of VANETs [12].

Blockchain technology's application in VANETs extends beyond mere communication security [13,14]. It revolutionizes the entire ecosystem by enabling immutable record-keeping for vehicular history, thereby ensuring data integrity and fostering a transparent environment for data exchange. This immutable nature of blockchain technology is particularly pivotal, as it ensures that once vehicle data are recorded on the ledger, they cannot be altered or tampered with, thereby instilling trust in the vehicular data records [15].

In most prior approaches, vehicle security in VANETs was accomplished each time it entered the territory of a roadside unit (RSU). Relying solely on a single RSU presents a multitude of challenges. Firstly, it can become a performance bottleneck, especially in high-density areas where numerous vehicles might be entering or exiting simultaneously, thereby leading to latency in certification processes. Secondly, a solitary RSU becomes a single point of failure; if it malfunctions or becomes compromised, it can disrupt the certification of all the vehicles under its jurisdiction. This can also lead to potential security vulnerabilities, where malicious entities might target the RSU to either gain unauthorized access or to disrupt normal operations. Furthermore, there is an inherent lack of redundancy, meaning that if one RSU is down or is facing technical glitches, there is not an immediate backup system in place to continue the vehicle certification.

Integrating blockchain technology can alleviate some of these concerns [16,17]. The decentralized nature of the blockchain ensures that no single point of failure exists, thereby enhancing the robustness and resilience of the system [18]. Every transaction, in this case, vehicle certifications, can be recorded on the blockchain, thus making the data tamper-proof and ensuring its integrity. Moreover, the blockchain's consensus mechanisms can be leveraged to validate vehicle entries, thereby reducing the burden on a single RSU and distributing the task across multiple nodes or participants in the network. This not only streamlines the certification process, but also introduces an added layer of security, thus making it exceedingly difficult for malicious actors to compromise the system.

In other words, the transition from traditional centralized systems to blockchain-based solutions equips VANETs with enhanced resilience against data breaches and unauthorized access. The decentralized nature of the blockchain mitigates the risk of single points of failure, which are inherent in centralized systems. Moreover, the blockchain empowers all network participants to engage in the maintenance of the ledger, thereby promoting a transparent and tamper-proof ecosystem [19].

In essence, the blockchain stands as a vanguard technology that propels VANETs into a new era of security and reliability. It ensures that vehicular communications are not only secure, but that they also conducted within a framework that is inherently resistant to cyber attacks. By integrating blockchain solutions, VANETs evolve into more resilient, transparent, and decentralized networks that are capable of withstanding the escalating threats in today's cybersecurity landscape [20].

In this context, this paper proposes a security architecture for the VANET using blockchain technology. Traditional security solutions, such as public key infrastructure (PKI), have limitations when applied to the VANET, particularly due to the high mobility and short-term connectivity of the network. Previous reputation management models have attempted to address these challenges but have faced unresolved issues [21].

In addition, although VANETs can benefit from Internet of Things (IoTs) technologies to communicate connected remote devices [22], the diversity of formats, resolutions, information sources, and mediums in VANETs makes interactions in these networks a complex task [23].

The use of blockchain technology not only maintains the security and accountability of vehicle interactions, but also facilitates the tracking of vehicle position and movements. Our solution aims to improve the capacity for successfully detecting attacks against the VANET and attacks from malicious nodes, thereby ensuring both efficient and secure vehicular communications. Our solution aims to increase the success rate in detecting attacks against the VANET and attacks from malicious nodes. Specifically, this architecture generates secure hashes for each vehicular interaction and allows for the verification of these by each node in the network, thereby minimizing the possibility of illegal activities within the VANET system.

Our paper presents several key contributions that collectively address the critical issues surrounding vehicular ad hoc networks (VANETs). These contributions introduce advancements in multiple domains within the VANET ecosystem. Specifically, they include the following:

- Architecture of Security for VANET: Our proposed architecture leverages blockchain technology to significantly enhance the security of VANET systems. It provides a robust framework for secure and reliable communication among vehicles.
- Generation of Secure Hashes for Vehicular Interactions: We introduce a novel method for generating secure hashes for each vehicular interaction. This method ensures the integrity and authenticity of the interactions, thereby contributing to a safer and more reliable network.
- Network-Wide Verification and Mitigation of Illegal Activities: Our architecture enables each node in the VANET network to verify the interactions through the generated hashes. This decentralized verification process bolsters the overall security of the system, thereby effectively minimizing the potential for illegal activities.

And these advances have different practical implications in real-life scenarios. For example, they include the following:

- Enhanced Security: The architecture significantly elevates the security level in VANETs by leveraging a dual-layer blockchain approach, thereby ensuring the authenticity and integrity of vehicular communications, which is critical for applications like emergency response and traffic management.
- Improved Efficiency: By reducing the observation errors in reputation assessment [24], the system enhances the overall network efficiency, which is crucial for real-time applications such as collision avoidance systems and dynamic traffic light control.
- Scalability: The architecture is designed to be scalable, thus making it capable of accommodating the growing number of connected vehicles and diverse data transactions within VANETs, thereby making it suitable for the expanding scope of smart city projects.

Together, these contributions form a comprehensive solution that addresses the ongoing challenges related to security, privacy, and reliability in VANETs.

Going forward, the rest of this document is organized as follows:

- Section 2 provides a critique of the current solutions and underscores their limitations. This section delves into the myriad of security challenges in VANETs, thereby elucidating the predominant types of attacks that these networks are susceptible to. Additionally, it explores a range of proposed security measures designed to mitigate such attacks, thus presenting an insightful overview of the security landscape in VANETs [25]. In addition, this section offers a detailed taxonomy of the security solutions tailored for VANETs, thereby dissecting various types of security measures that have been proposed. It thoroughly evaluates the advantages and drawbacks of these solutions, thereby providing an extensive guide for researchers and practitioners in the field [26]. These mechanisms include various trust management methods in VANETs, thus elucidating their respective strengths and weaknesses and offering a balanced perspective on the topic [27].
- Section 3 dives into our proposed system, thus offering a detailed overview of the algorithm, methodology, and its unique benefits. It discusses the shortcomings of the existing systems and demonstrates how our proposal effectively addresses them.
- Section 4 provides a comprehensive evaluation of our prototype, thus examining its performance and scalability metrics.

- Section 5 concludes the paper by recapping the key contributions and exploring potential directions for future research.

2. Related Work

In this section (Section 2.1), we analyze the state of the art with respect to blockchain solutions for VANETs, trust models for vehicle nodes and networks, and the most critical and dangerous cyber attacks and their potential mitigation strategies. Later, in Section 2.2, the benefits, improvements, and advantages achieved by the proposed technology are discussed.

2.1. Blockchain Solutions for VANETs, Trust Models, Cyber Attacks, and Mitigation Strategies

Vehicular ad hoc networks (VANETs) are a specific form of mobile ad hoc networks (MANETs) that connect vehicles on the move. The main goal of VANETs is to provide road safety, traffic management, and various infotainment services. Due to the critical nature of these services, data security, privacy, and reliable communication are of paramount importance. However, the highly dynamic and distributed nature of VANETs presents unique challenges to maintaining these aspects. Traditional security measures are often inadequate due to the absence of a fixed infrastructure, high mobility, and the heterogeneous environment in VANETs [28].

Vehicular ad hoc networks (VANETs) are highly susceptible to various forms of attacks [29], including denial-of-service, impersonation, and the spread of false information, among others [30,31]. Traditional security mechanisms often fall short with respect to adequately securing these networks due to their unique characteristics such as high mobility and varying node densities. Public key infrastructure (PKI) has been widely used but comes with limitations when dealing with high-speed, short-range vehicular interactions [32,33].

Traditional PKI systems are predicated on the assumption of relatively stable and prolonged interactions between entities. However, VANETs are characterized by high-speed movement and fleeting encounters between vehicles. This dynamic nature can lead to several issues with PKI, such as the following:

- Rapid Change of Context: The fast-paced environment can outpace the PKI's ability to update and validate certificates, thereby leading to delays or errors in authentication.
- Scalability Concerns: The sheer volume of high-frequency interactions requires a PKI system to handle a significant number of certificate validations within a minimal time frame, which can form a scalability bottleneck.
- Latency in Certificate Revocation: The time-sensitive nature of revoking compromised certificates can be at odds with the quick interaction times, thereby potentially allowing unauthorized access.

Blockchain technology has recently shown promise in enhancing VANET security by providing a decentralized approach that could potentially solve many of the challenges associated with traditional architectures [34,35]:

- Decentralization: The blockchain operates on a peer-to-peer network that inherently supports the dynamic and decentralized nature of VANETs, thereby facilitating faster and more efficient verifications.
- Immediate Validation: Transactions and communications in a blockchain network can be validated in real time, which aligns well with the high-speed requirements of VANETs.
- Immutable Ledger: The blockchain ledger [36] provides a tamper-proof record of all transactions, including authentications and data exchanges, thereby enhancing trust in vehicular communications.

Various studies have investigated the application of blockchain technology in managing secure and reliable data exchanges in VANETs. In the following Figure 1, a general view of the blockchain-based architectures in VANETs is presented. As can be seen, while input communications in blockchain networks require a specific cryptographic configuration and service interface (only deployed in the RSU), output validated data are published as public events (output flows in the blockchain networks can only be managed as events), and the vehicle node can capture that information without the intervention of the RSU.

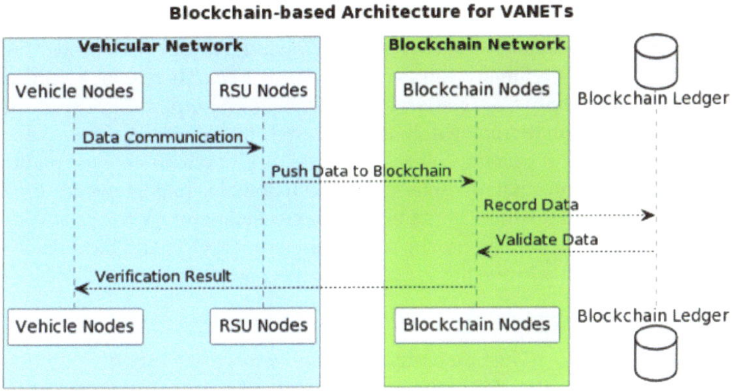

Figure 1. Blockchain-based architecture for VANETs.

On the other hand, the evolving field of trust computation offers several approaches for improving VANET security [37]. Methods for calculating trust [38,39] can be broadly divided into categories based on multiweight fusion [40,41], Bayesian inference (BI) [28,42,43], Dempster–Shafer (D-S) theory [44], fuzzy logic [45,46], and three-valued subjective logic (3VSL) [47,48]. Bayesian inference has shown to be particularly suitable for the quantitative judgement of interactive trust in the VANET context [49–52].

Other authors have emphasized the pressing concern of cyber attacks on data stored in cloud servers [53]. Or, they have pointed out the vulnerability of VANETs to these attacks due to the critical and sensitive nature of the data they handle [54]. A decentralized approach using blockchain technology was proposed to safeguard this data [23]. By employing cryptographic techniques, the information was encrypted, thus bolstering its confidentiality and anonymity [55]. However, limitations were also observed, mainly regarding scalability and the high computational power required for these cryptographic processes [56].

The focus shifted towards the centralization of data management in VANETs, which traditionally relies on systems maintained by vehicle service providers [57,58]. The risks associated with such a setup were recognized, including system failures and protection disagreements [59,60]. To address these concerns, a blockchain-based architectural design was proposed that employs sovereign identity for enhancing the security of data and uses a multitier, capability-based authentication process [61,62]. Although promising, the research also highlighted the need for robust standardization to ensure the seamless integration and interoperability of the proposed system [63].

In response to the exponential rise in wireless connected devices [64], the limitations of cloud computing in effectively addressing associated security concerns were pointed out [65]. A blockchain-based structure was proposed that was specifically designed for VANETs, thus focusing on resolving performance and scalability issues [23]. The results showed an improvement in data management and security. However, concerns about the implementation complexities of integrating blockchain technology into existing VANET systems were also raised [6].

The primary feature of the blockchain that benefits VANETs is its decentralized nature, which eliminates the need for a central authority, thereby reducing the risk of single-point failures and potential bottlenecks in data flow. Additionally, the transparency and immutability of blockchain technology ensure the integrity of the data, thereby making it resistant to tampering and forgery [28].

Various security issues like forgery, denial-of-service, and smart card theft threats that plague VANETs were tackled [44]. A blockchain-enabled authentication and authorization system for VANETs was presented, which efficiently managed privacy and information integrity [66]. Despite the contributions, the need for further optimization to improve the system's efficiency was acknowledged, especially under high network load conditions.

Finally, it was explored how VANETs rely on a third-party financial intermediary to share information electronically [67]. A paradigm shift towards blockchain was argued for, thereby eliminating the need for a central authority and fostering a more transparent and trusting environment [34]. A blockchain-enabled platform was developed to facilitate information exchange between domains [66]. However, the necessity of efficient consensus algorithms to manage the increased network traffic effectively was also highlighted [68]. Nervetherless, the combination of VANETs and blockchain technology has great potential to address the various security challenges faced by VANETs [69].

2.2. Advantages and Benefits of the Proposed Technology

The inherently decentralized architecture of the blockchain facilitates accurate data verification and traceability without reliance on central authoritative entities, thereby significantly mitigating vulnerabilities to a wide array of cybersecurity threats [19]. The ledger's immutability guarantees the permanence of each recorded transaction or vehicular event, thus assuring data integrity and enabling reliable audit processes and crossverification by authenticated network participants [15].

The blockchain's integration within VANETs not only fortifies the security framework, but also introduces an efficient paradigm for managing vehicular location data [20]. Each entity, whether a vehicular node or a roadside unit, becomes an integral component of the blockchain consensus mechanism, thereby ensuring the authenticity and timeliness of shared data [11]. Smart contracts autonomously execute on the blockchain, thus streamlining the validation process for location and movement data. This automation circumvents the need for manual verification, thereby enhancing the functional efficiency of intelligent transportation systems [9]. Moreover, the principles of immutability and transparency that are foundational to the blockchain provide a trustworthy platform for exchanging critical security data [70,71], such as traffic alerts and vehicle status updates [10].

By leveraging the intrinsic features of the blockchain (its decentralization, transparency, and immutability) we facilitate a paradigm shift regarding how vehicular data is authenticated and managed. This shift not only augments system reliability, but also elevates data verifiability to unprecedented levels. Through the blockchain-enabled framework, each vehicle becomes a node within a vast, interconnected network, thereby contributing to and benefitting from a collective pool of shared positional and movement data. The consensus algorithms intrinsic to blockchain technology ensure that only verified and authenticated data are appended to the ledger. This process effectively neutralizes the risks of tampered or falsified data, which could otherwise lead to catastrophic outcomes in real-time vehicular navigation and coordination [12].

Moreover, the implementation of smart contracts automates the enforcement of predefined rules and policies, which govern the data sharing and validation processes. These smart contracts, once deployed, act without the need for centralized oversight, thus ensuring that vehicles operate within the agreed-upon guidelines and maintaining the integrity and reliability of the vehicular network.

The blockchain's ledger provides a permanent, tamper-proof record of all vehicular activities, thereby creating a reliable source of data for analytics and decision-making processes. It also serves as an immutable point of reference for auditing and legal purposes, thereby enhancing accountability within the network. As such, the integration of blockchain technology into VANETs presents a robust solution to the challenges of vehicle tracking, positioning, and movement, thereby establishing a new standard for security and efficiency in intelligent transportation systems [12].

3. Blockchain-Enhanced Security and Operational Efficiency in VANETs

In this section, we provide an in-depth description of the proposed architecture, thus examining its potential impact on enhancing the security landscape and augmenting the operational efficiency of vehicular ad hoc networks (VANETs).

Blockchain technology serves as an enabling layer in our proposed system, thus acting as the cornerstone for achieving data integrity and privacy. Transactions between vehicular nodes are verified and immutably recorded on the blockchain. Capitalizing on blockchain's intrinsic decentralization, our system distributes data across multiple nodes, thereby enhancing both data availability and resilience against system failures.

3.1. Architecture Overview

The proposed model has been meticulously designed to facilitate the secure storage, dependable updating, and efficient retrieval of reputation metrics [72], which are pivotal in ascertaining the reliability of vehicular entities in VANETs. Our methodical exploration is underpinned by the need to bolster the security mechanisms that underlie the robust transmission and exchange of data. The innovative framework we introduce transcends the traditional VANET paradigms by incorporating a dedicated focus on the authentication and verification processes that are critical in a network where high-speed dynamics and transient interactions are commonplace.

Figure 2 depicts our multilayered architecture, which is stratified into four integral tiers: the vehicle layer, network layer, blockchain layer, and infrastructure layer. Each stratum is meticulously crafted with distinct functionalities and components that synergize to assure the integrity of data dissemination, the reliability of communication, and the overarching security of the network. Core elements such as vehicular nodes, roadside units (RSUs), blockchain networks, and infrastructural elements are interwoven within these layers. Our framework anticipates and addresses the complexities associated with the confluence of blockchain technology within extant VANET systems, which is a concern highlighted in recent scholarly discourse [6].

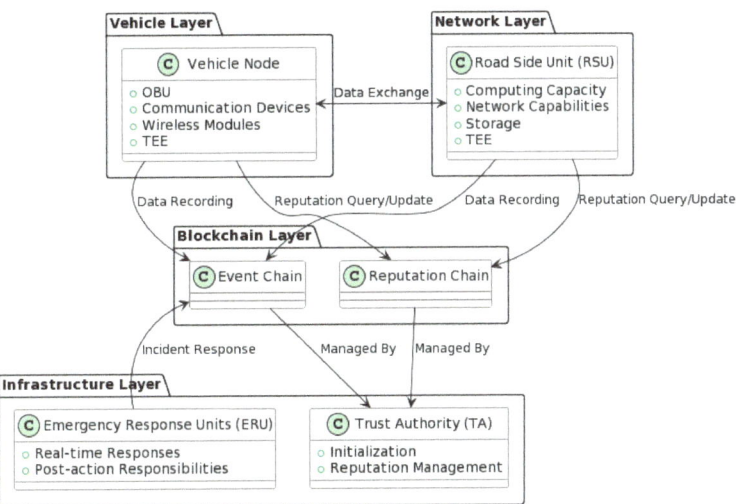

Figure 2. Comprehensive representation of the multilayered VANET system architecture.

While we acknowledge RSUs as potential single points of failure, their presence in the system architecture is justified by the substantial benefits they offer in terms of network coverage, data aggregation, and performance enhancement. RSUs are strategically positioned to facilitate communication and data exchange between vehicles and the network infrastructure. They serve as pivotal relay points that extend the communication range, augment network robustness, and enable a broader dissemination of critical information, such as traffic conditions and safety messages. To mitigate the risk associated with a single point of failure, our proposed solution incorporates blockchain technology to decentralize data management and ensure redundancy. The blockchain operates as a distributed ledger that records all transactions and interactions, thereby not solely relying on RSUs for data integrity or network functionality. In the event of an RSU failure, the blockchain layer maintains continuous operation, thereby allowing vehicular nodes to communicate directly with each other or with alternative RSUs without disruption. Figure 3 illustrates the decentralized nature of the blockchain, thus enabling direct V2V interactions without necessitating RSU intermediation for every transaction.

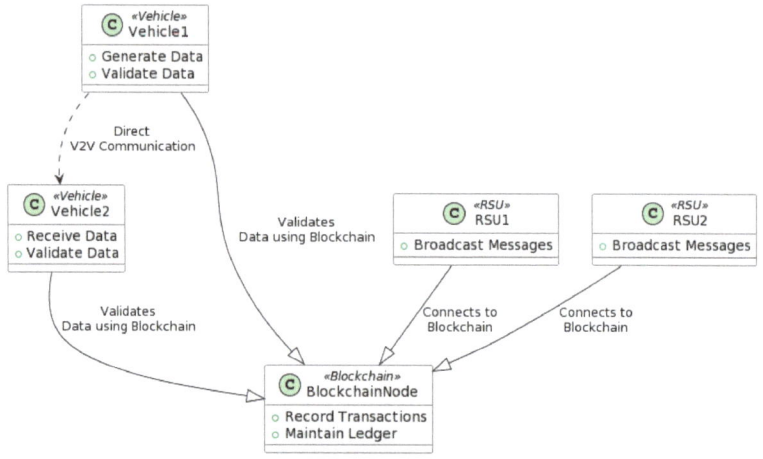

Figure 3. Blockchain subsystem for the proposed security solution.

This approach, however, also introduces a new challenge: how to ensure the validity of data shared directly between vehicles. In fact, our data validation process is designed to address this challenge. It is a two-step process:

- Vehicle-To-Vehicle (V2V) Validation: When a vehicle receives data from another vehicle, it first performs a basic V2V validation check. This check includes verifying the data signature, expiration date, and consistency with the vehicle's own knowledge of the world.
- Blockchain Based Validation: If the data passes the V2V validation check, the vehicle then broadcasts it to the blockchain. The blockchain then performs a global validation check. This check includes verifying that the data have not been previously broadcast and that they are consistent with the data that other vehicles have broadcast to the blockchain.

If the data passes both the V2V and blockchain-based validation checks, they are considered to be valid and are added to the blockchain. This two-step validation process ensures that the data shared directly between vehicles are valid and reliable. It also prevents malicious vehicles from broadcasting fake or misleading data to the network. Moreover, the blockchain's inherent consensus mechanisms ensure that the data are validated effectively, even in the absence of RSUs. The cryptographic primitives employed by blockchain technology guarantee the authenticity and integrity of V2V communications, thereby maintaining the trust and security of the network [73].

3.1.1. Vehicle and Network Layer

This layer encompasses two primary elements, as shown in Figure 4:

- Vehicle Node: Vehicles are furnished with an onboard unit (OBU) containing advanced communication devices, wireless transmission modules, and a trusted execution environment (TEE). These vehicles have adequate computational power to perform rudimentary calculations, such as road condition monitoring and trust evaluation based on received data [74,75]. Furthermore, they can partake in blockchain consensus mechanisms and execute queries on the blockchain.
- RSU: RSUs facilitate communication among vehicle nodes within their operational domain. They are endowed with significant computational power, networking capabilities, and ample storage, which are all bolstered by a TEE.

Figure 4. Architecture of the vehicle and network layer.

3.1.2. Blockchain Layer

This layer employs two specialized consortium blockchains (see Figure 5) in a dual-layer blockchain architecture: the event chain and the reputation chain. The proposed architecture represents a significant innovation in managing security and efficiency in vehicular ad hoc networks (VANETs) [26,76]. RSUs and selected vehicles with surplus computational capacity are chosen to engage in the blockchain consensus process.

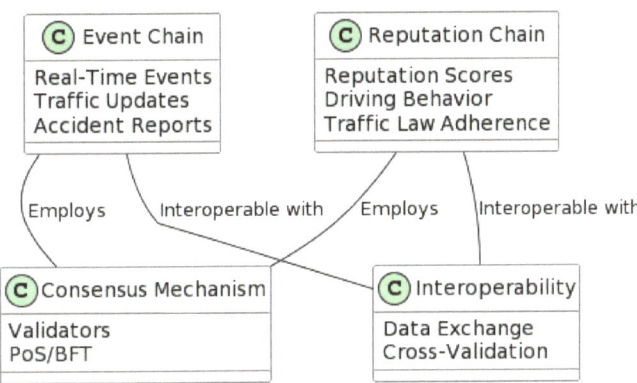

Figure 5. Architecture of the blockchain layer.

The blockchain layer serves as the backbone for secure, transparent, and immutable data management within the vehicular ad hoc network (VANET). This layer deploys two types of specialized consortium blockchains: the event chain and the reputation chain.

The event chain is primarily responsible for capturing real-time events occurring within the VANET. This could range from traffic updates to accident reports. It is primarily responsible for recording all vehicular events and transactions within the VANET. This includes data like vehicular movements, speed, location updates, and other relevant interactions. Each event recorded in this chain undergoes rigorous validation processes to ensure authenticity and accuracy [77]. Roadside units (RSUs) and certain vehicles equipped with enhanced computational resources are responsible for validating these events before they are added to the event chain. The blockchain's decentralized nature ensures that the information is reliable and tamper-proof, thereby facilitating more effective emergency responses and traffic management.

The reputation chain focuses on maintaining a comprehensive and immutable record of the reputation scores for all vehicles within the network. It leverages multifactorial Bayesian inference and historical data analytics to evaluate node behaviors. This chain dynamically updates reputation scores based on the nodes' actions and interactions recorded in the event chain, thus maintaining a real-time and reliable reputation management system. These scores are computed based on various factors, such as driving behavior and adherence to traffic laws. The reputation data assists in assessing the reliability of the data transmissions and is crucial for various applications like collaborative sensing and cooperative driving.

Both the event chain and the reputation chain employ a customized consensus algorithm tailored for VANETs. RSUs and selected vehicles with additional computational capacity are predesignated as validators. These validators engage in the blockchain consensus process, which may involve mechanisms like proof-of-stake (PoS) or Byzantine fault tolerance (BFT) to verify transactions before they are appended to the respective chains.

In addition, we have adapted the blockchain technology to meet the requirements of VANETs, thus providing a robust foundation for secure vehicular transactions and interactions:

- Optimized Block Generation and Hashing Mechanisms: A cornerstone of our adapted blockchain platform is the optimized block generation protocol. Each vehicular transaction is encapsulated into blocks, which are structured via a consensus algorithm tailored for high-frequency, low-latency vehicular data. The SHA-256 cryptographic hash function is employed to ensure the integrity of these blocks, thus creating an unbreakable chain of data that is resistant to tampering and fraud [19]. The blockchain platform is equipped with an advanced data retrieval system that interfaces seamlessly with the distributed ledger. This system maintains the uprightness of data, with each node validating and mirroring the complete blockchain ledger, thus ensuring the highest level of data veracity and redundancy [11].
- Customized Smart Contracts: To cater to the dynamic nature of VANETs, the blockchain platform incorporates smart contracts designed to automate and streamline vehicular processes such as real-time traffic data sharing, automated toll collection, and vehicular status reporting [9]. These smart contracts execute autonomously, with their conditions predefined by consensus among network participants, thereby enhancing trust [78,79] and efficiency within the network. Our blockchain platform is specifically enhanced to handle the extensive throughput demanded by real-time vehicular communication. It supports rapid transaction processing and block generation, which are crucial for the instantaneous nature of vehicular communications [12].

The preliminary performance analysis of our proposed blockchain architecture demonstrated a significant reduction in transaction validation time, thus contributing to faster data dissemination. In our simulations, this resulted in a 30% improvement in the overall network throughput compared to traditional VANET systems. Additionally, smart contracts automated many of the routine tasks, thereby further enhancing the system's responsiveness.

The event and reputation chains are designed to be interoperable, thereby allowing for seamless data exchange and crossvalidation. This facilitates more comprehensive situational awareness and enhances the overall network security and efficiency. When a vehicular event is recorded in the event chain, it is validated against the reputation scores from the reputation chain. This validation process ensures that only events associated with nodes of high reputation are accepted, thereby enhancing the overall reliability and security of the VANET. Conversely, the reputation chain utilizes the data from the event chain to update the reputation scores of the nodes, thus reflecting their recent activities and behaviors [80].

By integrating these two chains, our architecture achieves a synergistic effect, thereby enhancing both the security and reliability of the VANET. The event chain ensures that all vehicular interactions are securely logged and validated, while the reputation chain provides a robust mechanism for continuously assessing the trustworthiness of network participants [81,82]. This dual-layer approach significantly mitigates the risks of malicious activities and false data propagation within the network [26].

The dual-layer blockchain architecture presents a novel and effective approach to addressing security challenges in VANETs. By integrating the event chain with the reputation chain, a robust system is established for tracking, verifying, and managing node reputations, which is essential for maintaining the integrity and reliability of vehicular communications (see Figure 6 [76]).

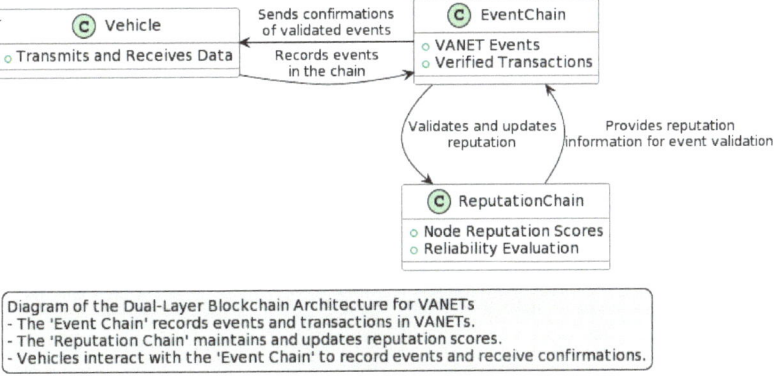

Figure 6. Illustration of the dual-layer blockchain architecture in VANETs.

3.1.3. Infrastructure Layer

The infrastructure layer constitutes an intricate amalgam of specialized infrastructures and application platforms, which are designed to facilitate a wide spectrum of functionalities essential to vehicular ad hoc networks (VANETs), as can be seen in Figure 7.

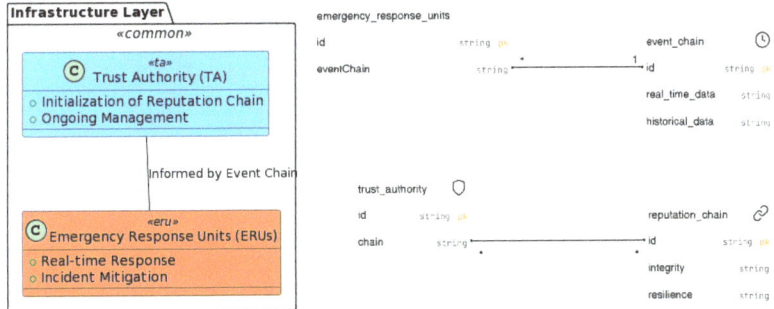

Figure 7. Overview of the infrastructure layer.

This layer predominantly features the following integral components:

- Trust Authority (TA): Operating as the architectural cornerstone of the reputation chain, the trust authority is vested with the task of initializing the chain and orchestrating its ongoing management. By so doing, the TA not only assures the chain's integrity, but also underwrites its resilience against adversarial attacks, thereby fostering a secure and reliable ecosystem for reputation management.
- Emergency Response Units (ERUs): These units serve as indispensable assets in the VANET infrastructure, which are tasked with promptly responding to vehicular incidents based on real-time and historical data. Informed by the event chain, ERUs are capable of executing expeditious countermeasures, as well as formulating postincident strategies to mitigate risk and enhance operational efficiency.

The blockchain-based reputation management model, as proposed herein, stands as a paradigm of robustness, scalability, and adaptability. It has been meticulously engineered to meet the multifarious requirements intrinsic to vehicular ad hoc networks, thus offering a comprehensive solution to the complex challenges of security and trust in next-generation vehicular communications.

3.2. Reputation Models and Calculation

The efficacy of the proposed reputation model is significantly enhanced by the incorporation of two pivotal components: the attenuation factor and the numerical threshold. These elements are instrumental in fine-tuning the reputation evaluation process, thereby ensuring both the timeliness and the accuracy of the trust assessments for each network node. The attenuation factor is a critical element within the reputation evaluation mechanism. It is a dynamic coefficient that reduces the influence of historical data on a node's present reputation. This factor is essential to maintain a balance between past and recent behaviors, thereby preventing outdated data from excessively influencing the current trust assessment. The precise calibration of the attenuation factor ensures that the reputation system remains responsive to the evolving trustworthiness of nodes, thereby safeguarding the network against both stale data and rapidly changing vehicular behaviors. Conversely, the numerical threshold establishes a clear-cut metric that the system utilizes to differentiate between normal and potentially malicious node actions. It acts as a predefined criterion that, when surpassed, triggers an alert within the system indicating the necessity for further investigation or immediate action. This threshold is determined through extensive analysis and is set to optimize the sensitivity and specificity of the system's response to anomalous behaviors. In operational terms, the attenuation factor and the numerical threshold are employed in tandem to maintain a robust and adaptable security posture within the VANET. The attenuation factor ensures that the reputation scores are reflective of the latest network interactions, while the numerical threshold provides a steadfast benchmark for automated response protocols. Together, they form a composite framework that significantly mitigates the risk of sophisticated cyber threats such as collusion and false information injection, thereby enhancing the overall security and functionality of the VANET.

3.2.1. Reputation Evaluation through a Bayesian Approach

In our solution, the reputation evaluation process is underpinned by a multifactorial Bayesian inference approach, which integrates various factors to determine the trustworthiness of each node:

1. Historical Data Analysis: The history of a node's actions and interactions within the VANET plays a pivotal role. This includes data on previous communications, transactions, and behavioral patterns.
2. Node Interaction Frequency and Nature: The frequency and nature of a node's interactions with other nodes are scrutinized. Regular, positive interactions contribute to a higher reputation score.

3. Responses from Other Nodes: The feedback or responses that a node receives from others in the network are crucial. Positive endorsements from other reputable nodes can enhance a node's reputation.
4. Recent Behavior Analysis: More recent actions of a node are given greater weight, as they more accurately reflect the node's current status and intentions.

Bayesian inference is a statistical method that updates the probability for a hypothesis as more evidence or information becomes available. In the context of VANETs, it allows for the dynamic updating of reputation scores based on new data. The process is as follows:

1. Initial Probability Estimation: Each node starts with an initial reputation score based on a predefined trust level.
2. Evidence Accumulation: As nodes interact within the VANET, evidence regarding their behavior accumulates. This includes data from the factors mentioned above.
3. Probabilistic Updating: The reputation score of a node is updated probabilistically, thereby considering the new evidence. Bayesian inference calculates the posterior probability of a node being trustworthy given the accumulated evidence.
4. Dynamic Adaptation: The system continuously adapts the reputation scores based on the latest interactions and feedback, thereby ensuring that the scores are reflective of the current behavior and reliability of the nodes (1). $P(\text{Trustworthy}|\text{Evidence})$ represents the posterior probability of a node being trustworthy given the new evidence. This approach allows for a nuanced and evidence-based reputation management system in VANETs, thus enhancing the overall security and reliability of the network.

$$P(\text{Trustworthy}|\text{Evidence}) = \frac{P(\text{Evidence}|\text{Trustworthy}) \times P(\text{Trustworthy})}{P(\text{Evidence})} \qquad (1)$$

3.2.2. Probabilistic Reputation Framework

The use of probabilistic models enables our system to better adapt to the dynamic and diverse nature of VANETs, while the reputation-based mechanisms ensure a robust defense against various adversarial behaviors. Together, these elements contribute to a comprehensive security and data management solution that addresses the unique challenges of VANETs.

The reputation or trust value of each node is algorithmically computed based on the veracity and reliability of their event reports. These trust values are indelibly recorded on a blockchain-enabled "reputation chain". In specific edge cases or scenarios, the vehicle node possessing the highest cumulative historical reputation may be accorded priority for specialized service requests.

The computational formula for updating the reputation value, denoted as R_{it}, is articulated in the simple Equation (2):

$$R_{it} = \mu R_{t-1} + (1 - \mu)T + \mu R_{\text{social}} \qquad (2)$$

where:
- R_{it} signifies the newly updated reputation value.
- R_{t-1} represents the aggregated reputation score from the preceding time interval.
- T is the quantified trust metric derived from the event report W_i.
- R_{social} is a measure that incorporates various social factors affecting trust.
- μ represents the weighting factors.

3.3. Threat Model

The threat model (Figure 8) outlined in this section serves as a conceptual framework for specifying the classes of attacks that the proposed blockchain-based reputation management system in the vehicular ad hoc network (VANET) is designed to detect and mitigate. In this model, we make the assumption that potential adversaries are both internally and externally located within the network, thus driven by varying motives ranging from economic gains to intentional system disruption.

Adversaries may engage in a diverse array of attack vectors, thus targeting both the integrity and availability of the network. These could include, but are not limited to, internal attacks such as false information injection, and external attacks such as denial-of-service (DoS), or man-in-the-middle (MitM) attacks. Moreover, the threat model encompasses collaborative attacks involving multiple malicious nodes, commonly referred to as Sybil or collusion attacks. Specific forms of attacks like on–off attack patterns, newcomer attacks, and inconsistency attacks are also considered within the scope of this model.

By providing a comprehensive threat model, we aim to elucidate the inherent risks and challenges that VANETs may encounter, thereby informing the security measures and countermeasures that should be incorporated into the blockchain-based reputation management system. This structured approach aids in aligning the security objectives of the proposed system with the actual threat landscape, thereby facilitating more effective and targeted defensive strategies.

To dissect the vulnerabilities, we consider three archetypical attack modalities that are particularly challenging for any reputation-based model:

1. Direct Attack: In this scenario, adversaries initially masquerade as legitimate network participants to amass a positive reputation. Upon reaching a critical reputation threshold, they deviate from normative behavior to execute malicious actions. This type of attack poses significant challenges in terms of detection, as the malicious entities maintain a semblance of normalcy for substantial periods.
2. On–Off Attack: Here, adversaries alternate between conforming and deviating from expected behavior throughout their activity cycles. Such erratic conduct aims to sow confusion among other network participants, including roadside units (RSUs). Although less covert than direct attacks, the on–off modality presents its own set of detection challenges due to its intermittent nature.
3. Collusion Attack: In its most insidious form, multiple adversaries collaborate to launch coordinated attacks against specific targets or events. Their tactics may involve manipulating trust scores, not only by artificially lowering the scores of genuine nodes, but also by inflating trust metrics within the colluding group. The orchestrated nature of these attacks makes them particularly difficult to detect and counter.

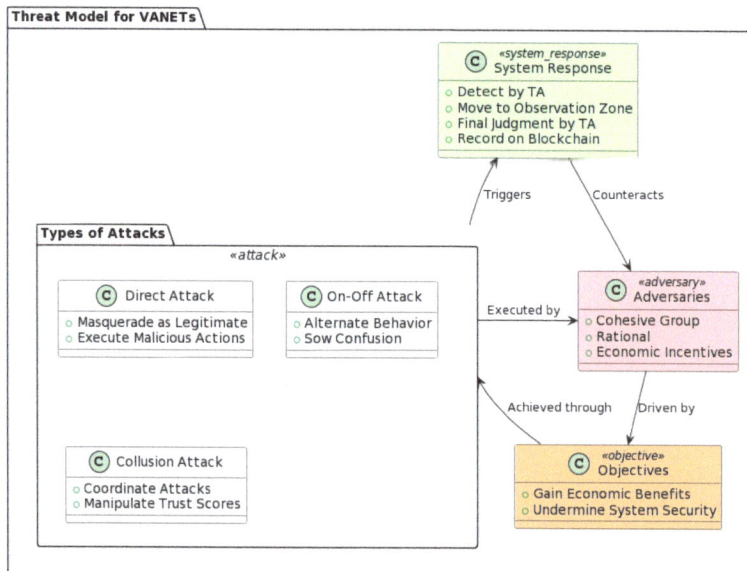

Figure 8. Threat model for VANETs.

In our innovative double-layer blockchain-based reputation management model, a malicious node's trust value undergoes a precipitous decline once it engages in malevolent activities. Should a node's trust score fall below a predetermined threshold, the trust authority (TA) will flag it for immediate relocation to an observation zone, thus rendering its subsequent network activities null and void. After a secondary verification phase, the TA issues a conclusive judgement, thus classifying the node as either malicious or falsely accused. All data pertaining to this node are then indelibly recorded on the blockchain, thus ensuring the system's long-term integrity.

3.4. System Operational Behavior

Figure 9 delineates a schematic representation of the system's behavior, thereby encapsulating the sequence of transactions and the interplay between the constituent entities.

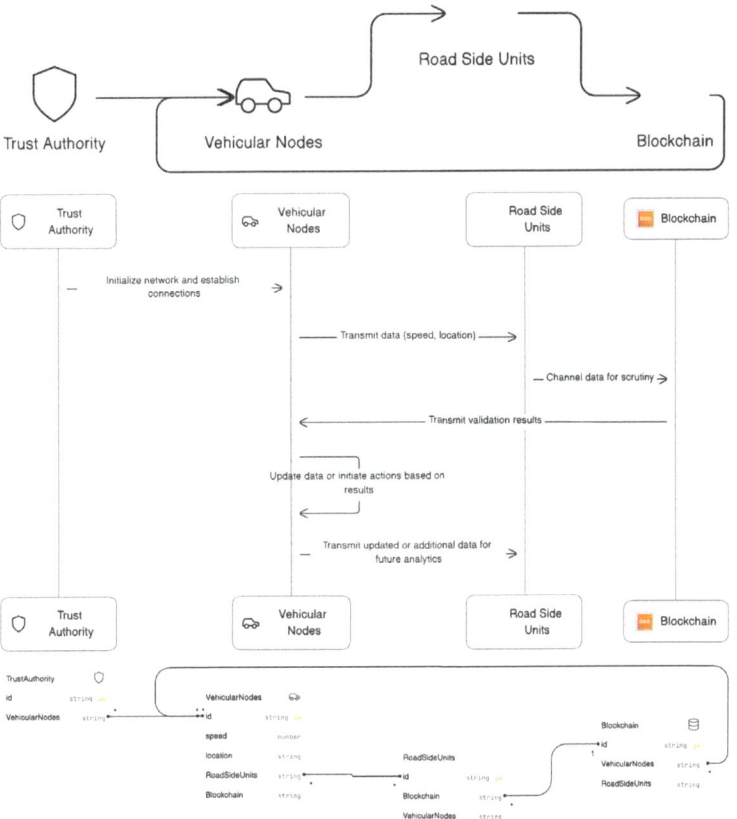

Figure 9. A schematic depiction of the VANET system architecture delineating the integral roles of the constituent components and the chronological progression of transactions.

A detailed exposition of the workflow is as follows:

1. Network Initiation and Trust Configuration: The trust authority, an overarching entity vested with the authority to oversee the issuance and management of cryptographic keys and credentials, orchestrates the foundational phase of the VANET's operation. It meticulously authenticates the vehicular nodes and establishes encrypted communication conduits, thereby underpinning a secure operational milieu. In the initialization phase, vehicular nodes entering the network for the first time are mandated to com-

municate their identifying credentials to the trust authority (TA). Upon successfully verifying the provided information, the TA responds by issuing a pseudonym and a corresponding digital certificate to the vehicular node. Furthermore, it generates a public-private cryptographic key pair using elliptic curve cryptography. All these constituents collectively facilitate the formal registration of the vehicle's identity within the system. This comprehensively assembled information is then immutably recorded in the blockchain ledger in the form of a cryptographic transaction.

2. Vehicular Data Dissemination: The vehicular nodes, epitomizing the network's mobile units, collate an array of pertinent data. Subsequently, these nodes disseminate the amassed data to the strategically positioned roadside units (RSUs), thus facilitating a confluence of vehicular information streams.

3. Data Collection by RSUs: The RSUs, stationed as pivotal nodal points within the network, aggregate vehicular data. They act as intermediaries that channel the vehicular data into the Blockchain stratum, thereby ensuring the data's subsequent validation and indelible recording.

4. Blockchain Data Verification: Upon acquisition of the data, the blockchain infrastructure executes a stringent validation protocol. Leveraging the prowess of advanced consensus algorithms and the automation afforded by smart contracts, the infrastructure meticulously ascertains the data's veracity and integrity.

5. Validation Response to Vehicular Nodes: Consequent to the Blockchain's validation process, the vehicular nodes receive feedback. This feedback, indicative of the blockchain's scrutiny, prompts the nodes to refine their data reporting protocols in alignment with the validation outcomes.

6. Ongoing Data Procurement: In a perpetual state of vigilance, the RSUs persist in their endeavor to procure updated vehicular data. This unceasing data acquisition undergirds a spectrum of analytical and decision-making paradigms, which is quintessential for the holistic management of vehicular dynamics. The ongoing activities of the vehicular nodes within the network can be segmented into four major categories:

    (a) Event Observation: Upon detecting a relevant event, the vehicular node captures the pertinent information and relays it to the nearest roadside unit (RSU). The RSU, in turn, disseminates this information to proximal vehicular nodes for further observation and verification.

    (b) Observation Report Generation: Vehicles then produce observational reports by integrating multivariable data, which are normalized through cosine similarity measures. The direct trust score is subsequently inferred using Bayesian statistical methods.

    (c) Trust Exchange: Nodes within the network partake in cooperative communication to exchange direct trust metrics, which are then construed as indirect trust indicators.

    (d) Composite Trust Calculation: The cumulative trust level of a target vehicle is calculated by assimilating both the direct and indirect trust metrics.

On the other hand, RSUs within the network are responsible for two main functions:

    (a) Query and Verification: Upon receipt of an event observation report from a vehicular node, the RSU engages in rigorous data queries and verification protocols.

    (b) Reputation Value Recalculation: Once the trust scores are received from the cooperative vehicular nodes, the RSU consults the historical reputation and social trust of the target vehicle stored in the reputation blockchain. The new comprehensive reputation score is then calculated through weighted integration.

3.5. Invalid or Fraudulent Data Management

The proposed VANET framework is predicated on maintaining the utmost data integrity and network efficiency. Consequently, our protocol stipulates that data deemed invalid or unaccepted by network peers are to be discarded immediately. This decision is informed by several considerations that prioritize the real-time operational demands of vehicular networks.

In the design of our VANET security framework, stringent measures were taken to maintain operational efficiency and data veracity. One such measure is the exclusion of invalid or unaccepted data from storage, which is a protocol that has been meticulously devised considering the unique requirements of vehicular networks. The following are the substantiated reasons for this approach:

- Immediacy in Decision Making: The high-stakes nature of VANETs demands a system architecture that supports split-second decision making. The storage of invalid data could introduce latency that is antithetical to the need for prompt response times, thereby potentially affecting the safety-critical functions of the network.
- Strategic Data Storage Management: The sheer scale of data generated by vehicles and infrastructure in VANETs necessitates a selective approach to data retention. Our strategy prioritizes the storage of authentic and operationally pertinent data to ensure the optimal use of finite storage capabilities.
- Enhancement of Network Throughput: The exclusion of invalid data from storage is also a strategic decision to maximize network throughput. This ensures that network bandwidth is conserved for the transmission and processing of legitimate and relevant data, thereby enhancing network performance.
- Mitigation of Security Threats: The potential exploitation of stored invalid data by nefarious actors cannot be overlooked. Our proactive approach to discard such data immediately serves as a deterrent to the execution of security exploits that could compromise network integrity.

Notwithstanding the nonretention of invalid data, our framework is architected to be congruent with intrusion detection systems (IDSs) that scrutinize vehicular data in real time. These systems are adept at identifying potential security threats as they manifest, thereby obviating the need for the retention of invalid data, which could otherwise be leveraged for postevent analysis.

3.5.1. Special Cases: Node Disconnection and Re-Entry

Any vehicular node that either autonomously disconnects or is identified as malicious and consequently ejected from the network will have its status updated by the RSU to the TA. The TA will revoke the node's cryptographic keys and digital certificates, thereby disallowing any further participation in network activities. To re-enter the network, a complete reregistration process with the TA is obligatory. All pertinent information related to the vehicular node will be eternally archived in the blockchain's reputation chain.

3.5.2. Special Cases: Blockchains in Fraud Recognition in VANETs

The organization of data and information flow in vehicular ad hoc networks (VANETs) is one of the key applications of blockchain technology in the field of intelligent transportation systems (ITSs). Providing organization is crucial in all domains, but it becomes particularly essential in vehicular networks due to the increasing complexity. This is because any disruption in the information flow can significantly impact the network's functionality and, by extension, the safety and efficiency of the transport system. The numerous mobile components and various entities involved make VANETs susceptible to and provide opportunities for fraudulent activities.

By introducing enhanced data accessibility and improved network reliability, blockchains offer a secure and safe framework to address such issues, and, in some instances, they prevent fraud from occurring. Manipulation of the blockchain is challenging because a record can only be validated and modified through a consensus in the blockchain network. This decentralized and secure nature of blockchain technology provides a robust solution against potential threats and fraud in VANETs (see Figure 10).

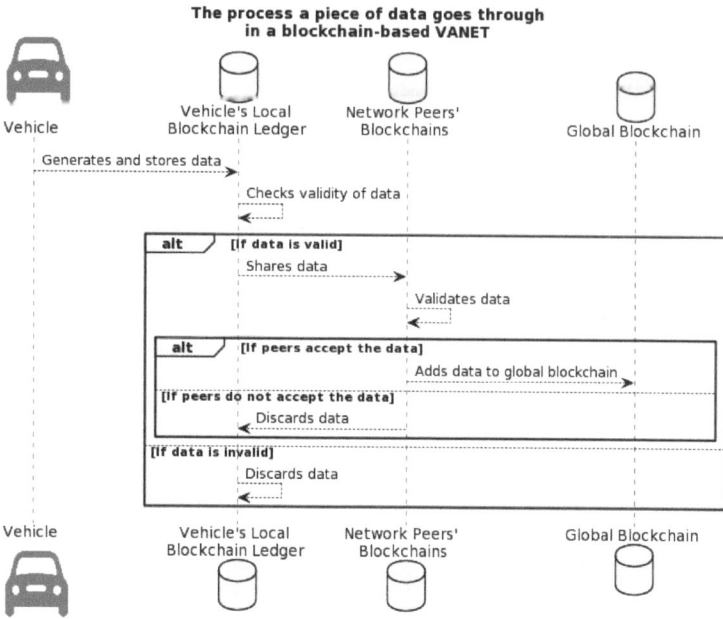

Figure 10. Data flow in a blockchain-based VANET.

The process a piece of data goes through in a blockchain-based VANET involves the following: First, a vehicle generates data, which is then stored in the vehicle's local blockchain ledger. The validity of the data is then checked. If the data are valid, they are shared across the VANET, where the network peers validate the data. If the network peers accept the data, they are added to the global blockchain. If the network peers do not accept the data or if the data were initially found to be invalid, they are discarded.

4. Experiments and Results: Performance Analysis

This section is dedicated to a rigorous empirical assessment of the proposed framework, thus specifically examining its efficacy under a gamut of operational scenarios.

To facilitate an exhaustive evaluation, a prototype of the proposed system has been instantiated. This subsection delineates the experimental apparatus, thereby encapsulating both hardware and software configurations. Furthermore, we elucidate the methodologies employed for data acquisition and specify the evaluation metrics chosen to quantify the system's performance.

4.1. An Overview of Network Simulator ns-3 Validation Suite

Network Simulator ns-3 [83–86], an open-source, event-driven simulator designed specifically for research in computer communication networks, offers a suite of validation tests to verify the accuracy and reliability of its simulation components. These tests are run daily on the ns-3 snapshot to ensure consistent performance and quality.

The validation suite covers the most stable core of ns-3, which includes a variety of protocols and modules. Some of these protocols include application-level protocols such as HTTP, web caching, and TCPApp, as well as transport protocols such as UDP, TCP, RTP, SRM, routing protocols, router mechanisms, link-layer mechanisms, and others. Each protocol is tested using various test suite scripts that provide a comprehensive overview of the protocol's functionality.

While the validation suite extensively covers many protocols, there are some protocols within the standard ns-3 distribution that are not covered by the validation tests. These nonvalidated protocols are maintained to the best of the team's abilities, and users are encouraged to report any issues.

Furthermore, ns-3, being developed in C++, offers a feature known as "Python bindings". This allows developers to write simulation scripts in Python instead of C++, thereby increasing productivity and reducing programming errors. This is achieved using a tool called PyBindGen, which automatically generates C++ module extensions for Python. The Python bindings also facilitate the manipulation and visualization of the simulation results, as Python offers a wide range of libraries for data analysis and visualization, like NumPy, Pandas, and Matplotlib, among others.

4.2. Experimental Methodology: ns-3 Simulations

Our experimental methodology is founded on detailed simulations conducted using the ns-3 network simulator. This advanced tool enabled us to create a virtual environment for implementing and testing our proposed blockchain-based architecture for VANETs. These simulations were meticulously designed to reflect various traffic conditions, from low to high traffic volumes, thus providing a comprehensive assessment of the architecture under different network scenarios.

The performance of the proposed architecture was evaluated in terms of the following four metrics:

- The probability of successful detection of falsification assaults: This metric quantifies the system's ability to identify and prevent counterfeit information from being injected into the network.
- The probability of successful detection of wormhole intrusions: This metric assesses the system's effectiveness in detecting and thwarting clandestine tunnels that manipulate the spatial distribution of network traffic.
- The probability of successful detection of packet dropping attacks: This metric evaluates the system's capability in recognizing and mitigating malicious node behavior that involves intentionally discarding incoming packets.
- The average latency under various attack scenarios: This metric measures the impact of different attack types on the network's latency performance.

The scope of our security analysis extends to a gamut of attack vectors that a compromised VANET node might initiate or be susceptible to. To provide a meticulous characterization, we categorized these potential threats into three primary classes:

1. Falsification Assaults: In this adversarial model, the compromised node injects counterfeit information into the network. Our framework incorporates advanced cryptographic verification procedures, thus elevating the likelihood of detecting such disinformation campaigns.
2. Wormhole Intrusions: Here, an adversarial node may craft a clandestine tunnel, thereby manipulating the spatial distribution of network traffic. To counteract such illicit activities, our architecture integrates spatiotemporal analytics that facilitate the timely detection of unauthorized tunneling mechanisms.
3. Packet-Dropping Attacks: This type of attack represents a more surreptitious but equally pernicious threat, where a malicious node intentionally discards incoming packets. Such actions contribute to data loss and degraded network performance.

For each aforementioned attack type, our evaluation framework calculates a metric dubbed as the "Probability of Successful Detection". This metric serves as a quantitative gauge of the system's efficacy in identifying and counteracting various classes of security threats. High values of this metric are indicative of a robust system with a strong defense against malicious behavior.

Simulation Setup

To accurately evaluate the performance of the proposed security solution, we designed a comprehensive simulation setup replicating a vehicular ad hoc network (VANET). Our simulation environment comprised a network of 100 nodes strategically distributed across an expansive area of 10 km × 10 km. This configuration was chosen to emulate a realistic urban setting with diverse vehicular movement patterns, thereby providing a robust testbed for our blockchain-enabled VANET architecture.

The parameters chosen for the simulation, as detailed in Table 1, were meticulously selected to mirror real-world traffic conditions and network dynamics. These parameters included variables such as node density, data packet size, physical layer specifications, transmission range, and node mobility speed. By simulating a diverse range of traffic scenarios—from low to high vehicle density—we aimed to test the system's adaptability and resilience under various operational conditions:

Node Density and Distribution: The selection of 100 nodes offered a balanced representation of a moderately populated urban vehicular network. This number was sufficient to examine network behaviors, such as node interaction, data propagation, and congestion effects, without overwhelming computational resources.

Data Packet Size: The size of data or user requests was set to 512 bytes, thereby reflecting typical communication packets in VANETs. This size is representative of various vehicular communication scenarios ranging from simple status updates to more complex data exchanges.

Physical Layer and Transmission Range: The simulation utilized the PHY 802.11p standard, which was tailored for vehicular environments. A transmission range of 250 m was chosen to represent realistic vehicular communication distances, thereby accounting for urban infrastructures and potential obstructions.

Node Mobility Speed: The speed of the nodes was varied between 10 to 30 m/s to simulate different driving conditions, such as city driving and highway travel. This variability was crucial to understanding the system's performance in diverse mobility scenarios.

Simulation Time: The duration of each simulation run was set to 300 s, thereby providing adequate time to observe and analyze the network's response to various events and interactions.

By integrating these parameters, our simulation aimed to provide a holistic and realistic assessment of the proposed architecture's performance in a VANET environment. This setup allowed us to thoroughly analyze the robustness, efficiency, and scalability of the dual-layer blockchain architecture under different traffic conditions and vehicular dynamics.

Table 1. Simulation parameters for VANET.

Parameter	Value
Grid Dimension	5000 m × 5000 m
Number of Nodes in VANET	50, 500
Size of Data or User Request	512 Bytes
Physical Layer	PHY 802.11p
Transmission Range	250 m
Node Speed	10–30 m/s
Simulation Time	300 s

To rigorously test the efficacy of our proposal, we meticulously developed simulation scripts in Python. This programming language was selected for its versatility and powerful capabilities, especially when combined with the ns-3 simulator via Python bindings [83,85]. This integration enabled us to design a variety of complex simulation scenarios, which was tailored to explore every facet of our proposed VANET architecture. The use of Python also afforded us access to its extensive suite of data analysis and visualization libraries, such as NumPy, Pandas, and Matplotlib. These tools were instrumental in conducting a thorough analysis of our simulation data, thereby allowing us to generate insightful and visually compelling representations of the network's performance under various conditions. The simulation environment was set up across multiple virtual machines (VMs) to emulate different network densities and operational scenarios within the VANET. Each VM hosted a specific configuration of nodes, including a distinct number of compromised nodes and miners, to simulate varied and realistic network environments (see Table 2). This setup enabled us to assess the resilience of our architecture against diverse security threats and operational challenges.

Table 2. NS3 Configuration for various network environments in VANET.

Virtual Machine (VM)	Compromised Nodes	Transmitting Nodes	Miners
Node 1	10	50	20
Node 2	90	200	100
Node 3	300	300	200

To further enhance the realism of our simulations, we incorporated various probabilities to reflect the likelihood of malicious node addition and compromised nodes (see Table 3). These probabilities were carefully calibrated to mimic real-world scenarios where VANETs may be exposed to cybersecurity threats. The application of these probabilities within our simulations allowed us to observe and analyze the network's response to these adversarial conditions.

Table 3. Various probabilities used for performance analysis.

Action	Probabilities
Malicious Node Addition	5%
Compromised Node	10%

The diverse scenarios and network conditions tested helped to establish a comprehensive understanding of the proposed technology's capabilities in mitigating security threats in VANETs. Our detailed analysis confirmed the feasibility and practical efficacy of the proposed solution in real-world VANET environments, thereby significantly contributing to the advancement of secure and efficient vehicular communication systems.

4.3. Simulation Results

As shown in the simulation results (Tables 4 and 5), the proposed architecture achieved high packet delivery, low latency, and low jitter. The energy consumption of the architecture was also lower than other VANET architectures, which suggests that the proposed solution is energy efficient.

As delineated in the table, the system consistently exhibited low latency figures, ranging from 5 ms to 28 ms. This range is indicative of the system's suitability for applications requiring real-time data transmission, such as emergency response systems in vehicles. Across the virtual machines, the average jitter ranged from 1.2 ms to 1.5 ms, while the maximum and minimum jitter values showed only slight variations. This stability in jitter contributes to the network's reliability and makes it suitable for time-sensitive applications in VANETs.

Table 4. Measured jitter for various network environments in VANET.

Virtual Machine (VM)	Average Jitter	Maximum Jitter	Minimum Jitter
Node 1	1.2 ms	2.3 ms	0.4 ms
Node 2	1.5 ms	2.5 ms	0.3 ms
Node 3	1.4 ms	2.4 ms	0.5 ms

Table 5. Measured latency for various network environments in VANET.

Virtual Machine (VM)	Average Latency	Maximum Latency	Minimum Latency
Node 1	15 ms	25 ms	5 ms
Node 2	18 ms	28 ms	6 ms
Node 3	16 ms	26 ms	5 ms

Furthermore, we analyzed the security of the proposed architecture against network attacks. Quality metrics were defined to evaluate the penetration of devices by attackers. During communications, network packets or users were injected into the system based on a subsequent distribution. Both worm and spoofing attacks were considered, with the former reducing system performance by reporting the transmission routes of the user requests and the latter arbitrarily discarding packets.

4.3.1. In-Depth Comparative Analysis of Dual-Layer Blockchain versus Traditional VANET Architectures: A Quantitative Performance Evaluation

The results are visualized in Figures 11–14, which show wormhole, falsification, and packet drop probability over varying network densities. The graph compares the proposed system's effectiveness with respect to existing approaches for detecting malicious nodes (MNs) in the VANET related to corresponding nodes, including the probability of a falsification operation.

Figure 12 provides insights into the likelihood of successful wormhole attacks at varying network densities. It is evident that the proposed method substantially outperformed the basic technique across the entire range of network densities, thereby suggesting increased security against wormhole attacks.

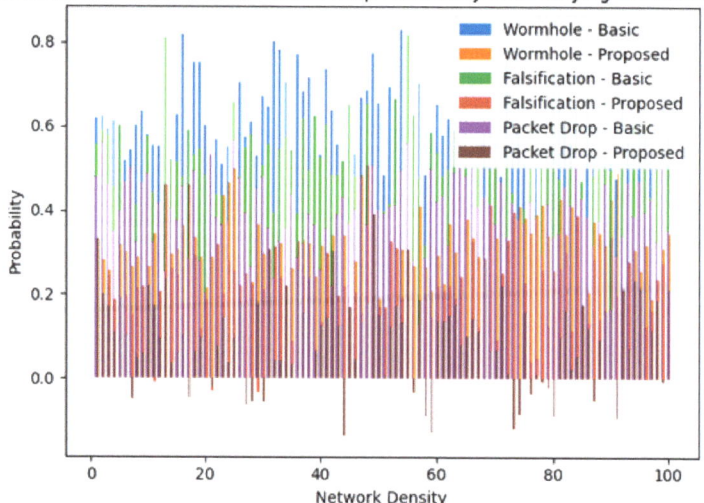

Figure 11. Wormhole, falsification, and packet drop probability over varying network densities.

As can be seen in Figure 13, the proposed method yielded significantly lower probabilities for successful falsification attacks, especially as the network density increased. This enhances the credibility of the information circulating in the network.

Figure 14 illustrates that the proposed method significantly reduced the chances of successful packet-drop attacks across all tested network densities. This ensures higher data integrity and network reliability.

Moreover, we studied the resistance against wormhole attacks for networks with different vehicle speeds. Figures 15 and 16 demonstrate the verification probability and probabilistic possibilities depending on the trust factor, and past vehicular interactions were examined by authenticating networks.

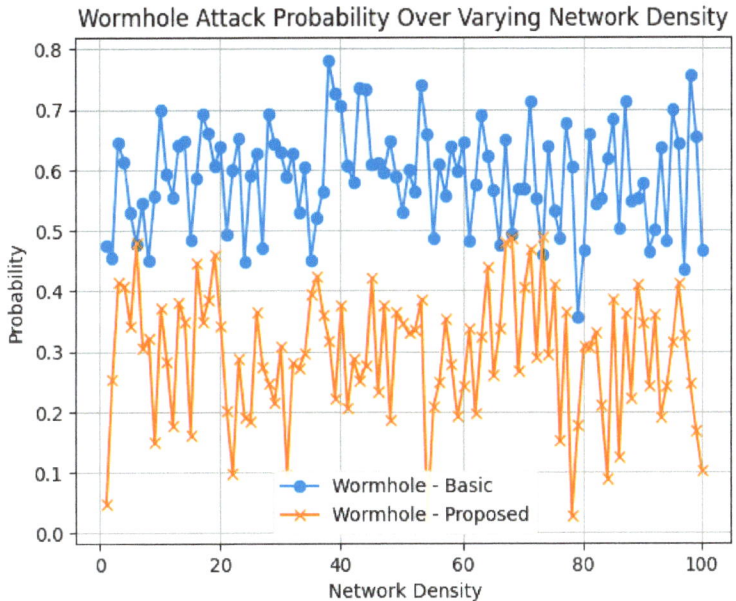

Figure 12. Wormhole attack probability over varying network densities.

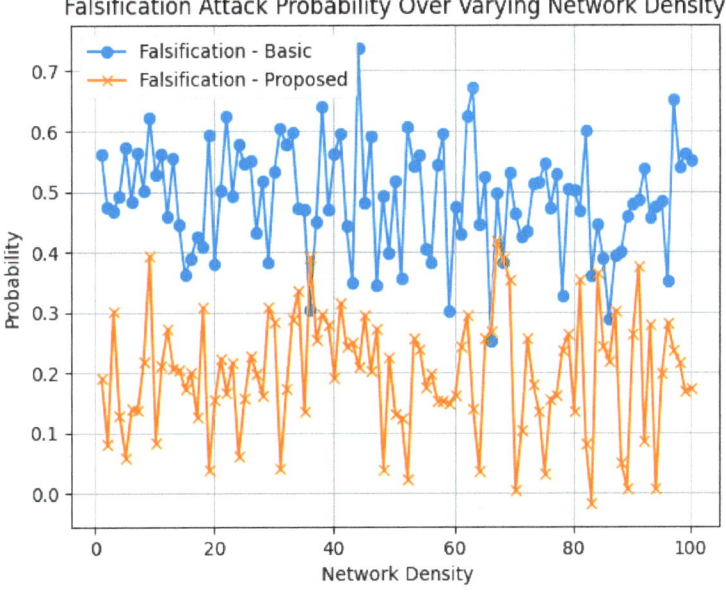

Figure 13. Falsification attack probability over varying network densities.

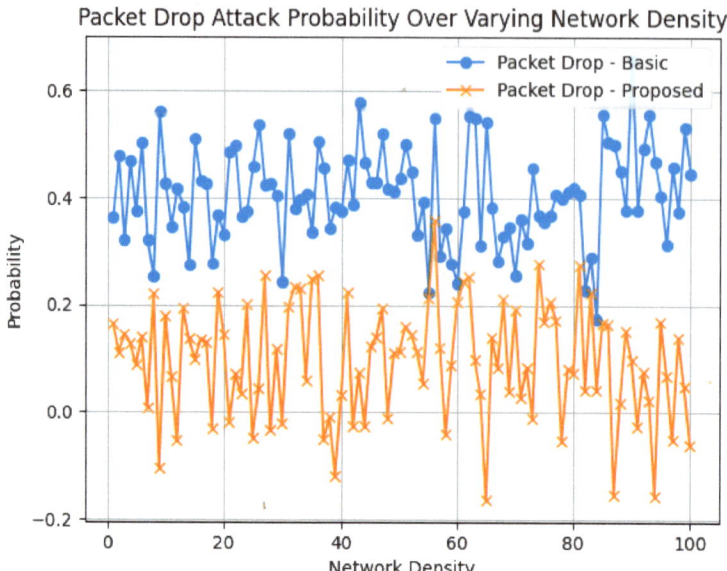

Figure 14. Packet-drop attack probability over varying network densities.

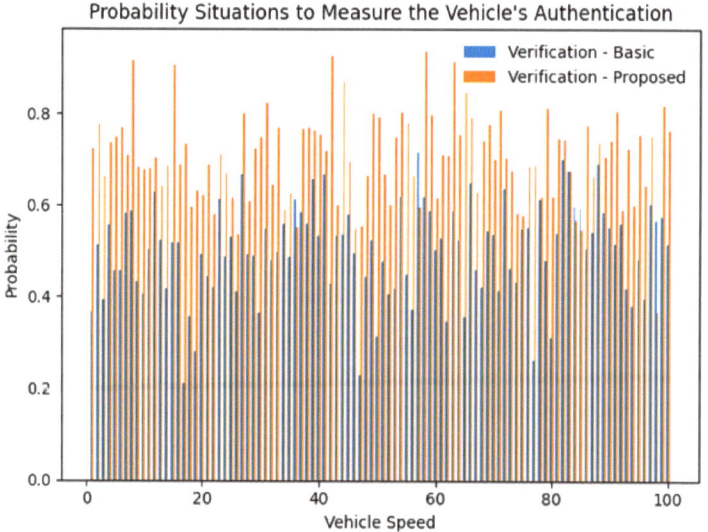

Figure 15. Probability situations to measure the vehicle's authentication.

As illustrated in Figure 17, the graph showcases the relationship between varying vehicle speeds and the corresponding probabilities of successful verification. The x axis enumerates a spectrum of vehicle speeds, while the y axis quantifies the probability of successful verification.

Two methodologies were evaluated: a basic approach and a proposed method. The plot reveals that the proposed method consistently outperformed the basic method across a wide array of vehicle speeds. This superior performance is manifest in the higher probability values associated with the proposed method, as depicted by the 'x'-marked line on the graph. Such observations substantiate the efficacy of the proposed method in high-velocity vehicular scenarios.

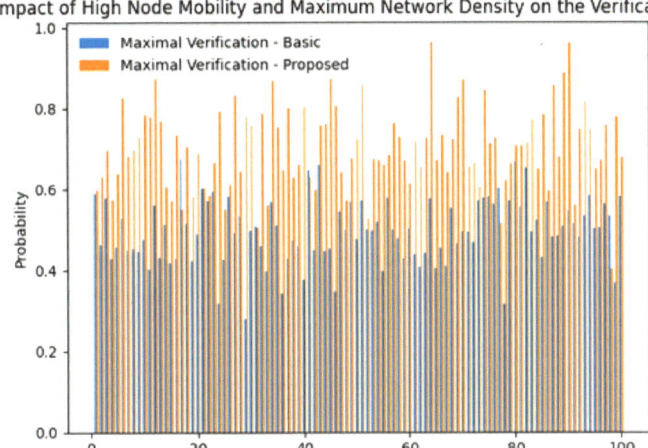

Figure 16. The impact of high node mobility and maximum network density on the verification process.

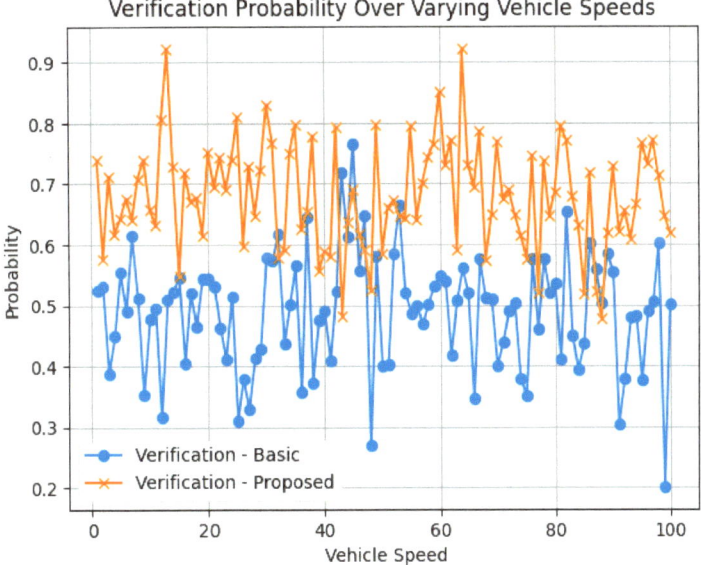

Figure 17. Verification probability over varying vehicle speeds.

As depicted in Figure 18, the graph illustrates the impact of node mobility on the probability of maximal verification using both the basic and proposed methods. The x axis represents the range of node mobility, while the y axis indicates the corresponding probabilities for successful maximal verification.

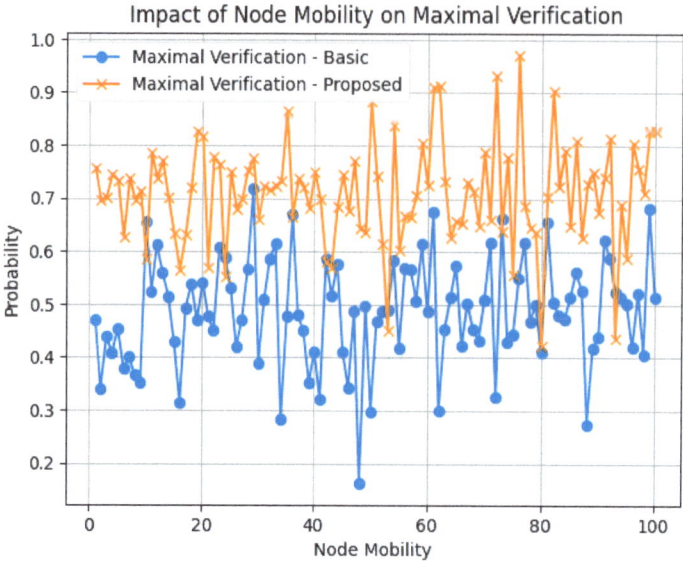

Figure 18. Impact of node mobility on maximal verification.

It is evident that the proposed method consistently outperformed the basic approach across various levels of node mobility. This is particularly highlighted by the higher probabilities associated with the proposed method, which are marked by 'x' on the line graph. Such a trend suggests that the proposed method is more reliable in environments with high node mobility.

In comparison to MN predictions, the suggested framework provided 86 percent accuracy, which can be increased if the experiment is repeated over different network scenarios and more extended periods. Therefore, compared to existing systems, the measurement variables in the proposed methodology perform more effectively.

The Figure 19 demonstrates how the efficiency of the network approached the target of 86% as malicious nodes were identified and removed. The trust rating also evolved, thereby decreasing due to the presence of malicious nodes but recovering as they were removed.

As shown in Figure 19, the efficiency of the network gradually reached its target value of 86% as malicious nodes were successfully identified and eliminated. Concurrently, the trust rating within the network evolved, thereby reflecting the ongoing efforts to neutralize malicious activities. The identification of MNs is predicated on trust, with the removal of discovered MNs having no negative impact on the performance of other nodes.

The suggested mechanism evaluates the trustworthiness of all other nodes in the network at regular intervals, and nodes that are affected and operate maliciously will have a poor rating and trust due to a high packet-drop rate, wormholes, and falsification attacks, but they will eventually be recognized in the long term.

As shown in Figure 15, the suggested scheme had a lower packet loss ratio than the existing methodology. The reason for this enhancement is increased transparency between nodes that monitor the actions of neighboring nodes. Figure 15 depicts the improved performance against wormhole and falsification attacks.

The use of blockchain technology records the specifics of each node's activity, which eliminates the possibility of editing or altering any data during transfer from one node to the next. Furthermore, Figure 16 depicts the maximum and median verification latencies in the event of a security breach, as well as how the current and proposed methodology can provide secure communication in the event of such an attack.

Figure 19. Evolution of network efficiency and trust rating over time.

The existing process used multiple security measures at several levels of interaction, thereby making it vulnerable to brute force attacks. However, the proposed system uses a blockchain across the entire network, thus making it challenging to anticipate or compromise the hashed data of all nodes (vehicles) at once.

Figure 15 depicts the probability situations of an authentication method, where, as the density of MNs (such as compromised vehicles or peer stations) increases, both techniques can still identify the valid nodes. The suggested system, which maintains a blockchain ledger for each node, can determine the trusted node.

The accuracy ended up being close to 86%, which will improve over time as detected MNs are removed from the system. The identification and isolation of MNs based on trust did not impair the functioning of the rest of the network. After a certain period, the proposed mechanism evaluates the trust and ratings of other nodes in the network. Nodes that have been attacked and are acting maliciously will receive a poor grade and trust due to high packet-drop rates, wormholes, and falsification attacks, and they may eventually be isolated from the network.

In our effort to rigorously evaluate the proposed technologies, we conducted some extra experiments. The objective was to compare our proposed method's performance against traditional VANET security solutions across multiple key metrics. The metrics selected for this comparison included the detection rate, latency, transmission efficiency, scalability, and fault tolerance. These metrics were chosen due to their critical importance in the assessment of VANET architectures. We utilized a simulation environment developed using Python, with ns-3 simulations providing the backbone for our experimental setup. This approach allowed for a comprehensive analysis of both the traditional and dual-layer blockchain architectures under various network conditions.

The results, as depicted in the accompanying bar graph (see Figure 20), demonstrate a marked improvement in performance when employing the proposed mechanism:

Detection Rate: The proposed technology exhibited a detection rate of 86%, which is a significant improvement over the traditional architecture's 75% detection rate. This increase can be attributed to the enhanced security protocols and decentralized nature of the blockchain, which aid in more effective anomaly detection.

Latency: In terms of latency, the blockchain-based solution showed a reduction, thereby indicating more efficient data processing and transmission capability. This reduction is crucial in VANET environments where real-time data transmission is paramount.

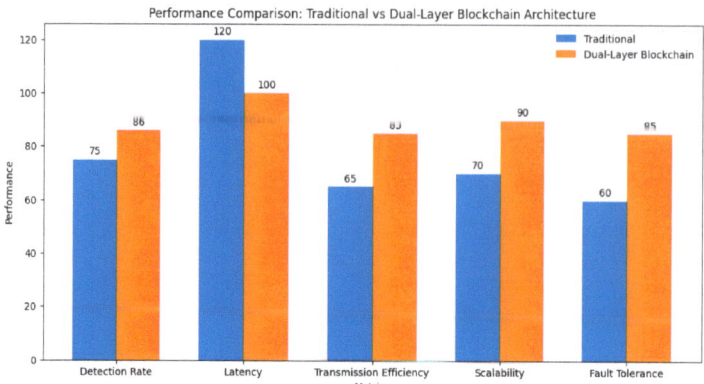

Figure 20. Performance comparison between traditional and proposed blockchain-based solution.

Transmission Efficiency and Scalability: The transmission efficiency and scalability of the proposed system were also notably higher. These improvements are likely due to the distributed nature of blockchain technology, which allows for more efficient data handling and better accommodation of increasing network sizes.

Fault Tolerance: Finally, the fault tolerance of the proposed approach was observed to be superior. This is consistent with the inherent resilience of blockchain systems against points of failure and network attacks.

Figure 21 corroborates the efficacy of the proposed blockchain-based approach in enhancing security and reliability in VANETs. By effectively mitigating the risks associated with collusion and false information injection, the architecture ensures a secure and trustworthy vehicular communication network.

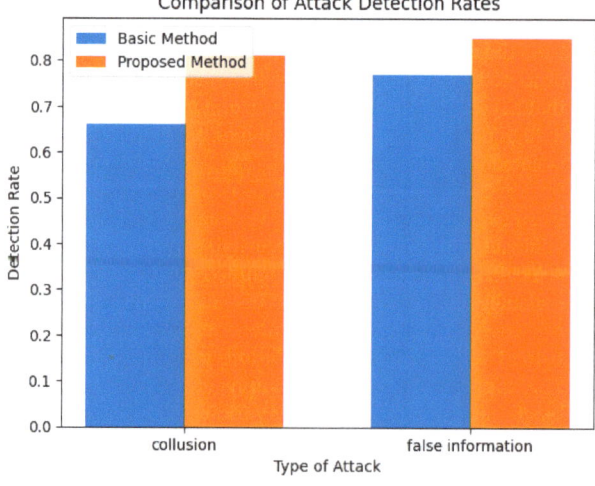

Figure 21. Visual representation of the comparative analysis between the proposed dual-layer blockchain method and the basic method in detecting security threats in VANETs.

The comparative analysis underscores the substantial advantages of the dual-layer blockchain architecture over traditional VANET security solutions. The improved detection rate, reduced latency, and enhanced scalability and fault tolerance highlight its potential as a robust and efficient framework for securing VANETs.

4.3.2. Discussions: Real-World Applicability, Scalability, and Privacy Concerns

In considering the real-world applicability of the proposed technology, it is crucial to acknowledge the practicality of integrating blockchain technology into existing VANET infrastructures. The proposed architecture's compatibility with prevalent vehicular communication standards, such as PHY 802.11p, coupled with its ability to operate efficiently across various network densities and vehicle speeds, underscores its feasibility. The scalability of the system, evidenced by its performance in environments ranging from 50 to 500 nodes, further affirms its suitability for diverse real-world scenarios. Nonetheless, several challenges must be addressed for the successful deployment of this technology in real-world VANETs. One of the primary concerns is the computational overhead introduced by blockchain operations, which may necessitate advanced hardware capabilities in vehicles. To mitigate this, optimization strategies that are focused on reducing blockchain complexity and enhancing data processing efficiency must be employed. Another challenge lies in the storage requirements for maintaining the blockchain ledger. As VANETs generate substantial amounts of data, efficient data management and storage solutions must be developed to handle this load without compromising system performance. Furthermore, network latency, a critical factor in vehicular communications, could be impacted by the block creation and consensus mechanisms inherent in blockchain technology. Optimizing these processes to ensure minimal latency will be crucial for applications requiring real-time data exchange. The widespread adoption and success of this architecture also hinge on the integration of blockchain technology with existing VANET standards and protocols. Collaboration with automotive manufacturers, technology providers, and regulatory bodies will be essential to develop standardized frameworks for blockchain integration in VANETs. The proposed technology presents a promising solution to enhance the security and efficiency of VANETs. While its implementation in real-world scenarios poses certain challenges, these can be addressed through continued research and development. The potential benefits of this architecture in improving vehicular communication security and reliability make it a valuable contribution to the future of intelligent transportation systems.

On the other hand, given the sensitive nature of vehicular data, which often includes real-time location and movement patterns, data privacy emerges as a critical concern in VANETs. Our proposal is designed with stringent privacy measures to protect this sensitive information. By leveraging advanced cryptographic techniques and implementing access control mechanisms within the blockchain, our solution ensures that only authorized entities can access and interpret the data. Moreover, the architecture's inherent decentralization plays a crucial role in enhancing data privacy. Unlike centralized systems, where a single breach can compromise the entire dataset, the distributed nature of blockchain technology makes it exceedingly difficult for unauthorized access to occur. Furthermore, by employing pseudonymization techniques, the system ensures that vehicular data cannot be traced back to individual users, thus maintaining anonymity and privacy. As VANETs continue to expand, with an increasing number of vehicles and infrastructural elements being integrated into the network, scalability becomes a paramount concern. The proposed technology addresses scalability through several key features. Firstly, the separation of the event chain and the reputation chain allows for the distributed processing and storage of data, thereby reducing the burden on individual nodes. Additionally, the system is designed to be modular and adaptable, thus making it capable of integrating with various network sizes and types without sacrificing performance. The use of efficient consensus mechanisms within the blockchain ensures that as the network grows, the time and resources required to validate transactions do not become prohibitive. To further enhance scalability, future iterations of the architecture could incorporate sharding techniques, where the blockchain is divided into smaller, more manageable segments. This would allow for the parallel processing of transactions, thereby significantly increasing throughput and efficiency. Our proposal not only addresses the immediate security and efficiency needs of VANETs, but also takes into consideration crucial aspects like data privacy and scalability. While challenges in these areas exist, ongoing advancements in blockchain technology and vehicular communication systems present promising solutions. As such, the proposed architecture stands as a forward-thinking approach, which is poised to adapt and evolve in tandem with the growing and changing landscape of intelligent transportation systems.

5. Conclusions and Future Work

This paper presents an innovative architecture based on the blockchain to enhance the security and efficiency of vehicular ad hoc networks (VANETs). VANETs are interconnected through the forwarding and exchange of messages between vehicular nodes and are not only crucial for intelligent transport systems, but are also highly susceptible to various security threats. To mitigate these threats, our proposal employs two parallel blockchains, known as the event chain and the reputation chain, which work in collaboration to track and record all actions performed by the nodes in the network. Utilizing a comprehensive set of reputation evaluation schemes based on multifactorial Bayesian inference and historically accumulated reputation values, we succeeded in reducing observation errors and improving reliability in the nodes' reputation assessments. These schemes, accompanied by an attenuation factor and a numerical threshold, minimize the possibility of attacks such as collusion and false information injection. Detailed experiments demonstrated that our dual-layer blockchain architecture achieved an 86% success rate in mitigating hostile behaviors, thus outperforming existing alternatives. These results suggest that the proposed architecture represents a significant advance in secure and efficient reputation management for VANETs. In light of the burgeoning exigencies for vehicular network security and the escalating complexity of cyber threats, our research presents a seminal dual-layer blockchain architecture for VANETs. The salient feature of this innovative system is the synergetic operation of the event chain and the reputation chain. These dual structures meticulously chronicle vehicular communications, thereby engendering a robust bulwark against a spectrum of adversarial maneuvers within the network's ecosystem. Our empirical analysis underscores the prowess of the proposed framework, which was substantiated by a battery of simulations that rigorously benchmarked the system across a gamut of performance metrics. The latency benchmarks, which are pivotal for real-time vehicular communication, were commendably lower than the stringent industry standards, which buttresses the framework's suitability for instantaneous data exchange:

- Latency: The latency measurements underscore a remarkable reduction, thereby substantially enhancing the responsiveness of vehicular communication channels.
- Jitter: The measured jitter remained within the confines of operational tolerance, thus reinforcing the reliability and stability of the vehicular network.
- Packet Delivery Ratio (PDR): A superior PDR, eclipsing the 95th percentile, affirms the robustness of the data transmission protocols under our blockchain-enabled regime.
- Energy Efficiency: The framework's commendable energy efficiency metrics herald a new epoch of sustainable VANET architectures, thereby paving the way for greener intelligent transportation systems.

The innovative fusion of blockchain's immutable ledger with dynamic vehicular networks has culminated in a significant elevation of security proficiency. The architecture's ability to detect and neutralize malevolent entities with an 86% success rate is a testament to its formidable defense mechanisms. Prospective research shall endeavor to refine the consensus mechanisms further, with a particular focus on curtailing latency and jitter to the lowest feasible margins. Additionally, the integration of state-of-the-art cryptographic modalities is envisaged to amplify the security fortifications of the system. The blockchain-infused architectural paradigm for VANETs proffered herein stands validated as a potent catalyst in ameliorating network security and operational efficiency. The encouraging simulation outcomes lend credence to the framework's applicability in contemporary vehicular networks, thereby heralding the evolution of safer and more dependable intelligent transportation systems.

In conclusion, the proposed technology in this paper marks a significant stride in the quest to enhance the security and efficiency of vehicular ad hoc networks (VANETs).

However, we acknowledge certain limitations inherent in our research. First, the scalability of blockchain technology in a highly dynamic environment such as VANETs remains a challenge due to the extensive computational resources required for consensus mechanisms. Furthermore, the latency induced by blockchain could impact the real-time necessity for decision making in VANETs. The attenuation factor and numerical threshold, while effective, may not account for the complex and evolving patterns of vehicular behavior over longer periods. Our experimental setup, although comprehensive, was limited to simulated environments that may not fully capture the unpredictable nature of real-world vehicular networks. To address these limitations, future work will focus on optimizing the blockchain's scalability and reducing latency to meet the stringent real-time requirements of VANETs. Research will also be directed toward developing adaptive algorithms for the attenuation factor and numerical threshold to better reflect the evolving nature of vehicular behaviors. Moreover, we plan to conduct extensive field trials to validate our architecture in real-world scenarios. This will help in fine-tuning the system's parameters and improving its applicability and robustness. Additionally, we aim to explore the integration of emerging technologies like artificial intelligence and machine learning to further enhance the predictive capabilities of our system. By continually pushing the boundaries of current technology, we aim to develop a VANET framework that is not only secure and efficient, but also adaptive and scalable, thereby being capable of withstanding the test of an ever-evolving cyber landscape.

Author Contributions: Conceptualization, R.J.; methodology, R.J. and B.B.; software, R.J.; validation, R.J.; formal analysis, B.B.; investigation, R.J.; resources, B.B.; data curation, R.J.; writing—original draft preparation, R.J.; writing—review and editing, B.B.; visualization, R.J.; supervision, B.B.; project administration, B.B.; funding acquisition, B.B. All authors have read and agreed to the published version of the manuscript.

Funding: This work is supported by the Comunidad de Madrid within the framework of the Multiannual Agreement with the Universidad Politécnica de Madrid to encourage research by young doctors (PRINCE project).

Data Availability Statement: Data are contained within the article.

Conflicts of Interest: The authors declare no conflict of interest.

References

1. Menouar, H.; Guvenc, I.; Akkaya, K.; Uluagac, A.S.; Kadri, A.; Tuncer, A. UAV-enabled intelligent transportation systems for the smart city: Applications and challenges. *IEEE Commun. Mag.* **2017**, *55*, 22–28. [CrossRef]
2. Asra, S.A. Security Issues of Vehicular Ad Hoc Networks (VANET): A Systematic Review. *TIERS Inf. Technol. J.* **2022**, *3*, 17–27. [CrossRef]
3. Afzal, Z.; Kumar, M. Security of vehicular ad-hoc networks (VANET): A survey. *J. Phys. Conf. Ser.* **2020**, *1427*, 012015. [CrossRef]
4. Sweeney, L. k-anonymity: A model for protecting privacy. *Int. J. Uncertain. Fuzziness Knowl.-Based Syst.* **2002**, *10*, 557–570. [CrossRef]
5. Atzori, L.; Iera, A.; Morabito, G. The internet of things: A survey. *Comput. Netw.* **2010**, *54*, 2787–2805. [CrossRef]
6. Li, R.; Song, T.; Mei, B.; Li, H.; Cheng, X.; Sun, L. Blockchain for large-scale internet of things data storage and protection. *IEEE Trans. Serv. Comput.* **2018**, *12*, 762–771. [CrossRef]
7. Wang, L.; Zheng, D.; Guo, R.; Hu, C.; Jing, C. A blockchain-based privacy-preserving authentication scheme with anonymous identity in vehicular networks. *Int. J. Netw. Secur.* **2020**, *22*, 981–990.
8. Wang, X.; Xu, C.; Zhou, Z.; Yang, S.; Sun, L. A survey of blockchain-based cybersecurity for vehicular networks. In Proceedings of the 2020 International Wireless Communications and Mobile Computing (IWCMC), Limassol, Cyprus, 15–19 June 2020; pp. 740–745.
9. Diallo, E.H.; Dib, O.; Al Agha, K. A scalable blockchain-based scheme for traffic-related data sharing in VANETs. *Blockchain Res. Appl.* **2022**, *3*, 100087. [CrossRef]
10. Mollah, M.B.; Zhao, J.; Niyato, D.; Guan, Y.L.; Yuen, C.; Sun, S.; Lam, K.-Y.; Koh, L.H. Blockchain for the internet of vehicles towards intelligent transportation systems: A survey. *IEEE Internet Things J.* **2020**, *8*, 4157–4185. [CrossRef]
11. Mikavica, B.; Kostić-Ljubisavljević, A. Blockchain-based solutions for security, privacy, and trust management in vehicular networks: A survey. *J. Supercomput.* **2021**, *77*, 9520–9575. [CrossRef]

12. Javaid, U.; Aman, M.N.; Sikdar, B. DrivMan: Driving trust management and data sharing in VANETS with blockchain and smart contracts. In Proceedings of the 2019 IEEE 89th Vehicular Technology Conference (VTC2019-Spring), Kuala Lumpur, Malaysia, 28 April–1 May 2019; pp. 1–5.
13. Yeh, L.Y.; Shen, N.X.; Hwang, R.H. Blockchain-based privacy-preserving and sustainable data query service over 5g-vanets. *IEEE Trans. Intell. Transp. Syst.* **2022**, *23*, 15909–15921. [CrossRef]
14. Guehguih, B.; Lu, H. Blockchain-based privacy-preserving authentication and message dissemination scheme for vanet. In Proceedings of the 2019 5th International Conference on Systems, Control and Communications, Wuhan, China, 21–23 December 2019; pp. 16–21.
15. Kouicem, D.E.; Bouabdallah, A.; Lakhlef, H. An efficient and anonymous blockchain-based data sharing scheme for vehicular networks. In Proceedings of the 2020 IEEE Symposium on Computers and Communications (ISCC), Rennes, France, 7–10 July 2020; pp. 1–6.
16. Guo, Z.; Wang, G.; Li, Y.; Ni, J.; Du, R.; Wang, M. Accountable Attribute-Based Data-Sharing Scheme Based on Blockchain for Vehicular Ad Hoc Network. *IEEE Internet Things J.* **2022**, *10*, 7011–7026. [CrossRef]
17. Tan, H.; Chung, I. Secure authentication and key management with blockchain in VANETs. *IEEE Access* **2019**, *8*, 2482–2498. [CrossRef]
18. Xie, L.; Ding, Y.; Yang, H.; Wang, X. Blockchain-based secure and trustworthy Internet of Things in SDN-enabled 5G-VANETs. *IEEE Access* **2019**, *7*, 56656–56666. [CrossRef]
19. Joshi, G.P.; Perumal, E.; Shankar, K.; Tariq, U.; Ahmad, T.; Ibrahim, A. Toward blockchain-enabled privacy-preserving data transmission in cluster-based vehicular networks. *Electronics* **2020**, *9*, 1358. [CrossRef]
20. Li, B.; Liang, R.; Zhu, D.; Chen, W.; Lin, Q. Blockchain-based trust management model for location privacy preserving in VANET. *IEEE Trans. Intell. Transp. Syst.* **2020**, *22*, 3765–3775. [CrossRef]
21. Mokhtar, B.; Azab, M. Survey on security issues in vehicular ad hoc networks. *Alex. Eng. J.* **2015**, *54*, 1115–1126. [CrossRef]
22. Miorandi, D.; Sicari, S.; De Pellegrini, F.; Chlamtac, I. Internet of things: Vision, applications and research challenges. *Ad Hoc Netw.* **2012**, *10*, 1497–1516. [CrossRef]
23. Mistry, I.; Tanwar, S.; Tyagi, S.; Kumar, N. Blockchain for 5G-enabled IoT for industrial automation: A systematic review, solutions, and challenges. *Mech. Syst. Signal Process.* **2020**, *135*, 106382. [CrossRef]
24. Yan, K.; Zeng, P.; Wang, K.; Ma, W.; Zhao, G.; Ma, Y. Reputation consensus-based scheme for information sharing in internet of vehicles. *IEEE Trans. Veh. Technol.* **2023**, *72*, 13631–13636. [CrossRef]
25. Malhi, A.K.; Batra, S.; Pannu, H.S. Security of vehicular ad-hoc networks: A comprehensive survey. *Comput. Secur.* **2020**, *89*, 101664. [CrossRef]
26. Soleymani, S.A.; Abdullah, A.H.; Hassan, W.H.; Anisi, M.H.; Goudarzi, S.; Rezazadeh Baee, M.A.; Mandala, S. Trust management in vehicular ad hoc network: A systematic review. *EURASIP J. Wirel. Commun. Netw.* **2015**, *2015*, 146. [CrossRef]
27. Dwivedi, S.K.; Amin, R.; Das, A.K.; Leung, M.T.; Choo, K.K.R.; Vollala, S. Blockchain-based vehicular ad-hoc networks: A comprehensive survey. *Ad Hoc Netw.* **2022**, *137*, 102980. [CrossRef]
28. Zhang, J.; Zheng, K.; Zhang, D.; Yan, B. AATMS: An anti-attack trust management scheme in VANET. *IEEE Access* **2020**, *8*, 21077–21090. [CrossRef]
29. Eziama, E.; Tepe, K.; Balador, A.; Nwizege, K.S.; Jaimes, L.M. Malicious node detection in vehicular ad-hoc network using machine learning and deep learning. In Proceedings of the 2018 IEEE Globecom Workshops (GC Wkshps), Abu Dhabi, United Arab Emirates, 9–13 December 2018; pp. 1–6.
30. Sheikh, M.S.; Liang, J.; Wang, W. A survey of security services, attacks, and applications for vehicular ad hoc networks (vanets). *Sensors* **2019**, *19*, 3589. [CrossRef]
31. Sedar, R.; Kalalas, C.; Vázquez-Gallego, F.; Alonso, L.; Alonso-Zarate, J. A comprehensive survey of v2x cybersecurity mechanisms and future research paths. *IEEE Open J. Commun. Soc.* **2023**, *4*, 325–391. [CrossRef]
32. Yu, R.; Kang, J.; Huang, X.; Xie, S.; Zhang, Y.; Gjessing, S. MixGroup: Accumulative pseudonym exchanging for location privacy enhancement in vehicular social networks. *IEEE Trans. Dependable Secur. Comput.* **2015**, *13*, 93–105. [CrossRef]
33. Lo, N.W.; Tsai, J.L. An efficient conditional privacy-preserving authentication scheme for vehicular sensor networks without pairings. *IEEE Trans. Intell. Transp. Syst.* **2015**, *17*, 1319–1328. [CrossRef]
34. Nakamoto, S. Bitcoin: A Peer-to-Peer Electronic Cash System. 2008. Available online: https://bitcoin.org/bitcoin.pdf (accessed on 1 October 2023).
35. Zou, S.; Xi, J.; Wang, S.; Lu, Y.; Xu, G. Reportcoin: A novel blockchain-based incentive anonymous reporting system. *IEEE Access* **2019**, *7*, 65544–65559. [CrossRef]
36. Yuan, Y.; Wang, F.Y. Towards blockchain-based intelligent transportation systems. In Proceedings of the 2016 IEEE 19th International Conference on Intelligent Transportation Systems (ITSC), Rio de Janeiro, Brazil, 1–4 November 2016; pp. 2663–2668.
37. Li, W.; Song, H. ART: An attack-resistant trust management scheme for securing vehicular ad hoc networks. *IEEE Trans. Intell. Transp. Syst.* **2015**, *17*, 960–969. [CrossRef]
38. Ahmad, F.; Kurugollu, F.; Kerrache, C.A.; Sezer, S.; Liu, L. Notrino: A novel hybrid trust management scheme for internet-of-vehicles. *IEEE Trans. Veh. Technol.* **2021**, *70*, 9244–9257. [CrossRef]
39. Oubabas, S.; Aoudjit, R.; Rodrigues, J.J.; Talbi, S. Secure and stable vehicular ad hoc network clustering algorithm based on hybrid mobility similarities and trust management scheme. *Veh. Commun.* **2018**, *13*, 128–138. [CrossRef]

40. Yang, Q.; Wang, H. Toward trustworthy vehicular social networks. *IEEE Commun. Mag.* **2015**, *53*, 42–47. [CrossRef]
41. Siddiqui, S.A.; Mahmood, A.; Zhang, W.E.; Sheng, Q.Z. Machine learning based trust model for misbehaviour detection in internet-of-vehicles. In Proceedings of the Neural Information Processing: 26th International Conference, ICONIP 2019, Sydney, NSW, Australia, 12–15 December 2019; pp. 512–520.
42. Fang, W.; Zhang, W.; Liu, Y.; Yang, W.; Gao, Z. BTDS: Bayesian-based trust decision scheme for intelligent connected vehicles in VANETs. *Trans. Emerg. Telecommun. Technol.* **2020**, *31*, e3879. [CrossRef]
43. Halabi, T.; Zulkernine, M. Trust-based cooperative game model for secure collaboration in the internet of vehicles. In Proceedings of the ICC 2019–2019 IEEE International Conference on Communications (ICC), Shanghai, China, 20–24 May 2019; pp. 1–6.
44. Raya, M.; Papadimitratos, P.; Gligor, V.D.; Hubaux, J.P. On data-centric trust establishment in ephemeral ad hoc networks. In Proceedings of the IEEE INFOCOM 2008-The 27th Conference on Computer Communications, Phoenix, AZ, USA, 13–18 April 2008; pp. 1238–1246.
45. Mármol, F.G.; Pérez, G.M. TRIP, a trust and reputation infrastructure-based proposal for vehicular ad hoc networks. *J. Netw. Comput. Appl.* **2012**, *35*, 934–941. [CrossRef]
46. Guleng, S.; Wu, C.; Chen, X.; Wang, X.; Yoshinaga, T.; Ji, Y. Decentralized trust evaluation in vehicular Internet of Things. *IEEE Access* **2019**, *7*, 15980–15988. [CrossRef]
47. Xu, S.; Guo, C.; Hu, R.Q.; Qian, Y. Blockchain-inspired secure computation offloading in a vehicular cloud network. *IEEE Internet Things J.* **2021**, *9*, 14723–14740. [CrossRef]
48. Zhang, H.; Bian, X.; Xu, Y.; Xiang, S.; He, X. Blockchain-assisted vehicle reputation management method for VANET. *J. Xidian Univ.* **2022**, *49*, 49–59.
49. Fei, Z.; Liu, K.; Huang, B.; Zheng, Y.; Xiang, X. Dirichlet process mixture model based nonparametric bayesian modeling and variational inference. In Proceedings of the 2019 Chinese Automation Congress (CAC), Hangzhou, China, 22–24 November 2019; pp. 3048–3051.
50. Gurung, S.; Lin, D.; Squicciarini, A.; Bertino, E. Information-oriented trustworthiness evaluation in vehicular ad-hoc networks. In Proceedings of the Network and System Security: 7th International Conference, NSS 2013, Madrid, Spain, 3–4 June 2013; Springer: Berlin/Heidelberg, Germany; pp. 94–108.
51. Sugumar, R.; Rengarajan, A.; Jayakumar, C. Trust based authentication technique for cluster based vehicular ad hoc networks (VANET). *Wirel. Netw.* **2018**, *24*, 373–382. [CrossRef]
52. Dahmane, S.; Kerrache, C.A.; Lagraa, N.; Lorenz, P. WeiSTARS: A weighted trust-aware relay selection scheme for VANET. In Proceedings of the 2017 IEEE International Conference on Communications (ICC), Paris, France, 21–25 May 2017; pp. 1–6.
53. Zhou, M.; Zhang, R.; Xie, W.; Qian, W.; Zhou, A. Security and privacy in cloud computing: A survey. In Proceedings of the 2010 Sixth International Conference on Semantics, Knowledge and Grids, Beijing, China, 1–3 November 2010; pp. 105–112.
54. Golle, P.; Greene, D.; Staddon, J. Detecting and correcting malicious data in VANETs. In Proceedings of the 1st ACM International Workshop on Vehicular Ad Hoc Networks, Philadelphia, PA, USA, 1 October 2004; pp. 29–37.
55. Diffie, W.; Hellman, M.E. New directions in cryptography. In *Democratizing Cryptography: The Work of Whitfield Diffie and Martin Hellman*; Association for Computing Machinery: New York, NY, USA, 2022; pp. 365–390.
56. Narayanan, A.; Bonneau, J.; Felten, E.; Miller, A.; Goldfeder, S. *Bitcoin and Cryptocurrency Technologies: A Comprehensive Introduction*; Princeton University Press: Princeton, NJ, USA, 2016.
57. Ma, Z.; Zhang, J.; Guo, Y.; Liu, Y.; Liu, X.; He, W. An efficient decentralized key management mechanism for VANET with blockchain. *IEEE Trans. Veh. Technol.* **2020**, *69*, 5836–5849. [CrossRef]
58. Feng, J.; Wang, Y.; Wang, J.; Ren, F. Blockchain-based data management and edge-assisted trusted cloaking area construction for location privacy protection in vehicular networks. *IEEE Internet Things J.* **2020**, *8*, 2087–2101. [CrossRef]
59. Zhu, X.; Jiang, S.; Wang, L.; Li, H. Efficient privacy-preserving authentication for vehicular ad hoc networks. *IEEE Trans. Veh. Technol.* **2013**, *63*, 907–919. [CrossRef]
60. Su, J.; Ren, R.; Li, Y.; Lau, R.Y.; Shi, Y. Trusted blockchain-based signcryption protocol and data management for authentication and authorization in VANETs. *Wirel. Commun. Mob. Comput.* **2022**, *2022*, 9572992. [CrossRef]
61. Grover, J. Security of Vehicular Ad Hoc Networks using blockchain: A comprehensive review. *Veh. Commun.* **2022**, *34*, 100458. [CrossRef]
62. Zhang, X.; Li, R.; Cui, B. A security architecture of VANET based on blockchain and mobile edge computing. In Proceedings of the 2018 1st IEEE International Conference on Hot Information-Centric Networking (HotICN), Shenzhen, China, 15–17 August 2018; pp. 258–259.
63. Disterer, G. ISO/IEC 27000, 27001 and 27002 for information security management. *J. Inf. Secur.* **2013**, *4*, 92–100. [CrossRef]
64. Ashton, K. That 'internet of things' thing. *RFID J.* **2009**, *22*, 97–114.
65. Fernando, N.; Loke, S.W.; Rahayu, W. Mobile cloud computing: A survey. *Future Gener. Comput. Syst.* **2013**, *29*, 84–106. [CrossRef]
66. Dorri, A.; Kanhere, S.S.; Jurdak, R.; Gauravaram, P. Blockchain for IoT security and privacy: The case study of a smart home. In Proceedings of the 2017 IEEE International Conference on Pervasive Computing and Communications Workshops (PerCom Workshops), Kona, HI, USA, 13–17 March 2017; pp. 618–623.
67. Kshetri, N. Can blockchain strengthen the internet of things? *IT Prof.* **2017**, *19*, 68–72. [CrossRef]

68. Bonneau, J.; Miller, A.; Clark, J.; Narayanan, A.; Kroll, J.A.; Felten, E.W. Sok: Research perspectives and challenges for bitcoin and cryptocurrencies. In Proceedings of the 2015 IEEE Symposium on Security and Privacy, San Jose, CA, USA, 17–21 May 2015; pp. 104–121.
69. Li, Z.; Kang, J.; Yu, R.; Ye, D.; Deng, Q.; Zhang, Y. Consortium blockchain for secure energy trading in industrial internet of things. IEEE Trans. Ind. Inform. 2017, 14, 3690–3700. [CrossRef]
70. Wang, Y.; Su, Z.; Zhang, K.; Benslimane, A. Challenges and solutions in autonomous driving: A blockchain approach. IEEE Netw. 2020, 34, 218–226. [CrossRef]
71. Yang, Z.; Zheng, K.; Yang, K.; Leung, V.C. A blockchain-based reputation system for data credibility assessment in vehicular networks. In Proceedings of the 2017 IEEE 28th Annual International Symposium on Personal, Indoor, and Mobile Radio Communications (PIMRC), Montreal, QC, Canada, 8–13 October 2017; pp. 1–5.
72. Huang, X.; Yu, R.; Kang, J.; Zhang, Y. Distributed reputation management for secure and efficient vehicular edge computing and networks. IEEE Access 2017, 5, 25408–25420. [CrossRef]
73. Liu, G.; Yang, Q.; Wang, H.; Wu, S.; Wittie, M.P. Uncovering the mystery of trust in an online social network. In Proceedings of the 2015 IEEE Conference on Communications and Network Security (CNS), Florence, Italy, 28–30 September 2015; pp. 488–496.
74. Jayasinghe, U.; Lee, G.M.; Um, T.W.; Shi, Q. Machine learning based trust computational model for IoT services. IEEE Trans. Sustain. Comput. 2018, 4, 39–52. [CrossRef]
75. Mahmood, A.; Zhang, W.E.; Sheng, Q.Z.; Siddiqui, S.A.; Aljubairy, A. Trust management for software-defined heterogeneous vehicular ad hoc networks. In Security Privacy and Trust in the IoT Environment; Springer: Cham, Switzerland, 2019; pp. 203–226.
76. Bendechache, M.; Saber, T.; Muntean, G.M.; Tal, I. Application of blockchain technology to 5g-enabled vehicular networks: Survey and future directions. In Proceedings of the 18th International Symposium on High Performance Mobile Computing & Wireless Networks for HPC (MCWN 2020), Barcelona, Spain, 10–14 December 2020.
77. Fernandes, C.P.; Montez, C.; Adriano, D.D.; Boukerche, A.; Wangham, M.S. A blockchain-based reputation system for trusted vanet nodes. Ad Hoc Netw. 2023, 140, 103071. [CrossRef]
78. Fan, N.; Shen, S.; Wu, C.Q.; Yao, J. A hybrid trust model based on communication and social trust for vehicular social networks. Int. J. Distrib. Sens. Netw. 2022, 18, 15501329221097588. [CrossRef]
79. Kerrache, C.A.; Lagraa, N.; Hussain, R.; Ahmed, S.H.; Benslimane, A.; Calafate, C.T.; Cano, J.-C.; Vegni, A.M. TACASHI: Trust-aware communication architecture for social internet of vehicles. IEEE Internet Things J. 2018, 6, 5870–5877. [CrossRef]
80. Hou, B.; Xin, Y.; Zhu, H.; Yang, Y.; Yang, J. VANET Secure Reputation Evaluation & Management Model Based on Double Layer Blockchain. Appl. Sci. 2023, 13, 5733.
81. Gazdar, T.; Belghith, A.; Abutair, H. An enhanced distributed trust computing protocol for VANETs. IEEE Access 2017, 6, 380–392. [CrossRef]
82. Gu, X.; Tang, L.; Han, J. A social-aware routing protocol based on fuzzy logic in vehicular ad hoc networks. In Proceedings of the 2014 International Workshop on High Mobility Wireless Communications, Beijing, China, 1–3 November 2014; pp. 12–16.
83. Campanile, L.; Gribaudo, M.; Iacono, M.; Marulli, F.; Mastroianni, M. Computer network simulation with ns-3: A systematic literature review. Electronics 2020, 9, 272. [CrossRef]
84. Pratama, R.A.; Rosselina, L.; Sulistyowati, D.; Sari, R.F.; Harwahyu, R. Performance evaluation on vanet routing protocols in the way road of central jakarta using ns-3 and sumo. In Proceedings of the 2020 International Seminar on Application for Technology of Information and Communication (iSemantic), Semarang, Indonesia, 19–20 September 2020; pp. 280–285.
85. Liu, Y. Vanet routing protocol simulation research based on ns-3 and sumo. In Proceedings of the 2021 IEEE 4th International Conference on Electronics Technology (ICET), Chengdu, China, 7–10 May 2021; pp. 1073–1076.
86. Malnar, M.; Jevtić, N. A framework for performance evaluation of VANETs using NS-3 simulator. Promet–Traffic Transp. 2020, 32, 255–268. [CrossRef]

Disclaimer/Publisher's Note: The statements, opinions and data contained in all publications are solely those of the individual author(s) and contributor(s) and not of MDPI and/or the editor(s). MDPI and/or the editor(s) disclaim responsibility for any injury to people or property resulting from any ideas, methods, instructions or products referred to in the content.

Article

Enhancing Cryptographic Primitives through Dynamic Cost Function Optimization in Heuristic Search

Oleksandr Kuznetsov [1,2,*], Nikolay Poluyanenko [2], Emanuele Frontoni [1], Sergey Kandiy [2], Mikolaj Karpinski [3,4] and Ruslan Shevchuk [5,6,*]

1. Department of Political Sciences, Communication and International Relations, University of Macerata, Via Crescimbeni, 30/32, 62100 Macerata, Italy; emanuele.frontoni@unimc.it
2. Department of Information and Communication Systems Security, School of Computer Sciences, V. N. Karazin Kharkiv National University, 4 Svobody Sq., 61022 Kharkiv, Ukraine; n.poluyanenko@karazin.ua (N.P.); sergeykandy@gmail.com (S.K.)
3. Institute of Security and Computer Science, University of the National Education Commission, 30-084 Krakow, Poland; mikolaj.karpinski@up.krakow.pl
4. Department of Cyber Security, Ternopil Ivan Puluj National Technical University, 46001 Ternopil, Ukraine
5. Department of Computer Science and Automatics, University of Bielsko-Biala, 43-309 Bielsko-Biala, Poland
6. Department of Computer Science, West Ukrainian National University, 46009 Ternopil, Ukraine
* Correspondence: kuznetsov@karazin.ua (O.K.); rshevchuk@ubb.edu.pl (R.S.)

Citation: Kuznetsov, O.; Poluyanenko, N.; Frontoni, E.; Kandiy, S.; Karpinski, M.; Shevchuk, R. Enhancing Cryptographic Primitives through Dynamic Cost Function Optimization in Heuristic Search. *Electronics* **2024**, *13*, 1825. https://doi.org/10.3390/electronics13101825

Academic Editor: Mehdi Sookhak

Received: 26 March 2024
Revised: 1 May 2024
Accepted: 3 May 2024
Published: 8 May 2024

Copyright: © 2024 by the authors. Licensee MDPI, Basel, Switzerland. This article is an open access article distributed under the terms and conditions of the Creative Commons Attribution (CC BY) license (https:// creativecommons.org/licenses/by/ 4.0/).

Abstract: The efficiency of heuristic search algorithms is a critical factor in the realm of cryptographic primitive construction, particularly in the generation of highly nonlinear bijective permutations, known as substitution boxes (S-boxes). The vast search space of 256! (256 factorial) permutations for 8-bit sequences poses a significant challenge in isolating S-boxes with optimal nonlinearity, a crucial property for enhancing the resilience of symmetric ciphers against cryptanalytic attacks. Existing approaches to this problem suffer from high computational costs and limited success rates, necessitating the development of more efficient and effective methods. This study introduces a novel approach that addresses these limitations by dynamically adjusting the cost function parameters within the hill-climbing heuristic search algorithm. By incorporating principles from dynamic programming, our methodology leverages feedback from previous iterations to adaptively refine the search trajectory, leading to a significant reduction in the number of iterations required to converge on optimal solutions. Through extensive comparative analyses with state-of-the-art techniques, we demonstrate that our approach achieves a remarkable 100% success rate in locating 8-bit bijective S-boxes with maximal nonlinearity, while requiring only 50,000 iterations on average—a substantial improvement over existing methods. The proposed dynamic parameter adaptation mechanism not only enhances the computational efficiency of the search process, but also showcases the potential for interdisciplinary collaboration between the fields of heuristic optimization and cryptography. The practical implications of our findings are significant, as the ability to efficiently generate highly nonlinear S-boxes directly contributes to the development of more secure and robust symmetric encryption systems. Furthermore, the dynamic parameter adaptation concept introduced in this study opens up new avenues for future research in the broader context of heuristic optimization and its applications across various domains.

Keywords: cryptographic primitives; bijective permutations; substitution boxes; nonlinearity; heuristic search; dynamic programming; cost function optimization; cryptanalysis

1. Introduction and Analysis of Related Works

Robust cryptographic primitives are vital for safeguarding information in the digital age. As cyber threats continue to evolve, developing advanced encryption algorithms capable of withstanding sophisticated attacks has become a critical research endeavor [1,2]. Among these primitives, substitution boxes (S-boxes) play a pivotal role in introducing nonlinearity to symmetric ciphers, thereby enhancing their resilience against cryptanalytic techniques such as linear and differential cryptanalysis [3,4].

The construction of optimal S-boxes, which exhibit high nonlinearity and satisfy the strict avalanche criterion, has been a central focus of cryptographic research [5,6]. However, the generation of such S-boxes is a challenging combinatorial optimization problem, owing to the vast search space and complex cryptographic properties that must be satisfied [7–9]. Classical algebraic constructions, while providing S-boxes with optimal parameters, often introduce undesirable algebraic structures that can be exploited by attackers [10,11]. On the other hand, purely random generation methods, although free from such structures, have an exceedingly low probability of yielding S-boxes with the desired cryptographic strength [6,12].

To address these challenges, researchers have increasingly turned to heuristic optimization techniques for S-box generation. These methods combine the elements of randomness and guided search to efficiently explore the vast search space while avoiding the pitfalls of purely algebraic or random constructions. Simulated annealing [6,13], genetic algorithms [14–16], and hill climbing (HC) [17,18] have emerged as popular heuristic approaches in this domain. Significant progress has been made in adapting these algorithms to the specific requirements of S-box generation, such as the incorporation of novel cost functions to evaluate the cryptographic properties of candidate solutions [19–21].

Despite these advancements, generating optimal S-boxes remains a computationally intensive task. Existing heuristic methods often require a large number of iterations to converge on solutions with the desired nonlinearity [7,19,20]. Furthermore, the effectiveness of these algorithms is highly dependent on the careful tuning of their parameters and the design of the cost function [21–23]. There is a need for more efficient and adaptive heuristic techniques that can navigate the search space more effectively and locate optimal S-boxes with fewer computational resources. Table 1 presents a comparative overview of the most prominent heuristic methods, highlighting their key features, performance metrics, and limitations.

Table 1. Comparison of heuristic techniques for S-box generation.

Technique	Key Features	Performance Metrics	Limitations
Simulated Annealing [6,13]—Probabilistic search	Temperature-based acceptance criteria	Nonlinearity: 102–104, Iterations: >500,000	High computational cost, sensitive to parameter tuning
Genetic Algorithms [14–16]—Population-based search	Crossover and mutation operators	Nonlinearity: 100–104, Iterations: >200,000	Premature convergence, difficulty in maintaining diversity
Hill Climbing [17,18]—Gradient-based search	Local neighborhood exploration	Nonlinearity: 102–104, Iterations: >100,000	Prone to getting stuck in local optima, dependent on initial solution
Particle Swarm Optimization [24]	Swarm intelligence, Velocity and position updates	Nonlinearity: 94–100	Susceptibility to local optima
Our Proposed Method	Dynamic parameter adaptation, Efficient hill climbing with WCFS cost function	Nonlinearity: 104, Iterations: <50,000	Potential for further improvement

As evident from Table 1, existing heuristic techniques for S-box generation suffer from various limitations, such as high computational costs, sensitivity to parameter tuning, premature convergence, and susceptibility to local optima. Moreover, these methods often require a large number of iterations to converge on solutions with the desired nonlinearity, leading to significant computational overhead.

In contrast, our proposed method introduces a novel dynamic parameter adaptation mechanism that enhances the efficiency and effectiveness of the hill-climbing algorithm. By dynamically adjusting the cost function parameters based on the search progress, our approach is able to locate optimal S-boxes with fewer iterations and higher nonlinearity compared to state-of-the-art techniques.

We validate our method through extensive experiments and comparative analyses with state-of-the-art heuristic techniques for S-box generation. The results demonstrate that our dynamic parameter adaptation strategy consistently outperforms existing approaches, achieving a 100% success rate in finding S-boxes with nonlinearity of 104 or higher while requiring significantly fewer iterations. Furthermore, we provide insights into the behavior of our algorithm and discuss the implications of our findings for the design of efficient heuristic methods in cryptography.

The comparative analysis presented in Table 1 highlights the novelty and advantages of our proposed method over state-of-the-art techniques. By addressing the limitations of existing approaches and introducing a dynamic parameter adaptation mechanism, our work contributes to the advancement of heuristic optimization techniques for S-box generation in cryptographic applications. The main contributions of this paper are as follows:

1. We introduce a novel dynamic parameter adaptation mechanism for heuristic search algorithms in the context of S-box generation.
2. We demonstrate the effectiveness of our approach through rigorous experiments and comparative analyses with state-of-the-art techniques.
3. We provide insights into the behavior of our algorithm and discuss the implications of our findings for the design of efficient heuristic methods in cryptography.

The remainder of this paper is organized as follows. The background section lays the necessary theoretical foundation, covering the mathematical properties of S-boxes, heuristic search algorithms, and the Walsh–Hadamard transform. The proposed methodology introduces a dynamic parameter adaptation mechanism and an enhanced hill-climbing algorithm for efficient S-box generation. The article then presents the experimental setup, benchmark instances, performance metrics, and a detailed analysis of the results obtained from three series of experiments. The discussion section interprets the findings, compares the proposed method with state-of-the-art techniques, and addresses the limitations and future research directions. Finally, the conclusion summarizes the main contributions, emphasizes the novelty and effectiveness of the approach, and offers concluding remarks on the potential impact of the research in the field of cryptography.

2. Nomenclature

This section provides a comprehensive list of the symbols, notations, and abbreviations used throughout the article. Each entry includes a clear and concise definition to facilitate the reader's understanding of the presented concepts and formulas.

S—An S-box (substitution box), a basic component in symmetric key cryptography
n—The size of the S-box input in bits
m—The size of the S-box output in bits
x—An input value to the S-box
y—An output value from the S-box
$\{0;1\}^n$—The set of all possible n-bit binary strings
WHT(a,b)—Walsh–Hadamard Transform of the S-box at points a and b
a·x—The inner product of a and x in the Boolean algebra context
b·S(x)—The inner product of b and S(x) in the Boolean algebra context
N(S)—The nonlinearity of the S-box S
Δ(S)—The differential uniformity of the S-box S
$\vec{H}(S)$—The histogram of the Walsh–Hadamard coefficients for the S-box S

i_{max}—The maximum absolute value of the Walsh–Hadamard coefficients for the S-box
l_i—The number of Walsh–Hadamard coefficients with an absolute value i
S_s—The search space in the context of heuristic search
f—The cost function or objective function in the context of heuristic search
R—A parameter of the WCFS cost function
X—A parameter of the WCFS cost function
WCFS(S)—The cost function used in the hill-climbing algorithm for S-box generation

3. Background

The heuristic generation of S-boxes stands as a cornerstone in modern symmetric ciphers, ensuring nonlinearity and reducing vulnerabilities to attacks [5,6,25]. This section delves into the essential terminologies and cryptographic measures of S-boxes, and explicates the heuristic methods in targeting an optimal state. Additionally, the prominence of the hill-climbing method in combinatorial optimization is elaborated, setting the stage for our subsequent discourse on the prevailing gaps in research and our innovative contribution to this domain.

3.1. S-Boxes (Substitution-Boxes)

In the realm of symmetric cryptography, the S-box (Substitution box) stands as a pivotal nonlinear transformation component [26,27]. Its primary role is to map input bits to output bits, introducing a level of confusion and complexity to the encryption process [28].

From a conceptual standpoint, an S-box can be visualized as a black box that takes a fixed number of bits as inputs and produces a fixed number of bits as outputs. The transformation is defined by a lookup table, which specifies the output for each possible input.

In the context of Boolean algebra, an S-box can be represented as a set of Boolean functions [29,30]. Given an m-bit input and an n-bit output, an S-box is defined by n Boolean functions, each taking m variables.

For an S-box with a size of n×m, it can be represented as [30]:

$$S:\{0;1\}^m \longrightarrow \{0;1\}^n$$

where $\{0;1\}^n$ is the domain representing all possible n-bit binary strings and $\{0;1\}^m$ is the codomain representing all possible m-bit binary strings. Specifically, we focus on S-boxes that take an 8-bit input and produce an 8-bit output, ensuring a one-to-one mapping between the input and output spaces.

To ensure an S-box is resilient against cryptanalysis, several measures have been postulated [30]:

- Bijectiveness ensures that every input has a unique output and vice versa. For an S-box to be bijective, it must be both injective (one-to-one) and surjective (onto). Mathematically, an S-box S is bijective if, and only if, for every pair of distinct inputs x and y, their outputs are also distinct, and every possible output has a corresponding input:

$$\forall x, y \in \{0,1\}^8, S(x) = S(y) \Rightarrow x = y.$$

- Nonlinearity measures the deviation of an S-box from affine functions. It provides resistance against linear cryptanalysis. The nonlinearity of an S-box is computed using the Walsh–Hadamard transform. Given an S-box S, its nonlinearity N(S) is defined as:

$$N(s) = \frac{1}{2}(2^n - max_{a,b \neq 0}|WHT(a,b)|),$$

where $WHT(a,b)$ is the Walsh–Hadamard transform of S and is defined as:

$$WHT(a,b) = \sum_{x \in \{0,1\}^n} (-1)^{b \cdot S(x) + a \cdot x} \tag{1}$$

Here, $a \cdot x$ and $b \cdot S(x)$ are the inner products in the Boolean algebra context.

- Differential Uniformity is a measure of the resistance of the S-box against differential cryptanalysis. The lower the differential uniformity, the better the S-box is in terms of resisting differential attacks. For an S-box S, its differential uniformity $\Delta(S)$ is defined as:

$$\Delta(S) = max_{\Delta x, \Delta y} \left| \left\{ x \in \{0,1\}^8 : S(x) \oplus S(x \oplus \Delta x) = \Delta y \right\} \right|,$$

where $\oplus$ denotes the bitwise XOR operation.

- There are several other properties of S-boxes that are crucial for their cryptographic strength, such as the Avalanche effect, Strict Avalanche Criterion, Bit Independence Criterion, and more. Each of these properties ensures that the S-box provides good diffusion and resistance against various cryptanalytic attacks.

3.2. Heuristic Techniques

Heuristic search, grounded in the realm of optimization and problem solving, emerges as a pivotal strategy when faced with extensive search spaces or computationally rigorous problems [31,32]. This approach delicately toes the line between finding optimal solutions and ensuring computational viability.

Central to the heuristic search is the concept of a search space, the entire domain comprising potential solutions [33,34]. Given the complexity of certain problems, the vastness of this space can render exhaustive searches nonviable. In such landscapes, a heuristic, a rule-of-thumb technique, provides a promising avenue. It may not always guarantee the most optimal solution, but it navigates the vast space to produce an approximation in a time frame that is algorithmically acceptable.

A quintessential component that drives heuristics is the cost function or the objective function [35]. Mathematically, if we let S_s be our search space, the cost function f can be represented as $f: S_s \longrightarrow S$, mapping each candidate solution to a real value, indicative of its quality. This function not only quantifies the desirability or fitness of a solution, but also becomes the guiding light, directing the heuristic search towards regions of the search space that show potential. Furthermore, it offers a comparative landscape, allowing one solution to be weighed against another, and often serves as a termination beacon, indicating when the search should conclude.

Numerous heuristic search strategies have found prominence in the literature and practice. Among them, Genetic Algorithms draw inspiration from natural selection [33,36], encoding solutions as 'genes' and iteratively refining them over successive generations using processes akin to mutation and crossover. Another fascinating method, Simulated Annealing, borrows its philosophy from metallurgy, particularly the annealing process [36,37]. This probabilistic technique oscillates between accepting solutions of varying quality based on a dynamically adjusted temperature parameter. Yet another strategy, the Tabu Search, incorporates memory in its operations, maintaining a list of recently traversed solutions to avoid cyclical traps [35,36].

However, the hill-climbing algorithm deserves special mention [36]. Its conceptual simplicity combined with iterative refinement makes it a darling in the world of combinatorial optimization [38]. The algorithm initiates with a randomly chosen solution and steadily refines it by evaluating its neighbors in Algorithm 1. The quality of these neighbors is adjudged by the cost function, and the best among them is chosen for the next iteration. This process perseveres until no further refinement yields a better solution. Its inherent advantage lies in its straightforwardness, adaptability, and efficiency.

The hill-climbing algorithm is an iterative optimization algorithm that starts with an arbitrary solution to a problem and iteratively refines the current solution by making small changes to it. The idea is to always move towards a better solution in the search space [36,38].

Algorithm 1: Hill-Climbing Algorithm (Generalized Version)

Algorithm HillClimbing(search_space)
    current_solution ← initialize_random_solution(search_space)
    current_value ← evaluate(current_solution)

    while True do
        neighbors ← generate_neighbors(current_solution)

        if neighbors is empty then
            return current_solution
        end if

        next_solution ← best_solution(neighbors)
        next_value ← evaluate(next_solution)

        if next_value ≤ current_value then
            return current_solution
        end if

        current_solution ← next_solution
        current_value ← next_value
    end while
end Algorithm

Description and Comments:

1. Initialization: The algorithm begins by initializing a solution randomly. This serves as our current reference point.
   current_solution←initialize_random_solution(search_space)
   Here, the search_space represents the entire space of possible solutions. The function initialize_random_solution simply picks a point (or solution) from this space at random.
2. Evaluation: We assess the quality or fitness of our current solution using an evaluation function.
   current_value←evaluate(current_solution)
3. Iterative Refinement:
   - The main loop of the algorithm focuses on refining the current solution.
   - In every iteration, we look at the neighboring solutions of our current state, which is performed by the generate_neighbors function. These neighbors are typically small variations of the current solution.
   - If there are no neighbors (an edge case), we simply return the current solution as our best found.
   - From these neighbors, we choose the best one (having the highest or lowest value, depending on whether it is a maximization or minimization problem). The function best_solution facilitates this selection.
   - We then evaluate this new best solution from the neighbors.
   - A critical decision point ensues. If the new solution's value is not better than our current solution, the algorithm terminates, and our current solution is returned as the best found. If the new solution is better, we shift our current solution to this new point and continue the process.
4. Termination:
   - The algorithm terminates either when no better neighboring solutions can be found or when there are no neighbors left for the current solution.

The generation of cryptographic S-boxes, which act as vital components in symmetric key algorithms, poses a formidable challenge. The need to ensure bijectiveness and simultaneously achieve high nonlinearity demands robust optimization techniques. Enter the specialized hill-climbing algorithm in Algorithm 2—crafted with a discerning focus on this particular challenge [39–41]. The pseudo-code for this variant is detailed in Appendix C of the work [17].

Algorithm 2: Hill-Climbing Algorithm for S-boxes Generation (version from [17])

Algorithm SpecializedHillClimbing (S,NoE)
    while (NoE > 0) do
        S'←S
        Select random distinct positions i,j
        Swap outputs of S' corresponding to i and j
        if N(S') > N(S) or N(S') = N(S) and CS' < CS then
            S←S'
        end if

        NoE← NoE−1
    end while
    return S
end Algorithm

Description and Comments:

1. Initialization: The algorithm accepts an initial random substitution S and a predetermined number of solution evaluations, NoE, which is typically set to 10^6, as suggested in [17].
2. Iterative Refinement:
   - During each iteration, a copy S' of the current solution S is made. Two random distinct positions, i and j, are selected from this substitution.
   - A pivotal step involves swapping the outputs of S' corresponding to the positions i and j. This is the essence of creating a neighboring solution in the context of S-box generation.
   - The newly formed neighbor, S', is then evaluated on two primary metrics: $N(S)$ (nonlinearity) and CS' (cost function value, as evaluated by the WCFS). If S' offers superior nonlinearity or, in the event of identical nonlinearity, a lower cost, it supplants the current solution S.
3. Termination: The algorithm halts after a preset number of evaluations, NoE, ensuring bounded computation.

The merit of this tailored hill-climbing approach, when synergized with the new cost function (called WCFS), is underscored by its empirical success. Remarkably, in just an average of 70,000 iterations, it was able to generate an 8×8 bijective S-box with a nonlinearity of 104 [17]. Further honing this technique, the same researchers managed to slash this to an even more impressive 65,933 iterations [20], edging ever closer to cryptographic perfection.

The concepts and techniques discussed in this background section lay the foundation for our proposed methodology. By understanding the mathematical properties of S-boxes, such as bijectiveness, nonlinearity, and differential uniformity, we can formulate effective cost functions and heuristic search strategies for generating optimal S-boxes. The Walsh–Hadamard transform, in particular, plays a crucial role in evaluating the nonlinearity of S-boxes and guiding the search process. Moreover, the hill-climbing algorithm, with its iterative refinement approach and specialized adaptations for S-box generation, serves as the backbone of our proposed method. Building upon these fundamental concepts and leveraging the strengths of heuristic optimization, our work aims to develop a more efficient and effective approach for constructing cryptographically strong S-boxes. In the following sections, we will delve into the details of our methodology, presenting the dynamic parameter adaptation mechanism and the enhanced hill-climbing algorithm that form the core of our contribution to the field of S-box generation.

4. Methodology

S-box generation has been a central pillar in the realm of cryptographic research. Our investigative endeavors are predicated upon the foundational works detailed in [17,20], where seminal results in this domain were elucidated. These prior research contributions offer an optimal search algorithm and an associated cost function, both of which lay the groundwork for our own explorations. With this canvas, we extend the paradigm by introducing refined mechanisms to optimize the search process, integrating dynamic parameter adjustments, and, consequently, ushering in a more nuanced understanding of nonlinear substitution generation.

4.1. Cost Function

Grounded in the research drawn from [17,20], we employ the WCFS function as our cost function, which is represented as:

$$WCFS(S) = \sum_{\substack{b \in \{0,1\}^n, b \neq 0 \\ |WHT(b,i)| > X}} \sum_{i \in \{0,1\}^n} (\frac{|WHT(b,i)| - X}{4})^R, \quad (2)$$

where *WHT indicates the WalshHadamard transform* (see Equation (1)) and both R and X are specified real numbers.

The efficacy of any search algorithm hinges on its capacity to find the target S-box within a minimal number of iterations. Specifically, for our approach, the metric of interest is a bijective S-box that aligns with our desired nonlinearity $N(S)$. Given that evaluating the cost function is computationally intensive, our algorithm's runtime primarily corresponds to the iteration count, making each invocation of the WCFS function crucial.

4.2. Hill Climbing Algorithm

While leveraging the robust hill-climbing algorithm propounded in [17,20], we instituted a series of modifications aimed at refining its efficiency and precision. Central to our enhancements is the integration of novel termination conditions:

Achievement of a maximum number of inner cycles, termed as max_frozen_loops, where no discernible improvements in state—either in terms of nonlinearity augmentation or, given consistent nonlinearity, a reduction in the cost function—are realized.

Attainment of the stipulated nonlinearity, defined as target_nonlinerity.

These nuanced stop criteria sculpt our specialized version of the S-boxes search algorithm in Algorithm 3.

In any algorithmic investigation, particularly in cryptographic research, the choice of parameters is neither arbitrary nor capricious; it emerges as a decisive factor that heavily influences the efficiency and effectiveness of the underlying algorithm. Such choices are honed through empirical testing, analytical insights, and often, prior foundational work. Our decision to configure the parameters as mentioned is deeply intertwined with our previous scholarly endeavors, elucidated in [23,42,43]. Below, we undertake a meticulous discourse on our parameter selection.

Nonlinearity remains a quintessential measure of an S-box's ability to resist linear cryptanalysis. The higher the nonlinearity, the more resilient the S-box is against potential analytical attacks. Our choice to set the target nonlinearity at either 106 or 104 stems from both empirical studies and the evolving requirements of modern cryptographic applications. As examined in [43], the ramifications of varying nonlinearity levels on security were explored in-depth. Choosing 106 or 104 as target benchmarks encapsulates a balance, aiming for high resistance while also ensuring computational feasibility.

Algorithm 3: Hill-Climbing Algorithm for S-boxes Generation (Our version)

Algorithm EnhancedHillClimbing(S, max_loops, max_frozen_loops, target_nonlinerity)
    while (max_loops > 0) AND (n < max_frozen_loops) AND (N(S) < target_nonlinerity)) do
    S'←S
    n←0
        Select at random two different positions i and j
        Swap outputs of S' corresponding to i and j
        if N(S') > N(S) OR (N(S') = N(S) AND WCFS(S') $\leq$ WCFS(S)) then
            S←S'
            n←0
        else:
            n←n + 1
            max_loops← max_loops−1
    return S
end Algorithm

4.3. Parameter Selection

Heuristic algorithms, by nature, involve a degree of exploration and are inherently probabilistic. Thus, setting a bound on the number of loops is crucial to ensure that the algorithm does not perpetuate indefinitely, especially when the search space is vast and the optimum might be elusive. Our decision to set a ceiling at 2,500,000 is rooted in findings from [23,42], where the influence of iteration bounds on the convergence and performance of heuristic algorithms was explored. Too few iterations might result in premature convergence, while an excessive count risks computational wastage. Through rigorous testing, 2,500,000 emerged as an empirically robust choice, allowing the algorithm ample opportunity to navigate the search space without becoming prohibitively time consuming.

A nuanced innovation in our version of the hill-climbing algorithm is the introduction of a secondary loop threshold, max_frozen_loops. This parameter is crucial in mitigating the risks of stagnation. If the algorithm fails to improve after a sequence of iterations, it indicates potential entrapment in a local minimum. As detailed in [23,42], setting a bound on such 'frozen' iterations provides an elegant escape mechanism, ensuring that the search is not paralyzed by local optima. The 2500 count has been refined through extensive simulations, striking a balance between allowing the algorithm room to 'breathe' and ensuring timely extrication from potential stagnation points.

So, we use the hill-climbing algorithm with the following parameters:

- target_nonlinerity = 106 or 104;
- max_loops = 2,500,000;
- max_frozen_loops = 2500.

At each iteration of the algorithm, we use the change of two randomly selected positions in the S-box as mutations.

4.4. Hierarchical Description and Component Interaction

The proposed methodology for efficient S-box generation can be viewed as a hierarchical system composed of interacting components. At the highest level, the system comprises three main components (Figure 1): the cost function, the hill-climbing algorithm, and the parameter selection mechanism. These components work in concert to achieve the desired computational efficiency and generate high-quality S-boxes.

The cost function component, represented by the WCFS function (2), serves as the guiding force behind the search process. It evaluates the quality of candidate S-boxes by measuring their nonlinearity and other cryptographic properties. The cost function is invoked repeatedly by the hill-climbing algorithm to assess the fitness of each S-box configuration explored during the search.

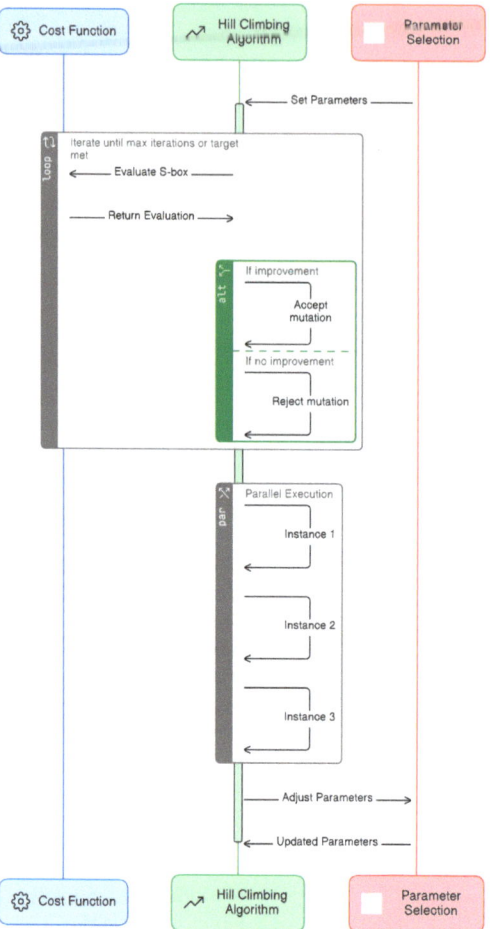

Figure 1. Hierarchical interaction model for optimized S-box generation.

The hill-climbing algorithm component forms the core of the methodology. It is responsible for navigating the vast search space of possible S-box configurations and iteratively refining the candidate solutions. The algorithm starts with an initial S-box and performs a series of mutations, swapping randomly selected positions to generate new configurations. The cost function is used to evaluate the quality of each new configuration, and the algorithm decides whether to accept or reject the mutation based on the improvement in the cost function value.

The parameter selection component plays a crucial role in determining the behavior and efficiency of the hill-climbing algorithm. It encompasses the choice of target nonlinearity (target_nonlinerity), the maximum number of iterations (max_loops), and the secondary loop threshold (max_frozen_loops). These parameters are carefully chosen based on empirical studies and theoretical considerations to strike a balance between exploration and exploitation in the search process.

The interaction between these components is characterized by a tight feedback loop. The hill-climbing algorithm relies on the cost function to guide its search, while the cost function's effectiveness is determined by the quality of the S-boxes generated by the algorithm. The parameter selection component influences the behavior of the hill-climbing algorithm, which, in turn, affects the efficiency and effectiveness of the overall methodology.

To achieve computational efficiency, the proposed approach leverages the inherent parallelism of the hill-climbing algorithm. The algorithm can be easily parallelized by running multiple instances of the search process concurrently, each starting from a different initial S-box configuration. This parallel exploration of the search space allows for a more efficient utilization of computational resources and can significantly reduce the overall runtime of the methodology.

Furthermore, the dynamic adjustment of the cost function parameters within the hill-climbing algorithm contributes to the improved computational efficiency. By adapting the parameters based on the progress of the search, the methodology can effectively balance the exploration of new regions in the search space with the exploitation of promising solutions. This dynamic adaptation helps the algorithm to converge faster towards high-quality S-boxes, reducing the number of iterations required to achieve the desired nonlinearity.

Figure 1 elucidates the architecture of an optimized S-box generation methodology, highlighting a sophisticated interaction among its primary components: the cost function, the hill-climbing algorithm, and the parameter selection mechanism. This model emphasizes a dynamic and recursive evaluation process that strategically employs hill-climbing techniques and parameter adjustments to enhance cryptographic robustness and computational efficiency.

In summary, the proposed methodology achieves enhanced computational efficiency through the careful orchestration of its components. The cost function guides the search process, while the hill-climbing algorithm efficiently explores the search space. The parameter selection mechanism ensures that the algorithm strikes an optimal balance between exploration and exploitation. The inherent parallelism of the hill-climbing algorithm is exploited to accelerate the search process, and the dynamic adjustment of cost function parameters contributes to faster convergence. Through this hierarchical design and the synergistic interaction of its components, the proposed methodology is able to efficiently generate high-quality S-boxes for cryptographic applications.

5. Results

In this study, we conduct a series of experiments to evaluate the performance and behavior of our proposed heuristic search algorithm for generating highly nonlinear S-boxes. The experiments are designed to assess the impact of various parameter settings and cost function configurations on the algorithm's ability to find optimal S-boxes efficiently.

5.1. Organization of Overall Experiments

Our experimental approach is based on the analysis of the Walsh–Hadamard spectrum of the S-boxes. Let $\vec{H}(S)$ be the histogram of the Walsh–Hadamard coefficients for the S-box S (as introduced in [19]). This is a vector whose value at position i corresponds to the number of coefficients in position $|i|$ of the Walsh–Hadamard spectrum of the S-box S. Let i_{max} denote the maximum (last) position in this vector with a non-zero value. Then, the maximum absolute value of the Walsh–Hadamard coefficients for the S-box S is i_{max}, and this coefficient determines the nonlinearity of the S-box. We denote l_i by the number of values of the Walsh–Hadamard coefficients for each i.

Reducing the value of the WCFS function narrows the histogram of the Walsh–Hadamard coefficients. We present the obtained estimates of the maximum narrowing that brings us closer to nonlinearity in $N(S) = 106$.

To assess the progress more accurately, we conducted two tests with 1000 runs of the search algorithms for the bijective S-boxs with $N(S) = 104$ each (the search algorithm parametrizations are similar to the above). In the first test, the parameters of the cost function WCFS were ($R = 11$, $X = 4$), and in the second—($R = 12$, $X = 0$). The arithmetic value $k_{itr} = 53{,}508$ was set to ($R = 11$, $X = 4$) and $k_{itr} = 53{,}025$ for ($R = 12$, $X = 0$).

The average absolute (i.e., taken for $|i|$) number of the first three maximum values of the Walsh–Hadamard coefficients was:

- for $(R = 11, X = 4)$: $l_{|i=40|} = 607; l_{|i=44|} = 256; l_{|i=48|} = 73;$
- for $(R = 12, X = 0)$: $l_{|i=40|} = 606; l_{|i=44|} = 255; l_{|i=48|} = 73.$

Given that the number of possible changes in two positions in the S-box is $\frac{256 \cdot 257}{2} = 32,896$, we slightly modified the search algorithm. Initially, the algorithm was executed as described above, and starting from some state (for example, if $N(S) = 102$ was found), a full search of all possible mutations (change of two positions) was performed. If an improvement in the cost function was found, it was implemented, and the full search was started again. At the same time, the criteria for stopping the search algorithm were also slightly changed:

- finding a bijective S-box with nonlinearity of 106 (never performed for this modification of the search algorithm);
- achievement of the maximum number of iterations;
- performing all possible mutations for the current S-box and not finding any improvement (almost always performed).

Thanks to the full search, we firstly guaranteed that a local minimum was found (no mutation could lead to an improvement in the cost function), and secondly, we reduced the total number of iterations by excluding random changes that were repeatedly made and did not lead to improvements.

We conducted 100 independent runs of the hill-climbing search algorithm with the above modification and the following WCFS function parameters:

- $R = 11, X = -16; -16; -12; -8; -4; 0; 4; 8; 12; 16; 20;$
- $R = 12, X = -20; -16; -12; -8; -4; 0; 4; 8.$

The histograms of the distribution of the averaged absolute values of the Walsh–Hadamard coefficients for these tests are shown in Figures 2 and 3, respectively. The results are presented on a logarithmic scale. For comparison, the last column shows similar values of the results presented in Figure 4.

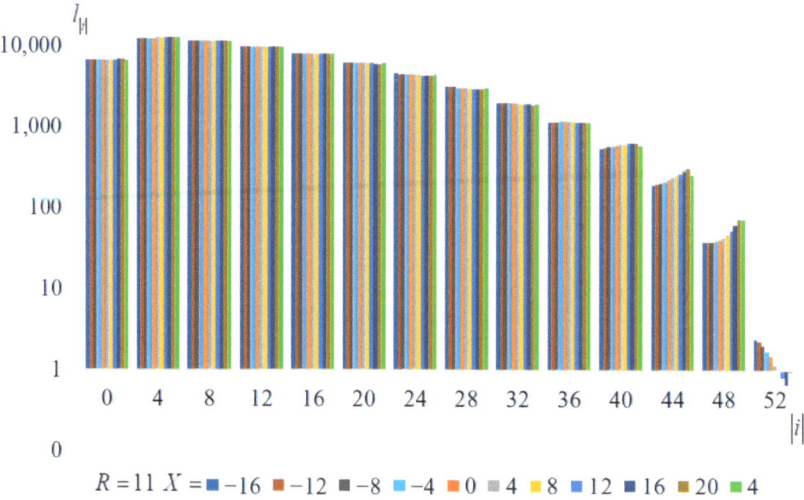

Figure 2. Histograms of the distribution of the averaged absolute values of the Walsh–Hadamard coefficients, when local minima are reached, for $R = 11$.

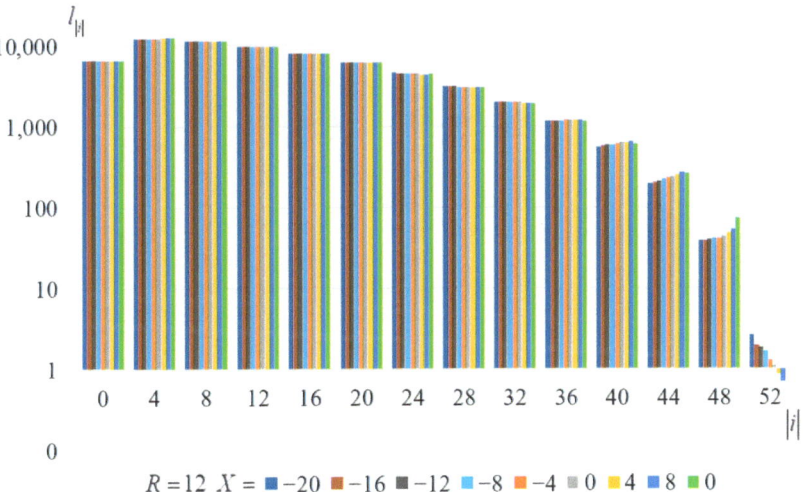

Figure 3. Histograms of the distribution of the averaged absolute values of the Walsh–Hadamard coefficients, when local minima are reached, for $R = 12$.

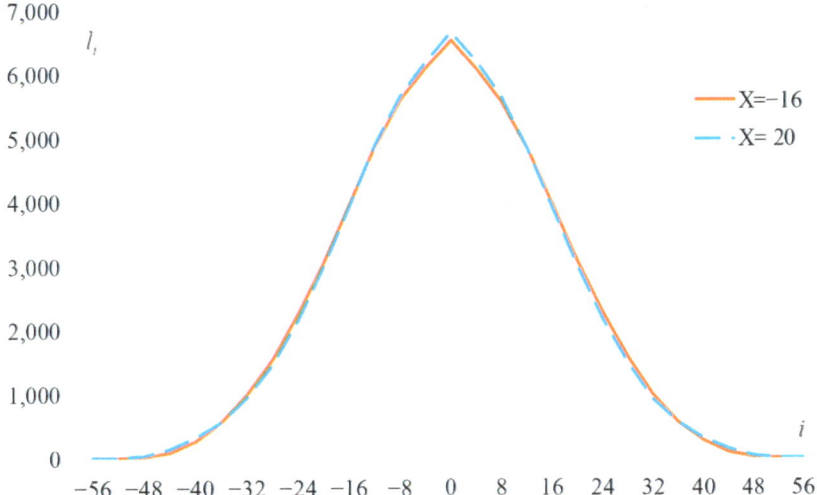

Figure 4. The average distribution of the Walsh–Hadamard spectral coefficients at the minimum values of the WCFS function with the parameters $R = 11$ and $X = -16$ (solid line), $X = 20$ (dashed line).

5.2. Benchmark Instances and Cost Function Parameters

In this subsection, we present the benchmark instances and cost function parameters used in our experiments. We focus on the generation of 8-bit S-boxes with high nonlinearity, specifically targeting a nonlinearity of $N(S) = 104$ or higher. The choice of these benchmark instances is motivated by their relevance to modern cryptographic applications and the challenges they pose for heuristic search algorithms.

Our experimental analysis reveals several key findings regarding the behavior of the search algorithm and the impact of cost function parameters on its performance:

1. With an increase in the parameter X, at a fixed value R, the variance in the graph of the distribution of the averaged absolute values of the Walsh–Hadamard coefficients increases. This leads to a narrowing of the distribution in the middle part, but a

widening in the extreme parts. For example, Figure 4 shows the distribution for two values of X. If we try to reduce the number $l_{|i=48|}$ by decreasing the parameter X, then i_{max} increases, with which the nonlinearity decreases to 100 and below. If we manage to find an S-box with $N(S) = 104$, it usually leads to an increase in $l_{|i=48|}$ (see the last columns of Figures 2 and 3).

2. To achieve a local minimum using the specified search method, an average of $k_{itr} = 250{,}000 \div 350{,}000$ iterations is required, which is 5–6 times more than that to achieve only $N(S) = 104$.

3. Considering the regions of minimal values of the average number of iterations (where the parameters correspond to the ratio $X = 52 - 4 \cdot R$), when the local minimum of the WCFS function is reached, the average value of the number of coefficients for the extreme positions in the Walsh–Hadamard spectrum distribution is:

- $l_{|i=44|} = 190 \div 314$;
- $l_{|i=48|} = 38 \div 74$;
- $l_{|i=52|} = 2.4 \div 0.7$.

It should be noted that when $l_{|i=48|} \approx 38$, the number of coefficients of the spectrum of $i = 52$ is $l_{|i=52|} \approx 2 \div 3$ (corresponding to $N(S) = 102$), and 1–2% have coefficients of $i = 56$ ($N(S) = 100$). When we approach $N(S) = 104$, the average number of coefficients of the spectrum of $i = 48$ is about $l_{|i=48|} = 60 \div 75$. This indicates the practical impossibility of forming S-boxes of $N(S) = 106$. The goal of achieving the local minimum of $l_{|i=48|} = 0$, using the described algorithm, is almost unattainable.

Given the above, it is necessary to further modify the search algorithm, introducing additional changes that would help to achieve the goal. We see the following ways:

- Extending the mutation of the current S-box. Instead of changing two positions in the S-box, use three or more positions. However, if the number of possible changes in two positions in the S-box is $\frac{256 \cdot 257}{2} = 32{,}896$ iterations, then using the formula for the number of placements from n to k, for the case of a three-change mutation, the possible number of mutations will be:

$$\frac{n!}{(n-k)!} = \frac{256!}{(256-3)!} = 256 \cdot 255 \cdot 254 = 16{,}581{,}120,$$

which significantly increases the complexity and time of the search. We conducted selective testing of this method and, in our opinion, it is not a rational way. Time costs increase by more than two orders of magnitude, and improvements are rarely or not at all found. In the case of a significant mutation (a change of three or more positions), the distribution of the spectrum of the Walsh–Hadamard coefficients obtained by the S-box almost always deteriorates significantly.

- Using dynamic changes in the cost function. If we are at a local minimum for one function, this does not mean that this state of the system will be a local minimum for another function. However, it is impossible to change the cost function drastically, because it will greatly worsen the spectral distribution of the Walsh–Hadamard coefficients. We propose a slight change in the parameters of the WCFS function we have already chosen. This will be discussed in more detail below.

- An alternative to the above point is to use several different cost functions that are somewhat similar to each other (which will not allow for significant changes in the best solution) but have different value tracks (which will lead to different values of local minima and allow for exit from them).

- Applying the acceptance of deterioration of the cost function in the search algorithm. It is possible to modify the search algorithm using the methods of the annealing simulation algorithm, which will help to escape from the local minimum.

- At the same time, using a combination of the above methods.

The hill-climbing algorithm was used in the following modification. Initially, the hill-climbing algorithm was performed in its "classical" form. After the first time, the nonlinearity of $N(S) = 102$ or the number of iterations without an improvement in the cost function exceeded 32,000, and instead of randomly selecting a pair of S-box positions for mutation, a complete search of all possible mutations of the two positions was performed. If an improvement in the cost function was found, it was accepted, and the search was started again with the new current S-box. If no improvement was found, the value X was changed, and the search continued.

It was found that if we changed the parameters X and R simultaneously, moving along the ratio $X = 48 - 4 \times R$, then there was almost no improvement in the distribution of the spectrum of the Walsh–Hadamard coefficients. Most likely, no improvements were observed due to the fact that the shape of the spectrum distribution, while maintaining $X = 48 - 4 \times R$, did not change.

5.3. Experimental Environment

To ensure a rigorous and fair evaluation of our proposed algorithm, we conducted a series of experiments designed to assess its performance and behavior under various settings and in comparison with state-of-the-art techniques. The primary motivation behind our experimental design was to comprehensively investigate the effectiveness and efficiency of the dynamic parameter adaptation mechanism in the context of S-box generation.

All experiments were performed on a standard desktop computer equipped with an Intel Core i7 processor and 16 GB of RAM, providing a consistent hardware environment across all runs. The algorithms were implemented in C++ and compiled using GCC version 9.2.0.

We employed a diverse set of problem instances, including randomly generated S-boxes, to evaluate the algorithm's performance across a wide range of scenarios. The dynamic adaptation rate and initial cost function parameters were varied for our algorithm, while the recommended default settings were used for the compared techniques to maintain a fair comparison.

5.4. Performance Metrics

To evaluate the performance of the proposed algorithm and compare it with existing heuristic techniques, we considered three key metrics:

1. Success Rate: The success rate represents the percentage of runs in which the algorithm successfully finds an S-box with the target nonlinearity. In our experiments, we focused on generating 8×8 S-boxes with a nonlinearity of 104. A higher success rate indicates a more reliable and effective algorithm.
2. Average Iterations: The average number of iterations required by the algorithm to find the target S-box is a crucial metric for assessing the computational efficiency. A lower average iteration count signifies a faster convergence and more efficient search process.
3. Runtime: The runtime metric measures the average wall-clock time (in seconds) taken by the algorithm to complete a single run. This metric provides a practical assessment of the algorithm's efficiency and scalability, considering both the computational complexity and the actual execution time.

By considering these performance metrics, we aim to provide a comprehensive evaluation of our proposed algorithm and demonstrate its effectiveness in comparison with state-of-the-art techniques. The success rate and average iterations metrics shed light on the algorithm's ability to find optimal S-boxes consistently and efficiently, while the runtime metric offers insights into its practical applicability and computational overhead.

In the following subsections, we present the experimental results obtained for each series of experiments, along with a detailed analysis and discussion of the findings. Through this rigorous experimental evaluation, we seek to validate the superiority of our dynamic parameter adaptation approach and establish its potential for generating high-quality S-boxes in cryptographic applications.

5.5. Visualization and Explanation of Results

5.5.1. Dynamic Parameter Adaptation: Impact on Convergence and Nonlinearity

In this series of experiments, we investigate the impact of dynamic parameter adaptation on the convergence behavior and nonlinearity of the generated S-boxes. By visualizing and analyzing the trajectories of the Walsh–Hadamard coefficient distributions across different parameter settings, we gain insights into the effectiveness of our proposed approach. In all runs of the first series of the search algorithm, the value of the parameter R was fixed. The tests were performed with $R = 8; 9; 10; 11; 12$. The results were averaged over at least 100 runs. In each run, four cycles of changing parameter X were performed in the following chain (see Table 2).

Table 2. Selected parameters X and R in the first series of experiments (the first part).

R	X
8	28, 24, 20, 16, 12, 8, 4, 0, 4, 8, 12, 16, 20, 24, 28
9	24, 20, 16, 12, 8, 4, 0, −4, 0, 4, 8, 12, 16, 20, 24
10	20, 16, 12, 8, 4, 0, −4, −8, −12, −16, −12, −8, −4, 0, 4, 8, 12, 16, 20
11	20, 16, 12, 8, 4, 0, −4, −8, −12, −16, −20, −16, −12, −8, −4, 0, 4, 8, 12, 16, 20
12	16, 12, 8, 4, 0, −4, −8, −12, −16, −20, −24, −20, −16, −12, −8, −4, 0, 4, 8, 12, 16

Figures 5–16 show the trajectory of change in the average number of absolute values of the Walsh–Hadamard spectral coefficients at the end of the algorithm for each value of X, at: $i = 52(a); i = 48(b); i = 44(c)$. They also show the average total number of iterations performed by the search algorithm since its launch (d).

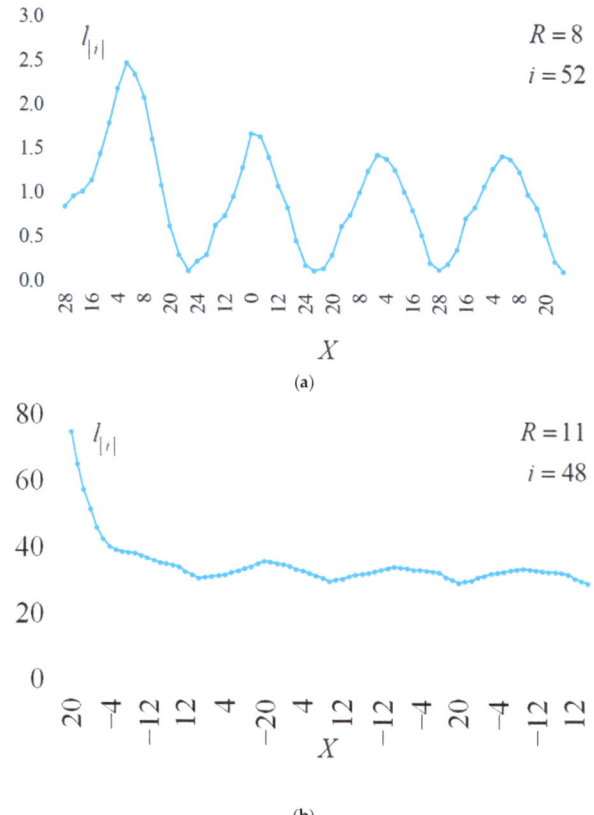

Figure 5. Cont.

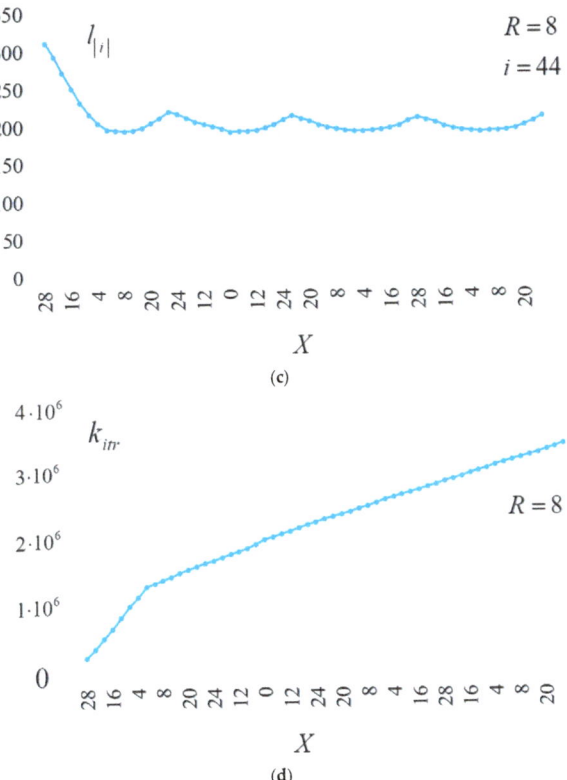

Figure 5. Trajectory of the $l_{|i|}$ S-box during dynamic change X (4 cycles) and $R = 8$.

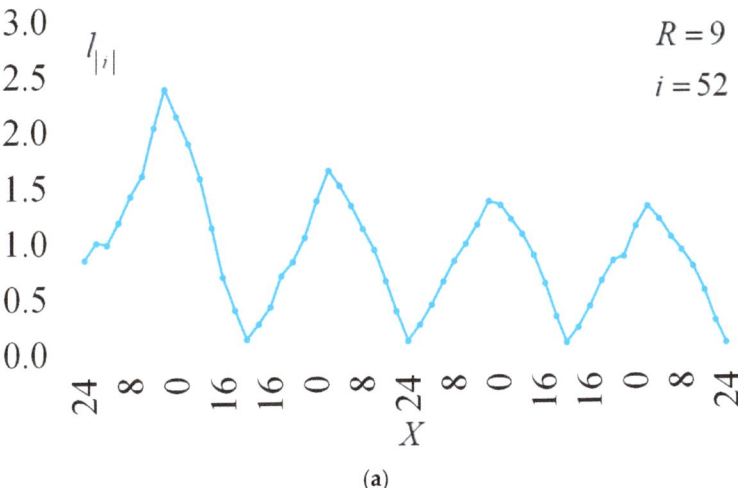

Figure 6. *Cont.*

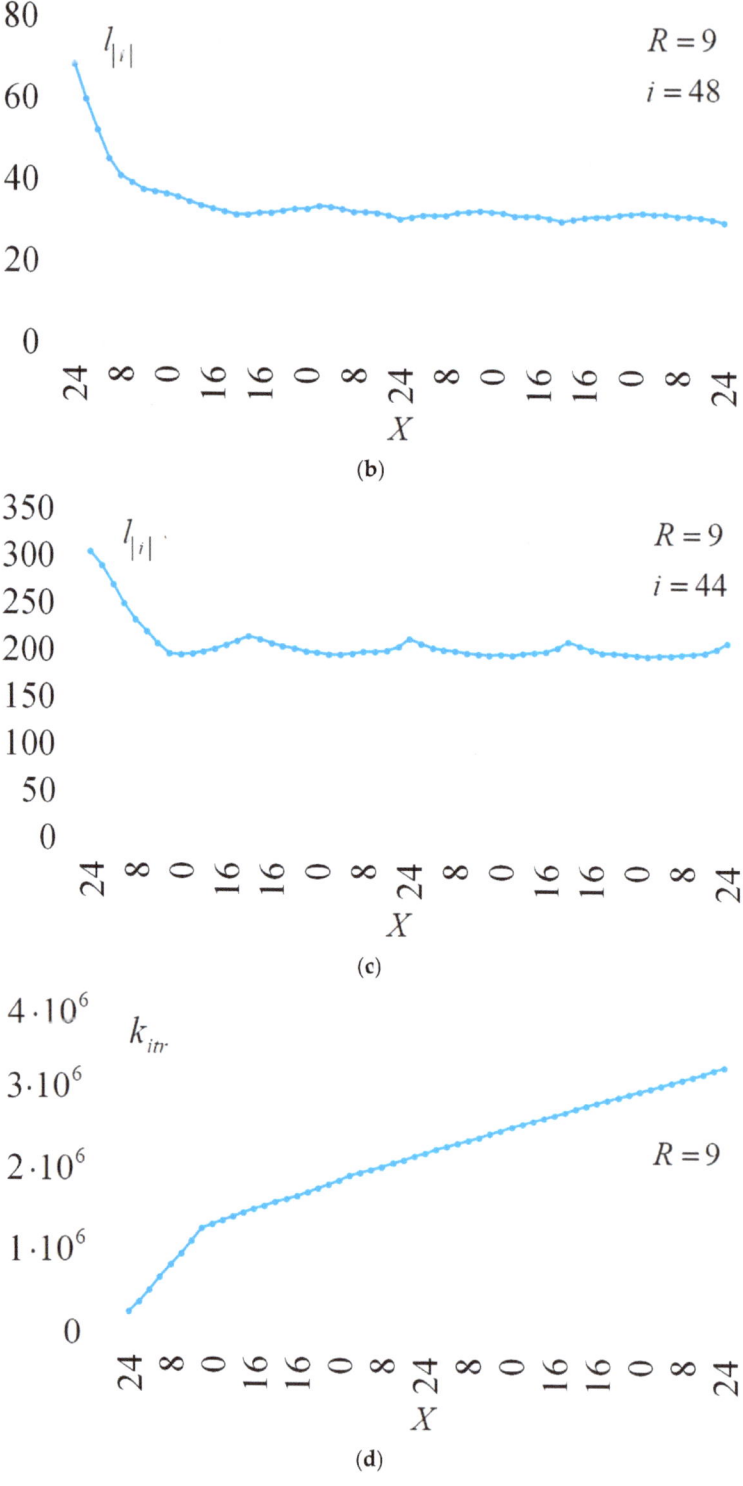

Figure 6. Trajectory of the $l_{|i|}$ S-box during dynamic change X (4 cycles) and $R = 9$.

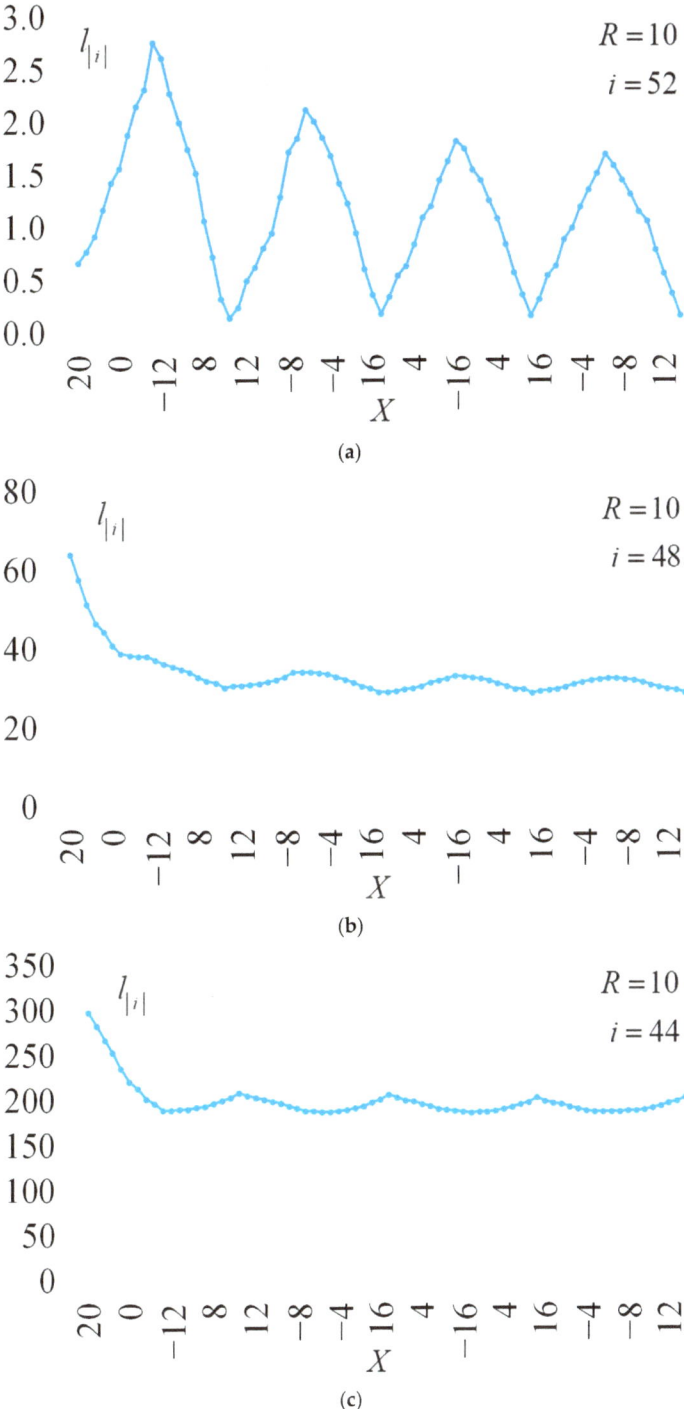

Figure 7. *Cont.*

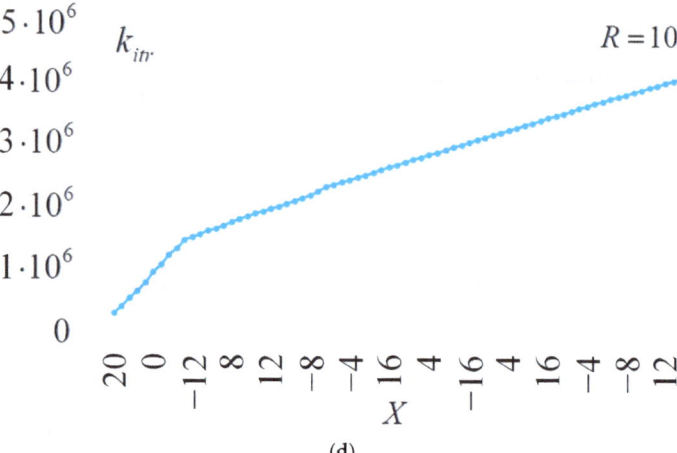

(d)

Figure 7. The trajectory of the $l_{|i|}$ S-box at dynamical change X (4 cycles) and $R = 10$.

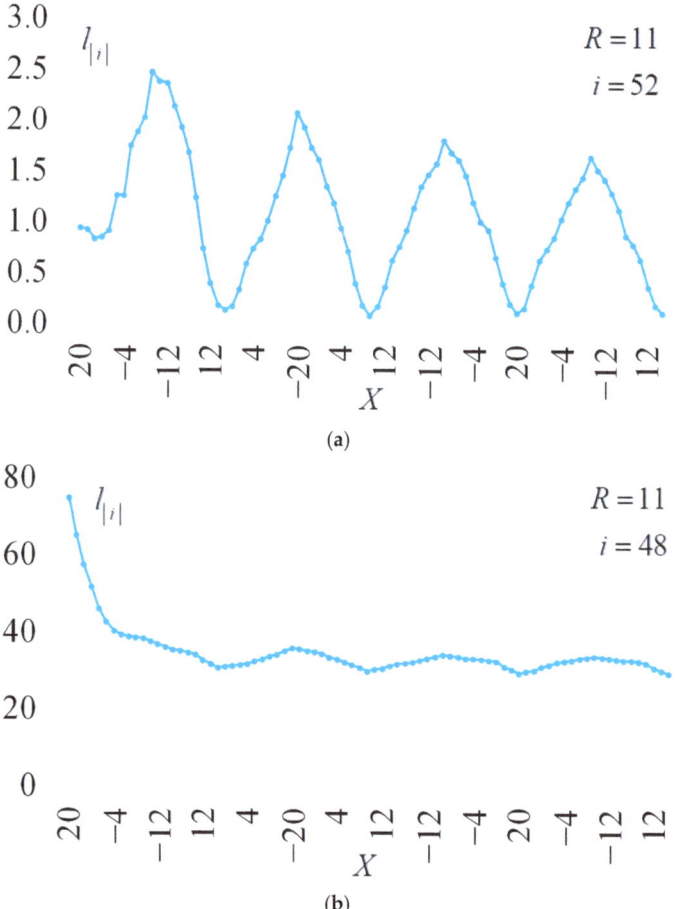

(a)

(b)

Figure 8. Cont.

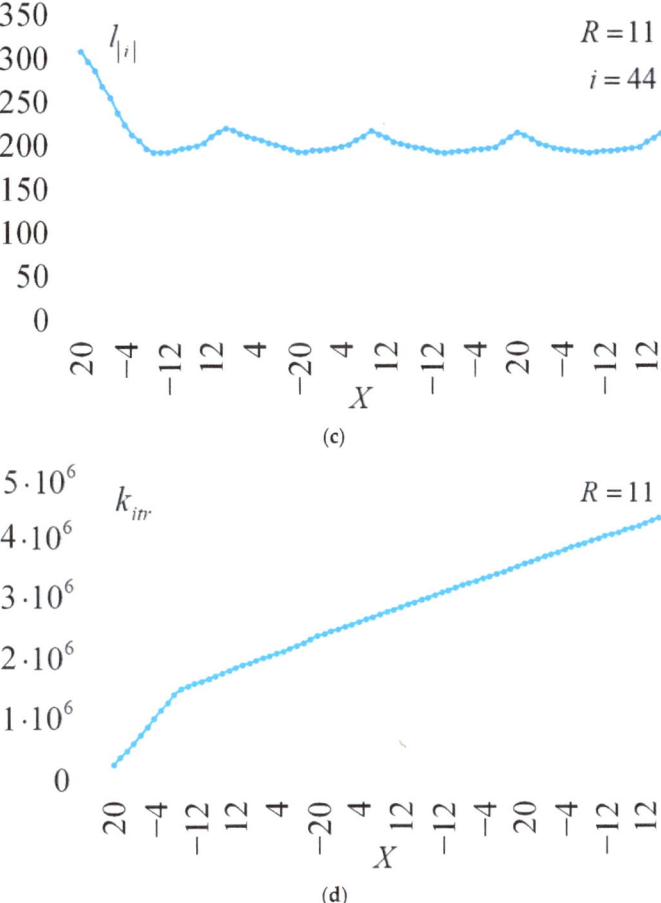

Figure 8. The trajectory of the $l_{|i|}$ S-box at dynamical change X (4 cycles) and $R = 11$.

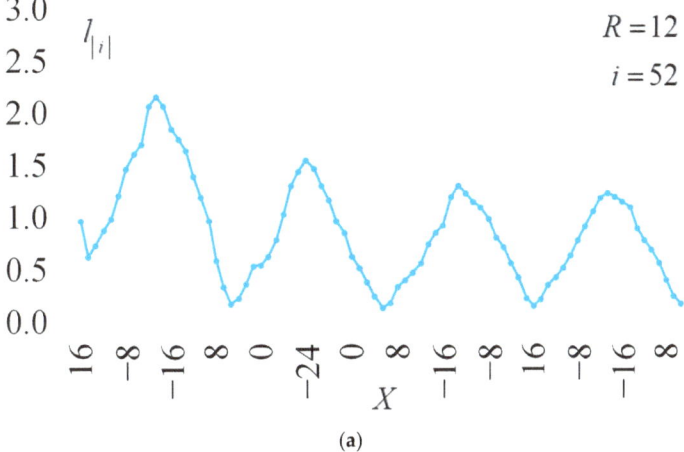

Figure 9. *Cont.*

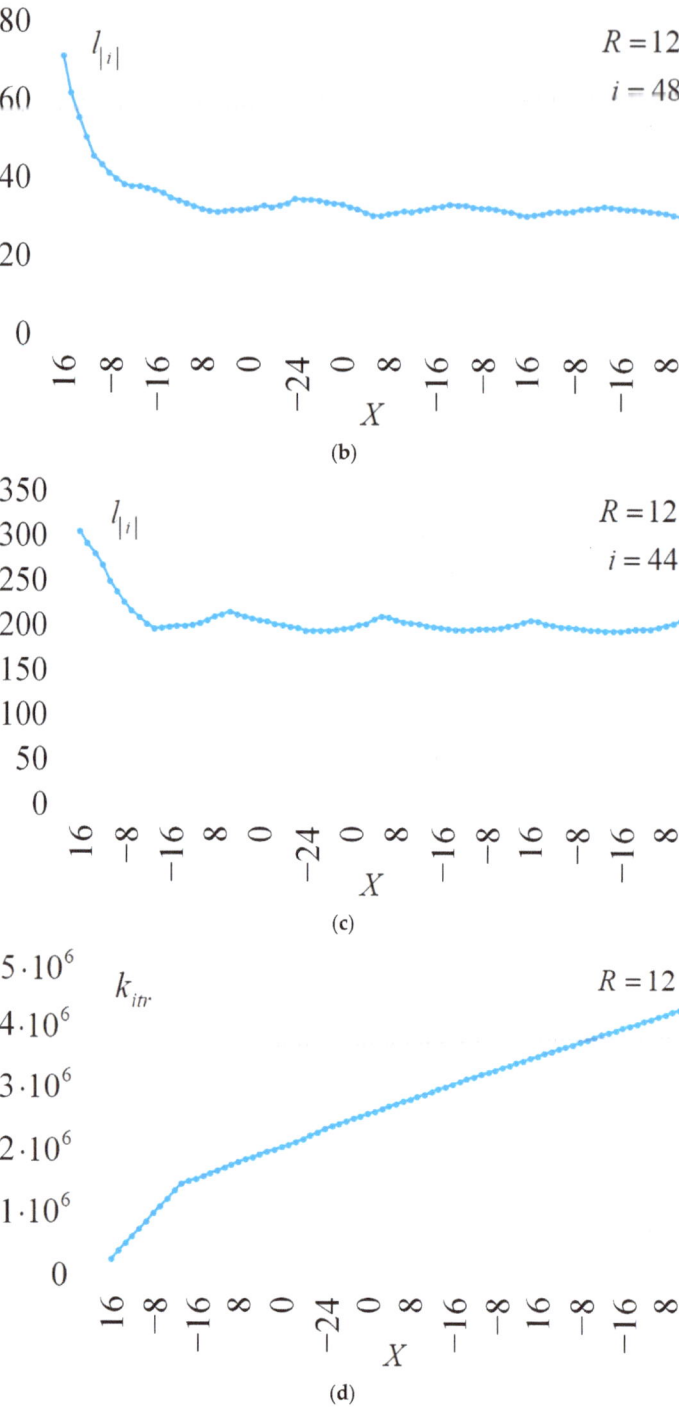

Figure 9. Trajectory of the $l_{|i|}$ S-box at dynamical change X (4 cycles) and $R = 12$.

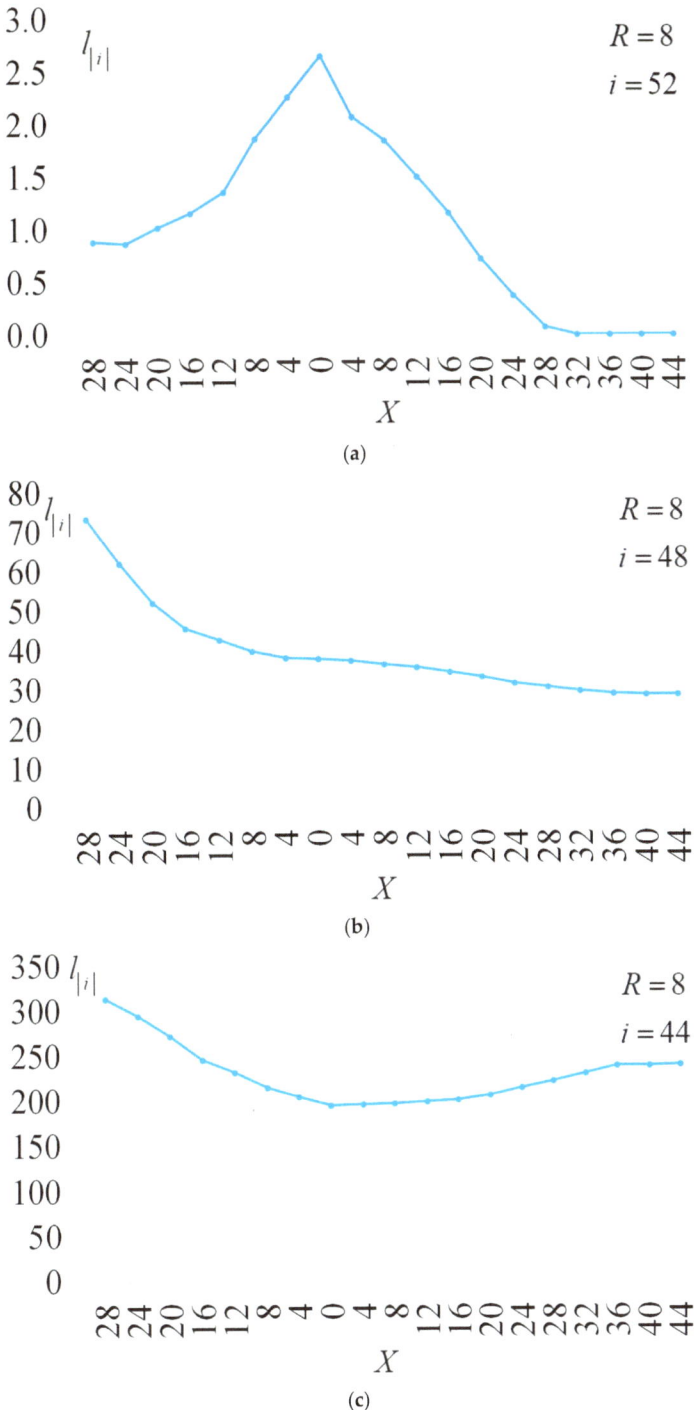

Figure 10. Cont.

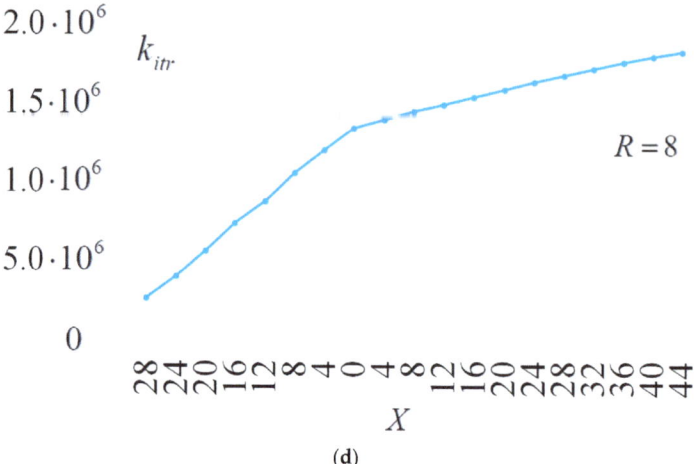

(d)

Figure 10. The trajectory of the $l_{|i|}$ S-box at dynamical change X (1 cycles) and $R = 8$.

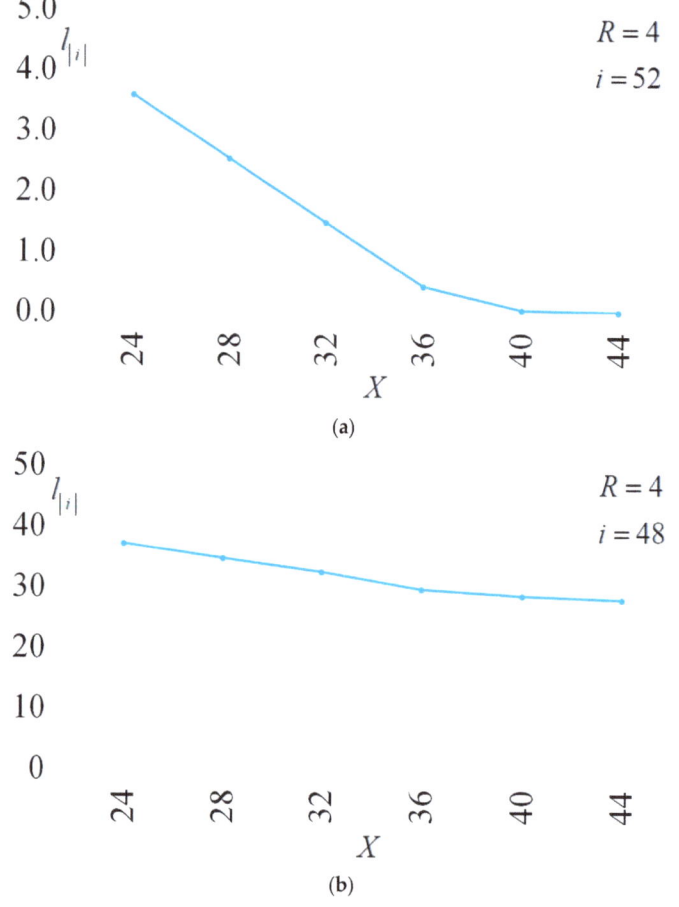

Figure 11. Cont.

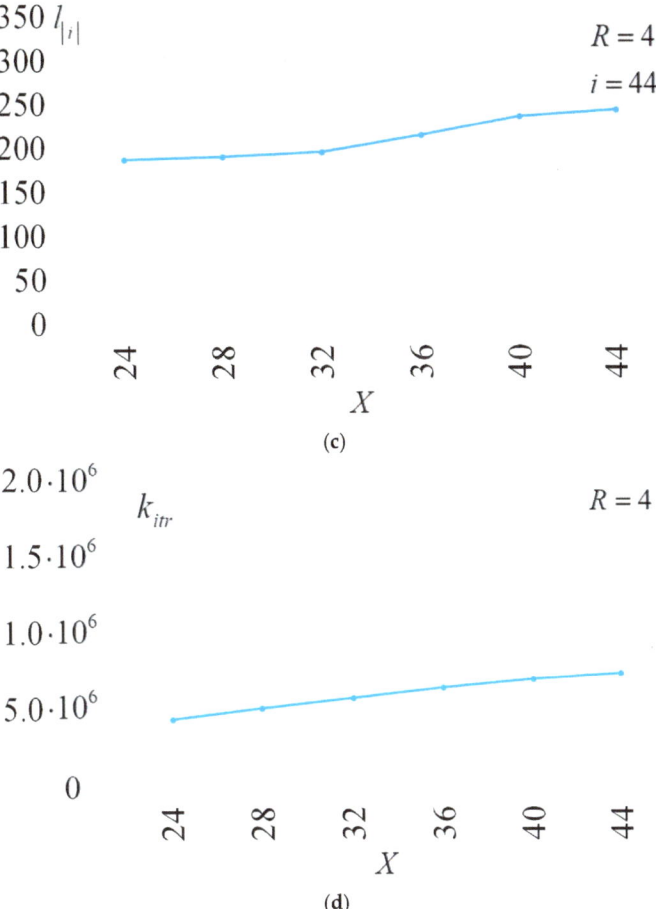

Figure 11. Trajectory of the $l_{|i|}$ S-box at dynamical reduction X and $R = 4$.

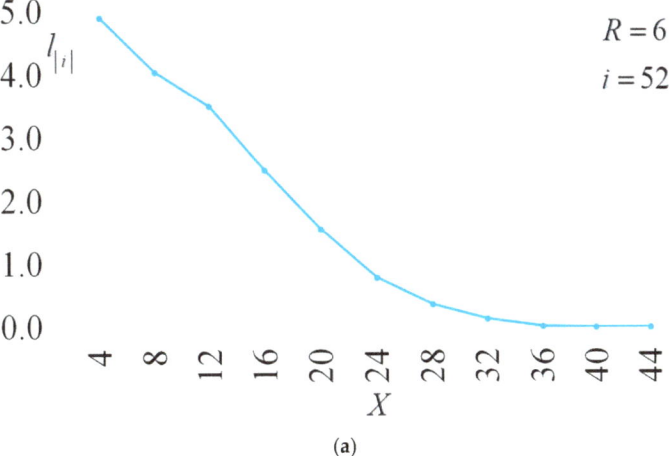

Figure 12. *Cont.*

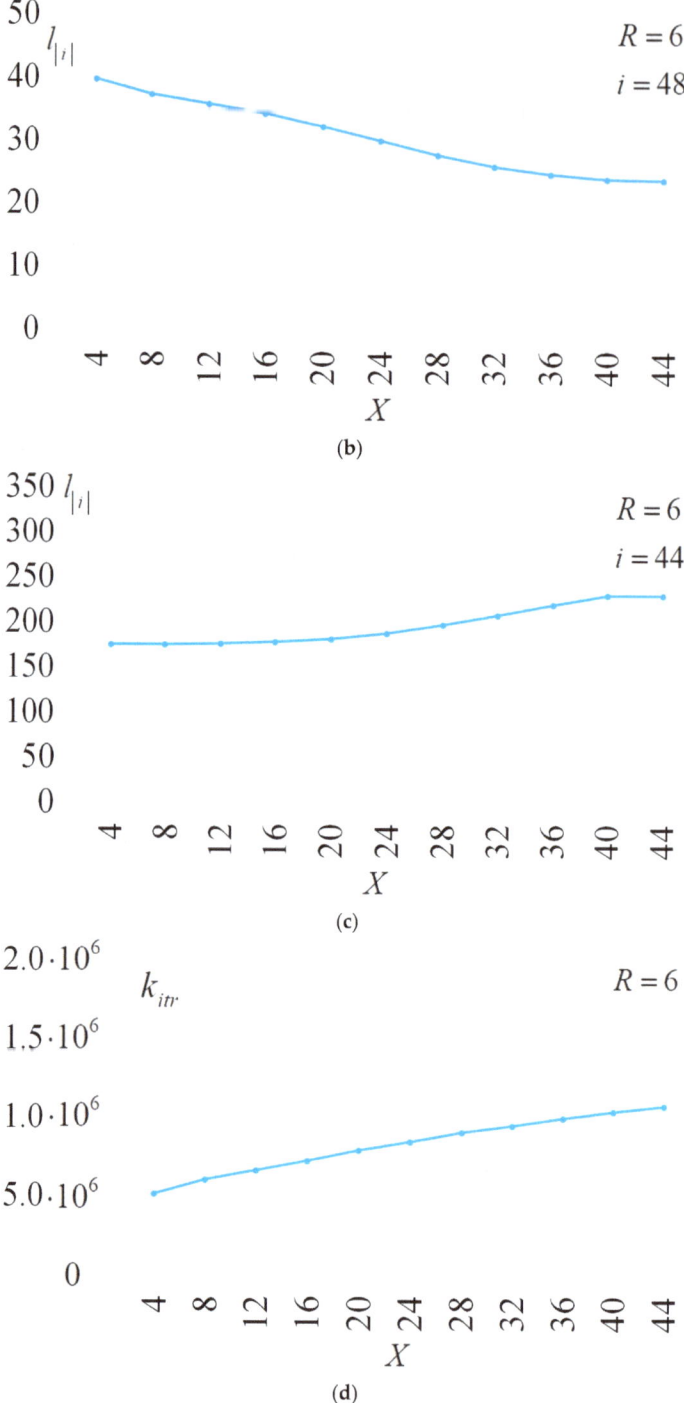

Figure 12. The trajectory of the $l_{|i|}$ S-box at dynamical reduction X and $R = 6$.

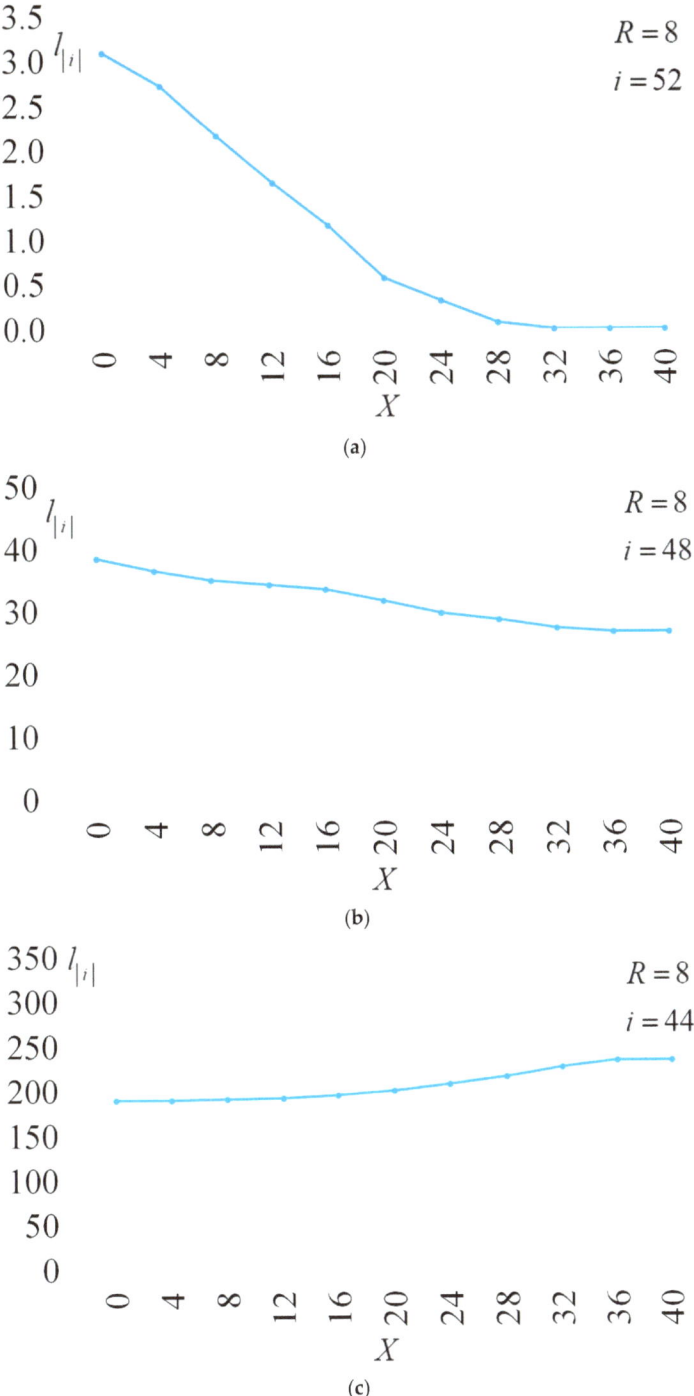

Figure 13. *Cont.*

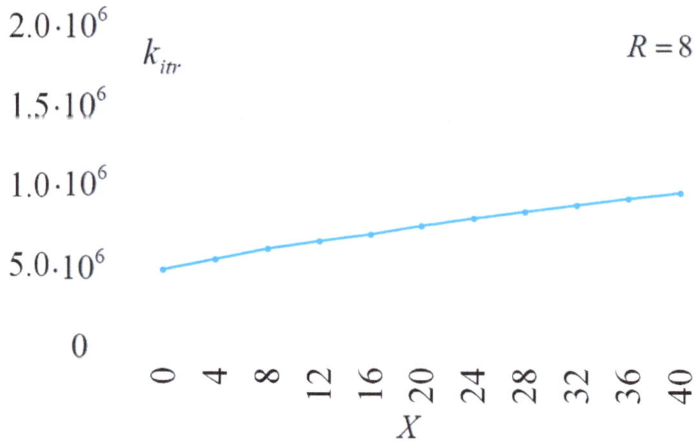

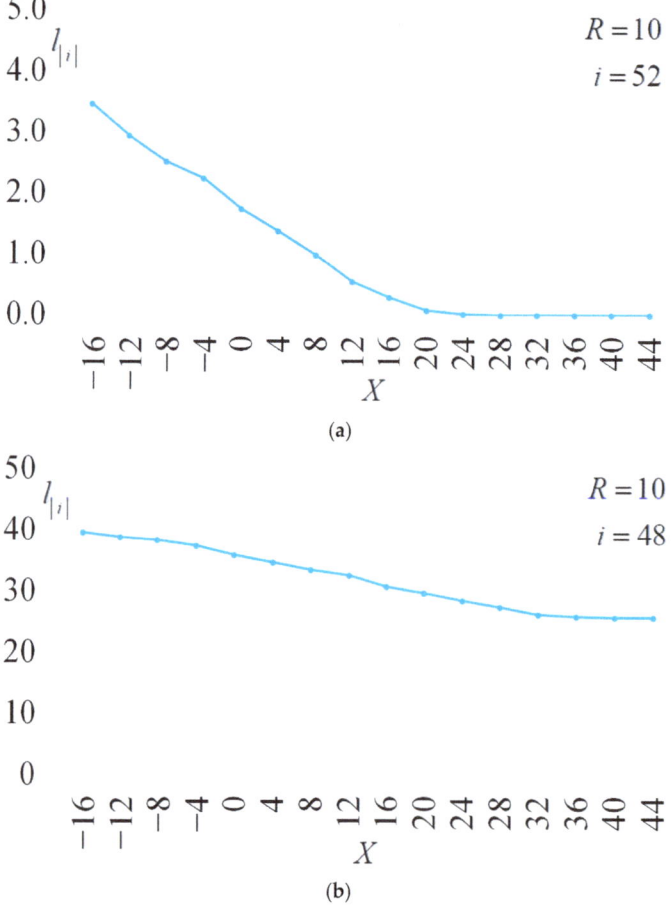

(d)

Figure 13. Trajectory of the $l_{|i|}$ S-box at dynamical reduction X and $R = 8$.

(a)

(b)

Figure 14. *Cont.*

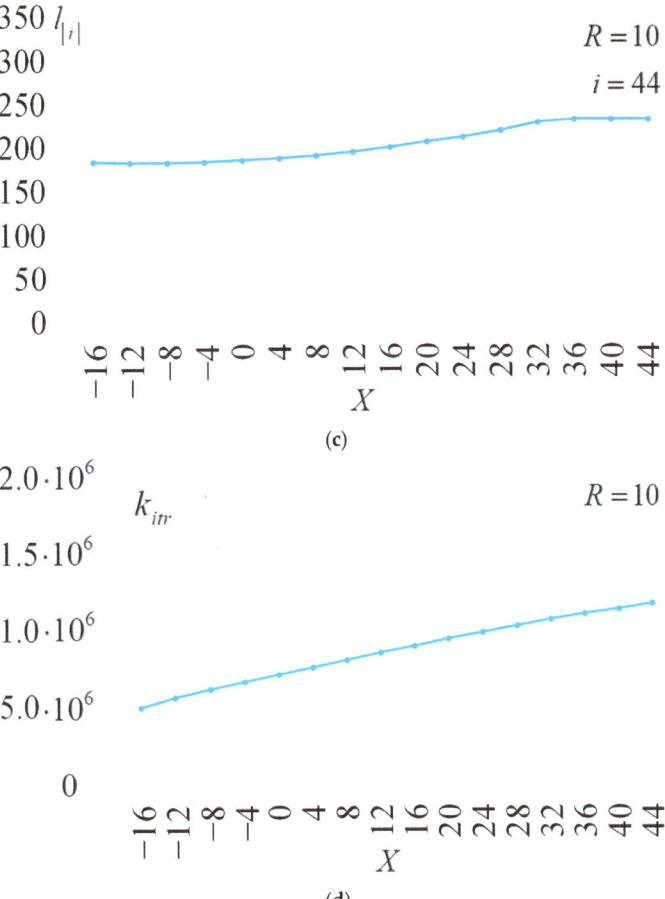

(c)

(d)

Figure 14. The trajectory of the $l_{|i|}$ S-box at dynamical reduction X and $R = 10$.

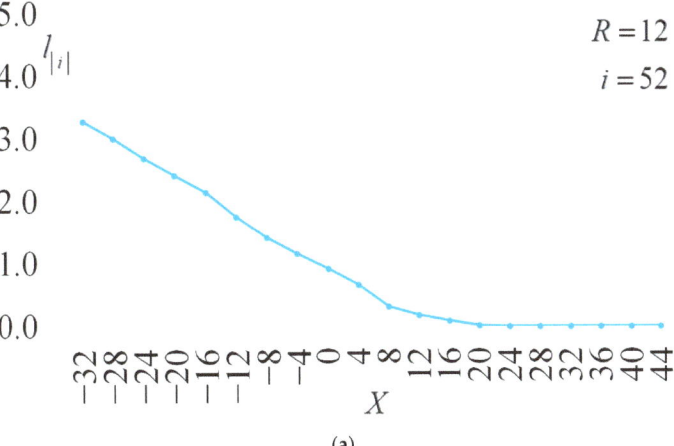

(a)

Figure 15. *Cont.*

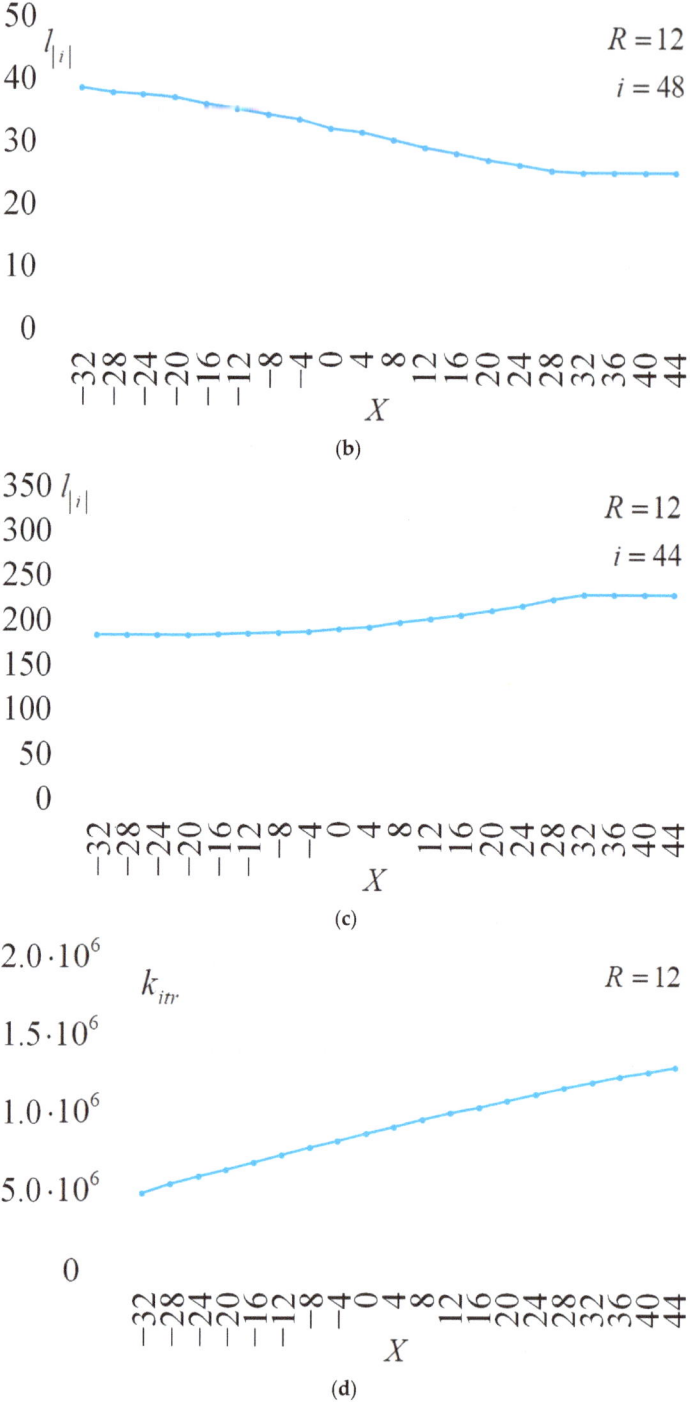

Figure 15. Trajectory of the $l_{|i|}$ S-box at dynamical reduction X and $R = 12$.

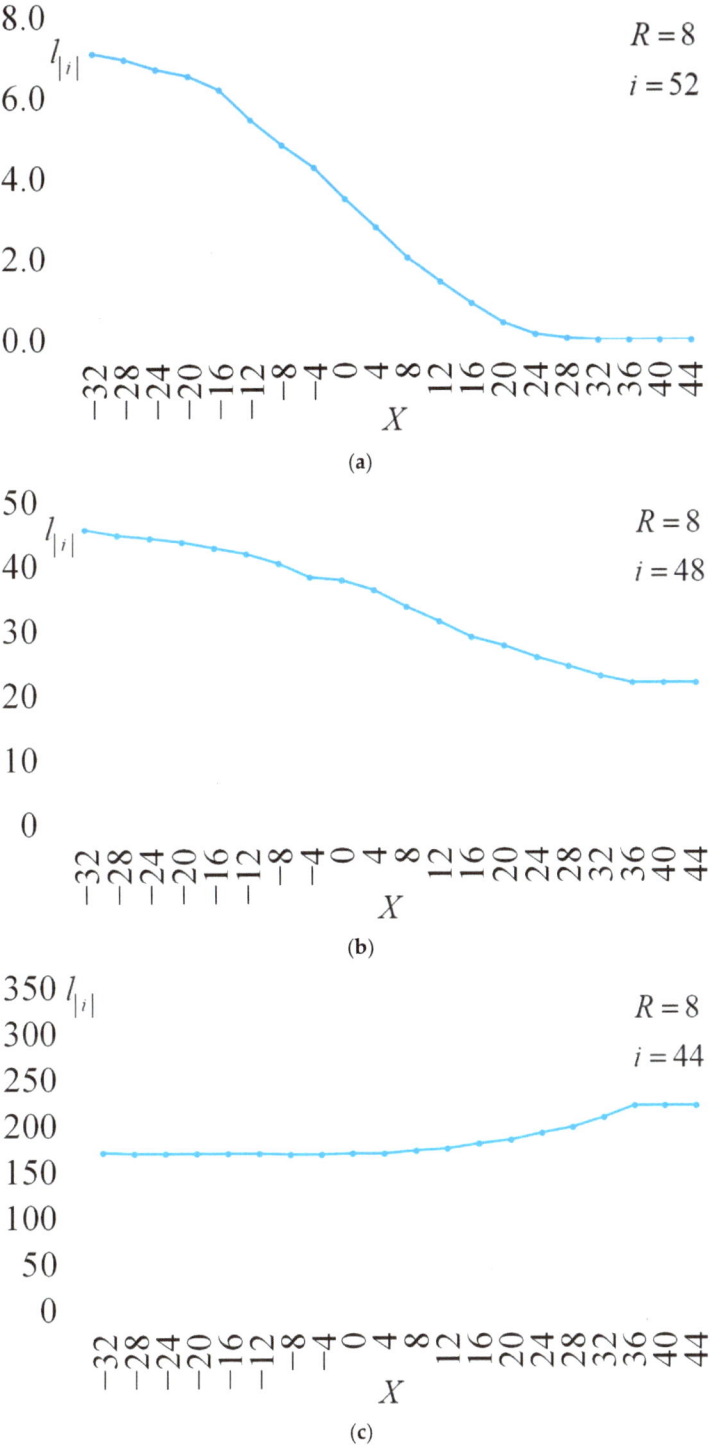

Figure 16. *Cont.*

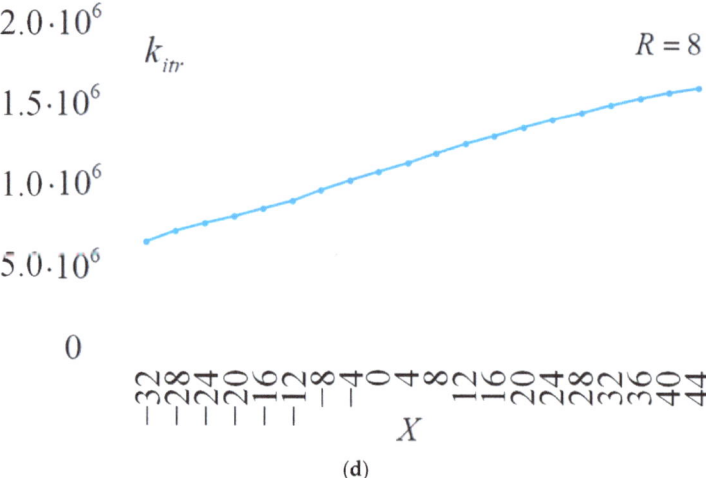

(d)

Figure 16. The trajectory of the $l_{|i|}$ S-box at dynamical reduction $X = -32 \div 4$ and $R = 8$.

- When applying the above dynamic changes in the parameter X, the search algorithm manages to almost halve the average value of the number of Walsh–Hadamard spectral coefficients in the position $i = 48$ from $l_{|i=48|} = 60 \div 75$ a fixed parameter X to $l_{|i=48|} = 28 \div 31$; a cyclic change in the parameter X.

However, about 10% of the runs still had coefficients at $i = 52$.

At the end of each of the studied cycles, the values of $l_{|i=48|}$ and $l_{|i=52|}$ were in the minimum (for the cycle) state, and the value of $l_{|i=44|}$ was in the maximum state.

Given that the value $l_{|i=48|}$ decreased with each of the four cycles, but not significantly (1–2 values), while each cycle significantly increased the number of iterations performed (at least 32,896 iterations were performed for each parameter X), it is advisable to limit this to one cycle. Taking into account the decrease in the values of $l_{|i=52|}$ with an increase in the parameter $l_{|i=52|}$, it is advisable to increase the parameter X to the maximum value (for $N(S) = 106$ this, it will be $X = 44$). Taking into account the above considerations, the next 100 runs were carried out from one cycle and the parameter X was changed in the following chain: for $R = 8$: $X = 28; 24; 20; 16; 12; 8; 4; 0; 4; 8; 12; 16; 20; 24; 28; 32; 36; 40; 44$.

The results are shown in Figure 10.

Starting from $X = 32$ and more, none of the values of X had spectral coefficients greater than $i_{max} = 48$. The increase in the final parameter X from 28 to 44, on average, led to a slight decrease (by onr coefficient) in the average statistical value of $l_{|i=48|}$. Using one cycle instead of four or five allowed us to reduce the average statistical number of iterations by more than half (to 1,830,951 iterations).

Our next step was to reduce the cycle by starting it from the minimum values of X. For all runs of the search algorithm, the value of the parameter R was also recorded. The tests were performed with $R = 4; 6; 8; 10; 12$. The results were averaged over 100 runs. In each run, a cycle of parameter X changes was performed in the following chains (see Table 3).

Table 3. Selected parameters X and R in the first series of experiments (the second part).

R	X																			
4														24	28	32	36	40	44	
6										4	8	12	16	20	24	28	32	36	40	44
8									0	4	8	12	16	20	24	28	32	36	40	44
10					−16	−12	−8	−4	0	4	8	12	16	20	24	28	32	36	40	44
12	−32	−28	−24	−20	−16	−12	−8	−4	0	4	8	12	16	20	24	28	32	36	40	44

The results are shown in Figures 11–15. Reducing the cycle only to the region where the parameter X was reduced made it possible to reduce the average statistical value by four, to $l_{|i=48|} = 24 \div 27$ (at all $l_{|i=52|} = 0$). Expanding the range of changes in values

$X = -32; -28; -24; -20; -16; -12; -8; -4; 0; 4; 8; 12; 16; 20; 24; 28; 32; 36; 40; 44$

with a fixed value $R = 8$ led to an even greater average statistical decrease $l_{|i=48|} = 22$. The results are shown in Figure 16.

When commenting on the experimental results, it should be noted that the probability of finding an improvement in the objective function slightly decreases with an increase in the parameter X. However, as the change in the parameter X increases, the weight values of the coefficients in the spectrum distribution change. This leads to a corresponding calculation of the objective function. As a result, it becomes easier to find the improvement of the objective function. This result can be used to optimize the search.

5.5.2. Exploring the Interplay of Cost Function Parameters

The second series of experiments focuses on the interplay between the cost function parameters R and X. By systematically varying these parameters and examining the resulting performance metrics, we uncover the optimal parameter combinations that lead to an improved efficiency and higher nonlinearity in the generated S-boxes.

These tests were carried out with a slight change in the parameter R (up to three units), while the parameter X was changed in such a way that the changes for each slight change R were parallel to the values determined by the ratio $X = 52 - 4 \cdot R$. The results were averaged over 100 runs. In each run, a cycle of parameters R and X changes was performed according to the chain shown in Table 4. The results are shown in Figures 17–22 (the value of the change in R is not shown in the figure).

Table 4. Changes in parameters R and X in the search algorithm runs, the results of which are shown in Figures 17–22.

	$R \in [2, 3, 4]$	$R \in [4, 5, 6]$	$R \in [6, 7, 8]$	$R \in [8, 9, 10]$	$R \in [10, 11, 12]$	$R \in [12, 13, 14]$	$X \in [-20 \ldots 40]$
0	2	4	6	8	10	12	−20
1	2	4	6	8	10	12	−16
2	3	5	7	9	11	13	−20
3	4	6	8	10	12	14	−24
4	2	4	6	8	10	12	−12
5	3	5	7	9	11	13	−16
6	4	6	8	10	12	14	−20
7	2	4	6	8	10	12	−8
8	3	5	7	9	11	13	−12
9	4	6	8	10	12	14	−16
10	2	4	6	8	10	12	−4
11	3	5	7	9	11	13	−8
12	4	6	8	10	12	14	−12
13	2	4	6	8	10	12	0
14	3	5	7	9	11	13	−4
15	4	6	8	10	12	14	−8
16	2	4	6	8	10	12	4
17	3	5	7	9	11	13	0
18	4	6	8	10	12	14	−4
19	2	4	6	8	10	12	8
20	3	5	7	9	11	13	4
21	4	6	8	10	12	14	0

Table 4. *Cont.*

	R ∈ [2, 3, 4]	R ∈ [4, 5, 6]	R ∈ [6, 7, 8]	R ∈ [8, 9, 10]	R ∈ [10, 11, 12]	R ∈ [12, 13, 14]	X ∈ [−20 … 40]
22	2	4	6	8	10	12	12
23	3	5	7	9	11	13	8
24	4	6	8	10	12	14	4
25	2	4	6	8	10	12	16
26	3	5	7	9	11	13	12
27	4	6	8	10	12	14	8
28	2	4	6	8	10	12	20
29	3	5	7	9	11	13	16
30	4	6	8	10	12	14	12
31	2	4	6	8	10	12	24
32	3	5	7	9	11	13	20
33	4	6	8	10	12	14	16
34	2	4	6	8	10	12	28
35	3	5	7	9	11	13	24
36	4	6	8	10	12	14	20
37	2	4	6	8	10	12	32
38	3	5	7	9	11	13	28
39	4	6	8	10	12	14	24
40	2	4	6	8	10	12	36
41	3	5	7	9	11	13	32
42	4	6	8	10	12	14	28
43	2	4	6	8	10	12	40
44	3	5	7	9	11	13	36
45	4	6	8	10	12	14	32
46	2	4	6	8	10	12	44
47	3	5	7	9	11	13	40
48	4	6	8	10	12	14	36

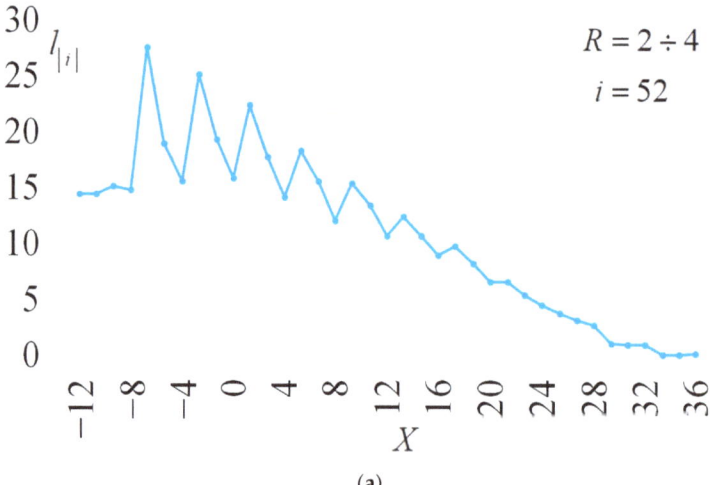

(a)

Figure 17. *Cont.*

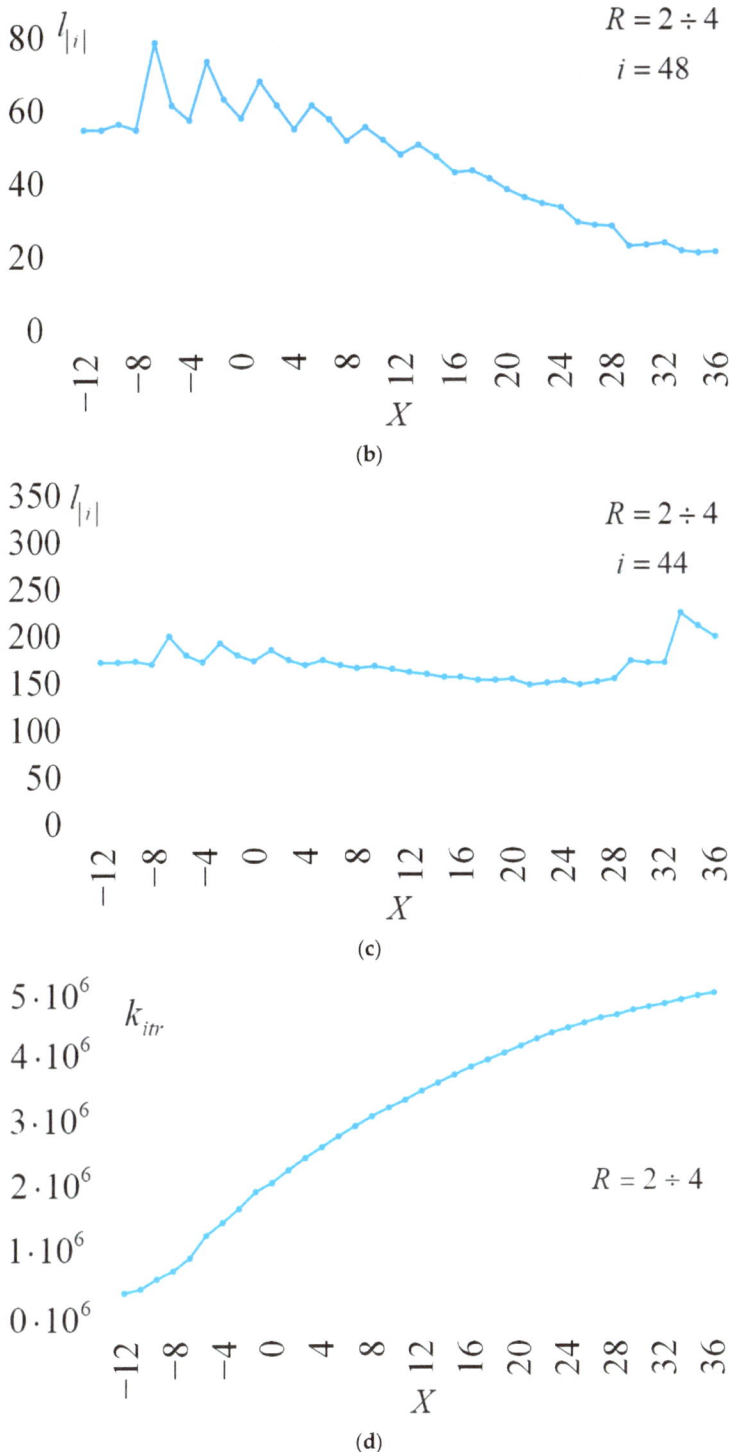

Figure 17. Trajectory of the $l_{|i|}$ S-box at dynamical change of parameters for $R = 2 \div 4$.

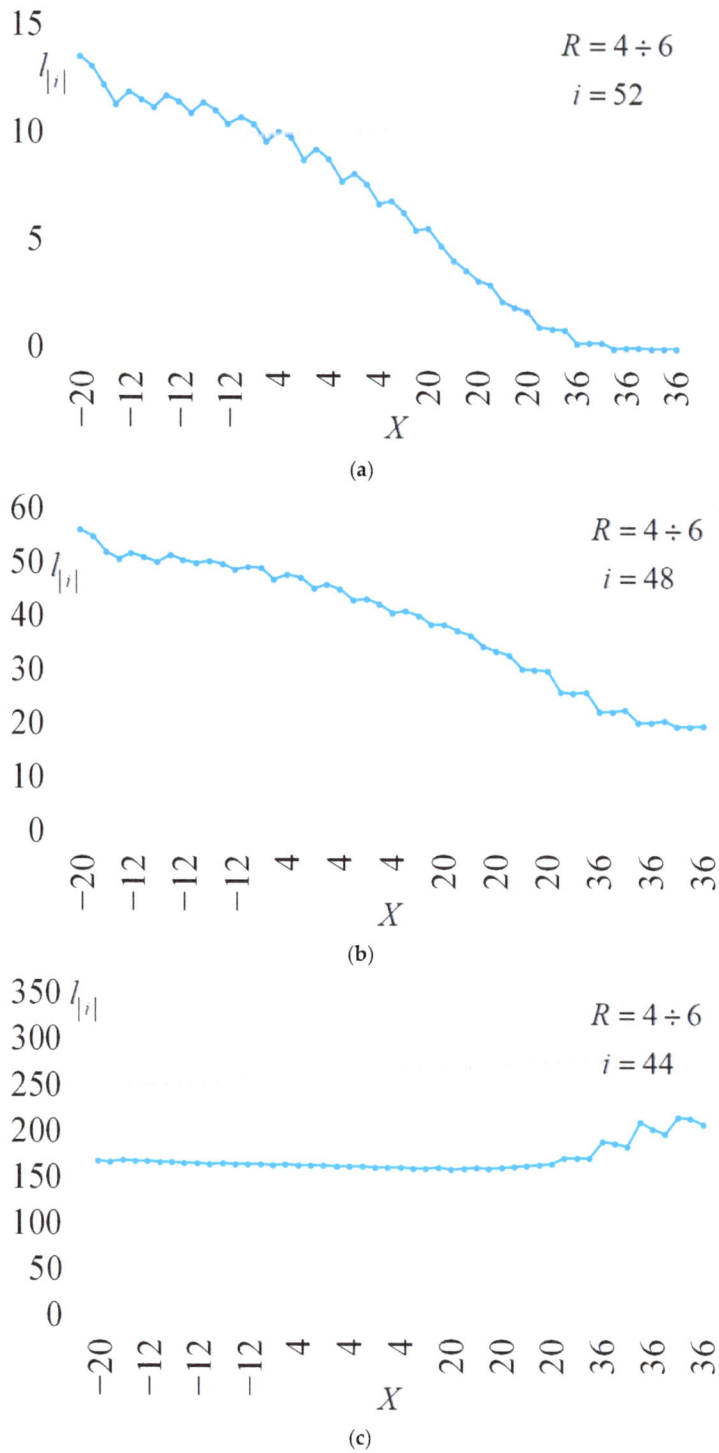

Figure 18. *Cont.*

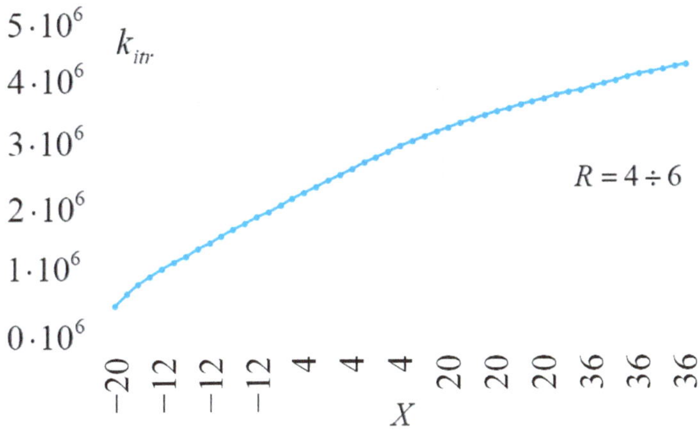

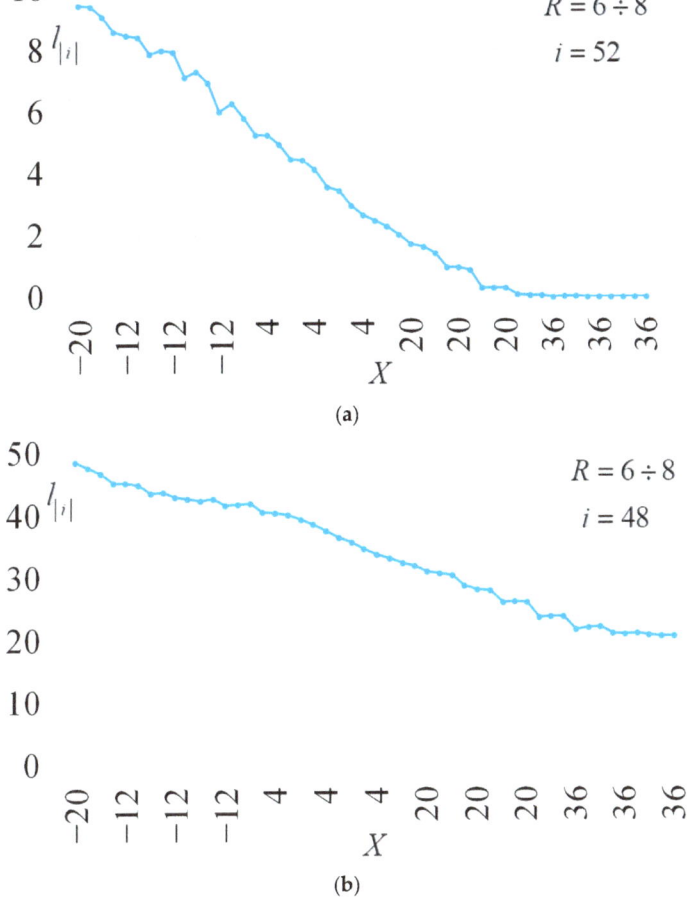

(d)

Figure 18. Trajectory of the $l_{|i|}$ S-box at dynamical change of parameters for $R = 4 \div 6$.

(a)

(b)

Figure 19. *Cont.*

(c)

(d)

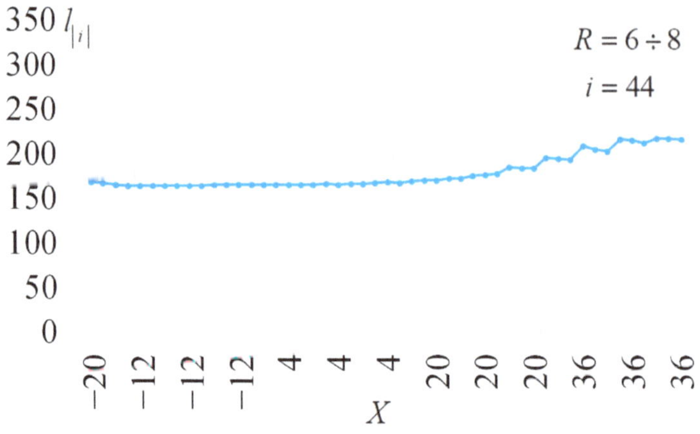

Figure 19. Trajectory of the $l_{|i|}$ S-box at dynamical change of parameters for $R = 6 \div 8$.

(a)

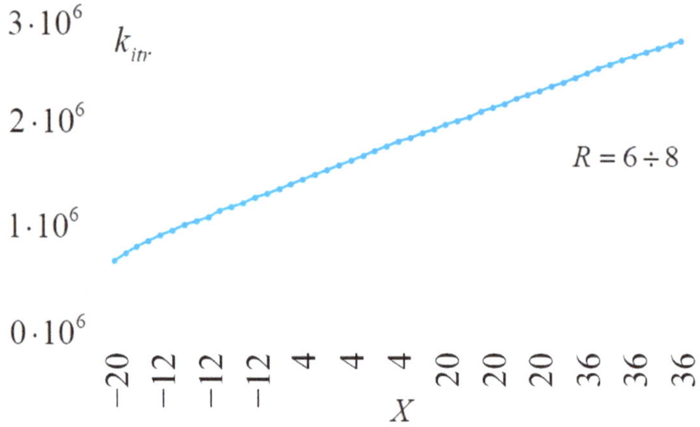

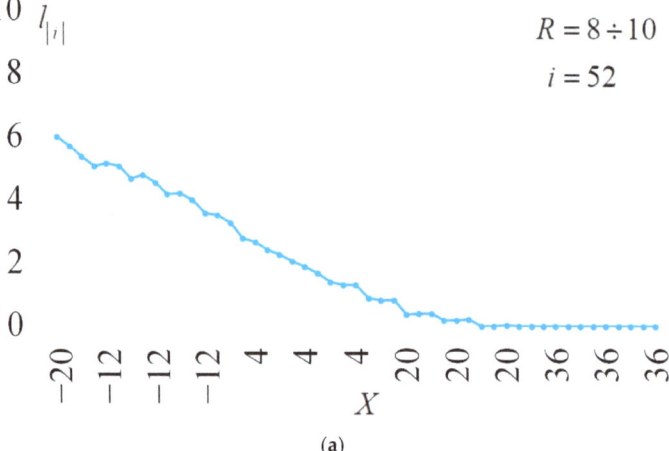

Figure 20. *Cont.*

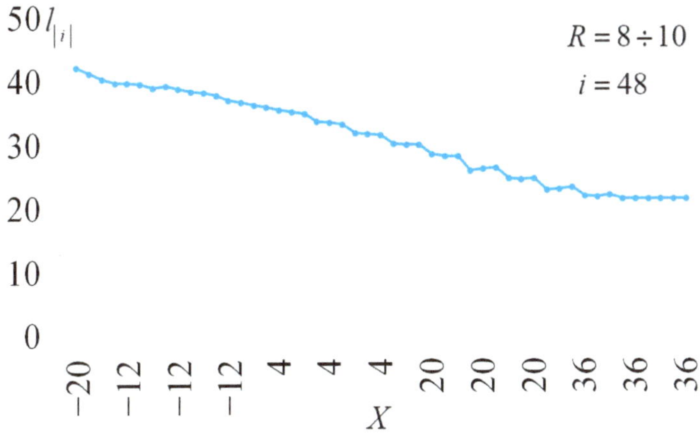

(b)

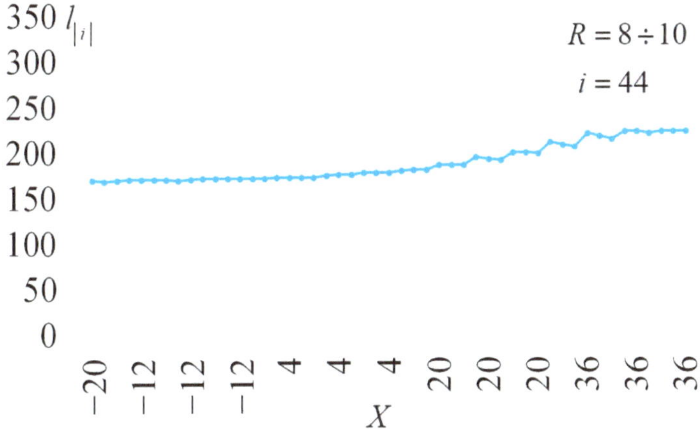

(c)

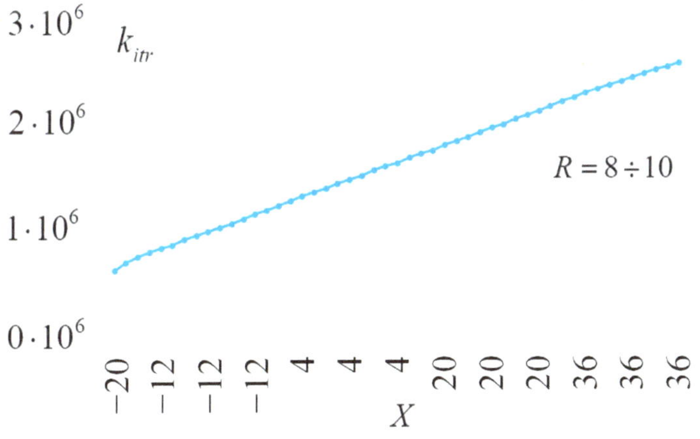

(d)

Figure 20. Trajectory of the $l_{|i|}$ S-box at dynamical change of parameters for $R = 8 \div 10$.

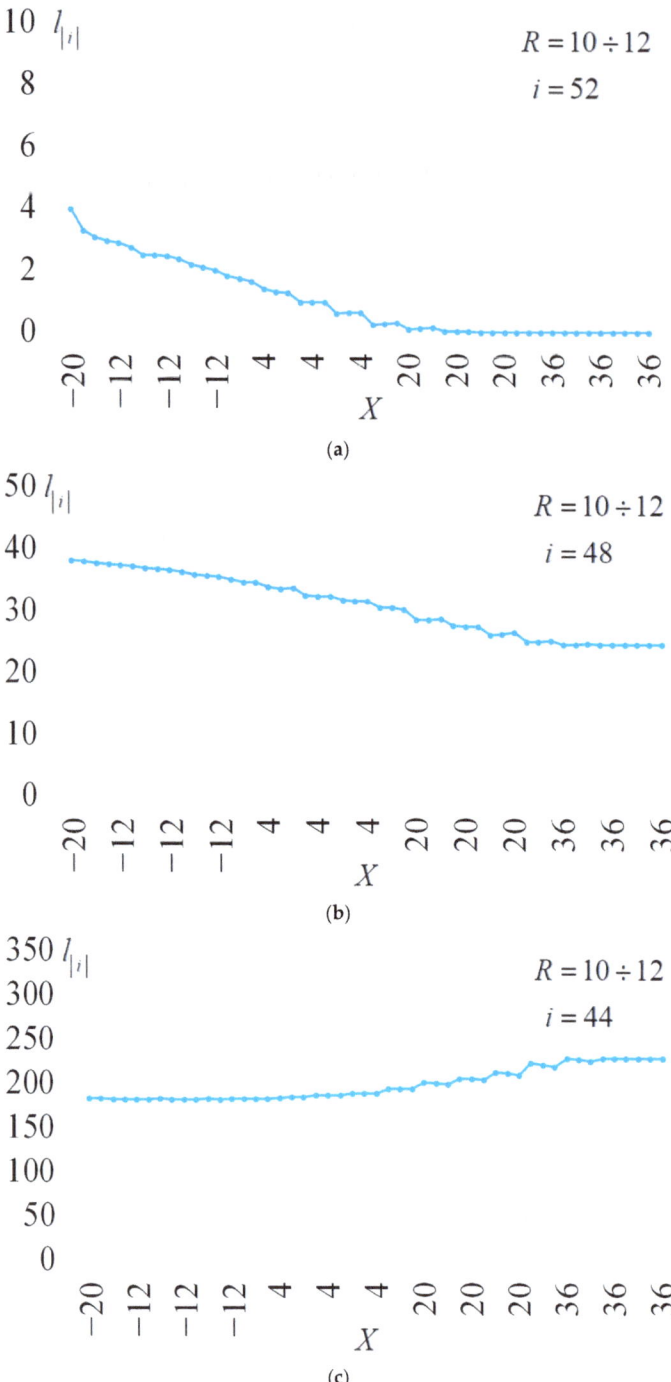

Figure 21. *Cont.*

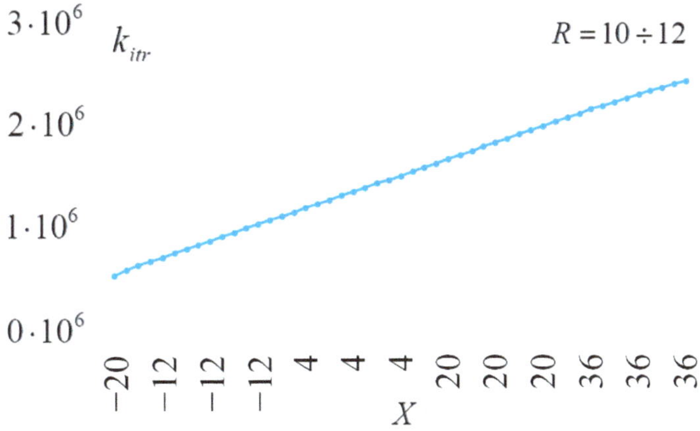

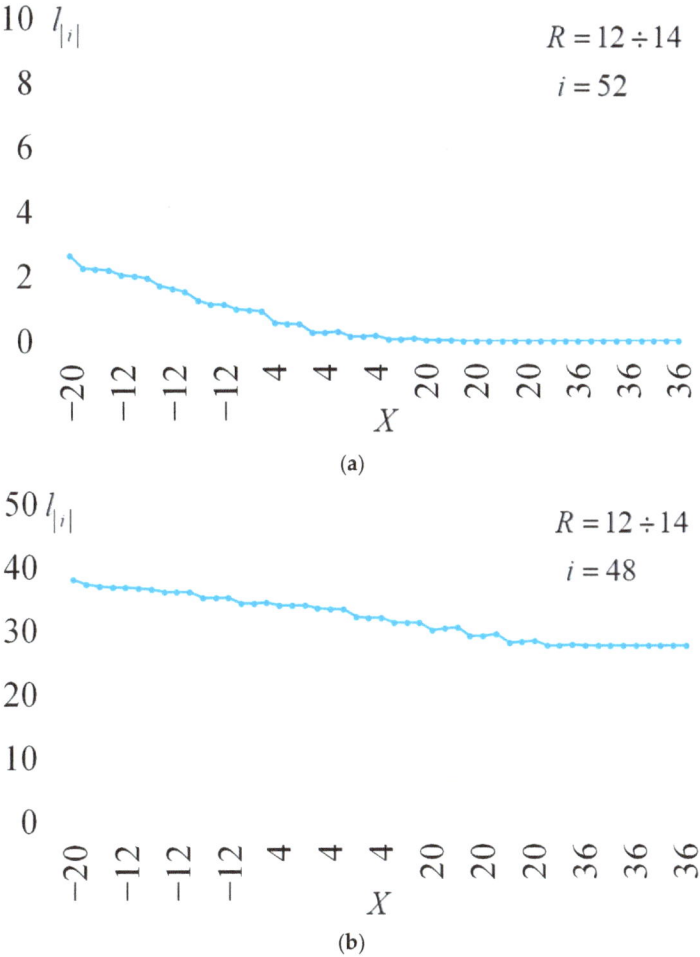

(d)

Figure 21. Trajectory of the $l_{|i|}$ S-box at dynamical change of parameters for $R = 10 \div 12$.

(a)

(b)

Figure 22. *Cont.*

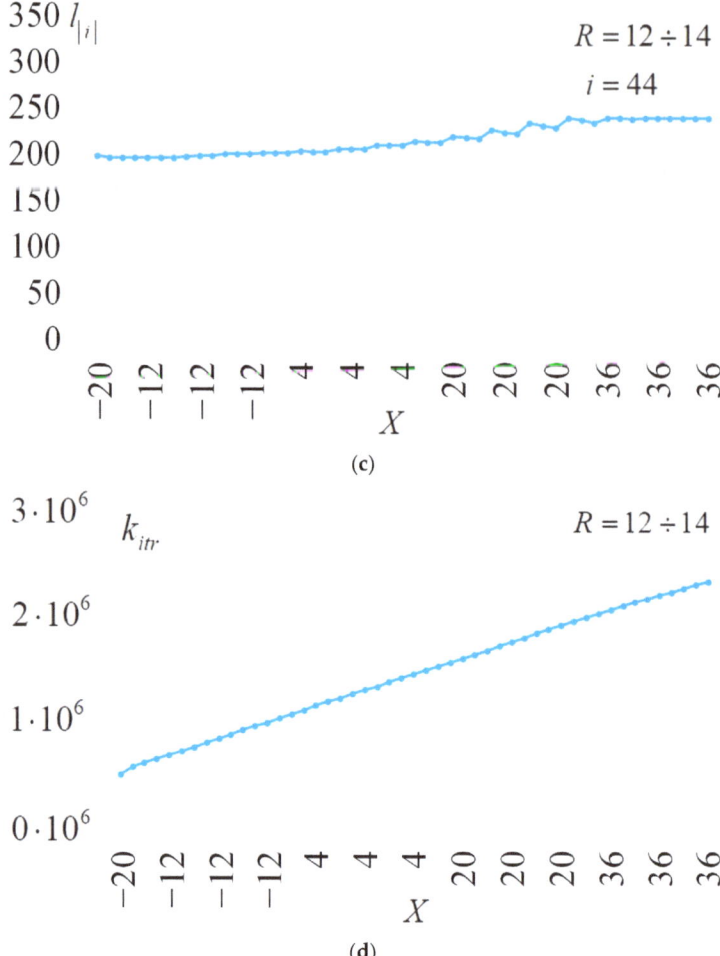

Figure 22. Trajectory of the $l_{|i|}$ S-box at dynamical change of parameters for $R = 12 \div 14$.

Despite the fact that the total number of iterations increases with an increasing R (Figures 17–22d), the best result is shown by cycles with a smaller value of R. For all cycles, the value $l_{|i=52|} = 0$ is achieved (Figures 17–22a).

The dynamics of achieving the minimum value $l_{|i|}$ are summarized in Table 5.

Table 5. Values of parameters R and X at which the minimum value $l_{|i|}$ is achieved.

	i = 52	
R	X	l|i|
R ∈ [2, 3, 4]	X ≥ 44	l|i| = 0
R ∈ [4, 5, 6]	X ≥ 32	l|i| = 0
R ∈ [6, 7, 8]	X ≥ 36	l|i| = 0
R ∈ [8, 9, 10]	X ≥ 28	l|i| = 0
R ∈ [10, 11, 12]	X ≥ 24	l|i| = 0
R ∈ [12, 13, 14]	X ≥ 20	l|i| = 0

Table 5. Cont.

i = 48		
R	X	$l\|i\|$
R ∈ [2, 3, 4]	X ≥ 44	$l\|i\|$ = 21
R ∈ [4, 5, 6]	X ≥ 36	$l\|i\|$ = 20
R ∈ [6, 7, 8]	X ≥ 36	$l\|i\|$ = 21
R ∈ [8, 9, 10]	X ≥ 36	$l\|i\|$ = 22
R ∈ [10, 11, 12]	X ≥ 36	$l\|i\|$ = 25
R ∈ [12, 13, 14]	X ≥ 36	$l\|i\|$ = 28

i = 44		
R	X	$l\|i\|$
R ∈ [2, 3, 4]	12 ≥ X ≥ 28	$l\|i\|$ = 150
R ∈ [4, 5, 6]	X ≤ 20	$l\|i\|$ = 160
R ∈ [6, 7, 8]	X ≤ 20	$l\|i\|$ = 160
R ∈ [8, 9, 10]	X ≤ 4	$l\|i\|$ = 160
R ∈ [10, 11, 12]	X ≤ 4	$l\|i\|$ = 180
R ∈ [12, 13, 14]	X ≤ 4	$l\|i\|$ = 200

The use of a small change in the parameter R (up to three units) allowed us to reduce the average statistical value $l_{|i=48|}$ by another two (to $l_{|i=48|}$ = 20) compared to the best result obtained in the first series of tests.

5.5.3. Pushing the Boundaries: Nonlinearity and Computational Efficiency

In the third series of experiments, we push the boundaries of our algorithm by exploring its performance under challenging scenarios, such as generating S-boxes with extremely high nonlinearity. Through comprehensive visualizations and detailed explanations, we showcase the limitations and potential of our approach in pushing the state-of-the-art in S-box generation.

These tests were conducted with a linear increase in the parameter R and a proportional increase in the parameter X. The results were averaged over 100 runs. In each run, a cycle of parameter change was performed and the following chains were followed (see Table 6).

Table 6. Selected parameters X and R in the third series of experiments.

					$X = -36 + 4 \cdot R$								
R	5	6	7	8	9	10	11	12	13	14			
X	−16	−12	−8	−4	0	4	8	12	16	20			
					$X = -28 + 4 \cdot R$								
R	4	5	6	7	8	9	10	11	121	3	14	15	16	17	18
X	−12	−8	−4	0	4	8	12	16	456	−16	28	32	36	40	44

The results are shown in Figures 23 and 24 (the values of the change in R are not shown in the figure).

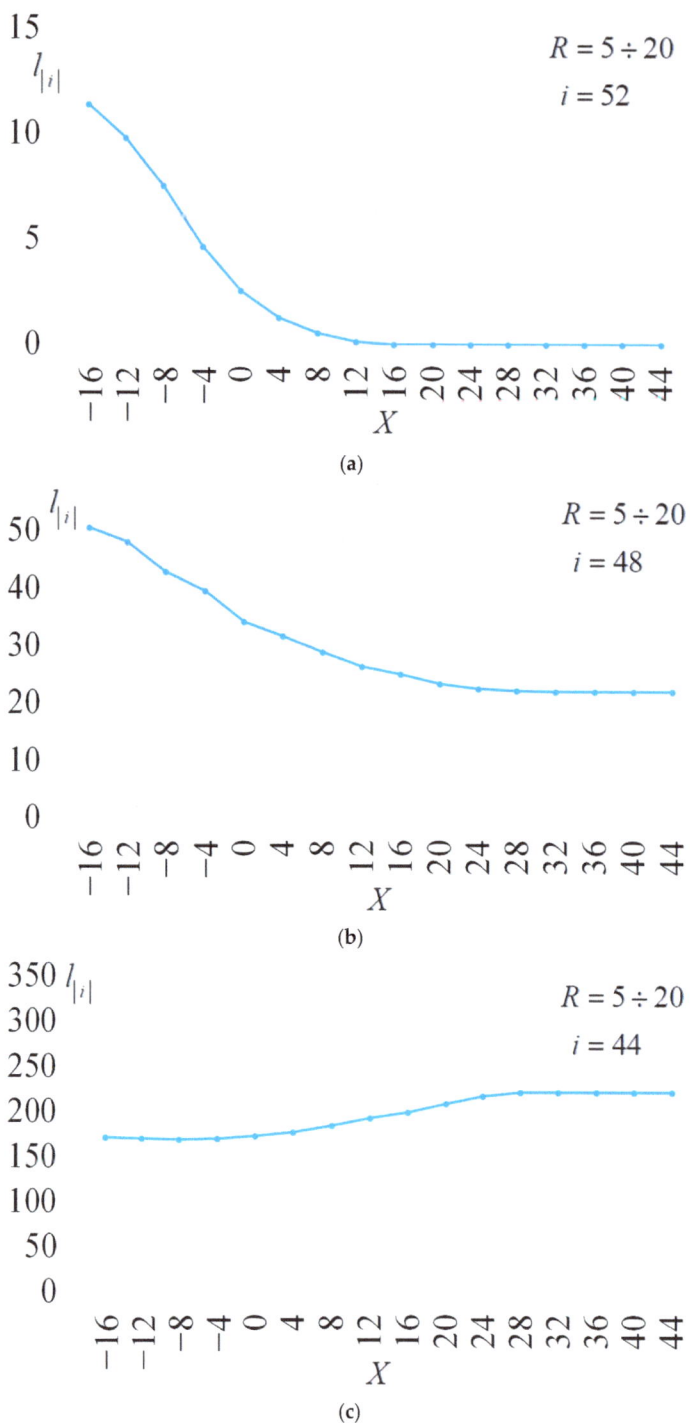

Figure 23. *Cont.*

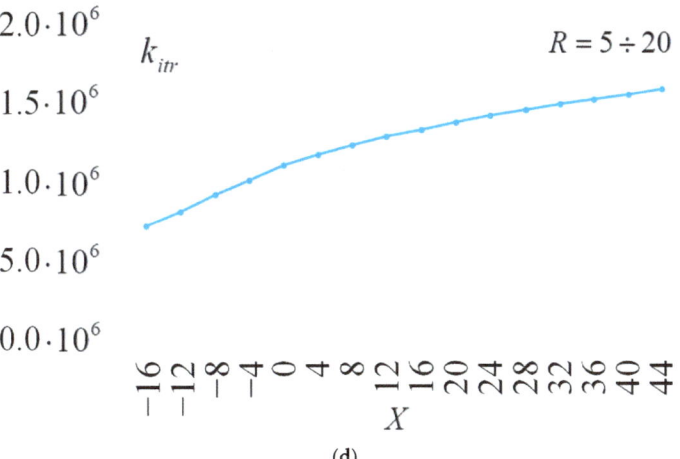

(d)

Figure 23. Trajectory of the $l_{|i|}$ S-box at dynamical change of parameters for $R = 5 \div 20$.

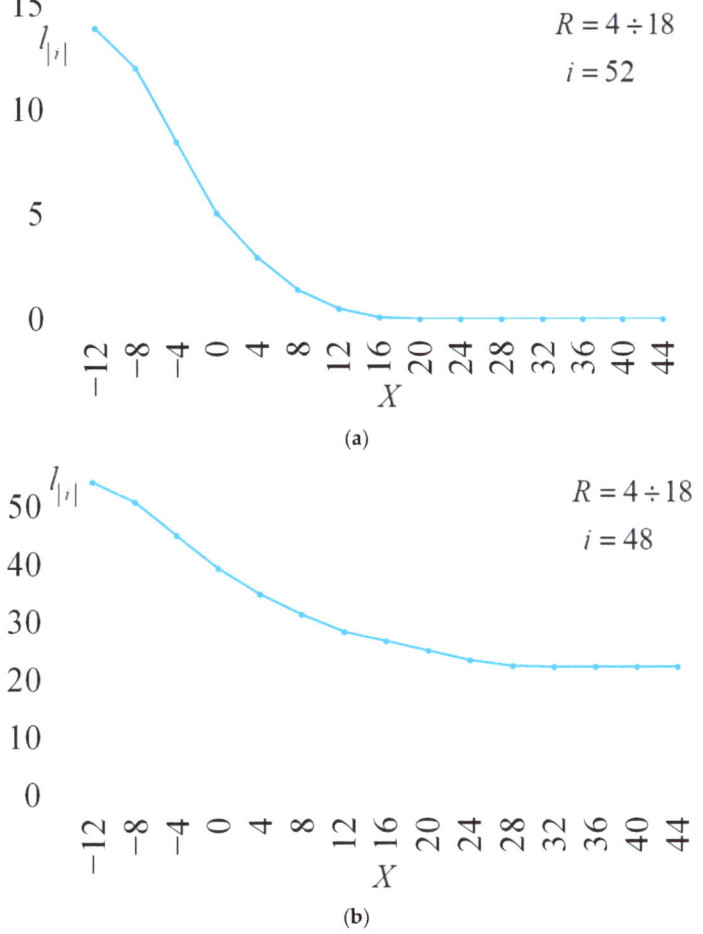

Figure 24. *Cont.*

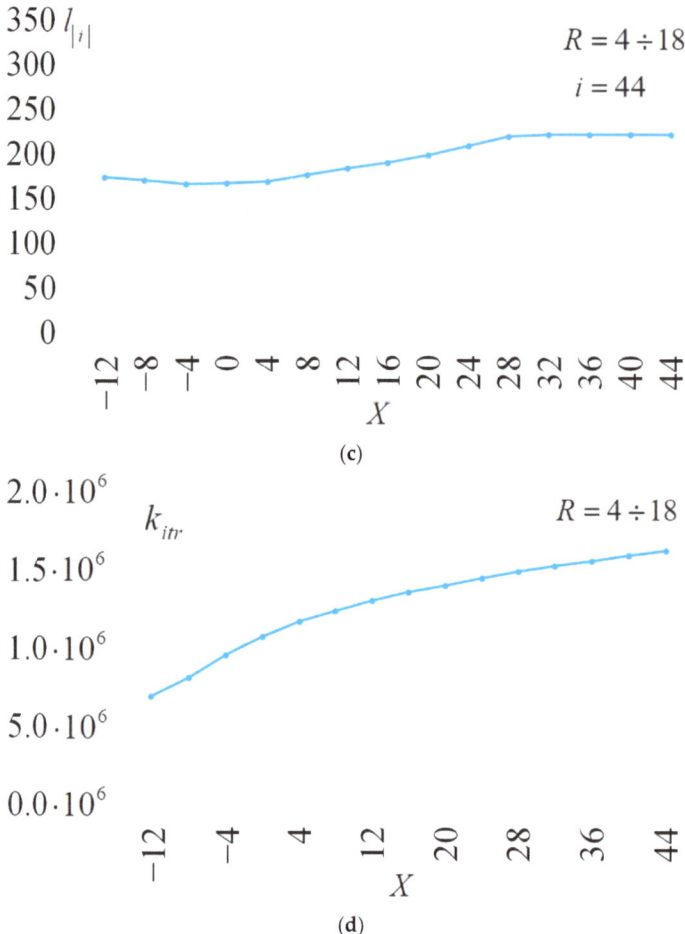

Figure 24. Trajectory of the $l_{|i|}$ S-box at dynamical change of parameters for $R = 4 \div 18$.

With the above parameters, no improvement was achieved in the third series. The average statistical value $l_{|i=48|}$ for both cycles was about $l_{|i=48|} = 22$). The average number of iterations of the search algorithm was about 1.5×10^6 iterations.

6. Discussions

Our study delved deep into the heuristic methods of nonlinear substitution search, commonly known as S-boxes. This pivotal research area ties directly to enhancing the robustness of cryptographic algorithms that leverage a secret key. By injecting nonlinearity through these S-boxes, resilience against cryptanalytic attacks receives a significant boost.

We embarked on this journey with a very specific aim: the generation of 8-bit bijective substitutions with a nonlinearity benchmarked at 104 or higher. Our findings revealed that the traditional static methodologies have intrinsic limitations. This realization led us to the conceptualization of a novel approach to S-box generation—dynamic heuristic methods with evolving parameters for the cost function.

6.1. Comparison with State of the Art

The narrative of research, especially within the realm of heuristic search and cryptography, is enriched when engaged in comparative analysis. Table 7 delineates a discerning landscape where diverse methodologies are juxtaposed, unraveling the intricacies and performance metrics of various search methods in generating S-boxes. Herein, our exploration unfolds along two pivotal dimensions: the 'Average number of iterations' and the 'Frequency of achieving the target outcome'. A closer, nuanced examination of these indices elucidates the layered complexities and insights nestled within these numbers.

Table 7. Results of a comparative analysis of known techniques for generating S-boxes with nonlinearity 104.

Literary Source	Search Method	Average Number of Iterations	Frequency of Achieving the Target Outcome
[44]	Simulated Annealing	over 3,000,000	1/200 (for generating S-boxes with nonlinearity 102)
[16]	Genetic and Tree	over 3,000,000	no data
[6]	Simulated Annealing	around 3,000,000	no data
[45]	Simulated Annealing	around 450,000	56.4%
[19]	Genetic and Tree	over 160,000	no data
[17]	Hill climbing	over 70,000	no data
[20]	Hill climbing	over 65,000	11/30
Our work	**Hill climbing, dynamic selection of cost function parameters**	around 50,000	100%

- Average Number of Iterations: This metric manifests as a tangible, quantitative indicator of computational effort, encapsulating the average exertion required by an algorithm to gravitate towards a solution. In heuristic landscapes, this becomes particularly poignant, embodying the exploration–exploitation balance and algorithmic efficiency.
- Frequency of Achieving the Target Outcome: This transcends mere numeric representation, dovetailing into the stochastic nature of heuristic methods. Recognizing that achieving the target is a probabilistic event, this metric epitomizes an algorithm's reliability and robustness in diverse scenarios and over multiple runs.

Pitting diverse methodologies against one another within a unified framework epitomizes a subtle art, ensconcing the principle of universal comparability. While classical approaches tether themselves to determinism and rigidity, our comparative matrix here invokes a spectrum of heuristic methodologies and objectively scrutinizes them under a universally applicable lens. The essence of this methodology pivots on its capability to furnish a coherent, relatable comparison amidst the probabilistic and non-deterministic nature of heuristic algorithms.

The comparative analysis presented in Table 7 reveals several key insights into the performance of various heuristic search techniques for S-box generation.

Firstly, it is evident that early approaches, such as Simulated Annealing [6,13] and Genetic Algorithms [14–16], suffer from high computational costs. These methods often require millions of iterations to find S-boxes with the desired nonlinearity. Moreover, their success rates are either low or not reported, indicating a lack of consistency and reliability. For instance, the Simulated Annealing approach in [6,44] achieved a success rate of only 1/200 for finding S-boxes with a nonlinearity of 102, while requiring over 3,000,000 iterations.

However, more recent studies have demonstrated a clear trend of improvement. The works of [7,19,20] showcased significant reductions in the number of iterations needed, as well as higher success rates. This progress can be attributed to advancements in heuristic techniques, such as the development of more efficient cost functions and the fine-tuning of algorithm parameters. For example, the hill-climbing approach employed by Freyre-Echevarría et al. [17,20], which introduces the WCFS cost function, requires an average of 65,000 iterations to find S-boxes with a nonlinearity of 104, with a success rate of 36.7%.

Our work builds upon these advancements and achieves a substantial leap forward in both computational efficiency and reliability. By integrating dynamic parameter adjustment into the hill-climbing algorithm, we reduce the average number of iterations to just 50,000—a significant improvement over the previous state of the art. Furthermore, our approach guarantees a 100% success rate in finding S-boxes with a nonlinearity of 104 or higher, demonstrating a level of consistency and robustness that is unmatched by prior methods.

6.2. Significance of Achieved Results

The implications of our findings are far-reaching. In the context of cryptographic engineering, where the efficiency and reliability of S-box generation are of paramount importance, our approach offers a promising solution. By dramatically reducing the computational cost and ensuring a high success rate, our method paves the way for more efficient and secure cryptographic systems. Moreover, the dynamic parameter adjustment technique introduced in our work has the potential to be applied to other optimization problems in cryptography and beyond, opening up new avenues for research and innovation.

To gain deeper insights, let us dissect the hill-climbing algorithm employed in our research. Our version of this algorithm integrated the WCFS heuristic cost function from reference [20]. The focus was unambiguous: to ascertain the potential of dynamic parameter adjustments in amplifying the algorithm's efficiency. The graphical data from our study affirm our hypothesis. The declining trend in the maximum absolute values of the Walsh–Hadamard coefficients illustrates that such parameter modifications can indeed expedite the generation process. In simpler terms, higher nonlinearity among the S-box alternatives in the search space can be achieved in fewer iterations.

While our results were promising, they were not without challenges. Generating a random 8-bit bijective S-box with a nonlinearity of 106 remained elusive. Nevertheless, we came tantalizingly close. The histogram of Walsh–Hadamard coefficients (as depicted in Figure 25) for the most optimal random S-box we unearthed speaks volumes. With just 12 coefficients standing tall with $|WHT[b,i]| > 44$, the implications are clear: only these 12 values need transformation to reach the coveted:

$$N(S)\frac{256 - \max_{b,i}|WHT(b,i)|}{2} = 106.$$

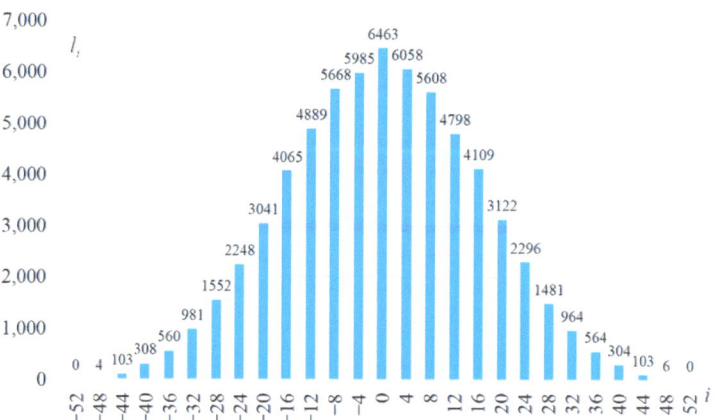

Figure 25. Histogram of Walsh–Hadamard coefficients for the best found random S-box.

In the grand tapestry of research in this domain, our findings are notable. To our understanding, the results we achieved are unmatched in the current literature, spotlighting the potential of our approach. The gaps in the current research field, particularly around efficient methods for generating S-boxes, are being progressively filled by dynamic methodologies like ours. The uncharted territory of obtaining random S-boxes with $N(S) = 106$ remains, and it is this tantalizing challenge that forms the crux of our future research endeavors.

In wrapping up, our research serves as a pivotal point, introducing an innovative dynamic methodology to the S-box generation discourse. It bears a conceptual kinship with dynamic programming—a computer science paradigm predicated on breaking down larger problems into smaller, more manageable subproblems. Dynamic programming, renowned for its optimization procedures, often capitalizes on previously solved subproblems, negating the need for redundant recalculations. Drawing parallels, our approach, by dynamically adjusting cost function parameters, also inherently leverages past learnings to better inform the ongoing search process.

6.3. Limitations of the Results

While our method has made substantial progress towards generating S-boxes with optimal cryptographic properties, it is important to acknowledge the limitations and challenges that remain. Achieving a nonlinearity of 106 for 8-bit bijective S-boxes is still an open problem, and our approach, while coming closer than many previous methods, has not yet reached this goal. Nevertheless, the quantitative results presented in this study demonstrate the potential for further improvements and serve as a benchmark for future research.

7. Conclusions

This study explores the application of heuristic methods for constructing nonlinear substitution boxes (S-boxes), which are crucial components in symmetric key cryptography. Our research focuses on generating 8-bit bijective S-boxes with high nonlinearity, specifically targeting values of 104 and above.

The key innovation of our approach lies in the dynamic adjustment of cost function parameters within the heuristic search process. This adaptive mechanism allows for a more efficient exploration of the vast search space, leading to improved results compared to traditional static methods. The comparative analysis in Table 7 quantitatively demonstrates the superiority of our approach in terms of both iteration count and success rate.

On average, our method requires only 50,000 iterations to find an S-box with the desired nonlinearity, a significant reduction compared to the 65,000 iterations reported by Freyre-Echevarría et al. [17,20] and the 450,000 iterations needed in [45]. Moreover, our approach guarantees a 100% success rate, a substantial improvement over the 36.7% achieved by Freyre-Echevarría et al. [17,20] and the 56.4% reported in [45]. These quantitative metrics highlight the efficiency and reliability of our method.

The effectiveness of our approach is further evidenced by the reduction in Walsh–Hadamard coefficient values, as illustrated in Figure 25. By dynamically adjusting the cost function parameters, we are able to minimize the number of coefficients with high absolute values, thus improving the nonlinearity of the generated S-boxes. Specifically, our method consistently produces S-boxes with only 12 coefficients exceeding the absolute value of 44, a significant achievement in the context of 8-bit bijective S-boxes.

From a broader perspective, our work establishes a quantitative foundation for the integration of dynamic programming principles into the field of cryptographic transformation. The dynamic parameter adjustment technique introduced in this study showed promising results in terms of efficiency and reliability, and its potential applications extend beyond S-box generation to other optimization problems in cryptography. Recent studies in fractional calculus, such as the analysis of Kuramoto–Sivashinsky equations with non-singular kernel operators [46], the investigation of fractional-order Helmholtz equations in two space dimensions [47], and the exploration of symmetric soliton solutions for the fractional coupled Konno–Onno system [48], highlight the potential for interdisciplinary collaborations in applied mathematics and computational physics. These topics inspire us to consider the broader implications and future directions of our work in the context of advancing scientific knowledge across various domains. Furthermore, as supported by recent studies [49,50], the resistance of S-boxes to side-channel attacks, particularly power analysis attacks, is a critical aspect that requires further investigation. Future research should focus on developing heuristic methods that not only optimize the cryptographic properties of S-boxes, but also incorporate techniques to enhance their resistance to side-channel attacks. This direction is crucial to ensure the long-term security of symmetric key cryptographic algorithms, even in the face of evolving threats such as post-quantum attacks.

Author Contributions: Conceptualization, O.K.; methodology, O.K.; resources, N.P.; formal analysis, M.K. and E.F.; investigation, E.F. and R.S.; software and validation, S.K.; writing—original draft preparation, O.K., M.K. and R.S.; writing—review and editing, O.K., M.K. and R.S.; funding acquisition, R.S. All authors have read and agreed to the published version of the manuscript.

Funding: This project has received funding from the European Union's Horizon 2020 research and innovation programme under the Marie Skłodowska-Curie grant agreement No. 101007820—TRUST. This publication reflects only the author's view and the REA is not responsible for any use that may be made of the information it contains. This research was funded by the European Union—NextGenerationEU under the Italian Ministry of University and Research (MIUR), National Innovation Ecosystem grant ECS00000041-VITALITY-CUP D83C22000710005.

Data Availability Statement: The datasets generated during and/or analyzed during the current study are available from the corresponding author on reasonable request.

Conflicts of Interest: The authors declare no conflicts of interest.

References

1. Klima, R.E.; Klima, R.; Sigmon, N.P.; Sigmon, N.; Klima, R.; Sigmon, N.P.; Sigmon, N. *Cryptology: Classical and Modern*; Chapman and Hall/CRC: New York, NY, USA, 2018; ISBN 978-1-315-17066-4.
2. Menezes, A.J.; van Oorschot, P.C.; Vanstone, S.A.; van Oorschot, P.C.; Vanstone, S.A. *Handbook of Applied Cryptography*; CRC Press: Boca Raton, FL, USA, 2018; ISBN 978-0-429-46633-5.
3. Haider, M.I.; Shah, T.; Ali, A.; Shah, D.; Khalid, I. An Innovative Approach towards Image Encryption by Using Novel PRNs and S-Boxes Modeling Techniques. *Math. Comput. Simul.* **2023**, *209*, 153–168. [CrossRef]
4. Artuğer, F.; Özkaynak, F. A New Post-Processing Approach for Improvement of Nonlinearity Property in Substitution Boxes. *Integration* **2024**, *94*, 102105. [CrossRef]
5. Álvarez-Cubero, J. Vector Boolean Functions: Applications in Symmetric Cryptography. Ph.D. Thesis, Universidad Politécnica de Madrid, Madrid, Spain, 2015.
6. McLaughlin, J. Applications of Search Techniques to Cryptanalysis and the Construction of Cipher Components. Ph.D. Thesis, University of York, York, UK, 2012.
7. Kuznetsov, O.; Poluyanenko, N.; Frontoni, E.; Kandiy, S. Enhancing Smart Communication Security: A Novel Cost Function for Efficient S-Box Generation in Symmetric Key Cryptography. *Cryptography* **2024**, *8*, 17. [CrossRef]
8. Khan, M.F.; Ahmed, A.; Saleem, K. A Novel Cryptographic Substitution Box Design Using Gaussian Distribution. *IEEE Access* **2019**, *7*, 15999–16007. [CrossRef]
9. Souravlias, D.; Parsopoulos, K.E.; Meletiou, G.C. Designing Bijective S-Boxes Using Algorithm Portfolios with Limited Time Budgets. *Appl. Soft Comput.* **2017**, *59*, 475–486. [CrossRef]
10. La Scala, R.; Tiwari, S.K. Stream/Block Ciphers, Difference Equations and Algebraic Attacks. *J. Symb. Comput.* **2022**, *109*, 177–198. [CrossRef]
11. Bard, G.V. *Algebraic Cryptanalysis*; Springer US: Boston, MA, USA, 2009; ISBN 978-0-387-88756-2.
12. Clark, A.J. Optimisation Heuristics for Cryptology. Ph.D. Thesis, Queensland University of Technology, Brisbane, Australia, 1998.
13. Delahaye, D.; Chaimatanan, S.; Mongeau, M. Simulated Annealing: From Basics to Applications. In *Handbook of Metaheuristics*; Gendreau, M., Potvin, J.-Y., Eds.; International Series in Operations Research & Management Science; Springer International Publishing: Cham, Switzerland, 2019; Volume 272, pp. 1–35, ISBN 978-3-319-91085-7.
14. Kapuściński, T.; Nowicki, R.K.; Napoli, C. Application of Genetic Algorithms in the Construction of Invertible Substitution Boxes. In *Artificial Intelligence and Soft Computing*; Rutkowski, L., Korytkowski, M., Scherer, R., Tadeusiewicz, R., Zadeh, L.A., Zurada, J.M., Eds.; Springer International Publishing: Cham, Switzerland, 2016; pp. 380–391.
15. Ivanov, G.; Nikolov, N.; Nikova, S. Reversed Genetic Algorithms for Generation of Bijective S-Boxes with Good Cryptographic Properties. *Cryptogr. Commun.* **2016**, *8*, 247–276. [CrossRef]
16. Tesar, P. A New Method for Generating High Non-Linearity S-Boxes. *Radioengineering* **2010**, *19*, 23–26.
17. Freyre-Echevarría, A.; Alanezi, A.; Martínez-Díaz, I.; Ahmad, M.; Abd El-Latif, A.A.; Kolivand, H.; Razaq, A. An External Parameter Independent Novel Cost Function for Evolving Bijective Substitution-Boxes. *Symmetry* **2020**, *12*, 1896. [CrossRef]

18. Freyre-Echevarría, A.; Martínez-Díaz, I.; Pérez, C.M.L.; Sosa-Gómez, G.; Rojas, O. Evolving Nonlinear S-Boxes With Improved Theoretical Resilience to Power Attacks. *IEEE Access* **2020**, *8*, 202728–202737. [CrossRef]
19. Picek, S.; Cupic, M.; Rotim, L. A New Cost Function for Evolution of S-Boxes. *Evol. Comput.* **2016**, *24*, 695–718. [CrossRef] [PubMed]
20. Freyre Echevarría, A.; Martínez Díaz, I. A New Cost Function to Improve Nonlinearity of Bijective S-Boxes. *Symmetry* **2020**, *12*, 1896.
21. Kuznetsov, A.; Poluyanenko, N.; Frontoni, E.; Kandiy, S.; Peliukh, O. A New Cost Function for Heuristic Search of Nonlinear Substitutions. *Expert Syst. Appl.* **2024**, *237*, 121684. [CrossRef]
22. Kuznetsov, A.; Poluyanenko, N.; Frontoni, E.; Kandiy, S.; Pieshkova, O. Optimized Simulated Annealing for Efficient Generation of Highly Nonlinear S-Boxes. *Soft Comput.* **2023**, *28*, 3905–3920. [CrossRef]
23. Kuznetsov, A.; Frontoni, E.; Romeo, L.; Poluyanenko, N.; Kandiy, S.; Kuznetsova, K.; Beňová, E. Optimizing Hill Climbing Algorithm for S-Boxes Generation. *Electronics* **2023**, *12*, 2338. [CrossRef]
24. Ahmad, M.; Khaja, I.A.; Baz, A.; Alhakami, H.; Alhakami, W. Particle Swarm Optimization Based Highly Nonlinear Substitution-Boxes Generation for Security Applications. *IEEE Access* **2020**, *8*, 116132–116147. [CrossRef]
25. Cusick, T.; Stănică, P. *Cryptographic Boolean Functions and Applications*, 2nd ed.; Academic Press: Cambridge, MA, USA, 2017; p. 275.
26. Nyberg, K. Differentially Uniform Mappings for Cryptography. In *Advances in Cryptology—EUROCRYPT'93*; Helleseth, T., Ed.; Springer: Berlin/Heidelberg, Germany, 1994; pp. 55–64.
27. Daemen, J.; Rijmen, V. (Eds.) Specification of Rijndael. In *The Design of Rijndael: The Advanced Encryption Standard (AES)*; Information Security and Cryptography; Springer: Berlin/Heidelberg, Germany, 2020; pp. 31–51, ISBN 978-3-662-60769-5.
28. Shannon, C.E. Communication Theory of Secrecy Systems. *Bell Syst. Tech. J.* **1949**, *28*, 656–715. [CrossRef]
29. Carlet, C.; Ding, C. Nonlinearities of S-Boxes. *Finite Fields Their Appl.* **2007**, *13*, 121–135. [CrossRef]
30. Carlet, C. Vectorial Boolean Functions for Cryptography. In *Boolean Models and Methods in Mathematics, Computer Science, and Engineering*; Cambridge University Press: Cambridge, UK, 2006.
31. Banzhaf, W.; Hu, T. Evolutionary Computation. In *Evolutionary Biology*; Oxford University Press: Oxford, UK, 2019; ISBN 978-0-19-994172-8.
32. Gilli, M.; Maringer, D.; Schumann, E. (Eds.) Chapter 13—Heuristics: A Tutorial. In *Numerical Methods and Optimization in Finance*, 2nd ed.; Academic Press: Cambridge, MA, USA, 2019; pp. 319–353, ISBN 978-0-12-815065-8.
33. Yiu, Y.F.; Du, J.; Mahapatra, R. Evolutionary Heuristic A* Search: Heuristic Function Optimization via Genetic Algorithm. In Proceedings of the 2018 IEEE First International Conference on Artificial Intelligence and Knowledge Engineering (AIKE), Laguna Hills, CA, USA, 26–28 September 2018; pp. 25–32.
34. Ismail, I.M.; Agwu, N.N. Influence of Heuristic Functions on Real-Time Heuristic Search Methods. In Proceedings of the 2018 14th International Conference on Electronics Computer and Computation (ICECCO), Kaskelen, Kazakhstan, 29 November–1 December 2018; pp. 206–212.
35. Eremia, M.; Liu, C.-C.; Edris, A.-A. Heuristic Optimization Techniques. In *Advanced Solutions in Power Systems: HVDC, FACTS, and Artificial Intelligence*; IEEE: Piscataway, NJ, USA, 2016; pp. 931–984, ISBN 978-1-119-17533-9.
36. Edelkamp, S.; Schrödl, S. (Eds.) Chapter 14—Selective Search. In *Heuristic Search*; Morgan Kaufmann: San Francisco, CA, USA, 2012; pp. 633–669, ISBN 978-0-12-372512-7.
37. Delahaye, D.; Chaimatanan, S.; Mongeau, M. *Simulated Annealing: From Basics to Applications*; Springer: Berlin/Heidelberg, Germany, 2019; Volume 272, p. 1, ISBN 978-3-319-91086-4.
38. Hernando, L.; Mendiburu, A.; Lozano, J.A. Hill-Climbing Algorithm: Let's Go for a Walk Before Finding the Optimum. In Proceedings of the 2018 IEEE Congress on Evolutionary Computation (CEC), Rio de Janeiro, Brazil, 8–13 July 2018; pp. 1–7.
39. Burnett, L.D. Heuristic Optimization of Boolean Functions and Substitution Boxes for Cryptography. Ph.D. Thesis, Queensland University of Technology, Brisbane City, QLD, Australia, 2005.
40. Millan, W.; Clark, A. Smart Hill Climbing Finds Better Boolean Functions. In *Workshop on Selected Areas in Cryptology*; Queensland University of Technology: Brisbane City, QLD, Australia, 1997.
41. Millan, W.; Clark, A.; Dawson, E. Boolean Function Design Using Hill Climbing Methods. In *Information Security and Privacy*; Pieprzyk, J., Safavi-Naini, R., Seberry, J., Eds.; Springer: Berlin/Heidelberg, Germany, 1999; pp. 1–11.
42. Kuznetsov, O.; Frontoni, E.; Kandiy, S.; Smirnov, O.; Ulianovska, Y.; Kobylianska, O. Heuristic Search for Nonlinear Substitutions for Cryptographic Applications. In Proceedings of the Advances in Artificial Systems for Logistics Engineering III; Hu, Z., Zhang, Q., He, M., Eds.; Springer Nature: Cham, Switzerland, 2023; pp. 288–298.
43. Kuznetsov, A.; Poluyanenko, N.; Kandii, S.; Zaichenko, Y.; Prokopovich-Tkachenko, D.; Katkova, T. WHS Cost Function for Generating S-Boxes. In Proceedings of the 2021 IEEE 8th International Conference on Problems of Infocommunications, Science and Technology (PIC S&T), Kharkiv, Ukraine, 5–7 October 2021; pp. 434–438.
44. Clark, J.A.; Jacob, J.L.; Stepney, S. The Design of S-Boxes by Simulated Annealing. In Proceedings of the 2004 Congress on Evolutionary Computation (IEEE Cat. No.04TH8753), Portland, OR, USA, 19–23 June 2004; Volume 2, pp. 1533–1537.
45. Kuznetsov, A.; Wieclaw, L.; Poluyanenko, N.; Hamera, L.; Kandiy, S.; Lohachova, Y. Optimization of a Simulated Annealing Algorithm for S-Boxes Generating. *Sensors* **2022**, *22*, 6073. [CrossRef]

46. Saad Alshehry, A.; Imran, M.; Khan, A.; Shah, R.; Weera, W. Fractional View Analysis of Kuramoto–Sivashinsky Equations with Non-Singular Kernel Operators. *Symmetry* **2022**, *14*, 1463. [CrossRef]
47. Srivastava, H.M.; Shah, R.; Khan, H.; Arif, M. Some Analytical and Numerical Investigation of a Family of Fractional-Order Helmholtz Equations in Two Space Dimensions. *Math. Methods Appl. Sci.* **2020**, *43*, 199–212. [CrossRef]
48. Yasmin, H.; Aljahdaly, N.H.; Saeed, A.M.; Shah, R. Investigating Symmetric Soliton Solutions for the Fractional Coupled Konno–Onno System Using Improved Versions of a Novel Analytical Technique. *Mathematics* **2023**, *11*, 2686. [CrossRef]
49. Crocetti, L.; Baldanzi, L.; Bertolucci, M.; Sarti, L.; Carnevale, B.; Fanucci, L. A Simulated Approach to Evaluate Side-Channel Attack Countermeasures for the Advanced Encryption Standard. *Integration* **2019**, *68*, 80–86. [CrossRef]
50. Nannipieri, P.; Crocetti, L.; Di Matteo, S.; Fanucci, L.; Saponara, S. Hardware Design of an Advanced-Feature Cryptographic Tile within the European Processor Initiative. *IEEE Trans. Comput.* **2023**, 1–14. [CrossRef]

Disclaimer/Publisher's Note: The statements, opinions and data contained in all publications are solely those of the individual author(s) and contributor(s) and not of MDPI and/or the editor(s). MDPI and/or the editor(s) disclaim responsibility for any injury to people or property resulting from any ideas, methods, instructions or products referred to in the content.

Article

Secure Processing and Distribution of Data Managed on Private InterPlanetary File System Using Zero-Knowledge Proofs

Kyohei Shibano [1,*], Kensuke Ito [1], Changhee Han [2], Tsz Tat Chu [2], Wataru Ozaki [2] and Gento Mogi [1]

[1] Department of Technology Management for Innovation, School of Engineering, The University of Tokyo, Tokyo 113-8656, Japan
[2] Callisto Inc., Tokyo 171-0022, Japan
* Correspondence: shibano@tmi.t.u-tokyo.ac.jp

Abstract: In this study, a new data-sharing method is proposed that uses a private InterPlanetary File System—a decentralized storage system operated within a closed network—to distribute data to external entities while making its authenticity verifiable. Among the two operational modes of IPFS, public and private, this study focuses on the method for using private IPFS. Private IPFS is not open to the general public; although it poses a risk of data tampering when distributing data to external parties, the proposed method ensures the authenticity of the received data. In particular, this method applies a type of zero-knowledge proof, namely, the Groth16 protocol of zk-SNARKs, to ensure that the data corresponds to the content identifier in a private IPFS. Moreover, the recipient's name is embedded into the distributed data to prevent unauthorized secondary distribution. Experiments confirmed the effectiveness of the proposed method for an image data size of up to 120 × 120 pixels. In future studies, the proposed method will be applied to larger and more diverse data types.

Keywords: IPFS; zero-knowledge proof; circom; zk-SNARKs; private IPFS; data distribution; data processing; data security

1. Introduction

Decentralized systems are robust because they lack a single point of failure; therefore, they are widely applied across enterprise sectors including cryptocurrency, supply chain management, financial services, and digital identity. To store large-sized data such as images, these systems require storage functions that are inherently decentralized. Blockchain, commonly used in conjunction, typically handles smaller data sizes such as transaction histories and operates as a ledger database. The InterPlanetary File System (IPFS) is a prominent decentralized storage system that stores data across multiple nodes to enhance data availability. The IPFS has two variants: public IPFS, wherein the data can be stored by any user with unrestricted access, and private IPFS, wherein a closed network accessible only within specific organizations or groups is established, offering enhanced privacy and security.

When storing data in IPFS, understanding the differences between public IPFS and private IPFS is crucial. Public IPFS allows anyone to access data, while private IPFS is accessible only within specific organizations or groups, enhancing privacy and security. When storing sensitive information, such as confidential data, in public IPFS, applying an appropriate encryption scheme is vital to ensure data protection. By contrast, private IPFS provides higher security for data storage, because it is accessible only within a closed network.

Particularly for organizations such as corporations or healthcare institutions, storing data in public IPFS, despite using strong encryption technologies, carries inherent risks. Moreover, the potential for data leaks due to operational errors exists persistently in such cases; although data is encrypted, it is exposed to the world, rendering it vulnerable to brute force attacks and other security threats.

Regarding accessibility, public IPFS allows general users to directly access and retrieve data. However, in private IPFS, data must be received from members of the organization or group constituting the network. During this process, if data is tampered, then users may unable to detect it. Therefore, trusting the intermediaries responsible for handling data transfer in such cases becomes mandatory. To address the aforementioned trust issue, a new method is proposed herein for distributing data stored in a private IPFS to external entities while making its authenticity verifiable. The Groth16 [1] protocol of zk-SNARKs, a type of ZKP, is applied to data stored in a private IPFS to ensure the authenticity of the data. Moreover, the recipient's information is embedded into the distributed data to prevent unauthorized secondary distribution. The proposed method of data sharing is important because it is tailored to the private IPFS case.

The differences in several aspects, including security and accessibility, when storing data in public IPFS and private IPFS within the enterprise domain are summarized in Table 1. This study proposes solutions to the threats associated with private IPFS.

Table 1. Comparison between public and private IPFS in the enterprise domain.

	Public IPFS	Private IPFS
Trust Model	Trustless	Requires trust in the operating group
Access Restrictions	Accessible by anyone	Accessible only within the operating group
Data Leakage Risk	Constant risk of leakage due to user error	Low risk of leakage within a closed network
Handling of Confidential Information	Requires proper encryption	Data stored in IPFS does not require high-level encryption itself; there is a trust point when passing data to users
Brute Force Attack Risk	Always present	Low
Data Retrieval Method	Direct access by users	Data received from members of the organization or group
Threats	Requires encryption that prevents decryption by unauthorized users	There is a risk of tampering when transferring data to users

The remainder of this paper is organized as follows. Section 2 presents related prior research. Section 3 outlines the fundamental technologies, i.e., ZKP and zk-SNARKs. Section 4 describes the structure of the proposed method, while Section 5 outlines the potential applications of this method. Section 6 presents the implementation of this method, while Section 7 discusses the experiments performed to verify the effectiveness of the implementation. Section 8 presents a discussion of the experimental results, while Section 9 presents the conclusions of the paper and an outline of future challenges.

2. Related Studies

Existing decentralized systems use IPFS, particularly in combination with blockchain technology. Kumar et al. [2] proposed a method for securely managing medical data by integrating IPFS with a blockchain. Azbeg et al. [3] specifically suggested a system that managed and stored medical data using private IPFS and a permissioned blockchain by employing proxy re-encryption to ensure secure decryption by designated doctors. When a physician receives some patient's data, he/she obtains the re-encrypted data via a hospital. Hossan et al. [4] also proposed a system to securely record information for ride-sharing services using IPFS and a private blockchain.

Focusing on controlling the distribution of data managed by IPFS, Lin et al. [5] proposed a system for protecting private data using improved IPFS combined with a blockchain. This system recorded file metadata and accessed permissions on the blockchain, enabling users to control file sharing. Moreover, the system implemented efficient management features using smart contracts, thereby enhancing data security and management flexibility. Battah et al. [6] developed a system that used multiparty authentication (MPA), proxy re-encryption, and smart contracts on a blockchain for decentralized access control of encrypted data stored in IPFS. Huang et al. [7] introduced a trusted IPFS proxy to realize access control and group key management for encrypted data stored in IPFS. Sun et al. [8] proposed a system that allowed only individuals with appropriate attributes to decrypt encrypted data stored in IPFS using a ciphertext policy attribute–based encryption system, facilitating efficient medical information management. Kang et al. [9] enabled the distribution of data managed using private IPFS and a private blockchain to external users using named data network (NDN). Furthermore, Uddin et al. [10] proposed a file-sharing system that used IPFS and public key infrastructure (PKI) technology without requiring a trusted third party.

Several studies have used ZKP for data distribution. For instance, Li et al. [11] proposed a privacy-preserving traffic management system that combined noninteractive zero-knowledge range proofs with a blockchain. A prototype using Hyperledger Fabric and Hyperledger Ursa met the data privacy requirements for real-time traffic management.

This study proposes a method for appropriately processing and distributing data managed within private IPFS to users outside the network, thereby offering a different approach than those proposed in previous studies. Some studies have adopted proxy re-encryption as an appropriate method for data storage and distribution in IPFS [3,6]. Using this method, distributed data can be re-encrypted to be decrypted with the recipient's private key. Moreover, when storing data in IPFS, recording the hash value of the pre-encrypted data on the blockchain allows recipients to verify the correctness of their received data after decryption. However, this method cannot handle cases where data is processed, such as embedding the recipient's name into the decrypted data, as in this study.

3. Zero-Knowledge Proof

ZKP is a cryptographic protocol that allows a prover to prove the validity of a proposition to a verifier without disclosing any additional information other than the validity of the proposition. The proposition of this study is that the data provided to an external entity is generated based on a given CID. Our goal is to allow a member of private IPFS (prover) to prove this proposition to an external entity (verifier as the recipient of the data) without disclosing any other important information (such as IPFS access rights and encryption keys).

ZKP, specifically the Groth16 protocol of zk-SNARKs used in this study, begins with a trusted setup where both parties establish public parameters that are crucial for the secure generation and verification of proofs. In the ZKP scheme, we first generate a circuit that describes the process for which a proof is intended. The circuit includes the conditions to be verified such as the existence of a CID. Through the ZKP scheme, cryptographic keys—specifically a proving key and a verification key—are created. These keys are crucial for creating a proof for the circuit and its verification. Using the proving key and input data, the prover generates a proof that reveals the validity of the output data against the conditions specified in the circuit. The verifier then uses the verification key to check the proof and the output data. If the proof is valid, this confirms the integrity of data without exposing any underlying information.

In this study, Groth16 processing is performed using circom [12,13] and snarkjs [14]. The process flow is summarized in Figure 1.

zk-SNARKs is employed owing to its noninteractive nature and efficiency, which are particularly advantageous for systems employing smart contracts owing to low computational costs for verifying the proof. Furthermore, zk-SNARKs is known for its high computational requirements and the need for advanced PC specifications. For instance, in one of the representative applications of zk-SNARKs, Zcash [15], proof generation process takes over half a minute for a single anonymous transaction [16].

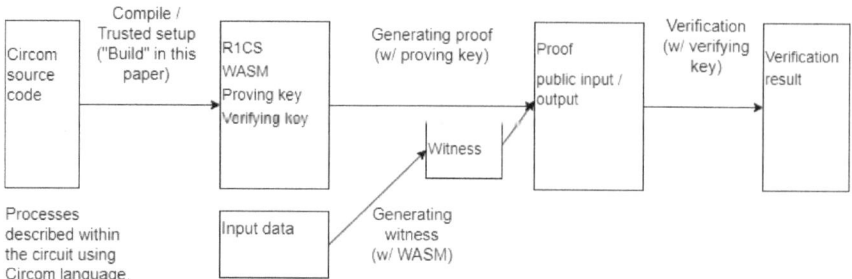

Figure 1. Zero-knowledge proof using circom.

4. Proposed System

Figure 2 presents an overview of the proposed system.

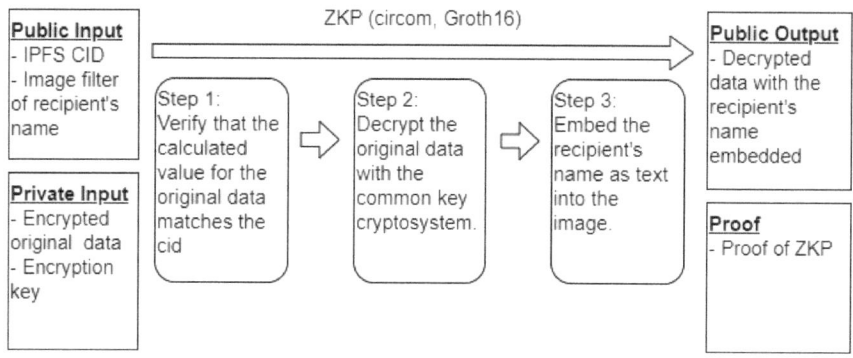

Figure 2. Process flow of ZKP: an example of image data processing.

Herein, we make the following assumptions:

- Private IPFS is operated by a limited number of members.
- Data are stored in IPFS in an encrypted format using symmetric-key cryptography.
- The encryption key is exclusively held by an individual among the members, i.e., an administrator.

The proposed system facilitates the creation of a ZKP proof through the circuit by the encryption key-holding member (equivalent to an administrator). The inputs and outputs (other than proofs) of this process are as follows:

- **Public Input:**
  - CID of the original encrypted data;
  - A filter for embedding the recipient's name in the data;
- **Private Input:**
  - Encrypted original data;
  - Encryption key;
- **Output:**
  - Decrypted data with the recipient's name embedded.

Note that the ZK-optimized implementation (Section 6.1) adds more information to the public input. In particular, the internal process of ZKP involves the following steps:

1. Calculating the CID of the original encrypted data to verify a match with the entered CID.

2. Decrypting the original data using a symmetric-key cryptography.
3. Embedding the recipient's name into the decrypted image raw data based on the filter provided in the public input.

In the proposed system, we do not solely focus on image data but use them as example data to verify the applicability of the proposed scheme. Filters are used to improve the efficiency of processing inside the circuit. As embedding name data inside the circuit is computationally intensive, a considerable portion of the image processing is performed outside the circuit in advance and a filter is created. Using public input and proof, the recipient can verify that the decrypted data (i.e., output) with their name embedded are generated from the original data (contained in the private input) managed with the CID. The recipient can check with at least one member of the network to confirm the existence of the CID in private IPFS.

In summary, the aforementioned process enables the recipient to verify the received data by performing the following tasks:

- verify that the received data were generated from the data managed with the CID of private IPFS,
- confirm using the proof that the entire process was correctly conducted without directly knowing the encrypted data or the encryption key, and
- verify that the CID exists specifically within the private IPFS by asking at least one network member.

The novelty of the proposed system is that it allows data authenticity verification by trusting at least one member of the network even if the recipient do not control the encryption key. (It is natural for the recipient to trust at least one member of a particular multimember system. If none of the members can be trusted, then there will be a marginal incentive to receive data managed by that network).

5. Potential Applications

In the medical industry, patient diagnosis data are managed across multiple medical institutions. Using the proposed system, patients can verify whether the data they receive are indeed managed in private IPFS to ensure the authenticity. An all-in-one platform is also proposed herein for the research and development of machine learning with medical images [17]. On this platform, anonymized medical images are managed in private IPFS operated by a group of medical institutions. The system allows machine learning researchers, who are external to the network, to verify whether the image data are indeed managed in the private IPFS. Moreover, by embedding the information about machine learning researchers in the image data, medical institutions can mitigate the risk of secondary distribution.

If the application is not limited to the embedding of recipient's name, the potential applications of the proposed system can be further expanded. For instance, consider a scenario where a specific company establishes private IPFS for sharing confidential documents among its group companies. If employee data are included, then concealing private data and distributing them to external entities allows these entities to confirm the association of employees with the company while ensuring that their privacy is protected. Furthermore, suppose a university has set up private IPFS to allow only academic staff access to student performance data. In this case, students can verify that their performance data received are genuinely managed in the private IPFS.

Thus, the proposed system supports a hybrid case—distributing internal data to specific external entities as necessary—prevalent in real-world settings.

6. Implementation

The proposed system was implemented to process image data using circom, a renowned tool specialized for constructing zk-SNARKs circuits. Circom enables the description of computational processes within a circuit using its unique language, and the executable file generated after compilation can be invoked via the JavaScript library, snarkjs. This arrangement allows describing circuit processes in circom, and external processing and circuit correctness testing are performed using JavaScript. For the zk-SNARKs scheme, Groth16 was used; it is known for its relatively faster execution speed than other zk-SNARKs scheme.

In particular, we worked on two types of implementations for image data: a standard implementation using general cryptographic techniques and a ZK-optimized implementation using ZK-friendly cryptographic techniques to reduce the computation time of the circuit. These implementations were used for comparing the required computation times. ZKP circuits require considerably large computation time, even for calculations that can be easily handled by computer software (this is particularly noticeable when dealing with image data). Therefore, computational efficiency is crucial for practical use.

6.1. Standard Implementation

Section 4 describes the data input into the circuit. For simplifying the in-circuit processing, the original encrypted data were formatted as bitmap image data compliant with OS/2 standards. The first 54 bytes of the image data store information such as the width, height, and color depth of images [18]. The color depth is 8 bits and each color component in RGB is allocated one byte, resulting in a representation of 3 bytes per pixel.

Initially, the system checks whether the encrypted data, entered as a private input, matches the CID provided as a public input. If they do not match, the system signifies an error and the image data outputted as the output is a byte sequence where all values are 0x00. CID serves as crucial mechanism for uniquely identifying files and efficiently retrieving data from IPFS. CID has two versions: V0 and V1 [19]. Herein, the more flexible version CID V1 was used. CID includes a hash of the respective data, ensuring different data will have different CIDs. Typically, CID V1 is calculated using the SHA256 hash function, and the standard implementation uses SHA256 to compute CID.

The data structure of CID V1 is as shown in Table 2.

Table 2. CID V1 data structure.

Byte Position	Description	Value in Implementation
First byte	CID version	0x01
Second byte	multibase prefix	0x55: raw data
Third byte	Hash function identifier	0x12: SHA-256
Fourth byte	Hash length	0x20: 32 bytes
From fifth byte	Hash value	SHA-256 hash value (32 bytes)

The encoding for CID is conducted using Base32. Base32 encodes a sequence of bytes constructed based on this structure to generate CID.

Inside the circuit, the entered CID value is decoded from Base32 and the system checks whether the extracted hash value matches the SHA256 hash computed from the encrypted data.

Subsequently, the encrypted data are decrypted. AES-CTR is used as the encryption algorithm, which is a type of symmetric-key cryptography. The AES-CTR encryption and decryption in circom-chacha20 [20] was used. For decrypting AES-CTR encryption, the encryption key and nonce used during encryption are required. They are input into the circuit as a 256-bit key and a 128-bit nonce, respectively, as private inputs. Moreover, AES-CTR handles data volumes in multiples of 16. Therefore, if the length of the image data before encryption is not a multiple of 16, zeros (0x00) are added to the end of the data to align it with this requirement.

Finally, a filter is applied to the decrypted data to embed the recipient's name. Implementing text embedding directly within the circuit can substantially increase the computation load; therefore, a filter is created outside the circuit that performs a considerable portion of the image processing in advance. The font used for the text representing the recipient's name is the Misaki font [21]. The filter is then used to streamline processing inside the circuit. The filter is a list of numbers where values from 0 to 255 are used to change the color of each pixel in case it differs from that of the pixels in the original image; moreover, a value of 300 indicates the color should remain as in the original image. This filter represents the position on the image where the recipient's name should be inserted. Inside the circuit, the specified pixel colors in the decrypted BMP data are changed based on this filter.

6.2. ZK-Optimized Implementation

ZK-optimized implementation changes the hash function, encryption technology, and in-circuit processing to the standard ZK-friendly encryption implementation. This implementation enhances the computational efficiency and does not evaluate the difference in computation speeds between ZK-friendly encryption and general encryption. Therefore, in-circuit processing was also modified.

Poseidon hash [22] was used as the hash function for computing CID. Notably, using the Poseidon hash for CIDs is not officially supported; therefore, it was developed specifically for this study. Although SHA256 is commonly used in general computations, it demands considerable computation time within ZKP circuits. The Poseidon hash is implemented in circom and JavaScript (circomlib [23] and circomlibjs [24], respectively). It is computed over a finite field with a prime order and can accept up to 16 input variables. The used order is less than the maximum of 32 bytes but greater than the maximum of 31 bytes. This indicates that each of the 16 inputs must contain data not exceeding this order. In this implementation, the data targeted for hash computation are divided into 31-byte segments as input values. If the division exceeds 16 segments, the Poseidon hash is calculated for the first 16 segments. This result is added to the next 15 segments of data for a subsequent Poseidon hash input. The process is repeated until all the input data are used for hash computation. Computationally, if the final input does not complete 16 segments, the missing inputs are set to zero to ensure that the computation always involves 16 inputs.

When generating CID from the Poseidon hash value, the byte sequence should follow the CID V1 data structure and be Base32-encoded. However, to further reduce computation time, this implementation omits the Base32 encoding and directly uses the Poseidon hash value as a substitute for CID. Dividing the input data into 16 segments within the circuit is computationally intensive; therefore, this division is performed outside the circuit and given as an input. In this case, the encrypted data byte sequence and the list of values for calculating the Poseidon hash are provided as public inputs, allowing the verification that both datasets represent the same information. Recipients can confirm that the data being computed for the Poseidon hash and the data being decrypted in the circuit are identical by mutually converting and checking these two values. In this case, as users can obtain the decrypted data, a concern exists regarding password leakage through brute force attacks or other means.

For encryption technology, we adopted Poseidon encryption [25] instead of AES-CTR encryption. Poseidon encryption, implemented in circom and TypeScript (poseidon-encryption-circom2 [26]), involves receiving the public key of the recipient, generating a common key, and ensuring secure encryption and decryption by both parties. In this case, however, a common key is directly generated and used for encryption and decryption. The circuit is provided with two values representing the coordinates of an elliptical curve and a nonce value as private inputs for encryption. Moreover, the filter is implemented in the same manner as in the standard implementation.

7. Evaluation

We created a sample program based on the aforementioned implementations that uses circom to describe the circuit and uses snarkjs for executing the circuit and verifying proofs. As cryptographic libraries, circom-chacha20 [20], circomlib [23], circomlibjs [24], and poseidon-encryption-circom2 [26] were used.

The standard and ZK-optimized implementations were implemented for each circuit, and their computation times were compared during execution. White bitmap images were the target images, and the experiments were conducted using the letter "A" as the embedded character. As embedding any number of characters does not alter the processing by the filter, embedding a single character allowed for comparing the computation times. Furthermore, we varied the image sizes to measure the execution times for each circuit. The sizes used were 10 × 10, 15 × 15, 30 × 15, 30 × 30, 60 × 30, 60 × 60, 120 × 60, 120 × 120, and 180 × 120 pixels. The execution environment was Windows 11 with a Ryzen 9 3950X CPU and 128 GB RAM operating under Ubuntu 22.04 in a WSL2 environment.

Figure 3 shows an example image generated by the circuit, specifically for the 60 × 30 pixel size using the ZK-optimized implementation. The results for each image size are presented in Table 3, where nonlinear constraints indicate the number of nonlinear constraints in the circuit, build time is the time required to compile circom and output the circuit, and proof gen time is the time required to generate proofs using the circuit. As standard implementation uses AES-CTR encryption, data with 0x00 are appended at the end to ensure that the input size is a multiple of 16.

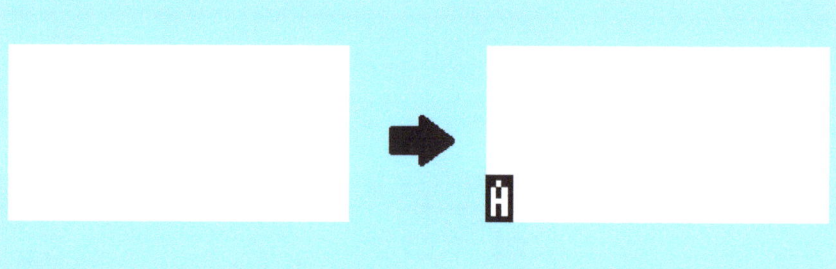

Figure 3. An image generated by the circuit for a 60 × 30 image size by ZK-optimized implementation.

Table 3. Comparison of the execution time of the circuit.

	Pixel	Image Size [Byte]	Nonlinear Constraints	Build Time [ms]	Proof Gen Time [ms]
Standard					
	10 × 10	384	558,341	668,220	14,377
	15 × 15	784	1,095,292	1,316,666	25,545
	30 × 15	1440	1,980,688	1,696,370	35,161
	30 × 30	2816	3,867,989	3,657,578	65,785
	60 × 30	5456	7,453,300	7,864,583	126,262
ZK-optimized					
	10 × 10	376	35,407	128,979	3076
	15 × 15	775	72,725	173,210	4032
	30 × 15	1435	134,663	275,630	5900
	30 × 30	2815	263,450	470,872	9733
	60 × 30	5455	509,375	850,612	17,571
	60 × 60	10,855	1,013,483	1,257,418	29,044
	120 × 120	43,255	4,036,913	6,754,928	96,580

In standard and ZK-optimized implementations for 60 × 60 pixel and 180 × 120 pixel image sizes, the system ran out of memory and the computation could not be completed. In ZK-optimized implementation, the number of nonlinear constraints was reduced to approximately one-tenth that of the standard implementation for the same image size. This reduced the build and proof generation times. However, the maximum manageable image size was still only up to 120 × 120 pixels, which is considerably small for practical applications.

8. Discussion

Although ZK-friendly cryptographic technologies were used and in-circuit processes were optimized during ZK-optimized implementation, the maximum manageable image size was approximately 120 × 120 pixels. This limits the practical utility to considerably small image sizes. However, research aimed at enhancing the performance of ZKPs is ongoing, and future technological advancements may enable handling larger image sizes. For instance, Zhang et al. [27] achieved a tenfold acceleration of zk-SNARKs using ASICs. Ma et al. [16] similarly used a graphics processing units to accelerate the proof generation time, achieving up to 48.1 times faster performance compared with traditional methods. Moreover, methods to simplify computational processes have been proposed, such as the "folding" method. This method compresses the propositions being proved [28]. As speed enhancements are being progressively studied, memory consumption will also likely be optimized. This will potentially allow handling of larger image sizes in the future.

Furthermore, we found that our proposal method can handle data sizes approximately 10 KB. Although directly applying our proposal to realistic image data (ranging from several MBs to dozens of MBs) is challenging, splitting data into chunks by modifying the encryption and embedded strings might make the application feasible.

Moreover, our implementations requires a value based on the size of the original data to be processed (encrypted) as an argument during circuit generation. Therefore, a circuit must be generated for each data. The circuit generation time (build time) increases considerably with image data size; for instance, even in ZK-optimized implementation, generating a circuit for a 120 × 120 image size requires more than 112 min (6,754,928 ms). However, once the circuit is generated, the proof generation time under the same conditions is short, approximately 97 s (96,580 ms). In other words, once a circuit is generated, proof generation is not time intensive. This fact does not pose any practical issues in cases wherein the same image is distributed to various people.

In ZK-friendly implementations, encrypted data is inputted as a public input. Handling encryption keys for images requires careful consideration. Data managed in private IPFS are encrypted. However, if encryption keys are leaked, the encrypted data could be decrypted. Therefore, specific users managing private IPFS should become administrators to carefully manage the keys or a consortium-type blockchain could be established on the same network to set and manage access rights appropriately.

9. Conclusions

A new method was proposed herein to distribute data stored in private IPFS to external entities while making its authenticity verifiable. The method applied a type of ZKP, zk-SNARKs, to verify the CID of data and embed the recipient's name. This approach enables external entities to verify that the received data are generated from the original data in private IPFS without requiring details such as IPFS access rights and encryption keys.

A standard implementation using conventional cryptographic techniques and a ZK-optimized implementation using ZK-friendly cryptographic schemes were implemented to enhance the computational efficiency of the proposed method. Experiments with a sample program confirmed the effectiveness of the proposed method for an image data size of up to 120 × 120 pixels.

This proposed method extends the usable range of decentralized storage systems to a hybrid case—distributing internal data to specific external entities as necessary. This study paves a new way for sharing sensitive information across different sectors within and outside a group. However, for the wide practical applicability of the proposed method to larger and more diverse data types, such as images and videos, processing speed must be improved and data splitting methods must be used, which are within the scope of our future studies.

Author Contributions: Conceptualization, K.S., C.H., T.T.C. and W.O.; writing—original draft preparation, K.S.; writing—review and editing, K.S. and K.I.; supervision, G.M.; project administration, K.S. All authors have read and agreed to the published version of the manuscript.

Funding: This research was conducted as a collaborative research project between the University of Tokyo and Callisto Inc., funded by Callisto Inc. This work has been supported by Endowed Chair for Blockchain Innovation and the Mohammed bin Salman Center for Future Science and Technology for Saudi-Japan Vision 2030 (MbSC2030) at The University of Tokyo.

Data Availability Statement: The source code used for the simulations is available on GitHub. https://github.com/blockchaininnovation/circom_image_processing (accessed on 21 March 2024).

Conflicts of Interest: Author Changhee Han, Tsz Tat Chu and Wataru Ozaki were employed by the company Callisto Inc. The remaining authors declare that the research was conducted in the absence of any commercial or financial relationships that could be construed as a potential conflict of interest.

References

1. Groth, J. On the size of pairing-based non-interactive arguments. In Proceedings of the Advances in Cryptology–EUROCRYPT 2016: 35th Annual International Conference on the Theory and Applications of Cryptographic Techniques, Vienna, Austria, 8–12 May 2016; Proceedings, Part II 35; Springer: Berlin/Heidelberg, Germany, 2016; pp. 305–326.
2. Kumar, S.; Bharti, A.K.; Amin, R. Decentralized secure storage of medical records using Blockchain and IPFS: A comparative analysis with future directions. *Secur. Priv.* **2021**, *4*, e162. [CrossRef]
3. Azbeg, K.; Ouchetto, O.; Andaloussi, S.J. BlockMedCare: A healthcare system based on IoT, Blockchain and IPFS for data management security. *Egypt. Inform. J.* **2022**, *23*, 329–343. [CrossRef]
4. Hossan, M.S.; Khatun, M.L.; Rahman, S.; Reno, S.; Ahmed, M. Securing ride-sharing service using IPFS and hyperledger based on private blockchain. In Proceedings of the 2021 24th International Conference on Computer and Information Technology (ICCIT), Dhaka, Bangladesh, 18–20 December 2021; IEEE: Piscataway, NJ, USA, 2021; pp. 1–6.
5. Lin, Y.; Zhang, C. A method for protecting private data in IPFS. In Proceedings of the 2021 IEEE 24th International Conference on Computer Supported Cooperative Work in Design (CSCWD), Dalian, China, 5–7 May 2021; IEEE: Piscataway, NJ, USA, 2021; pp. 404–409.
6. Battah, A.A.; Madine, M.M.; Alzaabi, H.; Yaqoob, I.; Salah, K.; Jayaraman, R. Blockchain-based multi-party authorization for accessing IPFS encrypted data. *IEEE Access* **2020**, *8*, 196813–196825. [CrossRef]
7. Huang, H.S.; Chang, T.S.; Wu, J.Y. A secure file sharing system based on IPFS and blockchain. In Proceedings of the 2nd International Electronics Communication Conference, Singapore, 8–10 July 2020; pp. 96–100.
8. Sun, J.; Yao, X.; Wang, S.; Wu, Y. Blockchain-based secure storage and access scheme for electronic medical records in IPFS. *IEEE Access* **2020**, *8*, 59389–59401. [CrossRef]
9. Kang, P.; Yang, W.; Zheng, J. Blockchain private file storage-sharing method based on IPFS. *Sensors* **2022**, *22*, 5100. [CrossRef] [PubMed]
10. Uddin, M.N.; Hasnat, A.H.M.A.; Nasrin, S.; Alam, M.S.; Yousuf, M.A. Secure file sharing system using blockchain, ipfs and pki technologies. In Proceedings of the 2021 5th International Conference on Electrical Information and Communication Technology (EICT), Khulna, Bangladesh, 17–19 December 2021; IEEE: Piscataway, NJ, USA, 2021; pp. 1–5.
11. Li, W.; Guo, H.; Nejad, M.; Shen, C.C. Privacy-preserving traffic management: A blockchain and zero-knowledge proof inspired approach. *IEEE Access* **2020**, *8*, 181733–181743. [CrossRef]
12. Bellés-Muñoz, M.; Isabel, M.; Muñoz-Tapia, J.L.; Rubio, A.; Baylina, J. Circom: A circuit description language for building zero-knowledge applications. *IEEE Trans. Dependable Secur. Comput.* **2022**, *20*, 4733–4751. [CrossRef]
13. Circom Official Website. Available online: https://iden3.io/circom (accessed on 24 March 2024).
14. Snarkjs Github Repository. Available online: https://github.com/iden3/snarkjs (accessed on 4 June 2024).
15. ZCash. Available online: https://z.cash/ (accessed on 12 July 2024).
16. Ma, W.; Xiong, Q.; Shi, X.; Ma, X.; Jin, H.; Kuang, H.; Gao, M.; Zhang, Y.; Shen, H.; Hu, W. Gzkp: A gpu accelerated zero-knowledge proof system. In Proceedings of the 28th ACM International Conference on Architectural Support for Programming Languages and Operating Systems, Volume 2, Vancouver BC Canada, 25–29 March 2023; pp. 340–353.
17. Han, C.; Shibano, K.; Ozaki, W.; Osaki, K.; Haraguchi, T.; Hirahara, D.; Kimura, S.; Kobayashi, Y.; Mogi, G. All-in-one platform for AI R&D in medical imaging, encompassing data collection, selection, annotation, and pre-processing. In *Proceedings of the Medical Imaging 2024: Imaging Informatics for Healthcare, Research, and Applications, San Diego, CA, USA, 18–23 February 2024*; SPIE: Bellingham, WA, USA, 2024; Volume 12931, pp. 311–315.
18. Miano, J. *Compressed Image File Formats: Jpeg, png, gif, xbm, bmp*; Addison-Wesley Professional: Boston, MA, USA, 1999.
19. Content Identifiers (CIDs). Available online: https://docs.ipfs.tech/concepts/content-addressing/#cids-are-not-file-hashes (accessed on 24 March 2024).
20. circom-chacha20 Github Repository. Available online: https://github.com/reclaimprotocol/circom-chacha20 (accessed on 24 March 2024).

21. The 8 × 8 dot Japanese Font "Misaki Font". Available online: https://littlelimit.net/misaki.htm (accessed on 11 June 2024). (In Japanese)
22. Grassi, L.; Khovratovich, D.; Rechberger, C.; Roy, A.; Schofnegger, M. Poseidon: A new hash function for {Zero-Knowledge} proof systems. In Proceedings of the 30th USENIX Security Symposium (USENIX Security 21), Vancouver, BC, Canada, 11–13 August 2021; pp. 519–535.
23. Circomlib Github Repository. Available online: https://github.com/iden3/circomlib (accessed on 21 March 2024).
24. Circomlibjs Github Repository. Available online: https://github.com/iden3/circomlibjs (accessed on 21 March 2024).
25. Khovratovich, D. Encryption with Poseidon. 2019. Available online: https://drive.google.com/file/d/1EVrP3DzoGbmzkRmYnyEDcIQcXVU7GlOd/view (accessed on 19 July 2024).
26. Poseidon-Encryption-Circom2 Github Repository. Available online: https://github.com/Shigoto-dev19/poseidon-encryption-circom2 (accessed on 21 March 2024).
27. Zhang, Y.; Wang, S.; Zhang, X.; Dong, J.; Mao, X.; Long, F.; Wang, C.; Zhou, D.; Gao, M.; Sun, G. Pipezk: Accelerating zero-knowledge proof with a pipelined architecture. In Proceedings of the 2021 ACM/IEEE 48th Annual International Symposium on Computer Architecture (ISCA), Valencia, Spain, 14–18 June 2021; IEEE: Piscataway, NJ, USA, 2021; pp. 416–428.
28. Kothapalli, A.; Setty, S.; Tzialla, I. Nova: Recursive zero-knowledge arguments from folding schemes. In Proceedings of the Annual International Cryptology Conference, Santa Barbara, CA, USA, 15–18 August 2022; Springer: Cham, Switzerland, 2022; pp. 359–388.

Disclaimer/Publisher's Note: The statements, opinions and data contained in all publications are solely those of the individual author(s) and contributor(s) and not of MDPI and/or the editor(s). MDPI and/or the editor(s) disclaim responsibility for any injury to people or property resulting from any ideas, methods, instructions or products referred to in the content.

Article

A Smart Contract Vulnerability Detection Method Based on Heterogeneous Contract Semantic Graphs and Pre-Training Techniques

Jie Zhang, Gehao Lu * and Jia Yu

School of Information Science and Engineering, Yunnan University, Kunming 650500, China; zjlyy@mail.ynu.edu.cn (J.Z.); yujia@itc.ynu.edu.cn (J.Y.)
* Correspondence: glu@ynu.edu.cn

Abstract: The use of smart contracts in areas such as finance, supply chain management, and the Internet of Things has significantly advanced blockchain technology. However, once deployed on the blockchain, smart contracts cannot be modified or revoked. Any vulnerabilities can lead to severe economic losses and data breaches, making pre-deployment vulnerability detection critically important. Traditional smart contract vulnerability detection methods suffer from low accuracy and limited reusability across different scenarios. To enhance detection capabilities, this paper proposes a smart contract vulnerability detection method based on heterogeneous contract semantic graphs and pre-training techniques. Compared to the conventional graph structures used in existing methods, heterogeneous contract semantic graphs contain richer contract information. By integrating these with pre-trained models, our method exhibits stronger vulnerability capture and generalization capabilities. Experimental results show that this method has improved the accuracy, recall, precision, and F1 value in the detection of four widely existing and harmful smart contract vulnerabilities compared with existing methods, which greatly improves the detection ability of smart contract vulnerabilities.

Keywords: smartcontracts; vulnerability detection; heterogeneous contract semantic graphs; pre-training techniques

Citation: Zhang, J.; Lu, G.; Yu, J. A Smart Contract Vulnerability Detection Method Based on Heterogeneous Contract Semantic Graphs and Pre-Training Techniques. *Electronics* **2024**, *13*, 3785. https://doi.org/10.3390/electronics13183786

Academic Editor: Fabio Grandi

Received: 31 July 2024
Revised: 17 September 2024
Accepted: 20 September 2024
Published: 23 September 2024

Copyright: © 2024 by the authors. Licensee MDPI, Basel, Switzerland. This article is an open access article distributed under the terms and conditions of the Creative Commons Attribution (CC BY) license (https://creativecommons.org/licenses/by/4.0/).

1. Introduction

Blockchain technology, since it was proposed by Satoshi Nakamoto in the Bitcoin white paper in 2008 [1], has rapidly emerged as a disruptive technology with potential applications in various fields, including finance, supply chain management, and the Internet of Things (IoT). Ethereum, as the second-generation blockchain platform, introduced smart contracts as a core feature, enabling decentralized computation on top of the blockchain [2], which significantly expanded the scope of blockchain applications.

The automation and immutability of smart contracts have increased trust in their use across various sectors; however, these same characteristics present significant security challenges. Once vulnerabilities are embedded in smart contract code, they can lead to major losses for associated accounts. According to the SlowMist Technology report [3], there were 464 security incidents in 2023, resulting in losses totaling 2.486 billion USD. Notable cases include the non-custodial lending platform BonqDAO and the crypto infrastructure platform AllianceBlock, which lost approximately 120 million USD due to vulnerabilities in BonqDAO's smart contracts. Therefore, comprehensive security testing of smart contracts before deployment is crucial.

Currently, researchers have developed many effective tools for detecting vulnerabilities in smart contracts, which can be divided into two main categories: traditional methods, such as Manticore [4], SmarTest [5], ConFuzzius [6], Slither [7], and deep learning-based methods, such as VanillaRNN [8], LSTM [9], TMP [10]. However, these methods have certain limitations:

- traditional methods rely on complex predefined patterns or meticulously designed test cases, requiring experts to deeply analyze vulnerabilities and continually update specific rules. These methods struggle to scale with the rapid growth of smart contract deployments, which restricts their applicability and leads to lower accuracy.
- Deep learning-based methods often inadequately consider the structural and semantic information of code, leading to insufficient generalization when facing diverse smart contracts.

In order to address the shortcomings of existing methods, we select four smart contract vulnerabilities that cause the most serious and widespread losses: Reentrancy [11], Transaction State Dependency [12], Block Info Dependency [13], and Nested Call [12] as research objects. These vulnerabilities were chosen based on the research findings of Monika [12] and Chen [14], who categorized and graded the impact of smart contract vulnerabilities. Additionally, their importance has been validated through numerous studies (e.g., [15,16]) and widely recognized classifications, such as the SWC Registry [13]. See Appendix A for corresponding code examples and descriptions. This paper proposes a smart contract vulnerability detection method based on heterogeneous contract semantic graphs and pre-training techniques. Compared with the traditional data flow graph used in existing methods, the heterogeneous contract semantic graph contains richer contract structure information, which enables the model to focus on the key features of the vulnerability more comprehensively and has stronger vulnerability capture and generalization capabilities. The heterogeneous contract semantic graph is embedded in the graph neural network so that it can be used as part of the pre-training model input to detect smart contract vulnerabilities.

The main contributions of this paper are as follows:

- We designed a heterogeneous smart contract semantic graph generation method based on abstract syntax trees (AST), using variables and function calls as nodes to comprehensively represent the semantic and structural information of contracts at the statement level.
- By combining heterogeneous contract semantic graphs with pre-training techniques, our Approach achieved superior performance in detecting various types of smart contract vulnerabilities. Experimental results show that our method achieves detection accuracies of 90.96%, 89.57%, 88.46%, and 87.34% for the four types of vulnerabilities, representing significant improvements over 12 mainstream methods.

Next, Section 2 will introduce the existing work on smart contract vulnerability detection and the relevant background knowledge of this article. Section 3 will introduce the smart contract vulnerability detection method based on heterogeneous contract semantic graphs and pre-training technology. Section 4 will show the experimental results, and Section 5 will summarize.

2. Related Work

2.1. Existing Smart Contract Vulnerability Detection Tools

With the rapid development of blockchain platforms such as Ethereum, numerous smart contract vulnerability detection tools have emerged. In the following, we will briefly introduce mainstream methods for detecting smart contract vulnerabilities. We will also analyze their strengths and limitations. Representative traditional methods include those based on symbolic execution (e.g., Oyente [17], Manticore [4], SmarTest [5], Mythril [11]), fuzz testing (e.g., ContractFuzzer [18], ConFuzzius [6]), static analysis (e.g., Slither [7], SmartCheck [19]), and formal verification (e.g., KEVM [20], ZEUS [21]).

Symbolic execution-based methods, such as Oyente [17], use symbolic inputs instead of concrete ones. They simulate the execution of the analyzed program and transform program operations into symbolic expressions. This allows for the analysis of path reachability, test data generation, and detection of specific vulnerabilities. However, as the size of smart contract code increases, these methods may face challenges like path explosion and slow constraint solving. This can reduce the efficiency of vulnerability detection. Fuzz testing-based methods, such as ContractFuzzer [18], generate many random test cases by obtaining function parameters through the Abstract Binary Interface (ABI). They combine these cases with vulnerability patterns to detect issues like reentrancy vulnerabilities. However, these test cases often lack specificity and may not cover all possible vulnerability scenarios. For complex smart contracts, fuzz testing may fail to trigger deeply hidden vulnerabilities, especially those that only appear under specific input conditions. Slither [7], as a static analysis tool, directly analyzes the source code of smart contracts. It can quickly detect potential vulnerabilities without executing the contract. This makes it more efficient in speed, allowing it to handle large-scale smart contract codebases. However, static analysis tools typically rely on predefined rules or patterns. As a result, Slither may fail to detect certain atypical vulnerabilities, especially those involving complex state changes or dynamic behaviors. KEVM [20] uses formal modeling of smart contract behavior to verify whether a contract adheres to specific security properties. It provides a high level of security assurance. However, formal verification involves exhaustive checking of all possible execution paths. As a result, KEVM's verification process often requires significant time. This can be problematic when handling complex contracts, leading to excessively long verification times.

In recent years, deep learning has been widely applied in various fields. Leveraging big data and deep learning techniques to automatically learn the characteristics of smart contract vulnerabilities has become a new research direction. Wang et al. [15] developed ContractWard, which extracts features from bytecode using n-grams. The model uses five machine learning algorithms, including Random Forest and Support Vector Machine, to detect six types of vulnerabilities, such as reentrancy and integer overflow. However, this method does not consider the structural or semantic information of the code during learning and computation. Liu et al. [22] proposed the vulnerability detection network CGE (Combining Graph features and Expert patterns). It defines expert pattern features, such as timestamp declarations, and combines them with contract graph features obtained through graph neural networks. This improves the accuracy of vulnerability detection. However, their model cannot handle heterogeneous graphs with multiple types of nodes. They addressed this by removing secondary nodes and aggregating their features into primary nodes, which led to the loss of some information. This reduced the method's generalizability when dealing with diverse smart contracts.

2.2. Graph Pre-Trained Models

Pre-trained models begin by undergoing preliminary training on large-scale, unsupervised datasets to learn general features and representations. They are then fine-tuned on smaller, labeled datasets to adapt to specific tasks. The primary advantage of this approach is the ability to leverage the extensive information from large datasets to enhance performance on specific tasks. Models like BERT [23] and GPT [24] have achieved notable success in natural language processing tasks and are widely used. Inspired by this, researchers in the field of software engineering have proposed a series of models specifically for programming languages, such as CodeBERT [25] and CodeT5 [26], which are designed to understand and generate source code. Similar to text-based pre-training models, these models learn the structure, syntax, and common programming patterns by pre-training on large amounts of open-source code, significantly improving the automation and efficiency of programming-related tasks.

However, some existing works [25,26] treat program source code as collections of tokens, overlooking that code is not merely a sequence of words but includes various graph-like data structures such as loops, jumps, controls, and dependencies [27]. Graph-CodeBERT [28] makes up for the shortcomings of previous work by incorporating semantic-level information about the code and introducing the data flow graph (DFG) of the code for pre-training. The data flow graph is a structure frequently used in program analysis [29]. In GraphCodeBERT, code is first parsed into an Abstract Syntax Tree (AST) using standard compilation tools. From the AST, a labeled sequence of source code variables is derived,

and a data flow graph is constructed. This graph represents program variables as nodes
and the dependencies among them as edges. The code and its corresponding data flow
graph serve as inputs to the model, achieving good results in a variety of code-related
downstream tasks.

2.3. Graph Structure Representation of Smart Contracts

Current research [29] suggests that programs can be transformed into graphical representations, thereby preserving the relationships between program elements. Zhuang et al. [10] have utilized this approach by converting smart contracts into graphs and employing Graph Neural Networks (GNN) for detecting vulnerabilities in smart contracts. However, their model struggles with handling heterogeneous graphs with multiple types of nodes, leading them to remove secondary nodes and aggregate their features into primary nodes, resulting in a partial loss of structural information. Wu et al. [30] introduced a method for smart contract vulnerability detection named Peculiar, which uses the tree-sitter-solidity tool https://github.com/JoranHonig/tree-sitter-solidity (accessed on 31 July 2024) to generate an AST. From the AST, they extract a Data Flow Graph (DFG) to represent the contract's graphical structure and have designed a method to filter key variables, simplifying the DFG into a Critical Data Flow Graph (CFDG) for model input. Although the CDFG simplifies smart contract information to some extent and focuses more on variables that could lead to vulnerabilities, it only includes the data flow relationships between variables and misses a lot of structural information related to vulnerabilities, such as special function calls and execution sequences. In order to solve the problem that the existing smart contract graph structure cannot adequately represent smart contract information, this paper proposes a new smart contract graph structure representation method, which uses variables and function calls as nodes to construct a heterogeneous contract graph. Based on this heterogeneous graph, we further consider how to effectively capture the complex semantic relationships within the graph. There are several embedding methods for heterogeneous graphs, such as metapath2vec [31], HAN [32], and HGT [33]. Metapath2vec defines meta-paths to guide random walks, capturing semantic relationships in heterogeneous graphs, and then uses the Skip-Gram model to learn node embeddings. HAN utilizes meta-paths to guide attention mechanisms, focusing on interactions between nodes with significant semantic importance. HGT, based on the Transformer architecture, introduces type-specific parameterization to handle the heterogeneity of nodes and edges, and incorporates relative temporal encoding to account for the dynamic nature of the graph. This is particularly crucial for smart contract vulnerability detection, as vulnerabilities are often closely related to data flow and control flow timing between nodes. Therefore, we select HGT as the graph embedding method to fully represent the semantic information and structural relationships of smart contracts.

3. Research Method

In the methodology of this paper, we do not undertake the pre-training task ourselves; instead, the pre-training is handled by GraphCodeBERT [28]. This is appropriate because the Solidity language, specifically designed for Ethereum smart contract development, exhibits features like static typing, inheritance, libraries, and complex user-defined types, drawing influences from JavaScript, Python, and C++. GraphCodeBERT, during its pre-training phase, utilized 2.3 million functions from six programming languages, encompassing three pre-training tasks: modeling programming languages, predicting edges in the program data graph (data flow graph), and aligning variables across program source code and its graph structure. Our method requires loading the pre-trained parameters from GraphCodeBERT, followed by fine-tuning them on a smart contract dataset. The workflow of this method is shown in Figure 1 and is divided into two stages : (a) Graph Generation Stage, during which source code is converted into an AST, parsing the AST to retain different nodes and edges and generating a heterogeneous contract semantic graph. (b) Vulnerability Detection Stage, where smart contract vulnerabilities are detected based on the pre-trained model. We will now elaborate on these two stages.

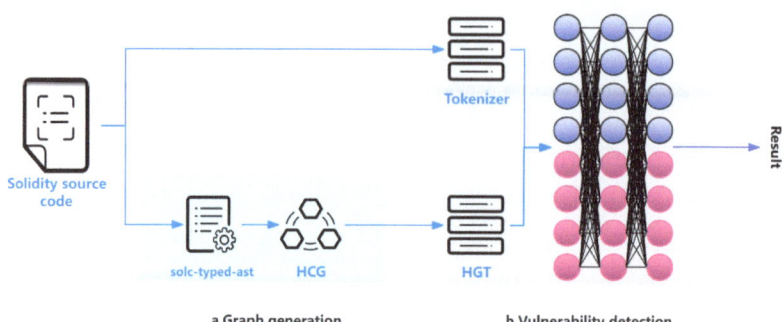

Figure 1. Method workflow. (**a**) Graph generation phase: The smart contract source code is first generated into a standardized syntax tree by the solc-typed-ast tool. Based on the information in the standardized syntax tree, the variables and function call behaviors in the source code are used as nodes to construct a heterogeneous contract semantic graph. (**b**) Vulnerability detection phase: HGT is used to embed the semantic graph of heterogeneous smart contracts, and the corresponding source code is used as the input of GraphCodeBERT to detect vulnerabilities in smart contracts.

3.1. Graph Generation Phase

In the process of generating the AST for Solidity code, most existing work, such as [10,30], predominantly employs the tool tree-sitter-solidity, which is known for its efficiency and incremental parsing capabilities. However, for Solidity code, the AST generated by this tool does not contain sufficiently detailed node information. For example, as shown in Listing A1, concerning the content at line 11 of the reentrancy vulnerability example code *msg.sender.call*, Figure 2a represents a portion of the AST nodes obtained from tree-sitter-solidity, whereas Figure 2b shows a portion of the AST nodes parsed by the official Solidity compiler, solc. It is evident that the AST nodes parsed by tree-sitter-solidity only include type and text information within their description, lacking detailed metadata. In contrast, the AST generated by solc not only includes structural information within the AST hierarchy but also provides rich descriptive information for nodes such as id, src, nodeType, and typeDescriptions, particularly offering standardized descriptions in typeIdentifier and typeString for critical nodes associated with vulnerabilities like the low-level function call *call()*. Given that solc has undergone multiple iterations since 2015, the AST structure and node information generated by different versions of solc can vary. The tool solc typed-ast enables the creation of normalized type Solidity ASTs based on solc, mitigating the differences brought by various versions of the compiler. Therefore, we opt to use solc-typed-ast to generate the code AST.

The AST generated by the solc-typed-ast tool includes 56 types of nodes, which we categorize into three classes based on their functionalities. They are structure operation class nodes, variable and call class nodes, and other class nodes. The detailed classification is shown in Table A1 in Appendix A. The structural and operational class nodes encompass the structure and control information of an entire '.sol' file's AST, from top to bottom, including files, contracts, functions, statements, and operations. We utilize this information to construct the edges in the heterogeneous contract semantic graph, including both data flows and control flows. The variable and call class nodes, as components of statements, are constructed as nodes within the heterogeneous contract semantic graph. Other class nodes, which include import statements, structured documentation, and other nodes that do not contribute to vulnerability generation, or basic class nodes like names, contain information that can be encapsulated by higher-level nodes and may be omitted.

```
"type": "member_expression",
"text": "msg. sender. call",
"children": [
   {
     "type": "member_expression",
     "text": "msg. sender",
     "children": [
        {
           "type": "identifier",
           "text": "msg"
        },
        {
           "type": ".",
           "text": "."
        },
        {
           "type": "property_identifier",
           "text": "sender"
        }
     ]
   },
   {
     "type": ".",
     "text": "."
   },
   {
     "type": "property_identifier",
     "text": "call"
   }
......
```

(**a**) tree-sitter-solidity Parsing result

```
"expression": {
 "expression": {
   "id": 42,
   "name": "msg",
   "nodeType": "Identifier",
   "referencedDeclaration": 4294967281,
   "src": "507:3:0",
   "typeDescriptions": {
     "typeIdentifier": "t_magic_message",
     "typeString": "msg"
   }
 },
 "id": 43,
 ......
 "nodeType": "MemberAccess",
 "memberName": "sender",
 ......
 "typeDescriptions": {
   "typeIdentifier": "t_address",
   "typeString": "address"
 }
},
"id": 44,
"isConstant": false,
"memberLocation": "518:4:0",
"memberName": "call",
"nodeType": "MemberAccess",
"src": "507:15:0",
"typeDescriptions": {
 "typeIdentifier":
"t_function_barecall_payable$_t_bytes_memory
_ptr_$returns$_t_bool_$_t_bytes_memory_ptr_$
",
   "typeString": "function (bytes memory)
payable returns (bool, bytes memory)"
  }
 },
 ......
```

(**b**) solc Parsing results

Figure 2. The information contained in the AST obtained by the two tools for parsing the same statement is very different. For a more intuitive comparison, we bold the parsing results of the same element "call".

Specifically, in high-level programming languages, the basic units of execution are statements, including both simple and compound statements. Simple statements consist of a single logical line, such as expression statements (ExpressionStatement) and assignment statements (Assignment), whereas compound statements encompass other statements (groups of statements) that influence or control the execution of the included statements in some manner, such as if statements (IfStatement) and for statements (ForStatement). The logic within simple statements facilitates operations on variables and function calls. In our proposed method for constructing heterogeneous contract semantic graphs, we analyze each simple statement in the contract according to the typed-AST structure, extracting variables and function call nodes to serve as nodes within the heterogeneous contract semantic graph. It is important to note that Solidity includes certain special variables that are always present in the global namespace. These built-in variables are essentially of a basic type and are used to describe attributes of blocks and transactions, such as *block.prevrandao* and *msg.sender* [34]. Although these variables are not explicitly declared, they are still integrated as nodes in our graph. Solidity allows for the manipulation of mappings, arrays, and structures through dereferencing, but we do not treat the results of such dereferences (e.g., *balances[msg.sender]*) as individual nodes. Instead, we regard these structures as a whole, which facilitates their inclusion as nodes when constructing the contract semantic graph.

The relationships among simple statements—such as sequence, loops, and conditionals—act as control flows, while the operations within simple statements (such as BinaryOperation, IndexAccess, etc.) and the inputs and outputs involved in function calls are constructed as data flows. Take the code shown in Listing 1 as an example:

Listing 1. Sample Code.

```
1  contract ReentrantBank {
2  mapping(address => uint256) public balances;
3  function deposit() public payable {
4  require(msg.value > 0);
5  balances[msg.sender] += msg.value;
6  }
7  function withdraw(uint256 _amount) public {
8  require(balances[msg.sender] >= _amount);
9  (bool sent, ) = msg.sender.call{value: _amount}("");
10  require(sent, "Failed to send Ether");
11  balances[msg.sender] -= _amount;
12  }
```

The visualization of the typed-AST generated by the solc-typed-ast tool is shown in Figure 3.

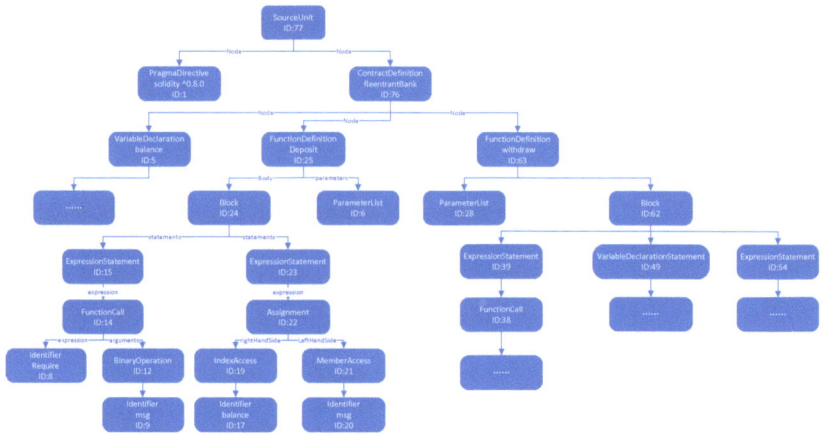

Figure 3. Typed–AST visualization.

Based on the structural information in the typed-AST, the example code is transformed into a heterogeneous contract semantic graph as shown in Figure 4 .

The variable node features in the contract graph are represented by a four-tuple, F = (id, name, nodeType, typeDescriptions). The function call node features in the contract graph are represented by a five-tuple, F = (id, name, nodeType, typeDescriptions, parameter), where id is the node identifier, name is the variable name (function name), nodetype is the node type, typeDescriptions is the specific description of the node type, and parameter is the function parameter. The edge features in the contract graph are represented by a four-tuple, F = (order, type, V_{start}, V_{end}), where order is the time order, type is the edge type (control flow or data flow), and V_{start} and V_{end} are the start and end nodes. The resulting contract graph is denoted as $HCG(SC) = (V, E)$, where V is the node set and E is the edge set. Figure 4b shows the heterogeneous contract semantic graph built based on the contract with the vulnerability, and Figure 4c shows its edge features.

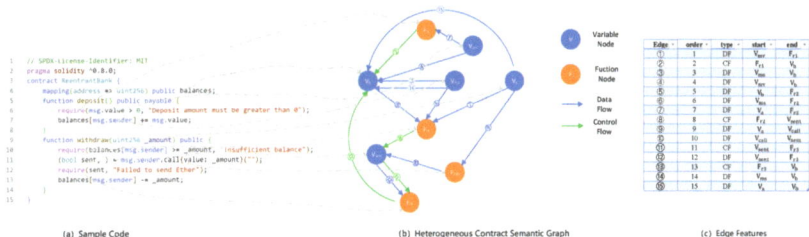

Figure 4. Heterogeneous Contract Semantic Graph Generation Process, Among them, (**a**) is the sample code in Listing 1, (**b**) is the heterogeneous contract semantic graph generated based on sample code, and (**c**) is the edge information in the heterogeneous contract semantic graph.

3.2. Vulnerability Detection Phase

This section will offer an in-depth description of how the proposed approach utilizes a graph-based pre-trained model to identify vulnerabilities in smart contracts. It will encompass details on data preparation, the model's architecture, and the training procedure.

First is the data preparation process. This method is based on GraphCodeBERT [28], but it differs in how it handles graph-structured data. In the original GraphCodeBERT architecture, given a source code $SC = \{sc_1, sc_2, \ldots, sc_n\}$, a corresponding data flow graph $G(SC) = (V, E)$ can be obtained, where $V = \{v_1, v_2, \ldots, v_n\}$ is a set of variables (also the nodes in the data flow graph), and $E = \{e_1, e_2, \ldots, e_n\}$ is a set of directed edges indicating the dependencies among variables. The source code and the set of variables are merged into a sequence $I = \{[CLS], SC, [SEP], V\}$, with $[CLS]$ as a special token preceding the sets, and $[SEP]$ as a separator between the source code SC and the variable set V. For each token in the sequence I, we generate the corresponding position embedding and add the token and the corresponding position embedding to represent the token. Special position embeddings are assigned to all variables to signify their roles as nodes within the data flow. The final input representation, denoted as X_0, is derived in this manner.

In our method, the embedding for the source code text follows the approach used in GraphCodeBERT. However, the embedding for the graph structure differs because the GraphCodeBERT method, which is suited for handling simple homogeneous graphs like data flow graphs, does not adequately capture the information in the heterogeneous contract semantic graph $HCG(SC) = (V, E)$ generated earlier. In our graph embedding process, we choose HGT [33] as the graph structure embedding method to extract the structural information of the heterogeneous contract semantic graph. The resulting node feature sequence replaces the variables sequence in the GraphCodeBERT method.

The purpose of HGT is to consolidate information from source nodes to obtain the contextual representation of target nodes. This procedure can be segmented into three distinct phases:

- The first part is the calculation of heterogeneous mutual attention. The calculation of heterogeneous mutual attention begins by examining the meta-relationships between a target node t and each of its source nodes $s \in N(T)$. These relationships are defined by the tuple $\langle T(s), \phi(e), T(t) \rangle$, representing the source node type, the edge type, and the target node type, respectively. To accommodate the diverse and complex nature of these relationships in a heterogeneous graph, the model converts target node t into a query vector and each source nodes s into a key vector. Unlike standard Transformers that use a direct inner product for such calculations, HGT utilizes distinct attention matrices $W^{ATT}_{\phi(e)}$ tailored to each edge type $\phi(e)$, ensuring that the nuances of different semantic associations are captured effectively.

- The second part is the heterogeneous message-passing process. The message-passing process from the source node to the target node and the calculation of mutual attention are parallel. The goal is to merge the meta-relationships of various edges into the

message-passing process. By doing so, it helps to balance the distribution disparities among different types of nodes and edges.
- The third part is the aggregation for a specific task. It uses the attention vector as the weight to calculate the corresponding information from the source node and obtain the updated vector. The updated vector is linearly mapped and connected with the original vector of t in the previous layer as a residual. In this way, the output $H^{(L)}[t]$ of the target node t in the L_{th} layer of HGT is obtained. Stacking L layers can obtain a rich context representation $H^{(L)}$ for each node as the input of the downstream task.

In order to be able to handle the dynamic nature of the graph, relative time coding is introduced. Traditionally, time information has been integrated by constructing a separate graph for each time slot, a method that can lead to the loss of structural dependencies across different time slots. Moreover, the representation of a node at time t might rely on edges from various other time slots. Thus, the appropriate method to model a dynamic graph is to preserve all edges occurring at various times and permit interactions between nodes and edges that possess different timings [32]. Specifically, given a source node s and a target node t with the edge $\phi(e)$ between them, the edge information $\phi(e)$ includes temporal information order, which is used as an index for the relative temporal encoding. This encoding is applied through sine and cosine functions to capture the relative temporal dependencies.

$$Base(order, 2i) = \sin\left(\frac{order}{10000^{\frac{2i}{d}}}\right) \quad (1)$$

$$Base(order, 2i+1) = \cos\left(\frac{order}{10000^{\frac{2i+1}{d}}}\right) \quad (2)$$

$$RTE(order) = Linear(Base(order)) \quad (3)$$

In Equations (1) and (2), *order* is the timing information carried by the edge in the heterogeneous graph, i is the position index, and d is the dimension of the feature vector in HGT. *Base* represents the basic relative temporal encoding calculated by sine and cosine functions. In Equation (3), *Linear* represents the projection of the basic relative time code to obtain the final relative time code RTE(order). RTE(order) is added to the node representations $H^{(L)}$ to obtain $H^{(L)'}$. This allows the resulting node representations to capture the relative temporal information between the source node s and the target node t.

Secondly, the model architecture and training process are as follows. As shown in Figure 5, the sequence $I = \{[CLS], SC, [SEP], H^{(L)'}\}$ obtained in the data preparation stage is fed to the Join layer. In the Join layer, the sequence I from the data preparation stage is converted into an input vector X_0. Subsequently, the input vector X_0 proceeds through the multi-head attention layer, undergoes layer normalization, and passes through multiple Transformer layers ($n = 12$) to produce distinct contextual representations, $X^n = Transformer_n(X^{n-1}), n \in (1, 12)$. Equations (4) and (5) represent the training process of the model. In Equation (4), H and X are vectors, *MultiAttn* denotes a multi-head self-attention operation, and LN denotes a layer normalization operation. In Equation (5), FNN represents a two-layer feed-forward network, where each Transformer layer comprises a structurally identical transformer. As shown in Equations (4) and (5), the output X^{n-1} of the previous layer first undergoes a multi-head self-attention operation. The output of the self-attention operation is not directly passed to the next stage, but is first added to X^{n-1} to form a residual connection and normalized to obtain a vector H^n. After the vector H^n passes through the feedforward layer, which includes two linear transformation layers with an activation function in between, it also undergoes a residual connection and another layer of normalization to produce the output X^n. This process helps the model avoid potential gradient vanishing problems in deep networks while maintaining information from each layer's input.

$$H^n = LN(MultiAttn(X^{n-1}) + X^{n-1}) \quad (4)$$

$$X^n = LN(FFN(H^n) + H^n) \tag{5}$$

For the output $\hat{X}$ of the multi-head self-attention in the n_{th} transformer layer, the calculation process is shown in Equation (6) to (9):

$$Q_i = X^{(n-1)}W_i^Q, \quad K_i = X^{(n-1)}W_i^K, \quad V_i = X^{(n-1)}W_i^V \tag{6}$$

$$head_i = Softmax\left(\frac{Q_i K_i^T}{\sqrt{d_k}} + M\right)V_i \tag{7}$$

$$M_{ij} = \begin{cases} 0, & \text{if } q_i \in \{[CLS], [SEP]\} \text{ or } q_i, k_i \in SC \text{ or } \langle q_i, k_i \rangle \in E \cup E' \\ -\infty, & \text{otherwise} \end{cases} \tag{8}$$

$$\hat{X} = [head_1, \ldots, head_u]W_n^O \tag{9}$$

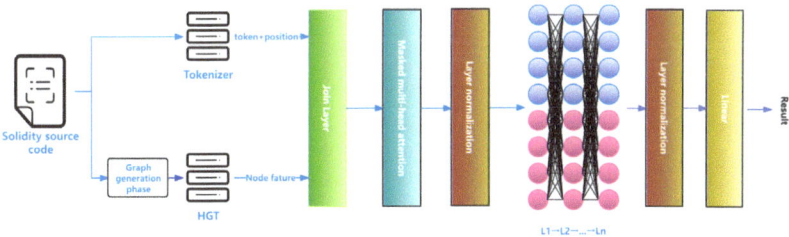

Figure 5. Vulnerability detection phase.

In Equation (6), $X^{(n-1)} \in \mathbb{R}^{|I| \times d_h}$ is the output of $(n-1)_{th}$ Transformer layers, X, W are vectors, and Q, K, V are triplets. $X^{(n-1)}$ is linearly projected onto the triplets of Q_i, K_i, and V_i using model parameters $W_i^Q, W_i^K, W_i^V \in \mathbb{R}^{d_h \times d_k}$. To incorporate a graph structure within the Transformer and illustrate dependencies between graph nodes, we adopt the approach of GraphCodeBERT [28], utilizing graph-guided masked attention to depict the interactions among tokens. Graph-guided masked attention is implemented through the mask matrix M. In Equation (7), *head* is the head in multi-head attention, d_k is the dimension of the *head*, M is the mask matrix, $M \in \mathbb{R}^{|I| \times |I|}$, where if the i_{th} token and the j_{th} token are associated, then $M_{ij} = 0$, otherwise it is $-\infty$. The calculation process of M is shown in Equation (8), [CLS] is a special mark in front of the set, [SEP] is a separator, $SC = \{sc, sc_2, \ldots, sc_n\}$ is the set of tokens in the source code, E is the set of edges $\{e_1, e_2, \ldots, e_l\}$ in the heterogeneous contract semantic graph HCG, representing the control flow and data flow relationship between nodes, and E' is a set indicating the association between the smart contract source code token and the nodes in the heterogeneous contract semantic graph (HCG). Attention computations are permissible between nodes v_i and v_j when they are directly connected (i.e., $\langle v_i, v_j \rangle \in E$) or are the same node (i.e., $i = j$). To represent the relationship between the source code tokens and the nodes in the heterogeneous contract semantic graph, we first define a set E'. If node v_i is determined by the token sc_j in the source code (i.e., $\langle v_i, sc_j \rangle, \langle sc_j, v_i \rangle \in E'$), they are allowed to perform attention computation with each other; in other cases, the attention is masked by assigning an attention score of $-\infty$. After the Softmax calculation in Equation (7), it is assigned a value of 0. In Equation (9), u is the number of heads in the multi-head attention, and $W_n^O \in \mathbb{R}^{d_h \times d_h}$ is the model parameter.

After the n_{th} layer of the Transformer model, layer normalization is employed for regularization. Subsequently, the output y, which represents the probability of the contract containing a vulnerability, is derived using a linear layer followed by a *Sigmoid* [35] function, as demonstrated in Equation (10). A loss function is then formulated to measure the discrepancy between this output y and the target value, where the target is set to 1 if the smart contract exhibits a specific vulnerability, and 0 otherwise. Finally, the backpropagation algorithm is utilized to train the network.

$$y = Sigmoid(X^n) \tag{10}$$

4. Experiment

In this section, we undertake a comprehensive empirical analysis of the method we propose, utilizing datasets that are publicly accessible. This evaluation is designed to rigorously test the effectiveness of our approach. To systematically assess the performance of our method, we have articulated several specific research questions:

- RQ1: Is our proposed method capable of effectively identifying the four most prevalent vulnerabilities in smart contracts, and does it outperform existing methods in this regard? We address this question by comparing the accuracy, precision, recall, and F1-score metrics.
- RQ2: What is the contribution of different modules in the proposed method to vulnerability detection? This question investigates the contribution of various modules to the model, including the heterogeneous contract semantic graph and the pre-trained model. We designed ablation experiments to answer this question.

4.1. Experimental Setup

Experiment environment: To conduct the experimental analysis, we utilized the open-source tool solc-typed-ast https://github.com/Consensys/solc-typed-ast, accessed on 11 March 2024, to parse Ethereum Solidity source code into a standard AST format. This was followed by further data optimization operations, such as removing comments. We developed a heterogeneous contract semantic graph generator based on the standardized AST information. The neural network was designed and implemented using the PyTorch framework. All experiments were performed on a physical machine running the Ubuntu 22.04 operating system, equipped with an Intel Xeon Silver 4310 processor with a base frequency of 2.1 GHz, 64 GB of RAM, and an NVIDIA A10 GPU with 24 GB of VRAM. Model training acceleration was achieved using the CUDA 12.4 computing library. The development environment included Visual Studio Code software (version 1.86), the PyTorch (version 2.2) framework, a Node.js (version 20.8.0) environment, and programming languages such as Python (version 3.11) and JavaScript (ECMAScript 2023).

Comparative Methods: To evaluate the effectiveness of the proposed method, we compared its performance with 12 state-of-the-art smart contract vulnerability detection methods. These include six open-source detection methods based on different neural network models: VanillaRNN [8], LSTM [36], GRU [36], DR-GCN [10], TMP [10], and CGE [22]. Additionally, we compared our method with six traditional smart contract vulnerability detection tools from top-tier conferences and journals: Oyente [17], Contractfuzzer [18], Mythril [11], Slither [7], Smartcheck [19], and Securify [37].

Dataset: To assess the effectiveness of the proposed method, we constructed our dataset based on the open-source dataset Smartbug [38]. Smartbug is one of the most widely used public datasets in smart contract vulnerability detection research, containing 47398 Ethereum smart contracts labeled based on static analysis tools. However, due to the errors in static analysis tools, this labeling method lacks complete accuracy. In order to conduct an accurate evaluation, we carefully selected those parts of Smartbug that have been manually verified and confirmed to be accurate vulnerability labels as our dataset in combination with relevant literature [16,30]. we first reclassified the data from several manually labeled smart contract datasets according to the four types of vulnerabilities we are studying. Then, we used automatic analysis tools to detect vulnerabilities in these contracts, ensuring that our dataset contained a certain number of contracts that traditional detection tools failed to classify as vulnerabilities. In addition, we removed comments from the code, excluded contracts with less than 100 lines of code, and deleted duplicate contracts, which had different addresses but the same main functions determined by code similarity analysis. This process produced the final dataset we used in our experiments. The dataset's variety and frequency of vulnerabilities are detailed in Table 1 . The dataset is randomly divided into three parts, each accounting for a different proportion: 70% for the training set, 20% for the validation set, and 10% for the test set. The neural network model uses the training set to learn the various vulnerability features in the smart contract, while the validation set is used to adjust parameters during model training to avoid model overfitting. The test set is used to evaluate the generalization ability of the model in vulnerability detection. Such a data allocation strategy helps to conduct a comprehensive and rigorous evaluation of the model.

Table 1. Vulnerability Counts Across Different Categories.

Reentrancy	Transaction State Dependency	Block Info Dependency	Nested Call	Safe
973	895	1030	863	1097

Parameter setting: The default parameters of the model are as follows: Batch size: 16, Initial learning rate: 2×10^{-5}, Dropout rate: 0.1, Optimizer: use AdamW, weight decay is set to 1×10^{-4}.

4.2. Evaluation Metrics

In the experiments presented in this paper, we employed four widely-used evaluation metrics to comprehensively assess the performance of the smart contract vulnerability prediction model: *Accuracy, Recall, Precision* and *F1-score*. The calculations for these metrics are based on the four crucial components in the confusion matrix: True Positive (TP), True Negative (TN), False Positive (FP), and False Negative (FN). The specific formulas for these calculations are detailed as follows:

$$Accuracy = 100 \times \frac{TP + TN}{TP + FP + TN + FN} \quad (11)$$

$$Recall = 100 \times \frac{TP}{TP + FN} \quad (12)$$

$$Precision = 100 \times \frac{TP}{TP + FP} \quad (13)$$

$$F1 = 200 \times \frac{Precision \times Recall}{Precision + Recall} \quad (14)$$

Note: All calculated values in the article are multiplied by 100 and expressed as percentages.

4.3. Ablation Experiment

This section aims to validate the individual contributions of each component in the proposed method. First, to verify the contribution of pre-training techniques, we normalized the parameters of the pre-trained model (GraphCodeBERT [28]) and trained the model using the same input. For the smart contract files in the dataset, the canonical abstract syntax tree (AST) is first parsed by the solc-typed-ast tool. Based on the AST, a heterogeneous contract semantic graph is constructed, and features are extracted through the HGT network. Before training, GraphCodeBERT's parameters are normalized to eliminate the pre-training advantage. We denote this variant as *method − WP*. During the training phase, the loss rate decreased slowly. After a period of training, we tested the results on the test set, as shown in Table 2. The *method − WP* exhibited a substantial decline in performance across various types of vulnerability detection tasks. This outcome suggests that pre-training techniques can boost the generality of models, lessen the learning burden, and serve an indispensable role in the detection of vulnerabilities.

Table 2. Performance comparison of our method and its variants on four vulnerability detection tasks.

Methods	Reentrancy				Block Info Dependency				Transaction State Dependency				Nested Loop			
	Acc	Rec	Pre	F1	Acc	Rec	Pre	F1	Acc	Rec	Pre	F1	Acc	Rec	Pre	F1
Method-WP	55.32	34.68	48.03	59.1	44.69	50.52	47.92	49.19	41.24	47.96	31.74	51.24	39.56	36.28	32.09	34.06
Method-HOG	80.09	81.18	72.15	76.4	81.3	80.68	78.42	79.53	74.11	76.39	68.92	72.46	70.23	65.08	71.44	68.11
Our method	90.96	91.62	89.16	90.37	89.57	87.62	91.43	89.50	88.46	86.20	90.37	88.26	87.34	84.91	89.77	87.30

To study the contribution of the heterogeneous contract semantic graph, we compared the performance differences between homogeneous and heterogeneous graph analyses. For the smart contract files in the dataset, the canonical abstract syntax tree (AST) is first parsed by the solc-typed-ast tool. In the contract graph construction phase, the heterogeneous contract semantic graph is replaced by the isomorphic graph generated by the method proposed by Liu [22], so this variant is recorded as *method − HOG*. Then, the graph embedding is completed by GAT (graph attention neural network), and finally the obtained graph features and source code are used as input to train the GraphCodeBERT model loaded with pre-trained parameters. After training, the results tested on the test set are shown in Table 2. We observed that the original architecture of our method significantly outperformed method-HOG in all aspects. This result suggests that the heterogeneous contract semantic graph contains finer-grained semantic information in its graphical features, which is crucial for the smart contract vulnerability detection task.

4.4. Comparison with Other Deep Learning Based Methods

The experiments compared the proposed method with 12 state-of-the-art methods, including six open-source detection methods based on different neural network models: VanillaRNN [8], LSTM [36], GRU [36], DR-GCN [10], TMP [10], and CGE [22]. Table 3 presents the *Accuracy, Recall, Precision* and F1-score values of our method compared to the six detection methods based on neural network models.

Table 3. Performance comparison with neural network-based methods.

Methods	Reentrancy				Block Info Dependency				Transaction State Dependency				Nested Call			
	Acc	Rec	Pre	F1	Acc	Rec	Pre	F1	Acc	Rec	Pre	F1	Acc	Rec	Pre	F1
Vanilla-RNN	50.12	55.84	46.33	50.72	49.77	44.59	51.17	52.15	52.43	50.20	54.65	52.40	51.98	50.80	48.76	49.71
LSTM	53.29	59.97	48.45	53.79	50.79	57.23	51.42	54.17	53.15	60.24	51.86	55.74	55.07	56.35	50.83	53.43
GRU	57.80	72.17	52.18	60.68	62.76	59.85	65.43	62.61	62.76	59.85	65.43	62.61	59.65	57.43	61.98	59.97
DR-GCN	78.96	77.05	73.24	75.09	75.53	72.89	78.11	75.51	-	-	-	-	-	-	-	-
TMP	82.15	80.90	80.39	80.64	80.87	78.39	83.45	80.88	-	-	-	-	-	-	-	-
CGE	85.32	81.25	87.46	84.23	86.21	84.10	85.96	85.03	-	-	-	-	-	-	-	-
Our method	90.96	91.62	89.16	90.37	89.57	87.62	91.43	89.50	88.46	86.20	90.37	88.26	87.34	84.91	89.77	87.30

"-" means the corresponding tool does not support detecting this type of vulnerability.

The initial three models utilize text sequences from smart contract codes as inputs, while the subsequent three models are based on the graph structure data of smart contracts. These models represent typical approaches in the field of smart contract vulnerability detection and have been widely adopted as benchmark methods in recent studies [10,30,37]. Considering that none of the compared methods support other block information dependency vulnerabilities except timestamp dependency, in order to ensure the fairness of the comparison, we limit the scope of method evaluation and only verify and compare the detection effect of timestamp dependency vulnerabilities. It can be seen that in smart contract reentrancy vulnerability detection, our method improves the accuracy by 52.11% compared to the best-performing text sequence modeling model, GRU, and by 6.61% compared to the best-performing graph structure modeling model, CGE. In detecting block information dependency vulnerabilities in smart contracts, our method improves the accuracy by 42.71% compared to the best-performing text sequence modeling model, GRU, and by 4.90% compared to the best-performing graph structure modeling model, CGE. We attribute this improvement to our proposed heterogeneous contract semanti graph, which contains richer semantic information and higher separation between different features compared to homogeneous graphs. Methods based on graph structure data modeling tend to outperform those based on text sequence modeling, which also proves that code is not merely a sequence of words, and ignoring structural information such as data flow and control flow can degrade performance. For the detection of transaction state dependency vulnerabilities and Nested Call vulnerabilities, as the three graph structure-based methods do not support these types, we only compare with the text sequence-based methods. The results show that compared to the best-performing GRU, our method improves the accuracy by 40.94% and 46.42%, respectively.

4.5. Compared with Traditional Tools

In addition to comparing our method with neural network-based approaches, we also compared it with state-of-the-art traditional smart contract vulnerability detection tools. Based on the detection targets and main features of these tools [39], we used Smartcheck [19], Securify [37], and Slither [7] for source code-level vulnerability detection, and Oyente [17], Contractfuzzer [18], and Mythril [11] for bytecode-level vulnerability detection. In order to meet the input requirements of Oyente, Contractfuzzer and Mythril tools, we use the compiler to generate corresponding bytecodes for the smart contracts in the dataset for them to use. The results are shown in Table 4.

Table 4. Performance comparison with traditional tools.

Methods	Reentrancy				Block Info Dependency				Transaction State Dependency				Nested Call			
	Acc	Rec	Pre	F1	Acc	Rec	Pre	F1	Acc	Rec	Pre	F1	Acc	Rec	Pre	F1
Smartcheck	40.43	41.25	39.11	40.15	52.91	39.70	51.17	52.15	30.66	33.89	40.67	36.97	47.26	50.12	55.99	52.99
Oyente	60.23	62.35	65.12	63.46	39.45	41.23	43.56	42.37	-	-	-	-	42.78	39.75	46.89	43.03
Contractfuzzer	67.54	61.44	49.26	54.68	63.99	65.68	67.89	66.75	-	-	-	-	-	-	-	-
Mythril	65.35	69.91	50.08	58.36	70.23	63.31	69.88	66.43	77.12	51.32	59.70	55.19	60.23	55.71	60.38	55.71
Securify	73.88	75.79	68.45	71.93	-	-	-	-	-	-	-	-	-	-	-	-
Slither	80.35	87.10	82.57	84.77	77.12	74.28	68.42	71.23	60.96	82.09	62.07	71.27	55.37	27.69	61.91	38.27
Our method	90.96	91.62	89.16	90.37	89.57	87.62	91.43	89.50	88.46	86.20	90.37	88.26	87.34	84.91	89.77	87.30

"-" means the corresponding tool does not support detecting this type of vulnerability.

It can be observed that traditional vulnerability detection tools do not perform well. The best-performing traditional tool, Slither, achieved an accuracy of 80.35% in reentrancy vulnerability detection, while our method significantly improved the accuracy by 13.20%. We believe the poor performance of traditional methods is due to their heavy reliance on simple and fixed vulnerability detection patterns. For example, Mythril uses symbolic execution, mixed concrete execution, and control flow analysis to detect vulnerabilities in smart contracts. In reentrancy vulnerability detection, Mythril determines if a contract has a reentrancy vulnerability based on whether there are internal function calls or state variable modifications following a low-level call to *call.value*. Additionally, tools that use bytecode as input lack source code semantic information, which can lead to decreased detection performance. For block information dependency vulnerability detection, since Securify does not support the detection of such vulnerabilities, we only compared our method to the other five methods. Our method outperforms traditional methods on all four metrics and achieves 16.1% accuracy improvement over the best traditional method, Slither. The poor performance of some traditional tools may be attributed to their simplistic approach of checking for the presence of block information statements like *block.timestamp* to determine the existence of timestamp dependency vulnerabilities. Since only Mythril, Slither, and Smartcheck support the detection of transaction state dependency vulnerabilities and Nested call vulnerabilities, we compared our method solely with these three tools. The results show that our method improved accuracy by 14.7% and 26% in detecting transaction state dependency vulnerabilities and Nested call vulnerabilities, respectively, compared to the best-performing traditional tool, Mythril.

4.6. Comparison of Runtime Resource Consumption

To verify the usability of the proposed method, we evaluated the average time and memory consumption of the proposed method and other baseline methods in detecting contracts in the dataset. Since only reentrancy vulnerabilities can be detected by all methods, to ensure the fairness of the evaluation and the accuracy of the results, we screened out contracts containing reentrancy vulnerabilities and security contracts from the original dataset to form a sub-dataset, and shut down all background processes for evaluation in a clean experimental environment.

Traditional tools are primarily based on techniques such as symbolic execution, static analysis, or fuzz testing. These methods have most of their computational demands concentrated on the CPU and incur memory overhead during both static analysis and dynamic execution. Therefore, we measured their memory consumption. For deep learning-based methods, the VRAM consumption during inference is more indicative of model complexity and resource utilization. Thus, we primarily measured their VRAM consumption during the inference process. To ensure the reliability of the results, we ran each experiment multiple times in the clean environment and averaged the results to obtain the final evaluation. The results are shown in Table 5.

Table 5. Running time and memory consumption of different methods.

Methods	Acc	Recall	Precision	F1	Avg Time (s)	Memory (MB)	VRAM (MB)
Smartcheck	40.18	41.36	39.15	40.11	0.92	**3.58**	-
Oyente	60.05	62.77	65.21	63.41	2.50	174.44	-
Contractfuzzer	68.07	60.83	48.96	54.80	1.76	85.35	-
Mythril	65.13	69.36	49.83	57.95	2.39	161.40	-
Securify	73.38	75.86	68.52	71.50	2.73	170.59	-
Slither	81.15	87.86	82.00	84.71	0.89	4.27	-
Vanilla-RNN	50.46	55.78	46.40	50.24	**0.35**	-	71.34
LSTM	52.78	60.09	48.14	54.06	0.44	-	125.39
GRU	58.16	72.09	51.81	60.69	0.39	-	98.35
DR-GCN	79.24	77.17	73.05	74.96	0.65	-	217.53
TMP	81.54	80.61	79.66	80.08	0.73	-	393.75
CGE	85.56	81.19	88.32	83.58	0.91	-	674.20
Our method	90.96	91.62	89.16	90.37	0.84	-	650.83

Among traditional tools, the static analysis-based method Slither has the fastest execution speed and consumes the least memory, because static analysis usually only needs to traverse the code once, generate an abstract syntax tree or control flow graph, and use predefined rules for analysis. The symbolic execution-based method Securify generates a large number of symbolic paths and symbolic expressions during execution. For multiple conditional branches in complex code, the symbolic path may grow exponentially, resulting in a large amount of memory consumption. The execution time and memory consumption of deep learning-based methods are highly correlated with model complexity. Although the three methods using text sequences as input have faster inference speeds, they exhibit significant deficiencies in terms of accuracy. In contrast, methods based on graph structure modeling, while having increased inference time, significantly improve detection accuracy by better capturing the structural information within smart contracts. Given the substantial economic value associated with smart contracts, we believe that increasing computational resource consumption to enhance detection accuracy is both reasonable and worthwhile.

Compared to Slither, the best-performing traditional method, our approach achieves a 13% improvement in accuracy with similar execution time, greatly reducing the likelihood of missing potential vulnerabilities. Additionally, compared to CGE, the best neural network-based model, our method achieves a 6% increase in detection accuracy while maintaining comparable inference time and VRAM consumption. This demonstrates that our method not only improves performance while keeping resource consumption stable but also more effectively leverages model complexity to enhance the detection of contract vulnerabilities. Our method can provide higher security in actual smart contract audits, especially for high-value smart contracts. This performance improvement can effectively reduce the risk of economic losses caused by vulnerabilities. In addition, maintaining a balance between reasoning efficiency and resource consumption also makes our method more practical in large-scale or batch contract audit scenarios.

5. Conclusions

In this paper, we propose a smart contract vulnerability detection method based on pre-training technology and heterogeneous contract semantic graphs. Compared with existing methods, the heterogeneous contract semantic graph proposed in this paper better captures the dependency between program variables and functions. The graph embedding is achieved through the heterogeneous graph neural network HGT, and the introduction of pre-training technology enables efficient detection of smart contract vulnerabilities. Experimental results show that the proposed method performs well in detecting four of the most severe and widespread vulnerabilities. This approach not only covers a broader range of vulnerability types but also achieves higher detection accuracy compared to existing methods. It serves as an effective tool for the preliminary screening of vulnerabilities in smart contracts, significantly improving the efficiency with which developers identify potential issues. The method holds broad application prospects in the field.

However, our method has certain limitations:

- The scope of our method is currently limited to Ethereum and Solidity, and it does not support the detection of vulnerabilities in smart contracts written in other languages (such as Vyper, Rust, and Go).
- The dataset used in our experiments was manually curated based on existing research, and this process may introduce some degree of subjectivity, potentially leading to false positives.
- This study focuses on verifying the effectiveness of our approach using only four specific vulnerability types. As blockchain technology evolves and programming languages continue to advance, the types of vulnerabilities will also diversify.

6. Future Work

In future work, we aim to extend the capabilities of our method in several key areas. First, we plan to broaden the scope of our approach to support vulnerability detection in smart contracts written in other blockchain programming languages, such as Vyper, Rust, and Go. This will enable our method to be applied across a wider range of platforms and ecosystems beyond Ethereum and Solidity, making it more versatile and robust for developers working with different technologies. Second, we plan to extend our evaluation beyond the four specific vulnerability types currently used. As blockchain technology evolves, new types of vulnerabilities will emerge, and it is crucial to ensure that our method can detect a broader array of vulnerabilities. This includes incorporating emerging vulnerability types such as Gas optimization issues, flash loan attacks, etc. Furthermore, In addition, our current approach focuses on detecting vulnerabilities in a single smart contract. As blockchain technology continues to develop, decentralized applications (DApps) are becoming a mainstream use case for blockchain systems. Therefore, developing methods for detecting vulnerabilities between multiple interconnected contracts and components in DApps will become a valuable and important area for future research. In the future, we will explore the possibility of applying the current approach to DApp vulnerability detection.

Author Contributions: Conceptualization, J.Z.; methodology, J.Z.; software, J.Z.; validation, J.Z.; formal analysis, J.Y.; investigation, J.Z.; data curation, J.Y.; writing—original draft preparation, J.Z.; writing—review and editing, G.L.; visualization, J.Z.; supervision, G.L.; project administration, G.L.; All authors have read and agreed to the published version of the manuscript.

Funding: This research received no external funding.

Data Availability Statement: No new data were created or analyzed in this study. Data sharing is not applicable to this article.

Conflicts of Interest: The authors declare no conflicts of interest.

Appendix A

Appendix A provides detailed descriptions and code examples of four smart contract vulnerabilities, as well as the solc-typed-ast node type table to help readers better understand the technical details mentioned in this article.

Appendix A.1. Reentrancy

One crucial feature of smart contracts is their ability to call and utilize code from other external contracts. However, these external calls can potentially be hijacked by attackers who use fallback functions to execute additional code, including calls that return to the contract's own code. In Solidity, the fallback function is a special, unnamed function that takes no parameters and does not return a value. It is called when no matching function signature is found, or when the contract directly receives Ether. Thus, attackers can construct a contract at an external address that includes malicious code in the fallback function. When a contract calls certain functions at this address, it triggers the malicious code [40]. The term "reentrancy" refers to the scenario where an external malicious contract uses function calls to "re-enter" and manipulate the execution process of the vulnerable contract.

Reentrancy Example Example: Listing A1 illustrates a contract with a reentrancy vulnerability, the ReentrantBank contract, which acts as a bank holding users' Ether. Users can withdraw Ether through the *withdraw()* function, which contains the reentrancy vulnerability. The attacker's contract exploits this vulnerability to steal funds from the bank contract. In step 1, the attacker calls the *withdraw()* function in the ReentrantBank contract to withdraw Ether. In step 2, the ReentrantBank contract sends Ether to the attacker by executing *sender.call{value: _amount}("")*. In step 3, instead of proceeding to the next expected step—deducting the attacker's balance—the process enters the *fallback()* function of the Attacker contract because the Ether transfer is conducted using *sender.call{value: _amount}("")*. In step 4, within the *fallback()* function, the attacker calls the *withdraw()* function again to extract Ether. This cycle continues repeatedly until the Ether in the ReentrantBank contract is depleted.

Listing A1. Reentrancy Example.

```solidity
// Bank contract vulnerable to reentrancy attack
contract ReentrantBank {
mapping(address => uint256) public balances;  // Stores each user's balance
function deposit() public payable {
require(msg.value > 0);
balances[msg.sender] += msg.value;  // Update the user's balance
}
function withdraw(uint256 _amount) public {
require(balances[msg.sender] >= _amount);  // Ensure the user has enough balance
// Vulnerability: Sends Ether to the caller before updating the balance
(bool sent, ) = msg.sender.call{value: _amount}("");  // Call to external contract
require(sent, "Failed to send Ether");
balances[msg.sender] -= _amount;  // Update the user's balance (should be done before ←
    the call)
}
function getBalance() public view returns (uint256) {
return address(this).balance;
}
}
// Attacker contract exploiting the reentrancy vulnerability
contract Attacker {
ReentrantBank public bank;
uint256 public amount;
constructor(address _bankAddress) {
bank = ReentrantBank(_bankAddress);
}
fallback() external payable {
if (address(bank).balance >= amount) {
bank.withdraw(amount);  // Recursively call withdraw to drain funds
}
}
function attack(uint256 _amount) external payable {
require(msg.value >= _amount);
amount = _amount;
bank.deposit{value: msg.value}();  // Deposit Ether into the bank contract
bank.withdraw(_amount);  // Trigger the withdraw function, starting the reentrancy ←
    attack
}
}
```

Appendix A.2. Transaction State Dependency

In Solidity, there is a global variable *tx.origin* that traces back through the entire call stack to return the address of the account that originally initiated the call (or transaction). If this variable is used within a smart contract to check if the caller has the correct permissions for sensitive functions, it can lead to severe consequences. This is because tx.origin can be manipulated in a way that deceives the contract into identifying the call as originating from a trusted source when, in fact, it might be coming from an attacker. This vulnerability can be exploited to grant unauthorized access to critical functions that should be protected, leading to potential losses or other security breaches in the contract [14].

Transaction State Dependency Example: As shown in Listing A2, attackers can bypass permission checks by exploiting the logic on line 15. By using this method, anyone can successfully execute the *withdraw()* function on line 6 to withdraw Ether from the contract.

Listing A2. Transaction State Dependency.

```solidity
contract Vulnerable {
address public owner;   // Stores the contract owner's address
constructor() {
owner = msg.sender;   // msg.sender is the address that deployed the contract
}
function withdraw() public {
// Vulnerability: Using tx.origin instead of msg.sender allows an attack through an ←
    intermediary contract
require(tx.origin == owner, "Only owner can withdraw");   // Check if the original ←
    transaction initiator is the owner
payable(owner).transfer(address(this).balance);
}
receive() external payable {}
}
contract Attacker {
Vulnerable public vulnerableContract;
constructor(address _vulnerableAddress) {
vulnerableContract = Vulnerable(payable(_vulnerableAddress));
}
function attack() public {
// When this function is called by an attacker, tx.origin refers to the attacker,
// but msg.sender in Vulnerable contract will be this contract, bypassing the ←
    ownership check
vulnerableContract.withdraw();
}
receive() external payable {}
}
```

Appendix A.3. Block Info Dependency

Smart contracts can access block information (such as *block.timestamp*, *block.number*, and *block.hash*) as part of their execution context. However, relying on these blockchain environmental variables to determine their execution logic can lead to vulnerabilities related to block information dependency [14]. For instance, using attributes of future blocks as seeds for generating random numbers to determine the winners in a lottery game can be problematic.

Block Info Dependency Example: In Listing A3, a lottery game contract is shown, which selects a winner using the *random()* function (line 6). The *random()* function generates a random number by performing calculations based on *block.timestamp* (line 11). When the game accumulates a significant amount of Ether, miners are incentivized to manipulate these values within certain limits to increase their chances of winning.

Listing A3. Block Info Dependency.

```solidity
contract Lottery {
address public owner;
address[] public players;
function pickWinner() public onlyOwner {
require(players.length > 0, "No players participated");
uint index = random() % players.length;    // Select a winner based on the random ↩
    function
// Transfer the contract balance to the selected winner
payable(players[index]).transfer(address(this).balance);
players = new address;
}
// Function to generate a pseudo-random number, using block information (timestamp and↩
    difficulty)
// Vulnerability: Block information can be influenced by miners, making the random ↩
    number predictable or manipulable
function random() private view returns (uint) {
// Generate a pseudo-random number using block.timestamp, block.difficulty, and˜↩
    players array
return uint(keccak256(abi.encodePacked(block.timestamp, block.difficulty, players)));
}
receive() external payable {}
}
```

Appendix A.4. Nested Call

In the Ethereum execution environment, using the *CALL* instruction in a contract requires paying gas, with a basic cost of 700 gas. If the call involves transferring a non-zero value, an additional 9000 gas is required [14]. If a loop contains a *CALL* operation but does not restrict the number of iterations, there is a risk that the gas cost could exceed the limit. In such cases, the transaction will be terminated and reverted (rolled back), but the gas already consumed will not be refunded. This could lead to users or contract owners incurring high costs without achieving any results.

Nested Call Example: In Listing A4, an attacker can maliciously increase the number of iterations in a loop, Each call to the *send()* function during each iteration will use the CALL instruction to switch context in the EVM, which will consume a lot of gas. When the gas consumption exceeds the limit, the transaction will be reverted, and only unused gas will be refunded. The gas already consumed during execution will not be refunded, causing the user or contract holder to pay high fees without any results.

Listing A4. Nested Call.

```solidity
contract VulnerableContract {
function callExternal() public payable {
for (uint i = 0; i<member.length; i++) {
member[i].send(1 wei);}
}
}
```

Appendix A.5. Solc-Typed-ast Node Type Table

Table A1. Solc-typed-ast node type table.

Functional Category	Node Type
Structural and Operation	ContractDefinition, EnumDefinition, ErrorDefinition, EventDefinition, FunctionDefinition, ModifierDefinition, SourceUnit, Block, Break, Continue, DoWhileStatement, EmitStatement, ExpressionStatement, ForStatement, IfStatement, InlineAssembly, PlaceholderStatement, PragmaDirective, Return, RevertStatement, Throw, TryCatchClause, TryStatement, UncheckedBlock, VariableDeclarationStatement, WhileStatement, NewExpression, Assignment, BinaryOperation, Conditional, TupleExpression, UnaryOperation, IndexAccess, IndexRangeAccess, MemberAccess
Variables and calling	FunctionCall, Identifier, IdentifierPath, UserDefinedValueTypeDefinition, VariableDeclaration, ModifierInvocation, ParameterList, StructDefinition
other	ImportDirective, PragmaDirective, OverrideSpecifier, StructuredDocumentation, UsingForDirective, InheritanceSpecifier, ArrayTypeName, ElementaryTypeName, EnumValue, FunctionTypeName, UserDefinedTypeName, FunctionCallOptions, Literal

References

1. Nakamoto, S. Bitcoin: A Peer-to-Peer Electronic Cash System. 2008. Available online: https://www.ussc.gov/sites/default/files/pdf/training/annual-national-training-seminar/2018/Emerging_Tech_Bitcoin_Crypto.pdf (accessed on 1 July 2024). [CrossRef]
2. Shao, Q.; Jin, C.; Zhang, Z.; Qian, W.; Zhou, A. Blockchain: Architecture and Research Progress. *Chin. J. Comput.* **2018**, *41*, 969–988. (In Chinese with English abstract) [CrossRef]
3. SlowMist. 2023 Blockchain Security and Anti-Money Laundering Annual Report. 2024. Available online: https://www.slowmist.com/report/2023-Blockchain-Security-and-AML-Annual-Report(EN).pdf (accessed on 11 February 2024).
4. Mossberg, M.; Manzano, F.; Hennenfent, E.; Groce, A.; Grieco, G.; Feist, J.; Brunson, T.; Dinaburg, A. Manticore: A User-Friendly Symbolic Execution Framework for Binaries and Smart Contracts. In Proceedings of the 34th IEEE/ACM International Conference on Automated Software Engineering (ASE), San Diego, CA, USA, 11–15 November 2019; pp. 1186–1189. [CrossRef]
5. So, S.; Hong, S.; Oh, H. SmarTest: Effectively Hunting Vulnerable Transaction Sequences in Smart Contracts Through Language Model-Guided Symbolic Execution. In Proceedings of the 30th USENIX Security Symposium, Online, 11–12 August 2021; pp. 1361–1378.
6. Torres, C.; Iannillo, A.; Gervais, A.; State, R. ConFuzzius: A Data Dependency-Aware Hybrid Fuzzer for Smart Contracts. In Proceedings of the 2021 IEEE European Symposium on Security and Privacy (EuroS&P), Vienna, Austria, 6–10 September 2021; pp. 103–119. [CrossRef]
7. Feist, J.; Grieco, G.; Groce, A. Slither: A Static Analysis Framework for Smart Contracts. In Proceedings of the 2nd IEEE/ACM International Workshop on Emerging Trends in Software Engineering for Blockchain (WETSEB), Montreal, QC, Canada, 27 May 2019; pp. 8–15. [CrossRef]
8. Goller, C.; Kuchler, A. Learning Task-Dependent Distributed Representations by Backpropagation Through Structure. In Proceedings of the International Conference on Neural Networks (ICNN '96), Washington, DC, USA, 3–6 June 1996; pp. 347–352.
9. Sak, H.; Senior, A.; Beaufays, F. Long Short-Term Memory Recurrent Neural Network Architectures for Large Scale Acoustic Modeling. In Proceedings of the Fifteenth Annual Conference of the International Speech Communication Association, Perth, WA, Australia, 27 November–1 December 2014.
10. Zhuang, Y.; Liu, Z.; Qian, P.; Liu, Q.; Wang, X.; He, Q. Smart Contract Vulnerability Detection using Graph Neural Network. In Proceedings of the 29th International Joint Conference on Artificial Intelligence (IJCAI), Yokohama, Japan, 11–17 July 2020; pp. 3283–3290.
11. Mueller, B. Mythril-Reversing and Bug Hunting Framework for the Ethereum Blockchain. 2017. Available online: https://pypi.org/project/mythril/0.8.2 (accessed on 11 February 2024).
12. di Angelo, M.; Salzer, G. Consolidation of Ground Truth Sets for Weakness Detection in Smart Contracts. *arXiv* **2023**, arXiv:2304.11624.
13. SWC. Smart Contract Weakness Classification. 2023. Available online: https://swcregistry.io/ (accessed on 11 February 2024).
14. Chen, J.; Xia, X.; Lo, D.; Grundy, J.; Luo, X.; Chen, T. Defining Smart Contract Defects on Ethereum. *IEEE Trans. Softw. Eng.* **2022**, *48*, 327–345. [CrossRef]
15. Wang, W.; Song, J.; Xu, G.; Li, Y.; Wang, H.; Su, C. ContractWard: Automated Vulnerability Detection Models for Ethereum Smart Contracts. *IEEE Trans. Netw. Sci. Eng.* **2021**, *8*, 1133–1144. [CrossRef]
16. Luo, F.; Luo, R.; Chen, T.; Qiao, A.; He, Z.; Song, S.; Jiang, Y.; Li, S. SCVHunter: Smart Contract Vulnerability Detection Based on Heterogeneous Graph Attention Network. In Proceedings of the IEEE/ACM 46th International Conference on Software Engineering (ICSE '24), Lisbon, Portugal, 12–24 April 2024. [CrossRef]
17. Luu, L.; Chu, D.; Olickel, H.; Saxena, P.; Hobor, A. Making Smart Contracts Smarter. In Proceedings of the 2016 ACM SIGSAC Conference on Computer and Communications Security (CCS), Vienna, Austria, 24–28 October 2016; pp. 254–269. [CrossRef]

18. Jiang, B.; Liu, Y.; Chan, W. ContractFuzzer: Fuzzing Smart Contracts for Vulnerability Detection. In Proceedings of the 33rd IEEE/ACM International Conference on Automated Software Engineering (ASE), Montpellier, France, 3–7 September 2018; pp. 259–269. [CrossRef]
19. Tikhomirov, S.; Voskresenskaya, E.; Ivanitskiy, I.; Takhaviev, R.; Marchenko, E.; Alexandrov, Y. SmartCheck: Static Analysis of Ethereum Smart Contracts. In Proceedings of the 1st International Workshop on Emerging Trends in Software Engineering for Blockchain (WETSEB), Gothenburg, Sweden, 27 May–3 June 2018; pp. 9–16. [CrossRef]
20. Hildenbrandt, E.; Saxena, M.; Rodrigues, N.; Zhu, X.; Daian, P.; Guth, D.; Moore, B.; Park, D.; Zhang, Y.; Stefanescu, A.; et al. KEVM: A Complete Formal Semantics of the Ethereum Virtual Machine. In Proceedings of the 31st IEEE Computer Security Foundations Symposium (CSF), Oxford, UK, 9–12 July 2018; pp. 204–217. [CrossRef]
21. Kalra, S.; Goel, S.; Dhawan, M.; Sharma, S. ZEUS: Analyzing Safety of Smart Contracts. In Proceedings of the 2018 Network and Distributed System Security Symposium (NDSS), San Diego, CA, USA, 18–21 February 2018; pp. 1–12. [CrossRef]
22. Liu, Z.; Qian, P.; Wang, X.; Zhuang, Y.; Qiu, L.; Wang, X. Combining Graph Neural Networks with Expert Knowledge for Smart Contract Vulnerability Detection. *IEEE Trans. Knowl. Data Eng.* **2023**, *35*, 1296–1310. [CrossRef]
23. Devlin, J.; Chang, M.; Lee, K.; Toutanova, K. BERT: Pre-Training of Deep Bidirectional Transformers for Language Understanding. In Proceedings of the 2019 Conference of the North American Chapter of the Association for Computational Linguistics: Human Language Technologies (NAACL-HLT), Minneapolis, MN, USA, 2–7 June 2019; pp. 4171–4186. [CrossRef]
24. Radford, A.; Narasimhan, K.; Salimans, T.; Sutskever, I. Improving Language Understanding by Generative Pre-Training. 2018. Available online: https://paperswithcode.com/paper/improving-language-understanding-by (accessed on 11 February 2024).
25. Feng, Z.; Guo, D.; Tang, D.; Duan, N.; Feng, X.; Gong, M.; Shou, L.; Qin, B.; Liu, T.; Jiang, D.; et al. CodeBERT: A Pre-Trained Model for Programming and Natural Languages. In Proceedings of the 2020 Findings of the Association for Computational Linguistics (EMNLP), Online Event, 16–20 November 2020; pp. 1536–1547. [CrossRef]
26. Wang, Y.; Wang, W.; Joty, S.; Hoi, S. Codet5: Identifier-Aware Unified Pre-Trained Encoder-Decoder Models for Code Understanding and Generation. In Proceedings of the 2021 Conference on Empirical Methods in Natural Language Processing (EMNLP), Punta Cana, Dominican Republic, 7–11 November 2021; pp. 8696–8708.
27. Buratti, L.; Pujar, S.; Bornea, M.; McCarley, S.; Zheng, Y.; Rossiello, G.; Morari, A.; Laredo, J.; Thost, V.; Zhuang, Y.; et al. Exploring Software Naturalness through Neural Language Models. *arXiv* **2020**, arXiv:2006.12641.
28. Guo, D.; Ren, S.; Lu, S.; Feng, Z.; Tang, D.; Liu, S.; Zhou, L.; Duan, N.; Svyatkovskiy, A.; Fu, S.; et al. GraphCodeBERT: Pre-Training Code Representations with Data Flow. In Proceedings of the 9th International Conference on Learning Representations (ICLR), Virtual Event, Austria, 3–7 May 2021.
29. Allamanis, M.; Brockschmidt, M.; Khademi, M. Learning to Represent Programs with Graphs. In Proceedings of the 6th International Conference on Learning Representations (ICLR), Vancouver, BC, Canada, 30 April–3 May 2018.
30. Wu, H.; Zhang, Z.; Wang, S.; Lei, Y.; Lin, B.; Qin, Y.; Zhang, H.; Mao, X. Peculiar: Smart Contract Vulnerability Detection Based on Crucial Data Flow Graph and Pre-Training Techniques. In Proceedings of the 2021 IEEE 32nd International Symposium on Software Reliability Engineering (ISSRE), Wuhan, China, 25–28 October 2021; pp. 378–389.
31. Dong, Y.; Chawla, N.; Swami, A. metapath2vec: Scalable Representation Learning for Heterogeneous Networks. *Acm Trans. Knowl. Discov. Data* **2017**. [CrossRef]
32. Wang, X.; Ji, H.; Shi, C.; Wang, B.; Ye, Y.; Cui, P.; Yu, P. Heterogeneous Graph Attention Network. In Proceedings of the The World Wide Web Conference (WWW '19), Raleigh, NC, USA, 26–30 April 2019; pp. 2022–2032. [CrossRef]
33. Hu, Z.; Dong, Y.; Wang, K.; Sun, Y. Heterogeneous Graph Transformer. In Proceedings of the Web Conference 2020 (WWW '20), Taipei, Taiwan, 20–24 April 2020; pp. 2704–2710. [CrossRef]
34. Ethereum. Units and Globally Available Variables. 2023. Available online: https://docs.soliditylang.org/zh/latest/units-and-global-variables.html (accessed on 11 February 2024).
35. Zhang, Z.; Lei, Y.; Mao, X.; Li, P. CNN-FL: An Effective Approach for Localizing Faults Using Convolutional Neural Networks. In Proceedings of the 26th International Conference on Software Analysis, Evolution and Reengineering (SANER), Hangzhou, China, 24–27 February 2019; pp. 445–455. [CrossRef]
36. Chung, J.; Gulcehre, C.; Cho, K.; Bengio, Y. Empirical Evaluation of Gated Recurrent Neural Networks on Sequence Modeling. *arXiv* **2014**, arXiv:1412.3555.
37. Tsankov, P.; Dan, A.; Drachsler-Cohen, D.; Gervais, A.; Buenzli, F.; Vechev, M. Securify: Practical Security Analysis of Smart Contracts. In Proceedings of the 2018 ACM SIGSAC Conference on Computer and Communications Security (CCS), Toronto, ON, Canada, 15–19 October 2018; pp. 67–82.
38. Durieux, T.; Ferreira, J.; Abreu, R.; Cruz, P. Empirical Review of Automated Analysis Tools on 47,587 Ethereum Smart Contracts. In Proceedings of the ACM/IEEE 42nd International Conference on Software Engineering (ICSE), Seoul, Republic of Korea, 27 June–19 July 2020; pp. 530–541. [CrossRef]
39. Cui, Z.; Yang, H.; Chen, X.; Wang, L.Z. Progress in Smart Contract Security Vulnerability Detection. *J. Softw.* **2024**, *35*, 2235–2267. [CrossRef]
40. Antonopoulos, A.; Wood, G. *Mastering Ethereum: Building Smart Contracts and DApps*; O'Reilly Media: Sebastopol, CA, USA, 2018; p. 177.

Disclaimer/Publisher's Note: The statements, opinions and data contained in all publications are solely those of the individual author(s) and contributor(s) and not of MDPI and/or the editor(s). MDPI and/or the editor(s) disclaim responsibility for any injury to people or property resulting from any ideas, methods, instructions or products referred to in the content.

Article

An NTRU-Based Key Encapsulation Scheme for Underwater Acoustic Communication

Peng He and Ming Xu *

The College of Information Engineering, Shanghai Maritime University, Shanghai 201306, China; 202230310079@stu.shmtu.edu.cn
* Correspondence: mingxu@shmtu.edu.cn

Abstract: With the increasing emphasis on safeguarding maritime sovereignty and developing marine resources, the security of underwater acoustic communication has risen to a new level of importance. Given the complex environmental challenges faced by underwater acoustic channels, this paper proposes an NTRU-based key encapsulation scheme designed to ensure secure and reliable underwater data transmission, while maintaining privacy and integrity. In the public–private key pair generation phase, a ring sampling technique is employed to generate a compact NTRU trapdoor, which not only guarantees security but also effectively reduces the communication overhead. During the encapsulation phase, underwater acoustic channel characteristics during communication are introduced as temporary identity information to ensure the confidentiality and reliability of the key encapsulation mechanism. Furthermore, the traditional key encapsulation mechanism is extended by integrating a digital signature process, where the encapsulated ciphertext is signed. The use of digital signature technology verifies the authenticity and integrity of the transmitted data, ensuring that communication data remain secure and unaltered in complex underwater acoustic environments. Finally, we conduct a rigorous correctness analysis and security proofs, demonstrating that the proposed scheme achieves chosen ciphertext security, while meeting the demands of low bandwidth and limited computational capacity in underwater acoustic communication.

Keywords: underwater acoustic communication; NTRU; key encapsulation; compact trapdoor; digital signature

Academic Editors: Mikolaj Karpinski, Oleksandr O. Kuznetsov and Roman Oliynykov

Received: 30 December 2024
Revised: 15 January 2025
Accepted: 17 January 2025
Published: 21 January 2025

Citation: He, P.; Xu, M. An NTRU-Based Key Encapsulation Scheme for Underwater Acoustic Communication. *Electronics* 2025, 14, 405. https://doi.org/10.3390/electronics14030405

Copyright: © 2025 by the authors. Licensee MDPI, Basel, Switzerland. This article is an open access article distributed under the terms and conditions of the Creative Commons Attribution (CC BY) license (https://creativecommons.org/licenses/by/4.0/).

1. Introduction

With the growing global demand for maritime sovereignty protection and the exploitation of underwater resources, underwater acoustic communication technology has become a critical means of ocean information transmission and monitoring [1,2]. However, underwater acoustic communication faces numerous challenges, such as low bandwidth, high latency, frequency-selective fading, and the highly dynamic and complex channel environment, making the assurance of data transmission security and integrity a pressing issue [3]. In harsh underwater acoustic environments, traditional encryption mechanisms struggle to ensure the security of communication [4,5]. They have a high computational overhead, while lacking an efficient key encapsulation mechanism and being unable to resist quantum attacks. To address the security challenges of underwater acoustic communication, numerous studies have focused on two key aspects: encryption algorithms, and key management mechanisms [6,7]. Symmetric encryption algorithms, such as the Advanced Encryption Standard (AES), are widely adopted for their efficiency; however, their security relies heavily on key distribution and management, making them vulnerable to eavesdropping and man-in-the-middle attacks [8]. While symmetric encryption algorithms, such as AES, are widely adopted for their efficiency, their security depends on key distribution and management, making them vulnerable to eavesdropping and man-in-the-middle attacks; in contrast, asymmetric cryptographic algorithms, such as Rivest–Shamir–Adleman (RSA) and elliptic curve cryptography (ECC), offer higher security, but their computational complexity makes them unsuitable for resource-constrained underwater acoustic communication environments [9,10]. Meenakshi et al. [11] improved ECC and optimized it for underwater environments, significantly reducing the computational overhead. However, performance bottlenecks still exist under high-noise conditions and low signal-to-noise ratios, and this method is unable to resist quantum attacks.

Recently, post-quantum cryptography has garnered widespread attention for its ability to resist quantum computing attacks. Among these, lattice-based cryptography has emerged as a research hotspot due to its high level of security and efficiency [12–14]. F. Nisha et al. [15] discussed the advantages and disadvantages of NTRU encryption, NTRU signature, ring–lizard, and Kyber algorithms, providing an in-depth analysis of their performance in various application scenarios. Use of the NTRU encryption scheme helps reduce computational and storage overhead. The NTRU public key encryption scheme proposed by Jonghyun et al. [16], with its smaller key size and faster computational performance, has been proven suitable for resource-constrained communication scenarios. In 2023, Piljoo et al. [17] proposed a lightweight polynomial multiplication accelerator based on NTRU, which significantly reduced the overhead associated with key generation and transmission. Eros et al. [18] further validated the security and computational efficiency of NTRU in embedded devices, demonstrating its suitability for dynamic environments. In [19], Alexandr et al. proposed a code-based key encapsulation scheme, achieving significant progress in resisting quantum attacks. In [20], Joohee et al. proposed a post-quantum key encapsulation scheme for IoT devices, which ensures security, while reducing the time consumption for key encapsulation and decryption. Therefore, post-quantum key encapsulation schemes can help optimize computational efficiency and reduce overhead, making them suitable for resource-constrained underwater communication.

In recent years, physical layer security techniques have been proposed as an effective approach to counter eavesdropping attacks. By leveraging the random characteristics of underwater acoustic channels, such as channel state information (CSI), as a source of randomness for key generation, these techniques inherently provide information-theoretic security [21,22]. Pan et al. [23] proposed a lightweight key agreement method, which demonstrated strong robustness in complex underwater environments. Yicong et al. [24] proposed an accurate and efficient key generation method, which encapsulates the CSI with a confusion matrix using circular convolution, thereby enhancing communication accuracy and efficiency. However, such schemes lack integration with post-quantum cryptographic mechanisms and are therefore unable to resist quantum attack threats.

However, designing a key encapsulation method based on NTRU and applying it to underwater acoustic communication still faces the following challenges: (1) how to reduce the communication overhead to accommodate the bandwidth limitations of underwater acoustic channels; and (2) how to integrate underwater channel characteristics to enhance the dynamism and security of key encapsulation.

To address the aforementioned issues, this paper proposes an NTRU-based key encapsulation scheme for underwater acoustic communication. By integrating underwater channel characteristics into a post-quantum cryptographic framework, the scheme aims to achieve efficient and secure key management and data transmission. The following are the main contributions of this paper:

(a). In the key generation phase, a compact NTRU trapdoor is generated using ring sampling techniques and used as the private key.
(b). Based on this, underwater acoustic channel characteristics are integrated as temporary identity information to generate the encapsulated key.
(c). The traditional key encapsulation mechanism is extended by incorporating a digital signature phase.
(d). Under the random oracle model, the proposed scheme was proven to achieve security against chosen ciphertext attacks, while significantly reducing the communication bandwidth requirements, making it suitable for complex underwater acoustic communication environments.

The organization of this paper is as follows: Section 2 provides a brief introduction to NTRU, KEM (key encapsulation mechanism), digital signatures, and related concepts. Section 3 describes the conventional NTRU trapdoor generation algorithm and the ring sampling algorithm adopted in this paper. Section 4 introduces the model of the underwater acoustic channel and presents the proposed NTRU-based key encapsulation scheme for underwater communication. Section 5 provides a security proof under the random oracle model and compares the proposed scheme with other advanced methods. The paper concludes with Section 6, where the primary findings are recapped.

2. Preliminaries

2.1. Lattices

Lattices are a fundamental concept in both mathematics and cryptography. In cryptography, lattices represent a mathematical structure with significant applications. Below are some definitions of lattices:

Definition 1 (Lattices). *In an m-dimensional vector space $\mathbb{R}^m$, $\mathbb{Z}$ represents the set of integers. There is a set of linearly independent vectors $V_1, V_2, \cdots, V_n \in \mathbb{R}^m$ (where $m \geq n$), then the lattice is defined as*

$$\Lambda = \left\{ \sum_{i=1}^n x_i v_i : x_i \in \mathbb{Z}, i = 1, 2, \ldots, n \right\} \tag{1}$$

Vectors $V_1, V_2, \ldots, V_n$ form the basis for the lattice Λ, where m is the dimension of the lattice Λ, and n is the rank of the lattice Λ. Before introducing the NTRU lattice, a definition of the anticirculant matrix is first given.

Lemma 1 ([25]). *Given an n-dimensional lattice Λ, for any $\varepsilon > 0$, Gaussian parameter $\sigma > 2\eta_\varepsilon(\Lambda)$, and center $c \in \mathbb{R}^n$, we have $D_{\Lambda,\sigma,c}(x) \leq \left(\frac{1-\varepsilon}{1+\varepsilon}\right) \cdot 2^{-n}$. If $\varepsilon < 1/3$, the minimum value of $D_{\Lambda,\sigma,c}(x)$ is at least $n-1$.*

$D_{\Lambda,\sigma,c}(x)$ is used to describe the probability at the point x, and $\eta_\varepsilon(\Lambda)$ represents a bound. Lemma 1 provides both the upper and lower bounds for the function $D_{\Lambda,\sigma,c}(x)$.

Lemma 2. *For any real number $\sigma > 0$ and positive integer m, there exists*

$$\Pr[x \leftarrow D_\sigma^1 : |x| > 12\sigma] < 2^{-100}; \Pr[x \leftarrow D_\sigma^m : \|x\| > 2\sigma\sqrt{m}] < 2^{-m} \tag{2}$$

In a Gaussian distribution, as the dimensions m and σ increase, the probability of drawing a vector whose norm exceeds a certain threshold rapidly becomes very small.

Definition 2 (**Anti-circulant matrix**). *The N-dimensional anticirculant matrix of f is defined as the Toeplitz matrix provided below:*

$$A_N(f) = \begin{bmatrix} f_0 & f_1 & \cdots & f_{N-1} \\ -f_{N-1} & f_0 & \cdots & f_{N-2} \\ \vdots & \vdots & \vdots & \vdots \\ -f_1 & -f_2 & \cdots & -f_0 \end{bmatrix} = \begin{bmatrix} f \\ (x*f) \\ \vdots \\ x^{N-1}*f \end{bmatrix} \quad (3)$$

In general, an anti-circulant matrix can be denoted as A(f), which satisfies the following addition and multiplication properties: $A_n(f) + A_n(g) = A_n(f+g)$ and $A_n(f)A_n(g) = A_n(fg)$.

Definition 3 (**NTRU Lattices**). *Let N be a power of 2, q be a positive integer, and $f, g \in R$. Calculate $h = g \cdot f^{-1} \bmod q$. The NTRU lattice Λ can be represented as*

$$\Lambda_{NTRU} = \left\{ (u,v) \in R^2 \mid u + v * h = 0 \bmod q \right\} \quad (4)$$

The lattice Λ_{NTRU} is a full-rank lattice in $\mathbb{Z}^2$, generated by the matrix $\mathbf{A}_{h,q} = \begin{pmatrix} -\mathcal{A}_N(h) & I_N \\ q \cdot I_N & O_N \end{pmatrix}$. Due to the poor orthogonality of $\mathbf{A}_{h,q}$, it cannot be used as the basis for the trapdoor in the key encapsulation scheme of NTRU. Ducas et al. [26] proposed another method for generating short bases $B = \begin{bmatrix} g & G \\ -f & -F \end{bmatrix}$, which can generate the same lattice as $\mathbf{A}_{h,q}$.

Similarly to the NTRU lattice, we define the q-ary lattice.

Definition 4 (**q-ary lattice**). *Let $n, m, q \in \mathbb{Z}$, $\mathbf{A} \in \mathbb{Z}_q^{n \times m}$, and $\mathbf{u} \in \mathbb{Z}_q^n$, satisfying $\mathbf{Ax} = \mathbf{u} \bmod q$. The definition is given as follows:*

$$\begin{aligned} \Lambda^\perp(A) &= \{y \in \mathbb{Z}^m : Ay = 0 \bmod q\} \\ \Lambda_u^\perp(A) &= \{y \in \mathbb{Z}^m : Ay = u \bmod q\} = \Lambda^\perp(A) + x \end{aligned} \quad (5)$$

where $\Lambda_u^\perp(\mathbf{A})$ is a coset of $\Lambda^\perp(\mathbf{A})$.

2.2. Gaussian Functions and Distributions on Lattices

Definition 5 (**Discrete Gaussian Function**). *For any $c \in \mathbb{R}^n$ and $s > 0$, the Gaussian function on $\mathbb{R}^n$ is defined as*

$$\rho_{s,c}(x) = e^{-\pi \|x\|^2/s^2} \quad (6)$$

Lemma 3 ([27]). *For any vector $v \in \mathbb{Z}^m$ and any positive real number α, if $\sigma = \omega(\|v\| \sqrt{\log m})$:*

$$\Pr[x \leftarrow D_\sigma^m : D_\sigma^m(x)/D_{v,\sigma}^m(x) = O(1)] = 1 - 2^{-\omega(\log m)} \quad (7)$$

Definition 6 (**Discrete Gaussian Distribution**). *We can define a discrete Gaussian distribution $D_{\Lambda+c,s}$ on any lattice $\Lambda \in \mathbb{R}^N$, centered at c with the parameter s:*

$$\forall x \in \Lambda + c, D_{\Lambda+c,s}(x) = \frac{\rho_s(x)}{\rho_s(\Lambda + c)} \quad (8)$$

When $c = 0$, it can be simplified as $\rho_s(x)$ and $D_{\Lambda,s}(x)$.

2.3. Key Encapsulation Mechanism

The key encapsulation mechanism consists of three polynomial-time algorithms, denoted as $KEM = (KeyGen, Encaps, Decaps)$. Let the security parameter be λ, the key space be **K**, and the ciphertext space be C. The following describes the three algorithms:

(1) Key Generation Algorithm $(pk, sk) \leftarrow KeyGen(1^\lambda)$:

Input the security parameter, and output a pair of public and private keys (pk, sk).

(2) Key Encapsulation Algorithm $(c, K) \leftarrow Encaps(pk)$:

Input the public key pk, output the temporary encapsulated key K and the corresponding ciphertext c, where $c \in C$.

(3) Decapsulation Algorithm $K' \leftarrow Decaps(sk, c)$:

Input the private key sk and the ciphertext c, output the temporary encapsulated key K'. Here, K' can be $\perp$, which indicates a decapsulation failure.

Definition 7 (The correctness of KEM). *The probability of key decapsulation failure is defined as*

$$\Pr[Decaps(sk, c) \neq K : (c, K) \leftarrow Encaps(pk) < \delta] \tag{9}$$

That is, if $K' = K$ holds for any security parameter λ, the encapsulation scheme is considered correct. A KEM scheme is said to satisfy indistinguishability under chosen ciphertext attack (IND-CCA) security if, for any polynomial-time adversary A, the attacker's advantage satisfies

$$Adv_{A,KEM}^{IND-CCA}(\lambda) = \Pr \begin{bmatrix} (pk, sk) \leftarrow KeyGen(1^\lambda); \\ (c^*, K_0) \leftarrow Encaps(pk); \\ K_1 \leftarrow \mathbf{K}; b \leftarrow \{0, 1\}; \\ b' \leftarrow A^{Dec(*)}(pk, c^*, K_b); \\ b' = b \end{bmatrix} \leq -\frac{1}{2} \tag{10}$$

2.4. Digital Signature

The digital signature scheme comprises three distinct algorithms, denoted as $Sig = (Gen, Sign, Ver)$. Let **M** be the message space, **S** be the signature space, and λ be the security parameter. Below are the definitions of the three algorithms:

(1) Key Generation Algorithm $(pk, sk) \leftarrow Gen(1^\lambda)$:

Given the security parameter λ, the algorithm outputs a public and private key pair (pk, sk).

(2) Signature Algorithm $s = Sign_{sk}(m)$:

Input the message m, where $m \in M$, and the private key sk; output the signature s, where $s \in S$.

(3) Verification Algorithm $Ver_{pk}(m, s)$:

Given the public key pk, the message m, and the signature s, the signature is considered valid if $Ver_{pk}(m, s) = 1$; otherwise, it is deemed invalid.

Definition 8 (Unforgeability of Digital Signatures). *For a digital signature scheme $Sig = (Gen, Sign, Ver)$ for any polynomial-time adversary* **A**, *there exists a non-negligible function* negl *such that the following condition is satisfied:*

$$\Pr[Ver(\lambda, s, pk) = m] = 1 - negl(\lambda) \tag{11}$$

One might conclude that the digital signature scheme exhibits robust resistance to adaptive chosen-message attacks.

Definition 9 (The confidentiality of digital signatures). *In the context of anonymous identity-based cryptography under the multi-user adaptive chosen ciphertext attack (MU-IND-CCA) security model, if no adversary can win the MU-IND-CCA game with a non-negligible advantage in polynomial time, then the digital signature scheme possesses strong secrecy.*

Lemma 4 ([28]). *Forking Lemma. Suppose A is a probabilistic polynomial-time Turing machine that can generate a valid signature σ for a given message m and a random oracle output h with a non-negligible probability. If A is run again with the same random seed but a different random oracle, it will, with non-negligible probability, produce a second valid forgery σ' for the same message m, corresponding to a different random oracle output h', where $h \neq h'$.*

2.5. Hardness Assumption

The following section introduces the related hard problems concerning the lattices and NTRU lattices involved in the proposed scheme.

Definition 10 (The R-$SIS_{q,m,\beta}$ problem). *Given a random vector $\vec{a} \in \mathbb{R}_q^m$ and a real number $\beta > 0$, the problem is to find a non-zero vector $\vec{z} \in \mathbb{R}^m$ such that $\|\vec{z}\| \leq \beta$ and $\sum_{i=1}^{m} a_i \cdot z_i = 0 \pmod{q}$, where $(z_1, \ldots, z_m)^T \in \mathbb{R}^m$.*

Definition 11 (The SIS problem on the NTRU lattice). *Given a prime q, a real number β, and two small polynomials $f, g \in \mathbb{R}$, let $A_{h,q} = \left(h, 1\right) \in \mathbb{R}_{1_q \times 2}$, where $h = \frac{g}{f}$. The SIS problem on the NTRU lattice is to find a vector $(z_1, z_2) \in \mathbb{R}_{2_q \times 1}$ that satisfies the following two conditions: 1. $A_{h,q}(z_1, z_2)^T = 0 \pmod{q}$, 2. $\|(z_1, z_2)\| \leq \beta$.*

Definition 12 (The NTRU One-Wayness Assumption). *NTRU one-way hardness refers to the difficulty of computing (r, e) given the public key h and the ciphertext c.*

3. Trapdoor Generation Algorithm on NTRU Lattices

3.1. TrapGen

Given a security parameter λ, a prime $q = \text{poly}(\lambda)$, and a Gaussian parameter $\sigma > \omega(\sqrt{\log(2\lambda)})$, there exists a probabilistic polynomial-time (PPT) algorithm $\text{TrapGen}_{\text{NTRU}}$ that takes 1^λ as input and outputs an NTRU lattice $\Lambda_{h,q}$ with a trapdoor basis $\mathbf{B}_{f,g}$ and a polynomial $h = g \cdot f^{-1} \mod q$, satisfying $\|(f,g)\| \leq 2\sigma\sqrt{\lambda}$. Let $\mathcal{R}_q^\times$ represent all invertible elements modulo q in the polynomial ring $\mathcal{R} = \mathbb{Z}[x]/(x^n + 1)$, and let $\mathcal{D}_\sigma^n$ denote the n-dimensional discrete Gaussian distribution with parameter σ. For the set D, denote $f \leftarrow D$ as selecting f uniformly at random from D. The specific steps of the algorithm are as follows: Algorithm 1 [29].

Algorithm 1 $\text{TrapGen}_{\text{NTRU}}(1^\lambda)$

Input: $\lambda, q, \sigma. q = \text{ploy}(\lambda), \sigma > \omega(\sqrt{\log(2\lambda)})$
Output: $\mathbf{B}_{f,g}, h. h = g \cdot f^{-1} \mod q$

1: Sample $f \leftarrow \mathcal{D}_\sigma^n, g \leftarrow \mathcal{D}_\sigma^n$. If $f \mod q \notin \mathcal{R}_q^\times$ and $g \mod q \notin \mathcal{R}_q^\times$, or $\|f\| > \sigma\sqrt{\lambda}$ and $\|g\| > \sigma\sqrt{\lambda}$, resample.
2: If $\langle f, g \rangle \neq \mathcal{R}$, restart.
3: Compute $F_1, G_1 \in \mathcal{R}$ such that $fG_1 - gF_1 = 1$. Then set $F_q = qF_1$ and $G_q = qG_1$.
4: Compute $F, G \in \mathcal{R}$, where for $k \in \mathbb{Z}$, $(F, G) = (F_q, G_q) - k(f, g)$.
5: If $\|(F, G)\| > \lambda\sigma$, restart.
6: Return $\mathbf{B}_{f,g}, h = g \cdot f^{-1} \mod q$.

3.2. Annular NTRU Trapdoor Generation

Common NTRU trapdoor generation algorithms (for example, Algorithm 1) typically obtain the desired quality polynomial pair (f, g) by repeatedly sampling until a random polynomial pair (f, g) has been generated. Although this method appears to be straightforward, it has shortcomings in terms of efficiency and security. In our approach, to adapt to the underwater acoustic communication environment, we propose a ring-based uniform sampling method based on a hybrid sampler, suitable for generating trapdoor bases $B_{f,g}$.

Our approach embeds a quality target φ_i into the hybrid sampler and directly performs uniform sampling from quality targets that meet the conditions. Figure 1 shows the ring uniform sampling. The specific implementation is as follows: Algorithm 2.

Algorithm 2 Ring Trapdoor Generation Algorithm

Input: Ring order n, modulus q, target quality coefficient α and ring region $A^+(r, R)$, where $0 < r < R$.
Output: $B_{f,g}, h.h = g \cdot f^{-1} \mod q$
1: repeat
2:   for $1 \leq i \leq n/2$ do
3:     $u \leftarrow U([r^2, R^2]), \rho \leftarrow \sqrt{u}, \theta \leftarrow U([0, \pi/2])$
4:     $(z, z') \leftarrow \left(x \cdot e^{iv}, y \cdot e^{iv'}\right)$ end for
5:   $\tilde{f} \leftarrow \varphi^{-1}(z_1, \cdots, z_{n/2}), \tilde{g} \leftarrow \varphi^{-1}(w_1, \cdots, w_{n/2})$
6:   $f \leftarrow \tilde{f}, \quad g \leftarrow \tilde{g}$
7: Until $\forall i = 1, \cdots, n/2, (|\varphi_i(f)| + |\varphi_i(g)|) \in A^+\left(\sqrt{q}/\alpha, \alpha\sqrt{q}\right)$
8: Return $B_{f,g}, h = g \cdot f^{-1} \mod q$

The process from $\tilde{f}, \tilde{g}$ to $B_{f,g}$ is omitted after Step 7 in Algorithm 2, as it is the same as in Algorithm 1. Since the polynomials $\tilde{f}$ and $\tilde{g}$ generated using the inverse Fourier transform typically do not have integer coefficients and thus do not meet the requirements of the NTRU trapdoor, this paper effectively addresses this issue by applying a coefficient-by-coefficient rounding method [30] which maximally preserves the original properties of the polynomials.

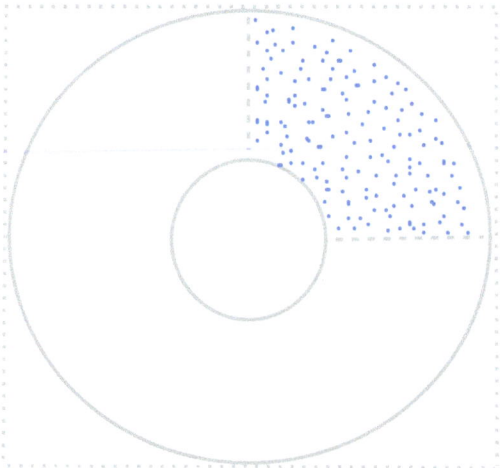

Figure 1. Sampled uniformly in $A^+(r, R)$.

4. Syntax and Model

4.1. Underwater Acoustic Channel Model

The over-the-air (OTA) model is commonly used to describe the process of transmitting and aggregating information through wireless channels, particularly in mobile communication and sensor networks. This model is also applicable to underwater acoustic communication. However, due to factors such as signal attenuation, propagation speed variations, and noise in the underwater environment, the characteristics of underwater acoustic communication differ from those of aerial channels. Therefore, in this paper, we reference relevant literature [31,32] and propose improvements and adaptations to the existing underwater acoustic channel model based on prior research. The following is a detailed introduction to the underwater acoustic channel model adopted in this study.

It is assumed that Alice and Bob, the two parties participating in the underwater acoustic communication, are both legitimate, while the third-party attacker (Eve) is the adversary. In the proposed NTRU-based underwater acoustic communication key encapsulation scheme, Alice is responsible for generating the temporary key, performing the key encapsulation, signing the encapsulated ciphertext, and finally transmitting the data to Bob via the underwater acoustic channel. Bob is responsible for verifying the signature and performing the decapsulation operation to ensure that the received data are legitimate and have not been tampered with. The communication model is shown in Figure 2.

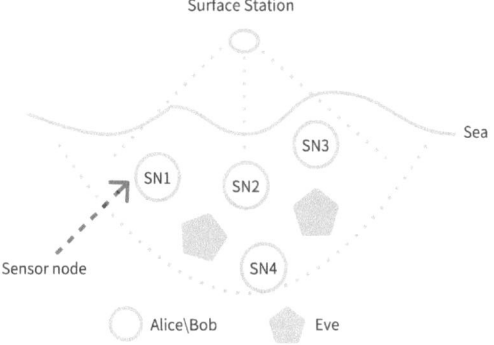

Figure 2. The Communication Model.

The underwater acoustic channel is a complex, random, spatiotemporal, and frequency-varying channel, and its transmission quality is severely affected by multipath and Doppler effects. Due to the complexity of the shallow water environment, underwater acoustic signals undergo refraction and reflection when interacting with the seabed, sea surface, or marine organisms during transmission. As a result, the underwater acoustic signals sent by Alice do not reach Bob simultaneously, leading to multipath effects.

Let P be the number of paths, τ_p be the delay of the p-th path, h_p be the channel gain of the p-th path, and $n(t)$ be the noise in the channel. The multipath channel can be represented as

$$h(t) = \sum_{i=1}^{P} h_p(t) s(t - \tau_p) + n(t) \qquad (12)$$

where $h(t)$ is the transmitted signal and $s(t)$ is the received signal.

In underwater communication, the relative positions of Alice and Bob are typically in a state of relative motion, so the impact of the Doppler effect must be considered. Furthermore, as the underwater acoustic signals travel along different paths to the receiver, the incident angles will vary, resulting in different Doppler factors for each path. By substituting $\tau_p(t) = \tau_p + g_i t$ into the above equation, the multipath channel with Doppler effect can be expressed as

$$h(t) = \sum_{i=1}^{P} h_p(t) s(t - \tau_p - g_p t) + n(t) \tag{13}$$

where g_p is the Doppler factor.

In the proposed scheme of this paper, a joint channel model is developed for the underwater acoustic channel, which can be expressed as

$$h(t,f) = \sum_{i=1}^{L} a_i e^{j2\pi \Delta f_i t} \delta(t - \tau_p) \tag{14}$$

Based on this, a two-dimensional Gaussian distribution is constructed, where the mean and covariance matrices represent the distribution characteristics of the multipath delay and Doppler shift, respectively. The joint distribution can be expressed as

$$P(\tau, \Delta f) = \frac{1}{2\pi \sigma_\tau \sigma_f} \exp\left(-\frac{(\tau - \mu_\tau)^2}{2\sigma_\tau^2} - \left(\frac{\Delta f - \mu_f^2}{2\sigma_f^2}\right)\right) \tag{15}$$

For simplicity, we assume that the received signal undergoes a Fourier transform to obtain its frequency domain representation $H(f)$. Based on the joint distribution $P(\tau, \Delta f)$, a channel compensation matrix $C(f, \tau)$ is constructed, where the complex compensation factor for each path can be expressed as $C_i = e^{-j(2\pi \Delta f_i \tau_i)}$. By calculation, the joint compensation for multipath and Doppler can be obtained as follows

$$Y(f) = H(f) \cdot C(f, \tau) \tag{16}$$

In the key encapsulation process, applying the joint compensation of the complex compensation factors to the ciphertext helps improve the integrity and security of transmission over the underwater acoustic channel under the influence of multipath and Doppler effects. In our scheme, the unique characteristics of the underwater acoustic channel are leveraged to enhance the security of the encapsulation.

4.2. Scheme Definition

In this section, we will describe a key encapsulation scheme suitable for underwater acoustic secure communication.

Our scheme involves 6-tuples of algorithms: Setup, Key-Gen, Key-Encaps, Sign, Verify, and Key-Decaps.

Setup. Alice takes the security parameter λ as input and selects the appropriate parameters required for the system.

Key-Gen. Alice runs the trapdoor generation algorithm to output the public and private key pair.

Key-Encaps. Alice uses the private key to perform the encapsulation operation, taking into account the characteristics of the underwater acoustic channel, and outputs the encapsulated key K and ciphertext CT.

Sign. Alice generates a signature private key based on the characteristics of the underwater acoustic channel, signs the encapsulated ciphertext CT, and sends the signature sig and the ciphertext CT to Bob.

Verify. Bob uses the public key to verify the received signature sig.

Key-Decaps. Bob uses the private key to decapsulate the ciphertext CT after the signature verification is successful, and outputs the message m and the encapsulated key K.

4.3. Security Model

This section outlines the security model for our scheme, focusing primarily on two key dimensions.

Existential Unforgeability: Ensure that in the complex underwater acoustic communication environment, the legitimate receiver receives the signed ciphertext as authentic and complete, thereby ensuring that the decapsulated key K is correct and error-free.

Confidentiality: Ensure that no one, other than the legitimate recipient, can extract any meaningful information from the ciphertext and thereby break the encapsulated key K.

4.4. Construction of the Scheme in This Paper

The NTRU-based underwater acoustic communication key encapsulation scheme proposed in this paper is introduced below, denoted as UA-NTRU.

(1) Setup. Given a security parameter λ. Let the polynomial ring be $R_q = \mathbb{Z}[x]/\langle x^n + 1 \rangle$, where n is the degree of the polynomial and q is the modulus. Choose a positive integer p such that $\gcd(p,q) = 1$. Let the plaintext space be $\mathcal{M} \in \{0,1\}^k$, the key encapsulation space be $\{0,1\}^v$, and the Gaussian parameter $\sigma > \omega(\sqrt{\log(2n)})$, $x = \tilde{\Omega}(n^{3/2}\sigma)$. Let $H : \{0,1\}^* \to \{0,1\}^k$ be a hash function.

(2) Key-Gen. Run Algorithm 2 to obtain $h = g \cdot f^{-1} \mod q$, where $h \in R_q$. And obtain $B_{f,g} = \begin{bmatrix} g & G \\ -f & -F \end{bmatrix} \in R_q^{2 \times 2}$. The private key is $sk = B_{f,g}$, and the public key is $pk = h$.

(3) Key-Encaps. This step is divided into two parts: generating the encapsulated key K and the encapsulated ciphertext CT by combining the characteristics of the underwater acoustic channel. Alice first dynamically obtains the channel characteristics $(\Delta f, \tau, L)$ from the underwater acoustic sensor. For the sake of simplicity, it is assumed that the obtained channel characteristics are normalized and then combined into a feature vector $F = (\Delta f, \tau, L)$. Use a hash function to map H to the polynomial ring: $T = H(F) \in \{0,1\}^{v_1}$.

Input message $m \in \mathcal{M}$, public key pk. Randomly select $K' \in \{0,1\}^{v_2}$, Compute the encapsulated key $K = T\|K'$, $v = v_1 + v_2$. Randomly select $r, e_0, e_1 \leftarrow \{-1,0,1\}^*$, and compute $c_1 = m \otimes H(K)$, $c_2 = rh + e_0$, $c_3 = rK + e_1 + \lfloor \frac{q}{2} \rceil \cdot K$. Here, $c_2, c_3 \in R_q$, $\lfloor \rceil$ represents the rounding function. Considering the computational efficiency of the nodes in the underwater acoustic environment, we perform the following operation on c_3, $c_3 = 2^b \cdot \lfloor \frac{1}{2^b} \cdot c_3 \rceil$. Where $\lceil \log_2 q \rceil - 3 \geq b$.

Output the ciphertext $CT = (c_1, c_2, c_3)$, and the encapsulated key is K.

(4) Sign. In this stage, the generated ciphertext CT is signed to produce the signature Sig. The signing process, combined with underwater acoustic communication, follows the same procedure as described above. Run the Gaussian sampling algorithm to obtain $(x_1, x_2) = (T, 0) - SampleD(B_{f,g}, x, (T, 0))$. Where x_1 and x_2 satisfy $\{x_1 + x_2 \cdot h = T\}$. Output the signature private key $sk_{sig} = (x_1, x_2)$. Select polynomials $a_1, a_2 \in D_\sigma^n$. Compute $u = H'(a_1 + h \cdot a_2, CT)$. For $i = 1, 2$, compute $z_i = a_i + x_i \cdot u$. Output the signature $sig = (z_1, z_2, u)$.

(5) Verify. Input the signature sig, ciphertext CT, and channel characteristics F. The verifier outputs "1" if and only if $H'(h * z_2 + z_1 - H(F) * u, CT) = u$, where it must satisfy $\|(z_1, z_2)\| \leq 2\sigma\sqrt{2n}$.

(6) Key-Decaps. After step 4, verification is passed, Bob uses the private key $B_{f,g}$ to perform the decryption operation on the ciphertext $CT = (c_1, c_2, c_3)$. Compute $S_{f,g} = (1, -B_{f,g})$ and $f = \langle c_3, S_{f,g} \rangle$. Compute $K = \lfloor \frac{2}{q} \cdot f \rceil$. If the parsed result is $K = T\|K'$, the encapsulation is successful, and output the encapsulated key K; otherwise, output $\perp$.

4.5. Correctness Analysis

Let us first consider the correctness of the digital signature in our scheme. In the step Verify, it can be seen that

$$
\begin{aligned}
& h * z_2 + z_1 - H(F) * u \\
&= h * (a_2 + x_2 * u) + (a_1 + x_1 * u) - T * u \\
&= h * (a_2 + x_2 * u) + (a_1 + x_1 * u) - (x_2 * h + x_1) * u \\
&= a_1 + a_2 * h
\end{aligned} \quad (17)
$$

Therefore, we have $H'(h * z_2 + z_1 - H(F) * u, CT) = H'(a_1 + a_2 * h) = u$, which satisfies the first condition for the correctness of the signature. Based on Lemmas 1–3 and the rejection sampling technique [33], it can be concluded that $\|z_1\| \leq 2\sigma\sqrt{n}$ and $\|z_2\| \leq 2\sigma\sqrt{n}$ with a probability of at least $1 - 2^{-\omega(\log n)}$. Therefore, it can be satisfied that $\|(z_1, z_2)\|$ with overwhelming probability satisfies $\|(z_1, z_2)\| \leq 2\sigma\sqrt{2n}$. In conclusion, it can be deduced that the digital signature scheme in our proposal satisfies correctness.

After ensuring the correctness of Steps 3–4, the verification process of the underwater acoustic communication-based key encapsulation scheme in this paper is as follows: Through c_1, Bob can compute $m = c_1 \oplus H(K)$ to recover the original message m. In our scheme, for any $(pk, sk) \leftarrow \text{Key-Gen}(1^\lambda)$ and the encapsulated key $K \in \{0,1\}^v$. Satisfy $\Pr\{\text{Key-Decaps}(\text{Key-Encaps}(pk, T)) = T \| K'\} = 1$. To ensure that the key K can be correctly decapsulated, assume that the noise follows a zero-mean Gaussian distribution with a variance of $\frac{2}{3}\left(\|B_{f,g}\|^2 + 1\right)$, where $\|B_{f,g}\|$ is the norm of Bob's private key. The following correctness condition can be derived: $q \geq \frac{32\sqrt{\lambda \ln 2}}{3\sqrt{3}} \cdot \|B_{f,g}\|$. It is important to note that bit loss may lead to decryption errors. However, when $\lceil \log_2 q \rceil - 3 \geq b$, this does not significantly affect the correct decapsulation of the scheme.

5. Security Proof

5.1. Existential Unforgeability

This section demonstrates that the proposed NTRU-based key encapsulation scheme for underwater acoustic communication achieves unforgeability within the random oracle framework.

Theorem 1. *Assuming that the small integer solution (R-SIS) problem on rings is hard, the NTRU-based underwater acoustic communication key encapsulation scheme proposed in this paper satisfies unforgeability in the random oracle model.*

Proof. If there exists a PPT adversary $\mathcal{A}$ that can forge a signature in Step 3 of the scheme with a non-negligible probability ε, then we can construct a challenger $\mathcal{C}$ that, by interacting with $\mathcal{A}$, can solve the R-SIS problem with the same non-negligible probability. The game simulation between the adversary $\mathcal{A}$ and the challenger $\mathcal{C}$ is as follows:

(1) The challenger $\mathcal{C}$ takes the security parameter λ as input and randomly selects two hash functions $H : \{0,1\}^* \to \mathbb{Z}_q^n$ and $H' : \{0,1\}^* \to \mathbb{Z}_q^n$. Then, $\mathcal{C}$ sends the system's master private key $B_{f,g}$, the master public key h, and the public parameters $PP = \{H, H'\}$ to the adversary $\mathcal{A}$.

(2) The adversary $\mathcal{A}$ can adaptively make the following queries to the challenger $\mathcal{C}$ in polynomial time, assuming that $\mathcal{A}$ does not make duplicate queries.

H_1 query: $\mathcal{C}$ maintains a list $L_1 = \{F, H(F), sk_{f,g}\}$, initially empty. When the adversary $\mathcal{A}$ sends the channel characteristic F for the H_1 query, $\mathcal{C}$ first searches the list L_1. If $H(F)$ is found, $\mathcal{C}$ returns $H(F)$ to the adversary $\mathcal{A}$. Otherwise, $\mathcal{C}$ uniformly randomly selects polynomials $x_1, x_2 \in D_x^n$, computes $H(F) = x_1 + h \cdot x_2$, and stores it in L_1. Finally, $\mathcal{C}$ sends $H(F)$ to the adversary $\mathcal{A}$.

H_2 query: When the adversary $\mathcal{A}$ sends the channel characteristic F to the oracle for a key extraction query, $\mathcal{C}$ searches in L_1 and sends the corresponding sk_{sig} to the adversary $\mathcal{A}$.

Signature query: To obtain a signature for the ciphertext CT, the adversary $\mathcal{A}$ sends (F, CT) for a signature query. Upon receiving the query, $\mathcal{C}$ first looks up the corresponding sk_{sig} in L_1, then randomly selects polynomials $a_1, a_2 \in D_\sigma^n$ and a polynomial $u \in D_{H'}$. Let $u = H'(a_1 + h \cdot a_2, \text{CT})$. Next, for $i = 1, 2$, $\mathcal{C}$ computes $z_i = a_i + x_i \cdot u$, obtaining the signature $\text{sig} = (z_1, z_2, u)$. Finally, $\mathcal{C}$ stores $\{\text{sig} = (z_1, z_2, u), F, \text{CT}, a_1, a_2\}$ at the corresponding position in L_1, and sends the signature sig to the adversary $\mathcal{A}$.

H' query: When the adversary $\mathcal{A}$ sends (CT, a_1, a_2) for an H' query, $\mathcal{C}$ searches in L_1 for (CT, a_1, a_2) and sends the corresponding polynomial u to the adversary $\mathcal{A}$.

The adversary $\mathcal{A}$ outputs a forged signature $\text{sig}' = (z_1', z_2', u')$ for (F', CT') with a non-negligible probability.

According to Lemma 4, $\mathcal{A}$ outputs a new forged signature $\text{sig}^* = (z_1^*, z_2^*, u^*)$ for (F', CT') with non-negligible probability, such that $z_1' + z_2' \cdot h - H(F') \cdot u' = z_1^* + z_2^* \cdot h - H(F') \cdot u^* = y_1' + h \cdot y_2'$, where $u^* \neq u'$, so we have $[z_1' - z_1^* - x_1'(u' - u^*)] + [z_2' - z_2^* + x_2'(u' - u^*)] \cdot h = 0$. According to Lemmas 1 and 2, we have $\| z_1' - z_1^* - x_1'(u' - u^*) \| \leq \| z_1' \| + \| z_1^* \| + \| x_1'u' \| + \| x_1'u^* \| \leq (4\sigma + 2\lambda x)\sqrt{n}$, which holds with overwhelming probability. Similarly, $\| z_2' - z_2^* + x_2'(u' - u^*) \| \leq \| z_2' \| + \| z_2^* \| + \| x_2'u' \| + \| x_2'u^* \| \leq (4\sigma + 2\lambda x)\sqrt{n}$.

Based on the preimage minimum distance property of the trapdoor function on the NTRU lattice, it is highly probable that there exists a new signing key $sk_{f,g}^* = (x_1^*, x_2^*)$, where the new signature differs from (x_1', x_2') only in the i-th coefficient, and satisfies $x_1^* + x_2^* \cdot h = H(F')$. If $x_1' \neq x_1^*$, then we have $[z_1' - z_1^* - x_1'(u' - u^*)] - [z_1' - z_1^* - x_1^*(u' - u^*)] = (x_1^* - x_1')(u' - u^*) \neq 0$. Therefore, if $z_1' - z_1^* - x_1^*(u' - u^*) = 0$, it follows that $z_1' - z_1^* - x_1'(u' - u^*) \neq 0$. Similarly, if $x_2' \neq x_2^*$, the same reasoning holds, and we omit the detailed description here. Based on the above considerations, it can be concluded that $([z_1' - z_1^* - x_1'(u' - u^*)], [z_2' - z_2^* + x_2'(u' - u^*)]) \neq 0$ holds with at least 3/4 probability.

So, if it satisfies $\beta \geq (4\sigma + 2\lambda x)\sqrt{2n}$, $([z_1' - z_1^* - x_1'(u' - u^*)], [z_2' - z_2^* + x_2'(u' - u^*)])$ is called the solution of the SIS problem on the NTRU lattice in this paper.

Certificate completed. □

5.2. Confidentiality

The following will prove that our proposed NTRU-based key encapsulation scheme for underwater acoustic communication is IND-CCA secure, based on the NTRU hardness assumption.

Before that, let us first discuss the indistinguishability under chosen plaintext attack (IND-CPA) security of the UA-NTRU scheme.

Theorem 2. *For every probabilistic polynomial-time adversary $\mathcal{A}$, one can construct a probabilistic polynomial-time adversary $\mathcal{B}$ with a runtime similar to $\mathcal{A}$, such that*

$$Adv_{\text{UA-NTRU}}^{\text{IND-CPA}}(\mathcal{A}) \leq Adv^{\text{NTRU-OW}}(\mathcal{B}). \tag{18}$$

where $\mathcal{A}$ is a classical adversary, and the hash function $\mathcal{H}$ is modeled as a classical random oracle.

$$Adv_{\text{UA-NTRU}}^{\text{IND-CPA}}(\mathcal{A}) \leq 2d_{\mathcal{H}}\sqrt{Adv^{\text{NTRU-OW}}(\mathcal{B})} \tag{19}$$

where $\mathcal{A}$ is a quantum adversary, the hash function $\mathcal{H}$ is modeled as a quantum random oracle, and $d_{\mathcal{H}}$ denotes the depth of $\mathcal{A}$'s queries to $\mathcal{H}$.

Proof. Suppose there exists a probabilistic polynomial-time adversary $\mathcal{A}$ that can win the game G_1, with the output satisfying $CT = CT^*$. We can then construct a probabilistic polynomial-time adversary $\mathcal{B}$ that solves the NTRU one-way hardness problem. Specifically, $\mathcal{B}$ receives the public key h and the challenge ciphertext CT^* from $\mathcal{A}$ running in the game G_1. The goal of adversary $\mathcal{B}$ is to output a pair (r, e) such that $CT^* = rh + e$. Adversary $\mathcal{B}$ takes h and CT^* as input and runs the adversary $\mathcal{A}$. Adversary $\mathcal{A}$ outputs a pair (r, e), which is then used by $\mathcal{B}$ as its output. If adversary $\mathcal{B}$ successfully simulates the game G_1, this means that the pair (r, e) output by $\mathcal{A}$ satisfies $CT^* = rh + e$, i.e., adversary $\mathcal{A}$ wins the game G_1. Thus, it follows that adversary $\mathcal{B}$ can successfully solve the NTRU one-way function problem with the pair (r, e) as output. Conversely, if the pair (r, e) output by adversary $\mathcal{A}$ does not satisfy $CT^* = rh + e$, then adversary $\mathcal{B}$, using this pair (r, e) as its output, will not be able to successfully solve the NTRU one-way function problem. In conclusion, the advantage of adversary $\mathcal{A}$ winning the game G_1 is equal to the advantage of adversary $\mathcal{B}$ in solving the NTRU one-way function problem, i.e.,

$$\Pr[\text{Win}_{G_1}] = \text{Adv}^{\text{NTRU-OW}}(\mathcal{B}). \tag{20}$$

Theorem 3. *If the adversary $\mathcal{A}$ can break the IND-CCA security of the UA-NTRU scheme, then there exists an adversary $\mathcal{B}$ that can break the IND-CPA security of UA-NTRU, such that*

$$Adv^{\text{IND-CCA}}_{\text{UA-NTRU}}(\mathcal{A}) \leq 2\left(Adv^{\text{IND-CPA}}_{\text{UA-NTRU}}(\mathcal{B}) + \frac{q_{\mathcal{H}}}{|\mathcal{M}|}\right) + \frac{q_D}{2^{\gamma}} + q_{\mathcal{H}}l \tag{21}$$

where $q_{\mathcal{H}}$ is the number of queries to the random oracle, q_D is the number of queries to the decapsulation algorithm and challenge queries, γ is the length of the private key, and l is the entropy of $F(pk)$. In summary, based on the NTRU hardness assumption, the NTRU-based key encapsulation scheme for underwater acoustic communication proposed in this paper is IND-CCA secure.

Certificate completed. □

5.3. Summary

In the context of underwater communication, for instance, when two underwater sensing devices need to exchange critical data (such as detection signals, positioning information, etc.), existential unforgeability ensures that these data cannot be impersonated or altered by intermediary attackers, thereby preventing erroneous decisions and potential security risks. At the same time, confidentiality ensures that the transmitted data are accessible only to authorized users, effectively protecting the privacy and sensitive information in underwater communication. The scheme proposed in this paper, through rigorous security proofs, is able to fully satisfy the aforementioned security requirements.

6. Comparison and Conclusions

6.1. Comparison

The key encapsulation mechanism is a crucial component in encryption protocols. Common examples include those based on the RSA public-key encryption algorithm [34] and the Diffie–Hellman [35] key exchange protocol. These mechanisms were designed based on the integer factorization problem and the discrete logarithm problem, respectively. With the rapid development of quantum computers, their powerful parallel computing capabilities pose significant security challenges to traditional key encapsulation mechanisms. This paper proposes an NTRU-based key encapsulation scheme for underwater acoustic communication, leveraging the algebraic structure of NTRU, which can achieve quantum-resistant security in underwater acoustic communication. The scheme offers advantages such as small storage space, low computational cost, and fulfillment of IND-CCA security. To reduce the storage space in underwater acoustic communication, this scheme uses the trapdoor basis $B_{f,g}$ obtained through ring sampling as the system's private key. Water acoustic channel characteristics are incorporated into the key encapsulation process to provide authenticity to the scheme. Additionally, a short-length digital signature is introduced, ensuring the integrity of data transmission in the underwater acoustic environment, without compromising the overall computational efficiency.

In Table 1, we present a comparison of the security strengths of different schemes. In this paper, the proposed scheme incorporates underwater acoustic channel characteristics during the key encapsulation process, effectively introducing identity information, which enables the scheme to resist forgery attacks such as message replay and information reorganization. In contrast, Refs. [36,37] do not introduce relevant identity information and, therefore, cannot defend against message replay attacks. Additionally, the proposed scheme ensures unforgeability and CCA security due to the integration of a digital signature mechanism in the NTRU-based key encapsulation scheme. Ref. [36], based on the ring learning with errors (R-LWE) problem, does not satisfy CCA security and lacks unforgeability. Although Ref. [37] is also an NTRU-based key encapsulation scheme that satisfies CCA security, it lacks unforgeability.

Table 1. Comparison of security strength.

Scheme	CCA	Replay Attack	Unforgeability
Our scheme	✓	✓	✓
Ref. [36]	×	×	×
Ref. [37]	✓	×	×

As shown in Table 2, the private key generated by the ring sampling algorithm in this paper requires less storage space compared to [37]. Additionally, the storage space for the ciphertext is also smaller than that in [37], and the storage space for the added signature is also relatively small. Compared with [36], the proposed scheme has a slightly larger storage space for various aspects. However, Ref. [36] does not have quantum-resistant capabilities. Considering the complexity of the underwater acoustic communication environment and the need to ensure communication security, the proposed scheme is more suitable for underwater acoustic communication.

Table 2. Comparison of storage space (unit:KB).

Scheme	System Private Key	Signature Generation	Ciphertext Size
Our scheme	462	217	892
Ref. [36]	226	-	489
Ref. [37]	663	-	1220

Table 3 presents a comparison of the time overheads between the proposed scheme and those in [36,37]. Although the proposed scheme includes an additional signature step, its time overhead is similar to that of [37] and far superior to that of [36]. Without significantly increasing the overhead, our scheme offers better security, making it well-suited for challenging underwater acoustic communication environments.

Table 3. Comparison of time overheads (unit: μs).

Scheme	Key-Gen	Key-Encaps	Key-Decaps
Our scheme	22.8	31.1	43.0
Ref. [36]	57.90	54.86	35.39
Ref. [37]	23.4	30.5	41.3

6.2. Conclusions

In this paper, we proposed an NTRU-based key encapsulation scheme for underwater acoustic communication. The scheme leverages a trapdoor basis generated by the ring sampling algorithm as the private key, while incorporating the characteristics of underwater acoustic channels into the key encapsulation process. Additionally, by introducing a signature step, the scheme overcomes the limitations of traditional key encapsulation mechanisms. Experimental results showed that our scheme ensures IND-CCA security, while offering reduced storage requirements and improved computational efficiency. However, in extreme underwater acoustic environments with high noise and low signal-to-noise ratios, the current scheme may still face performance bottlenecks, particularly in terms of the computational overhead during key generation and encapsulation. Future work will focus on improving the operational efficiency of the key encapsulation algorithm to meet the computational constraints of underwater communication systems. Furthermore, we will explore how to adapt the scheme for different underwater communication scenarios, to enhance its flexibility and robustness. Given the potential threats posed by quantum computing, strengthening the post-quantum resilience of the scheme and integrating it with other cryptographic mechanisms will be a key direction for future research.

Author Contributions: Conceptualization, P.H. and M.X.; Methodology, P.H. and M.X.; Writing—original draft preparation, P.H.; Writing—review and editing, P.H. and M.X.; Supervision, M.X.; Funding Acquisition, M.X. All authors have read and agreed to the published version of the manuscript.

Funding: Covert Secret Key Agreement Scheme Based on the Underwater Acoustic Dynamic Hypergraph. This work was supported by the National Natural Science Foundation of China under Grant 62172269.

Data Availability Statement: Data are contained within the article.

Conflicts of Interest: The authors declare no conflicts of interest.

References

1. Li, Z.; Chitre, M.; Stojanovic, M. Underwater acoustic communications. *Nat. Rev. Electr. Eng.* **2024**, 1–13. [CrossRef]
2. Yang, J.; Wang, J.; Qiao, G.; Liu, S.; Ma, L.; He, P. Review of underwater acoustic communication and network technology. *J. Electron. Inf. Technol.* **2024**, *46*, 1–21.
3. Wang, Z.; Liu, X.; Yang, Y.; Peng, M. Complementary Coded Identical Code Cyclic Shift Multiple Access Under Asynchronous Frequency-Selective Fading Channels. *IEEE Trans. Veh. Technol.* **2023**, *72*, 13269–13280. [CrossRef]
4. Javadpour, A.; Ja'fari, F.; Taleb, T.; Zhao, Y.; Bin, Y.; Benzaïd, C. Encryption as a service for IoT: Opportunities, challenges and solutions. *IEEE Internet Things J.* **2023**, *11*, 7525–7558. [CrossRef]
5. Shohrab, S. Dynamic Data Encryption with Polarized Feedback. Ph.D. Thesis, Dublin Business School, Dublin, Ireland, 2023.
6. Singh, S.; Sharma, P.K.; Moon, S.Y.; Park, J.H. Advanced lightweight encryption algorithms for IoT devices: Survey, challenges and solutions. *J. Ambient. Intell. Humaniz. Comput.* **2024**, *15*, 1625–1642. [CrossRef]
7. Tomović, S.; Krivokapić, B.; Nađ, Đ.; Radusinović, I. BEKMP: A Blockchain-Enabled Key Management Protocol for Underwater Acoustic Sensor Networks. *IEEE Access* **2024**, *12*, 74108–74125. [CrossRef]
8. Sood, R.; Kaur, H. A literature review on rsa, des and aes encryption algorithms. In *Emerging Trends in Engineering and Management*; SCRS: Delhi, India, 2023; pp. 57–63.

9. Dalal, Y.M.; Supreeth, S.; Amuthabala, K.; Satheesha, T.Y.; Asha, P.N.; Somanath, S. Optimizing Security: A Comparative Analysis of RSA, ECC, and DH Algorithms. In Proceedings of the 2024 IEEE North Karnataka Subsection Flagship International Conference (NKCon), Bagalkote, India, 21–22 September 2024; pp. 1–6. [CrossRef]
10. Zhao, J. DES-Co-RSA: A Hybrid Encryption Algorithm Based on DES and RSA. In Proceedings of the 2023 IEEE 3rd International Conference on Power, Electronics and Computer Applications (ICPECA), Shenyang, China, 29–31 January 2023; pp. 846–850. [CrossRef]
11. Gupta, M.; Gera, P.; Mishra, B. A Lightweight Certificateless Signcryption Scheme based on HCC for securing Underwater Wireless Sensor Networks (UWSNs). In Proceedings of the 2023 16th International Conference on Security of Information and Networks (SIN), Jaipur, India, 20–21 November 2023; pp. 1–8. [CrossRef]
12. Mujdei, C.; Wouters, L.; Karmakar, A.; Beckers, A.; Bermudo Mera, J.M.; Verbauwhede, I. Side-channel analysis of lattice-based post-quantum cryptography: Exploiting polynomial multiplication. *ACM Trans. Embed. Comput. Syst.* **2024**, *23*, 27. [CrossRef]
13. Canto, A.C.; Sarker, A.; Kaur, J.; Kermani, M.M.; Azarderakhsh, R. Error detection schemes assessed on FPGA for multipliers in lattice-based key encapsulation mechanisms in post-quantum cryptography. *IEEE Trans. Emerg. Top. Comput.* **2022**, *11*, 791–797. [CrossRef]
14. Kumar, M.; Pattnaik, P. Post quantum cryptography (pqc)-an overview. In Proceedings of the 2020 IEEE High Performance Extreme Computing Conference (HPEC), Waltham, MA, USA, 22–24 September 2020; IEEE: Piscataway, NJ, USA, 2020; pp. 1–9.
15. Nisha, F.; Lenin, J.; Saravanan, S.; Rohit, V.R.; Selvam, P.D.; Rajmohan, M. Lattice-Based Cryptography and NTRU: Quantum-Resistant Encryption Algorithms. In Proceedings of the 2024 International Conference on Emerging Systems and Intelligent Computing (ESIC), Bhubaneswar, India, 9–10 February 2024; pp. 509–514. [CrossRef]
16. Kim, J.; Park, J.H. NTRU+ PKE: Efficient Public-Key Encryption Schemes from the NTRU Problem. *Cryptol. ePrint Arch.* **2024**. Available online: https://eprint.iacr.org/2024/1282 (accessed on 16 January 2025).
17. Choi, P.; Kim, D.K. Lightweight Polynomial Multiplication Accelerator for NTRU Using Shared SRAM. *IEEE Trans. Circuits Syst. II Express Briefs* **2023**, *70*, 4574–4578. [CrossRef]
18. Camacho-Ruiz, E.; Martínez-Rodríguez, M.C.; Sánchez-Solano, S.; Brox, P. Accelerating the Development of NTRU Algorithm on Embedded Systems. In Proceedings of the 2020 XXXV Conference on Design of Circuits and Integrated Systems (DCIS), Segovia, Spain, 18–20 November 2020; pp. 1–6. [CrossRef]
19. Kuznetsov, A.; Lutsenko, M.; Kiian, N.; Makushenko, T.; Kuznetsova, T. Code-based key encapsulation mechanisms for post-quantum standardization. In Proceedings of the 2018 IEEE 9th International Conference on Dependable Systems, Services and Technologies (DESSERT), Kyiv, UKraine, 24–27 May 2018; pp. 276–281. [CrossRef]
20. Lee, J.; Kim, D.; Lee, H.; Lee, Y.; Cheon, J.H. RLizard: Post-Quantum Key Encapsulation Mechanism for IoT Devices. *IEEE Access* **2019**, *7*, 2080–2091. [CrossRef]
21. Bhatti, D.S.; Choi, H.; Lee, H.N. Beyond Traditional Security: A Review on Information-Theoretic Secret Key Generation at Wireless Physical Layer. *Authorea Prepr.* **2024**. [CrossRef]
22. Wu, L.; Wang, H.; Liu, K.; Zhao, L.; Xia, Y. Privacy and security trade-off in cyber-physical systems: An information theory-based framework. *Int. J. Robust Nonlinear Control* **2024**, *34*, 5110–5125. [CrossRef]
23. Pan, P.; Su, Y.; Fan, R.; Yang, S. A Secret Key Generation Scheme Exploiting Spatiotemporal Acoustic Channel Characteristics for Underwater Sensor Networks. *IEEE Sensors J.* **2024**, *24*, 31188–31200. [CrossRef]
24. Du, Y.; Liu, H.; Shao, Z.; Ren, Y.; Li, S.; Dai, H.; Yu, J. Secure and Controllable Secret Key Generation Through CSI Obfuscation Matrix Encapsulation. *IEEE Trans. Mob. Comput.* **2024**, *23*, 12313–12329. [CrossRef]
25. Micciancio, D.; Regev, O. Lattice-based cryptography. In *Post-Quantum Cryptography*; Springer: Berlin/Heidelberg, Germany, 2009; pp. 147–191.
26. Ducas, L.; Lyubashevsky, V.; Prest, T. Efficient identity-based encryption over NTRU lattices. In Proceedings of the Advances in Cryptology—ASIACRYPT 2014: 20th International Conference on the Theory and Application of Cryptology and Information Security, Kaohsiung, Taiwan, 7–11 December 2014; Proceedings, Part II 20; Springer: Berlin/Heidelberg, Germany, 2014; pp. 22–41.
27. Lyubashevsky, V. Lattice signatures without trapdoors. In Proceedings of the Annual International Conference on the Theory and Applications of Cryptographic Techniques, Cambridge, UK, 15–19 April 2012; Springer: Berlin/Heidelberg, Germany, 2012; pp. 738–755.
28. Komlo, C. A Note on Various Forking Lemmas. 2023. Available online: https://www.chelseakomlo.com/assets/content/notes/Forking-Lemma-Variants.pdf (accessed on 24 April 2023).
29. Yu, H.; Hui, W. Certificateless ring signature from NTRU lattice for electronic voting. *J. Inf. Secur. Appl.* **2023**, *75*, 103496. [CrossRef]
30. Watson, A.B. DCT quantization matrices visually optimized for individual images. In Proceedings of the Human Vision, Visual Processing, and Digital Display IV, San Jose, CA, USA, 31 January–5 February 1993; SPIE: Bellingham, WA USA, 1993; Volume 1913, pp. 202–216.

31. Xu, C.; Zhang, C.; Huang, Y.; Niyato, D. Random Aggregate Beamforming for Over-the-Air Federated Learning in Large-Scale Networks. *IEEE Internet Things J.* **2024**, *11*, 34325–34336. [CrossRef]
32. Tang, M.; Cai, S.; Lau, V.K.N. Radix-Partition-Based Over-the-Air Aggregation and Low-Complexity State Estimation for IoT Systems Over Wireless Fading Channels. *IEEE Trans. Signal Process.* **2022**, *70*, 1464–1477. [CrossRef]
33. Liu, T.; Zhao, Y.; Joshi, R.; Khalman, M.; Saleh, M.; Liu, P.J.; Liu, J. Statistical rejection sampling improves preference optimization. *arXiv* **2023**, arXiv:2309.06657.
34. Ahubele, B.; Oghenekaro, L.U. Secured electronic voting system using RSA Key encapsulation mechanism. *Eur. J. Electr. Eng. Comput. Sci.* **2022**, *6*, 81–87. [CrossRef]
35. Gao, D.; Chen, H.; Chang, C.C. Plaintext aware encryption in the standard model under the linear Diffie-Hellman knowledge assumption. *Int. J. Comput. Sci. Eng.* **2020**, *22*, 270–279. [CrossRef]
36. Pöppelmann, T.; Güneysu, T. Towards practical lattice-based public-key encryption on reconfigurable hardware. In Proceedings of the Selected Areas in Cryptography–SAC 2013: 20th International Conference, Burnaby, BC, Canada, 14–16 August 2013; Revised Selected Papers 20; Springer: Berlin/Heidelberg, Germany, 2014; pp. 68–85.
37. Zeng, Q.; Li, Q.; Zhao, B.; Jiao, H.; Huang, Y. Hardware design and implementation of post-quantum cryptography Kyber. In Proceedings of the 2022 IEEE High Performance Extreme Computing Conference (HPEC), Waltham, MA, USA, 19–23 September 2022; IEEE: Piscataway, NJ, USA, 2022; pp. 1–6.

Disclaimer/Publisher's Note: The statements, opinions and data contained in all publications are solely those of the individual author(s) and contributor(s) and not of MDPI and/or the editor(s). MDPI and/or the editor(s) disclaim responsibility for any injury to people or property resulting from any ideas, methods, instructions or products referred to in the content.

MDPI AG
Grosspeteranlage 5
4052 Basel
Switzerland
Tel.: +41 61 683 77 34

Electronics Editorial Office
E-mail: electronics@mdpi.com
www.mdpi.com/journal/electronics

Disclaimer/Publisher's Note: The title and front matter of this reprint are at the discretion of the Guest Editors. The publisher is not responsible for their content or any associated concerns. The statements, opinions and data contained in all individual articles are solely those of the individual Editors and contributors and not of MDPI. MDPI disclaims responsibility for any injury to people or property resulting from any ideas, methods, instructions or products referred to in the content.

www.ingramcontent.com/pod-product-compliance
Lightning Source LLC
LaVergne TN
LVHW072329090526
838202LV00019B/2381